CW00747106

# Morocco
## OVERLAND

**ROUTE GUIDE – FROM THE ATLAS TO THE SAHARA**

**4WD – MOTORCYCLE – VAN – MOUNTAIN BIKE**

# CHRIS SCOTT

with contributions from
**JOSÉ BRITO & TIM CULLIS**
and additional material by
**ERIC DE NADAI, FRANCK SIMONNET
& RAF VERBEELEN**

## TRAILBLAZER PUBLICATIONS

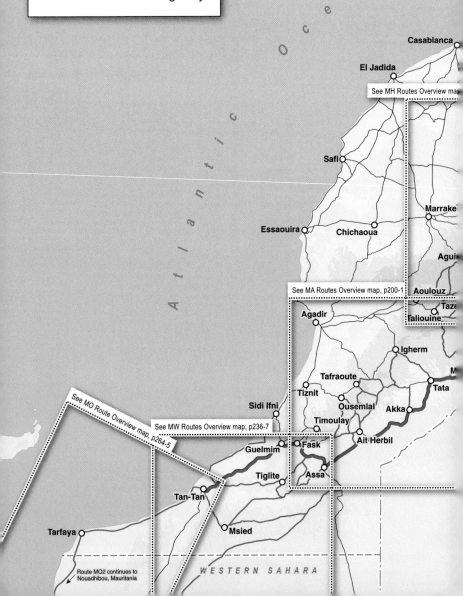

# Morocco Overland Routes

**MA** – Anti Atlas routes
**ME** – Eastern routes
**MH** – High Atlas routes
**MO** – Ocean routes
**MS** – Saharan routes
**MW** – Western routes
▬▬ – MS10 Desert Highway

Atlantic Ocean

Casablanca

El Jadida

See MH Routes Overview map

Safi

Marrake

Essaouira    Chichaoua

Aguir

See MA Routes Overview map, p200-1

Aoulouz

Taze

Agadir

Taliouine

Igherm

M

Tafraoute

Tata

Tiznit

Sidi Ifni    Ousemlal    Akka

Timoulay

See MW Routes Overview map, p236-7    Ait Herbil

See MO Route Overview map, p264-5

Fask

Guelmim

Tiglite    Assa

Tan-Tan

Tarfaya    Msied

Route MO2 continues to
Nouadhibou, Mauritania

WESTERN SAHARA

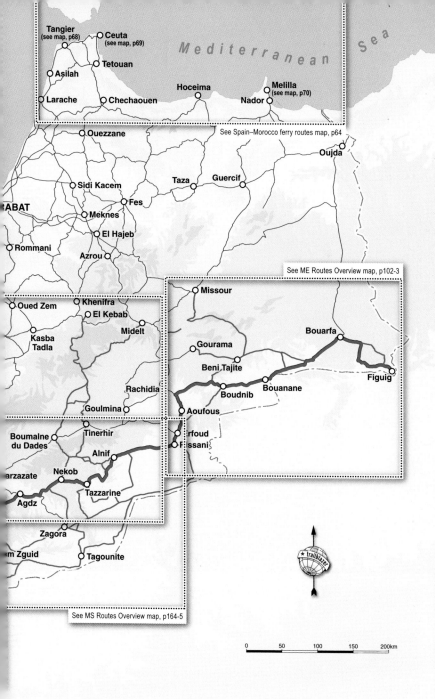

See Spain–Morocco ferry routes map, p64

See ME Routes Overview map, p102-3

See MS Routes Overview map, p164-5

Mediterranean Sea

Tangier
(see map, p68)

Ceuta
(see map, p69)

Tetouan

Asilah

Larache

Chechaouen

Hoceima

Melilla
(see map, p70)

Nador

Ouezzane

Oujda

Sidi Kacem

Taza

Guercif

RABAT

Fes

Meknes

El Hajeb

Rommani

Azrou

Missour

Oued Zem

Khenifra

El Kebab

Midelt

Gourama

Bouarfa

Kasba
Tadla

Beni Tajite

Figuig

Rachidia

Boudnib

Bouanane

Goulmina

Aoufous

Boumalne
du Dades

Tinerhir

rfoud

Alnif

Fssani

arzazate

Nekob

Agdz

Tazzarine

Zagora

m Zguid

Tagounite

ALGERIA

0    50    100    150    200km

soyez le bienvenu au

CAFE RESTAURANT **OASIS**

**CHRIS SCOTT** first passed through Morocco in 1981 on an XT500 motorcycle while returning from his first aborted Sahara trip, an adventure he relates in his early memoir, *Desert Travels*. Since that time he's undertaken several other aborted trips in the Sahara, including *Desert Riders* in 2005 (on DVD) and the second known crossing of the Majabat al Koubra in 2006. For the full list of his other achievements go to www.sahara-overland.com and click the picture.

His other books for Trailblazer include the *Adventure Motorcycling Handbook*, *Sahara Overland* and the *Overlanders' Handbook* (due 2010).

# CONTENTS

## INTRODUCTION

## PART 1: PLANNING

## PART 2: VEHICLE CHOICE & PREPARATION

## PART 3: GETTING THERE

## PART 4: AT THE BORDER

## PART 5: ON THE ROAD

## PART 6: OFF THE ROAD

## PARTS 7-12: ROUTE GUIDES     [see p100 for detailed list]

**Morocco Overland – Route guide: from the Atlas to the Sahara**
First edition: June 2009

**Publisher**
Trailblazer Publications
The Old Manse, Tower Rd, Hindhead, Surrey, GU26 6SU, UK
Fax (+44) 01428-607571
info@trailblazer-guides.com
www.trailblazer-guides.com


**British Library Cataloguing in Publication Data**
A catalogue record for this book is available from the British Library


**ISBN 978-1-905864-20-1**

© **Chris Scott 2009**
Text, maps and photographs (unless otherwise credited)
The right of Chris Scott to be identified as the author of this work has been asserted
by him in accordance with the Copyright, Designs and Patents Act 1988

**Editor**: Jim Manthorpe
**Series Editor**: Patricia Major
**Editorial assistant**: Nicky Slade
**Typesetting and layout**: Chris Scott
**Cartography**: Nick Hill
**Index**: Patrick D Hummingbird


**Additional acknowledgements**
As well as those included on the title page, thanks to Peter B at Bikershome for a couple of ideas
and to Peter Hartleb, Manfred Schweda, Daniel Hunter and Rob & Ally Ford for pictures


**Photos**
© Chris Scott 2009 (unless otherwise credited)
**Cover**: KM74, Route MA3; **p1**: Reporting for duty on Route MW3;
**p4**: Café by the palmerie in Taghjijt

All rights reserved. Other than brief extracts for the purposes of review
no part of this publication may be reproduced in any form without the written
consent of the publisher and copyright owner.


**Mountain and desert travel is unpredictable and can be dangerous.**
**Every effort has been made by the author, contributors and the publisher to ensure that**
**the information contained herein is as accurate as possible. However, they are unable**
**to accept responsibility for any inconvenience, loss or injury sustained by anyone**
**as a result of the advice and information given in this guide.**

Printed on chlorine-free paper by D2Print (☎ +65-6295 5598), Singapore

# INTRODUCTION

*'...had to get away to see what we could find.'* **Marrakech Express**

As a tourist destination Morocco is well established. Long before Crosby, Stills, Nash & Young sang their carefree Sixties hit, and half a century before Bergman turned away from Bogart on that foggy airstrip in *Casablanca*, European tourists had lifted the veil on the 'African Orient'. They crossed the Straits of Gibraltar, intrigued by the mysterious medieval allure of cities like Tangier, Fes and Marrakech, a traditional Islamic culture that had fiercely resisted colonisation, and the promise of the mountains and desert beyond.

Today our fascination with Morocco, so close and yet so different, shows no sign of abating. 'Sand, sea and souks' coach tours continue to ply the well-worn tourist tramlines, while cheap air fares have popularised weekend city breaks to upmarket Marrakech *riads* or villas.

*Morocco Overland* shows you another side of Morocco, where the adventurous driver, rider or cyclist can safely explore the snowbound passes of the High Atlas or the dusty *pistes* of the Sahara. In between visiting the well-known highlights, the sites, cities and beachside resorts, you can trace a network of easily navigable routes far from the hassle-prone, trinket-clad tourist hotspots.

In doing so you have a chance to experience the wilderness of southern Morocco at your own pace and on your own terms. Explore the jebels, palmeries and ruined kasbahs of canyon-bound Berber villages lost in time, and by doing so encounter a traditional and hospitable people, light years from the populated, Europeanised north.

Along the way you'll also learn the capabilities of your own machine and acquire many other new skills, all while lunching on a grassy meadow by a mountain stream or overnighting at the base of

a dune with little more than the wind, sand and stars between you and Timbuktu.

# 1 PLANNING

## When to go

Morocco is a **year-round destination** but, depending on the season, some regions will be more agreeable or accessible than others. The short version is this: in summer the desert will be extremely hot; in winter tracks over the High Atlas may be closed, and at any time of year heavy rain can render mountain tracks impassable. **Flooding** or its consequent damage is the least predictable but most likely cause of inaccessible tracks and briefly closed main roads in southern Morocco.

Some guidebooks suggest the spring thaw sees a high risk of floods across the Atlas. It sounds plausible but in fact anywhere in the world, mountain snow melts steadily and there's not that much of it in Morocco anyway. A sustained period of heavy rains will have a much greater impact and this can happen at any time of year, but most commonly in late summer-early autumn. In September and October 2008 the north-east corner of Africa was hit by weeks of extremely heavy rains which led to scores of fatalities along Morocco's Mediterranean coast and in the east of the country.

There's not much you can do about flooding, but unless you know better or are habituated to high temperatures (as bikers from the Iberian peninsula might be), on a **bike** you'd do well to **avoid Morocco in mid-summer**, or at least plan to stay in the mountains.

### Climate patterns

The Atlas mountains, the Sahara and the Atlantic Ocean, along with the Mediterranean Sea, all help make the Moroccan climate as regionally diverse as its landscapes. The snow-bound summit of Jebel Toubkal (North Africa's highest mountain) is just 200km from the dunes of Chegaga and many routes in this book can take you from 2500m (8000ft-plus) passes down to the baking desert in a couple of hours. On one trip in April I experienced scorching 40°C winds south of Foum Zguid and met some bikers a few days later who were riding through snow over the Rif Mountains at around the same time. In a car with air-con, heating and wipers, the weather is not such a big deal, but on a bike – with or without an engine – it certainly is.

North of the High Atlas the country experiences a predominantly Mediterranean climate of hot, dry summers and cool, wet winters. Snowfall is likely in the Middle Atlas with winter rainfall most prominent north of Casablanca and particularly in the Rif. Heading south from the Mediterranean ports from November to March there's a one-in-three chance you'll get rained on any one day. By the time you get to Marrakech it's less than one-in-five and over the Atlas in Ouarzazate the chances of getting wet are negligible. Ouarzazate is Morocco's **driest and hottest** big town and can experience temperature extremes of 58°C (though not necessarily in the same year) and an annual average of less than half an inch (< 12mm) of rain. Places further from the sea and at lower elevation like Figuig or Zagora are probably a little drier and hotter still.

The **wettest and coldest** town is the alpine-style resort of Ifrane at 1665m/5463ft in the Middle Atlas, with average daily lows barely above freezing from December to March and with a lot of rain and snow from November to April. If you find yourself heat struck in mid-summer Morocco, head for Midelt (1515m/4970ft) or the cool cedar forests of the Middle Atlas.

## The desert wind
In the desert, winds are almost always present and when strong and from a certain direction can take the edge off your experience by reducing visibility to a few kilometres and rendering all landscapes hazy. The season begins in February with hot **sand winds** blowing for days at a time. As the months progress and temperatures rise, summer skies are often muddied by the heat-borne, dusty haze.

In my experience the term sandstorm is often misused for conditions that are merely very windy with some dust and sand blowing about; a pretty permanent situation in the Sahara which occasionally escalates to the sand wind described above. Just like a regular thunderstorm, a true **sandstorm** is a relatively short and intense event, lasting maybe a few hours. It will be associated with a wall of sand coming at you and engulfing you briefly in zero visibility. A sprinkle of rain often accompanies this dramatic event. Although, like thunderstorms, they're more common at the height or end of summer, in 30 years I've only experienced this twice in the Sahara. One time was in May 2008 near Merzouga when with little warning, a tsunami of sand hundreds of feet high rolled towards us and wrapped the rocking car in a sandy fog.

In southern Morocco I find the most violent sand winds seem to come pre-

---

### DAYLIGHT HOURS IN WINTER

When the clocks go back in the UK in late October, Moroccan time is the same but because it's more or less halfway to the equator from the UK, daylight hours vary less with the seasons. So it is that while the sun may set at 5.45pm in late October or February, it's also light enough to travel from 6am onwards. By getting into a 'farmer's' schedule of sleeping and rising early, you can still make use of up to 12 hours of daylight at these times of year. Moroccan hotel staff may not see it this way of course, and getting an early breakfast may take some persuading.

In mid-winter the **shortest days** are still about 10 hours long, with sunrise around Christmas in Ouarzazate at 7.20am and sunset at 5.30pm. Depending on your **altitude**, when camping at this time of year, it can be the dawn temperatures that decide how early you manage to get up, but with the way the clocks are set in Morocco, it pays to get going soon after dawn and so make the most of the best part of the day.

dominantly from the south or south-east in the **transient seasons** of spring and autumn, bringing with them the dust from the Western Sahara plateau. Such a day can often end in rain which quickly rinses the skies, bringing a following day of ragged clouds and clear air until the next front comes through.

## The Atlantic influence

While the Atlantic coast of Morocco sees the Sahara unroll to its very shore from Tan-Tan southwards, temperature extremes are mitigated by ocean currents. Places like Essaouira and particularly Agadir have the most agreeable climates in Morocco, with moderate rainfall and temperatures all helping make Agadir the country's main beach resort. Down in the Western Sahara, Laayoune recorded 44°C one day in June 2007, but generally the ocean suppresses such extremes and summer temperatures here don't usually exceed the mid-30s. Dakhla (a special case, situated as it is on the end of a peninsula) never sees frost and gets temperatures above 30°C on no more than a couple of days a year. At this time, however, right along the Atlantic Route **strong winds** as well as cloud and fog are regular features.

## And when not to go

Particularly on a motorbike or bicycle, avoid the **Moroccan Sahara** between June and September. At this time from Tangier southwards anywhere in Morocco below 1500m can have a 40°C day and south of the Atlas these sorts of temperatures occur daily for a month or two.

© Eric De Nadai

In winter expect to get **rained on** in the north as well as in the High- and Middle Atlas ranges where **snow** is also a distinct possibility above 2000m. However bad that might get, at this time at least you have the benefit of knowing that this book's routes south of the High Atlas (ie: most of them) will probably experience near ideal conditions: clear skies but with little chance of getting dangerously dehydrated while riding a bike.

In between these seasons – **October to November** and **February to March** – you have the greatest chance of exploring anywhere without getting comprehensively frozen, soaked or baked. Late autumn in particular can be a good time with light winds, warm temperatures and clear skies.

Good **weather websites** covering Morocco include 🖥 www.weather online.co.uk/Morocco.htm and 🖥 uk.weather.com/global (click 'North Africa') which features sunrise and sunset times (see box on previous page).

PLANNING YOUR TRIP

# Where to go

Even if this is not your first visit to Morocco, chances are you'll want to see something of the north during your visit, at the very least one of the big cities like Fes or Marrakech, or more manageable large towns like Asilah or Chefchaouen, both an hour or two south of Tangier.

## The Standard Morocco Tour

For car drivers and motorbikers, the standard trip to Morocco involves crossing the Straits on a quick ferry to **Ceuta** or Tangier, heading down towards the Middle Atlas or **Marrakech**, crossing the **Atlas**, often via the popular **Aït Benhaddou** piste (see p162) then heading over to the east to pay one's respects to the **Todra Gorge** and maybe have a crack at Gorge-to-Gorge; Route MH3. From there it's common to cross over **Jebel Sarhro** to Nekob via Route MH4 and either continue south to **Zagora** to take Route MS6 east to Merzouga, or find some other way to end up visiting **Erg Chebbi**. A return might include a crossing of the Atlas such as MH2 or via Midelt with a stop in **Fes**. **Essaouira** on the coast north of Agadir might be thrown in the mix too, somehow.

A tour like this is manageable in a fortnight and hits just about all the buttons in Morocco. It could also be described as following the main tourism axis with the most chance of encountering high prices and hassle in the bigger towns and cities. In the busy seasons it can also feel a bit like a procession at times, reducing the impression that you're out exploring in the wilds, though if it's your first time, knowing you're not alone can actually be comforting.

For Morocco, Erg Chebbi is a natural wonder for sure, but other than that, consider using this book to find a creative way to cover the same regions, or break off the axis altogether to do your own thing. There is more on the regions at the start of each of the six zones from p101.

---

### ... AND WHERE YOU MIGHT NOT WANT TO GO: THE RIF

Although no one will stop you going there, one region worth being aware of is the cannabis cultivation area of the **Rif mountains**, centred around the town of Ketama on the N2 junction, east of Chefchaouen.

Following a post-independence Berber rebellion in the 1950s (and a brief 'Republic' in the 1920s, crushed by France and Spain), the government turned its back on the Rif, stifling economic development in the area. As a result cannabis, once grown all over Morocco, has boomed here making it the biggest source of hash in the world, with cannabis pollen recorded on the Spanish mainland and the ever expanding cultivation threatening local forests.

Despite EU pressure, the state turns a blind eye to the illegal enterprise, but deprivation has led to poverty, crumbling roads and neglected towns of hostile people. It may be a lucrative business but the peasants who do all the work are as poor as any in Morocco.

There are no armed drug gangs terrorising each other as elsewhere in the world, but those travellers who don't blunder in naively regularly report that their initial curiosity soon vanishes on being chased by youths in an aggressively-driven Mercedes trying to sell a block of hash or inviting them for a smoke – usually in exchange for their valuables.

## What can I do in...

These suggestions assume you're UK-based. If you're in Portugal or Spain you can do a bit more; if you live 70km east of Murmansk your options are much more limited. Even then, many recognise once they get back that they **planned over-ambitiously** and tried to do **too much in too short a time**.

For ideas of what can be done in a **two-day rental** see p85. For suggestions on combining many of these routes into 25 **day trips** by returning to the same place in the evening – particularly aimed at motorbikers looking to enjoy a ride without carting full baggage – see p92-96.

### A week or less

Quite a lot actually, but you'll need to fly in and rent a vehicle out of Agadir, Marrakech or Ouarzazate (see p83) to make the most of your time. All three cities are well placed to make the most of their adjacent regions, giving you up to five great days on the piste. Doing it this way will be a bit hectic of course, but the costs may well be the same as trying to cram a fortnight in with your

---

### FIRST TIME IN MOROCCO

In the current climate of what some call Islamophobia, it's normal to feel apprehensive about travelling to Morocco if you've never visited a Muslim country or have had much of a chance to meet Muslim people.

Particularly around Algeciras port in southern Spain or in Ceuta, the flavour of what lies ahead can start to get intimidating, which is one reason why the alternative Spanish ports of Tarifa, Málaga and Almería can be more relaxed departure points.

Once off the boat and with the immigration formalities completed, the biggest hurdle is behind you, but the culture shock still requires some acclimatisation. Until you get your bearings, or even when you do, the relatively crowded north may not be to everyone's taste. South of the Atlas it's altogether another world and is partly why a book like this got written.

If you're unsure about dealing with it all it's not a bad idea to head directly south and get a feel for the country and the people. Then dally through the north on your way back by which time you're a little more streetwise.

#### Islamic customs

It's worth recognising that not all Muslim countries follow the strict mores of places like Saudi Arabia or Iran. North African countries in particular interpret religious strictures much more leniently and even meld Islam with older, pre-Islamic practices.

This moderate form of Islam partly accounts for the success of tourism in places like Morocco, Tunisia and Egypt.

When you start to meet genuine people (as opposed to the irritating touts who'll zone in on you) there are some customs worth adopting. They really add up to no more than politeness and local etiquette.

- When asking directions or initiating a conversation with a stranger, slow down, turn off a noisy engine, then start with a *bonjour* or *salaam aleikum* and shake hands, rather than yelling '*Oi, which way to Ouarzazate!?*'.
- In remote and traditional settings such enquiries have the most successful and accurate results with older men.
- If you speak in French there's more chance of being understood. In the remote villages women may not speak French.
- If invited into someone's living room or tent, take your shoes off.
- For anything more than a tea, for example a meal, a lift or some other form of help, offer payment or some sort of gift. It does not have to be extravagant.
- If eating communally from a bowl (as one does with cous-cous) do not use the left hand.
- If the talk turns to Islam, as it can do, it's better to profess some religious belief than being an atheist or agnostic.
- If in doubt, do as others do.

own vehicle. A more relaxed alternative is having a normal week's holiday and renting for a couple of days to do some routes. It's a great way to dip your toe in the sand and see if you even like the idea of overlanding in Morocco.

## Two weeks

This is the practical limit for a visit in your own vehicle from the UK or northern Europe. Falling within a typical holiday allocation, it's what many people try, usually just once. You'll need to get cracking and have a good plan; from London to Algeciras is 2350km or nearly 1500 miles. To squeeze every last hour from what are technically 16 days off, if the ferries line up and by leaving work on a Friday night, you could be in Morocco by Monday lunchtime and in the desert a day or two later, This could give you, at the very best, nine days in the Atlas and the Sahara, or more reasonably a week on the piste with a rest day or two or a visit to a big city or a resort. Although this is an intense schedule, a week on the piste is actually a pretty satisfying immersion as long as the weather remains good and you have no vehicle problems.

Renting a decent 4WD like a Toyota 105 for two weeks gets pretty pricey unless you have a car full of people to share the cost or if you choose to hire a well-used and inexpensive 4WD with all the risks that entails off the highway. The cheapest motorbike rentals out of Marrakech add up to around €1000 or so for a fortnight, still pretty good compared to a ride in mid-winter but sometimes frustrating when it comes to gear.

## A month

With up to four weeks at your disposal you need not dash from the office to the ferry port like a lunatic and so can enjoy a relaxing tour, ticking off your pick of the routes in this book as well as taking the chance to visit some other places in Morocco, Spain and France. Between Figuig and the Atlantic you could easily explore a dozen routes as well as a few of your own, highlighting the full potential or the region and without needing a holiday afterwards to get over it. Or of course you could make a mad dash to Mauritania and Timbuktu.

## More than a month

By choosing the right season and using your typical three-month Moroccan visa to the limit, you can slowly explore the Atlas ranges and the Saharan plains, park up in remote spots or villages that take your fancy, get to know some locals, go trekking with them or go mountain biking and generally immerse yourself in the Moroccan experience. Or head off to West Africa for the winter. All you need is the time, the money and the inclination.

# Documents, money, costs and phones

For Morocco your paperwork adds up to no more than your **passport** and your **vehicle ownership document** as well as possible motor- and travel insurance documents. Your passport must be valid for at least six months after the date you expect to leave Morocco and, unlike some other North African countries, the presence of Israeli stamps is not a problem.

Your **vehicle ownership documents** – in the UK called the V5 or 'logbook' – are your vehicle's 'passport' and even though back home you may only ever see it when buying and selling a vehicle, to enter Morocco it's **essential**. If for some reason the vehicle is not in your name you'll need a letter of explanation in French and better still Arabic with official-looking stamps stating you have permission from the owner, but even then you can expect problems.

In general the owner of the vehicle must be present at the Moroccan border and this particularly goes for someone else's motorbikes in the back of a van. If vehicle owners are not present, even with the vehicle logbooks and written permission from the owners, you can expect long delays at the port while you persuade them you're not an unlicensed tour operator or transporting stolen bikes to Mauritania. It can be done but lately has become a lot harder; you have been warned.

## Visas

Currently citizens of EU member states as well as Canadians, Americans and Australians don't need a visa and can stay in Morocco for up to **90 days**. This period can be renewed at police stations or by simply leaving the country and coming back in. Some east European nationals as well as South Africans will require a visa which must be applied for in advance and which lasts a month. In the UK they cost about £16. Apply at your nearest Moroccan embassy well before your planned departure.

## Motor insurance

A few years ago in the UK it used to be easy to get a Green Card extension of your domestic motor insurance to cover Morocco, just as you can still do for Europe (although your basic insurance will cover you in the EU, even without a Green Card). Low-risk **UK campervan** drivers have less difficulty with Moroccan cover and the situation is better on the continent, but nowadays it seems regular UK motor insurance companies don't offer this service. However, buying insurance in Morocco is easy enough and costs the same.

Some entry ports like Tangier and Nador (see map on p68 and 70) but not Fnideq at Ceuta have insurance booths selling *Assurance aux Frontières*. It's also said to be possible to buy it at Algerciras port. If not, you can buy it once out of the port in an adjacent town (from Fnideq it's Tetouan – look out for the blue '*Axa Assurance*'). If you get stopped by the police as you leave a port – a not uncommon occurrence – explain you're heading for- or even ask for the nearest '*bureau d'assurance*'. It may seem unorthodox to venture out on the streets without motor insurance but this, as you're about to find out, is Africa.

The cost of insurance is the same fixed rate wherever you buy it and the periods are fixed at one or three months with prices at the time of writing as follows:

|  | 10 days | 1 month | 3 months |
| --- | --- | --- | --- |
| Cars and motorcycles | 574 dirhams (dh) | 876 dh | 1768 dh |
| Camping cars | 1500 dh (est) | 2518 dh | 4609 dh |

For **exchange rates** see the opposite page. A document will be printed out not unlike your D16 (see p68) with your details alongside French and Arabic explanations. Keep it with your D16 to present if asked at a roadside checkpoint.

What is actually covered in the event of an accident you'd hope never to find out, but it's most probably no more than the legal minimum protection to a Third Party, or more realistically something to show at a police checkpoint to avoid a fine.

Some people worry that this does not cover **damage** to or **theft** from or of their vehicle and is one good reason to resist decking out your Defender like the Battlestar Gallactica. Such insurance can be bought from expedition specialists in the UK but it can be extremely expensive (on the continent it's less so). When overnighting in big cities, if your hotel has no parking (often the case in the traditional small hotels in the city-centre medina or old quarter) you're best off paying for **secure parking** in attended lots or garages while taking the usual precautions you'd take anywhere else. The guidebooks on pp25-26 give basic details of secure parking sites in cities like Fes or Marrakech.

In the UK at least, insurance cover for breakdowns, repairs or **vehicle recovery** is not available as it is say, for Dutch members of the Royal Dutch Automobil Club and probably other continental nationals. This does mean you can be on your own if you strike vehicle trouble and is where the true and not so glamourous meaning of the word 'adventure' can become apparent. For ideas on what to do when things go wrong, see p74.

## Money and costs

At the time of writing exchange rates for major currencies against the Moroccan dirhams were as follows:

| £1 | 12.4 dirhams (dh) |
|---|---|
| €1 | 11.2 dh |
| US$1 | 8.6 dh |

Officially it's not possible to buy Moroccan dirhams outside the country but there'll be exchange bureaux or banks at Algeciras, on some ferries and at the ports. They're all legitimate, offer the same rate and provide you with a receipt, but as anywhere it pays not to let your guard down when the notes are being dished out and to count them back in front of the seller. There's **no black market** for currency in Morocco, though that won't stop shady individuals at the ports or in bigger cities trying to suggest otherwise.

Once on the road it's easy to withdraw further funds with credit or debit cards from banks or **ATMs** outside banks in many Moroccan towns. It's not unusual to find that, despite guarantees in advance, on arrival one of your UK bank cards is not recognised in a Moroccan ATM (or even mainland Europe) so if you have several cards, **bring a few** to be on the safe side and try them out sooner rather than later. Some of these ATMs even recognise and accept major foreign currency bank notes (as opposed to plastic cards) and will return a receipt plus dirhams in notes and a tinkle of coins. In the deep south ATMs will only be found in the biggest towns like Erfoud and Rissani, Zagora, Tata and Guelmim.

Away from ATMs, **credit or debit cards** are not widely used for purchases in the south of Morocco, certainly not in local stores, most fuel stations or at less than high-end hotels. Travellers' cheques leave you dependent on finding a bank that's open and so good, old-fashioned **cash** in the form of **euros** or of course dirhams is the best currency in Morocco. If you run out of dirhams, in places it may be possible to pay in euros.

## Some costs

As a tourist, and certainly in touristy places down south such as Boumalne du Dades, Erfoud and Zagora, you can expect to be overcharged a little for ordinary purchases where prices are not clearly marked. Overall though it's not something worth getting worked up about as the **cost of living** is less than half that of the UK.

Remember too that, as anywhere in the world, costs will be higher and the range of products less in remote places. Very occasionally, in places not normally visited by tourists you may be charged a local rate for something like a meal which can come as quite a shock. Then again, at other times a kind local may offer a service or assistance for nothing or humbly request 'whatever you think it's worth'. Even in tourist souks, getting blatantly ripped off is as rare as getting robbed and depends partly on your attitude, gullibility, patience and sometimes, your proficiency in French.

### Motoring

| | |
|---|---|
| Straits ferry; 4WD and 2 pax | from €200 return |
| Motorcycle and rider | from €80 return |
| Diesel | 7.4 dh/litre |
| Unleaded petrol | 11.4 dh |
| 5L motor oil | from 90 dh |
| Car tyre repair | from 30 dh |
| DIY car wash | from 20 dh |
| Replace broken leaf spring | around 500 dh |
| Motorcycle rental | around 3500–5000 dh/week |
| 4WD rental | from 9000 dh/week |

Diesel prices in 'mainland' Morocco (see also p76) are currently about the same as in the two Spanish port enclaves, though unleaded may work out less here. In Western Sahara they are about 30% less than the north: see p61.

---

### BARGAINING FOR SOUVENIRS

Despite what some may assume, bartering over regular daily purchases and services is not the norm. Haggling over a **souvenir** in a *souk* or market is another game altogether.

You may read about memorising cunning equations such as: offer a third of the initial price and settle on half, but if you don't want to feel you've been cheated or made a fool of, the simplest advice is:

- take your time (take *days* to think it over if you have the chance) and
- pay what you think it's worth.

Ask youself would you *really* pay €25 for a studded leather camel skull ash tray back home? Moroccan vendors are world-class masters in the art of selling overpriced handicrafts to tourists. But so-called 'Moroccan chic' and design are world class too, and many of the products you'll admire in the souks would proudly be seen adorning the homes of locals.

My own tactic on seeing something I like but don't need is this: first, mull it over for days. If possible, ask a local what it's worth. Then fix a fair price in your head, stick to it **with good humour** through all the spiel and 'buy two get one half price', and be prepared to walk away if you don't get it.

The back of the current *Lonely Planet Morocco* guide allocates a full page of sound advice for the wary buyer.

## Eating

| | |
|---|---|
| Bread | from 0.2 dh |
| Bottled water 1.5 lt | around 5–7 dh |
| Soft drink | around 4–6 dh |
| Cup of coffee or tea | from 5 dh |
| Salad | around 10 dh |
| Brochette (kebab) | from 40 dh |
| Omelette and chips | from 20 dh |
| Tajine | from 30–60 dh |

## Accommodation

Morocco has a huge range of inexpensive, unclassified hotels as well as basic tourist-oriented *auberges*. In the bigger cities they're often in the charismatic but also run-down and noisy old quarter or *medina* with attendant parking limitations and, away from the tourist axis in the south, basic hotels like this may be all you'll find. At these places booking ahead is unnecessary; very often you'll be the only person staying there.

In the cities or in the countryside you'll not get much more, pound for pound, by paying over 250dh for a hotel room unless you've been roughing it for days and are looking for some sort of lavish treat. Anything with 'kasbah' in the name will usually be in this category. The better **guidebooks** (see pp25-26) can fill you in on other costs and practicalities of accommodation and this book's website has a link to a growing thread of recommendations.

| | |
|---|---|
| Basic hotel (shared bathroom) | from 50 dh – half board from 90 dh |
| Moderate (en suite) | from 120 dh – half board from 170 dh |
| Upmarket kasbah-auberge | from 180 dh – half board from 250 dh |

### BUSINESS HOURS, RAMADAN & TIME ZONE

Morocco is an Islamic country but follows the Western model for business hours.

Things may change in the annual month-long festival of **Ramadan**, when the devout don't eat, drink or even smoke during daylight hours. Shops are still open but in general business becomes dormant, with long siestas to allow people to rest. Many restaurants and cafés close in the daytime, when it can be hard to get a meal.

It's not quite correct to call Ramadan a **fast**, as a whole lot of eating and drinking goes on once the *muezzins* (prayer callers) or sirens have signalled sunset. The fast is often broken with a light snack of dates and milk, with a big feed late at night and another an hour or two before dawn.

For the non-Muslim traveller, Ramadan in Morocco can be an inconvenience in the daytime, at which time it's good form not to eat or drink publicly. Be discrete; most people are tolerant of non-Muslim foreigners.

Although it's fun to get caught up in the evening's anticipation as the daily fast is broken, perhaps the biggest factor to travellers is that by the end of Ramadan people are pretty exhausted and can get ratty. At this time it should be you who exercises some tolerance.

Every year Ramadan falls about 11 days earlier and currently it's moving towards August which will see it coinciding with the longer, hotter days of summer. The exact timings are governed by the moon sightings in Mecca. Future predictions are as follows:

| | | |
|---|---|---|
| 2009 | 21 August | 19 September |
| 2010 | 10 August | 8 September |
| 2011 | 1 August | 29 August |
| 2012 | 21 July | 20 August |

Despite a brief experiment in 2008, Morocco now follows **GMT**. This means in winter it's an hour behind Spanish time (ie: the same as the UK) and in summer is two hours behind Spain. Remember that the Spanish enclaves and ferry ports of Ceuta and Melilla will run on Spanish time. Don't miss the boat!

## MOBILE PHONES

Bring a mobile to Morocco even if you don't plan to turn it on. Disregarding its day to day utility, a mobile is a very useful tool out there in case of emergency. As with many North African countries, the market penetration of mobiles is among the highest in the world and far exceeds land lines. Your mobile should work in any sizeable town.

The two main mobile phone service providers are *Maroc Telecom* and *Méditel*, and both have kept pace by erecting masts across the country to keep up with demand. At ⌨ gsmworld.com/roaming/gsminfo/ (click 'Morocco') or the Méditel website (⌨ www.meditel.ma/cvr/nat) you can scan a map to get a good idea of the national coverage, but bear in mind these maps are probably optimistic. Obviously you need to make sure your **roaming** has been enabled before leaving home and it's important to recognise that on many of the routes in this book you'll be out of range.

The Meditel map will reveal that **south of the Atlas**, and on the Atlantic coast south of Tan-Tan, coverage along highways drops off about 20km from a town with a mast. Nevertheless, if you're desperate, besides setting your phone to re-scan manually for local providers, it's worth walking around, getting on high ground or on a line-of-sight towards where you think a mast or town might be to try and get a signal. And as for who you're going to call...? See p75.

If you find your home service isn't working in Morocco or just want to save money on local calls (and even calls home) it's easy to buy a local SIM card from the above providers' many agencies for just a couple of pounds and get some credit. To do this you mobile phone may need 'unlocking', but chances are the shop that sells you the SIM can do this for you for a few dirhams. Moroccan mobile numbers start with 06 or 07 but see the website's update page for **new phone codes** which were introduced in March 2009.

Public phones do exist but as elsewhere in the world, their days are numbered. More prolific and reliable are taxi phone boutiques; private enterprises with a bank of phones for those too poor to afford a mobile. The **international country code** is 212.

# Maps

You'll need one of these maps in Morocco but the following reviews (updated on the website) only relate to a map's utility on the pistes of the Atlas and the Sahara. The north of Morocco is not considered, though one can safely assume that a map's general characteristics will not vary much either side of the Atlas.

## COUNTRY MAPS

There are up to a dozen Morocco country maps in print and taking into account scale, price, clarity, availability, date of publication and presence of a longitude/latitude grid to enable rough positioning with a roamer (see picture p21), half a dozen can be considered useful for independent overland travel in the south of Morocco.

Using them in the field one thing quickly became clear to me: while you won't get lost and die of thirst relying on these maps, scrutinise them closely and they're surprisingly inaccurate when it comes to verifying and differentiating a road from a track and even a *piste* from a footpath. They also tend to copy each other's mistakes which hints at how some get updated.

Some minor routes shown as sealed are in fact little-used pistes not likely to be sealed anytime soon, and some tracks depicted identically on several maps do not exist or match the orientation shown. Unlike with most guidebooks, it seems unlikely that an operative from the map publisher drives around checking for mistakes or that anyone takes much notice of updates sent in by users. Instead they may rely on information on road-building programmes issued by government ministries.

In other words, for navigating along the main 'N' or *route nationale* highways in an RV, in most cases the following maps are fine, but using even this short-listed selection for reliable navigation and accurate position-finding on southern Moroccan tracks is likely to be a hit and miss affair. Once you've accepted this limitation these maps aren't so bad; without other navigational aids just be ready not to always be sure exactly where you are or where a given piste not covered in this book may end up. By Saharan standards Moroccan tracks are short (rarely over 200km) so this uncertainty is not much of a problem in cars or even on motorcycles with a 15-litre-plus fuel tank.

What also became evident over the weeks was how many more interesting and easily navigable pistes there are in Morocco which never make it onto these maps. The same can be said for villages; many established settlements on a par with other locally-depicted places were missing while some towns are given inconsistent prominence.

I used all these maps on both research trips and soon became familiar with their strengths and weaknesses. It's worth remembering that appreciating a map's style and design can be objective so don't take my word for what follows, or indeed any other opinion given in this book!

## Michelin 742 (2008)

### 1:1 million
Michelin, the best map for Morocco, right? It's OK but the thin paper Michelin uses does not lend itself to regular use, not helped by the fact that, at over 1.5m wide, the 742 is a big map. Rather than city insets you get five useful sub regions at 600k scale (notably Jebel Sirwa south of Marrakech), as well as some useful climate statistics.

The best thing about this map is the intuitive 1:1m scale (a millimetre = a kilometre), the clear, functional Michelin design and the fact that the main map goes right down to Laayoune which means you can view all this book's routes at once (apart from the lower halves of Routes MO2 and MW6). At under a fiver in the UK it's also the cheapest of the Morocco maps.

With the exception of a suspiciously straight piste heading west out of Taouz, roads and pistes wind around with believable intricacy (unlike the lazier RKH map, see p21). You get Michelin's well-known scenic 'green road' feature (imitated on the GeoCentre and IGN maps) which is pretty reliable, but elsewhere they go too far: if you're a woodpecker then the forest cover is not to be relied on too closely unless for example, the Taliouine region has experienced a recent epidemic of Dutch Elm disease. Depictions of dunes get the same artistic interpretation and this is the sort of base detail that you feel will never get updated.

As for the accuracy of secondary roads and pistes – a common failing on all these maps – look carefully at the Key (in five languages including Arabic – nice touch). Unconventionally, uncoloured (white) roads with solid borders on both sides signify 'Road surfaced' (*route revêtue* or 'covered', as opposed to *goudronée*; tarred) but one dashed edge means an all-out piste. Surfaced with what you wonder? It's a conveniently ambiguous way of saying they could be surfaced with steaming asphalt, gravel, Nutella or rocks. Some of these 'white roads' are major two-lane highways where the regular yellow colouring would be correct. As on other maps, a few pistes and even white roads don't exist, while of course many more are missing. In places this data is up to eight years out of date but overall they don't get it as badly- or as blatantly wrong as the *RKH* (see p21).

Conspicuous by its absence is a long/lat grid for use with a roamer (see picture opposite). A possible reason why Michelin have not got round to this in this age of widespread GPS use becomes apparent when you try and draw a grid on it yourself. It soon transpires the map is actually aligned quite a few degrees east of north, most probably because it's based on the top left corner of their 'North and West Africa' 953 map which is north-centred on E16°. Without presumably expensive correction, printing a grid over a 742 would expose this lean all the more clearly and might put customers off. Don't know what I'm on about? Don't worry, it's not that important.

Overall, you can forgive the out-of-date detail because of the good design, but instead of banging out so-called 'new editions' with the legal minimum of alterations, Michelin should take a bold step and print double-sided on plastic paper with grid lines – or at least use better paper. That is never going to happen so in my experience the 742 is not significantly better for back-country or piste driving than a more robust and gridded RKH or IGN/Geo Centre.

## GeoCentre (2006)

### 1:800,000

After the Michelin the design of the GeoCentre map works best; an off-white background on comfortingly thick paper and with muted relief shading making roads and tracks clearer. It also has a long/lat grid at no less than half-degree intervals which, with a ruler or the right-sized roamer (see opposite), makes estimating your position from a GPS waypoint easy.

Road information was pretty out-of-date compared to other maps reviewed here, although GeoCentre imitate Michelin's green bands to designate scenic drives. It's an objective thing but what 'green roads' I drove on the Geo were indeed scenic, though so were a lot of other plainly marked byways.

Insets include three northern cities and the Western Sahara but the bottom edge of the main map ends quite high at Sidi Ifni (The 742, by comparison reaches down well below Smara).

You get an index booklet (does anyone ever use these?), a key in several languages, but like the F&B they don't give a publication date. The identical IGN version claims to be from 2006.

## IGN (2006)

### 1:800,000

This map is the same as the GeoCentre described opposite but with a slightly darker tone (just as the RKH appears darker compared to the Rough Guide version). The paper may be a tad thinner and you don't get the index booklet or the multi-lingual key. In short it's a compact and so less expensive Geo Centre with the main sheet reaching down only to Sidi Ifni. The remainder is an inset at 2.5m which is not so good for use in the 'MW' region (see p234).

## Reise Know-How (2007)

### 1:1 million

When you recognise all these maps are flawed, the RKH is the most practical because, unlike the better Michelin, it won't fall apart after less than an hour's accumulated use. Cartographically the RKH wasn't the best design but the double-sided printing made it compact and easy to use inside a car, a lift or out in a gale. Try that with a TPC or the Michelin. The 1:1m scale is intuitive for quick distance estimates and the grid lines work well with a roamer*. They even manage to squeeze an index round the edges.

If necessary you can eat your lunch off an RKH, use it as an umbrella, origami it into a pet bath and generally treat it rough without it ending up like Michelin's self-confetti-ing map. Unless they have the environmental notoriety of UPVC windows, plastic paper maps are the way to go.

The RKH's biggest flaw is the vague alignment of roads and tracks and unprofessional assumptions about which pistes have been sealed. Heading for a sealed road on the map that is actually still a piste and will never be a road is more irritating and time-wasting than merely not knowing the full extent of asphalting and may be why Michelin plays it down by using less conspicuous 'white roads'.

This map is not widely sold in the UK. You can also download a pre-calibrated digital version of this map from the RKH website to import into a computer and so track your

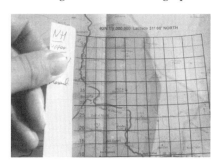

* In the sense used here (as opposed to the commercial examples found online) **roamers** are one-degree-square grids printed on clear acetate (pictured above) to help approximate your position on a 1:1m scale map with a long/lat grid.

They're only accurate on a particular band of latitude which for most of the routes in this book is 'NH'. You can download roamers to print off from the *Morocco Overland* website.

movements using GPS software for PCs. See the *Morocco Overland* website for a direct link.

## Freytag & Berndt (2005)

### 1:900,000

The F&B does not print a publication date on this map apart from a misleading '06/2008' next to the ISBN (possibly the next edition that didn't happen?). Amazon lists it as a 2005. Once an earlier edition of the *Rough Guide* map was dropped in favour of the identical but (at that time) newer *RKH*, the *F&B* was the map I referred to last and after a while did not bother at all. While there's a possibly useful index on the back and insets of five northern cities as well as Western Sahara, for some reason the main body of the map has a dull yellow background making the detail less legible. Add to that road information that's not especially up-to-date and a mushy style used to show the relief and you begin to lose interest. Worst of all, pistes are depicted with a vague, dashed line and even change midway into a dotted line ('footpath' according to the key – on a 1m-scale country map!) which did not inspire confidence.

## Rough Guide (2009)

### 1:1 million

Released just as this book went to print, the Rough Guide updates the 2007 RKH reviewed on p21, though a few new errors are added in classifying road surfaces. The German version prints the relief with more contrast or ink which helps clarity but the Rough Guide edition is easier to find in the UK and can even be ordered from the *Morocco Overland* website where you'll find a fuller review.

## Other maps and topographical imagery

You certainly don't want to travel around Morocco without one of the maps on pp19-22 but below are some other mapping resources. For reviews of **older paper maps** including IGN one millions, American 500,000 TPCs and Soviet-era topos in three scales, as well as new editions of the above sheets, see the website.

### French 1:250,000 series

These colonial-era maps are so old they don't show a border between Morocco and Algeria, but a '250' will almost always identify some obscure mountain piste that you'll find yourself on (even if it's just a thin black line) and will depict the topography with clarity and colour. Along with many disused pistes that time forgot, most of today's 'N' highways are there, showing how little has changed in the south and proving that most pistes were established in the French era, even if many have got sealed in the last decade.

They are apparently available in paper format in Morocco from some ministry or other but it may take some persuading to get a set; you can't buy them from a shop. However, the whole series of 62 full-colour sheets are available on bootleg CD. Once they're calibrated with GPS software they become very useful navigational back-up in Morocco, even if it means carrying a laptop around. With a set of calibrated 250s and a GPS you can confidently wander around the outback of Morocco and never be lost, and by reducing the size/scale of the digital files slightly to fit on to standard A0 paper size (841 x 1189mm) you can get a set printed inexpensively.

## Morocco GPS vector map: 'Olaf'

'Olaf' is my abbreviation for the free downloadable Marokko Topo GPS vector map (💻 www.island-olaf.de/travel/marokko/gps.html) produced by a German guy called Olaf Kähler – don't ask me how he does it. If you could import maps like the French 250s into a handheld GPS (as opposed to an in-car navigator like a Tom Tom) there wouldn't be so much of a need for Olaf, but you can't (at least not into a £200 Garmin). Olaf improves greatly on the base map of Morocco you get in a standard hiking

Olaf on the silver screen.
Who needs a book then?

GPS (not hard) but crucially is enhanced by adding tracks which have been GPS'ed and sent in as track logs by contributors to the project.

My appreciation of 'Olaf' was rather limited as I don't use a PC. With a PC you can view the full range of routes on a computer screen using Garmin MapSource software. I've only experienced Olaf on the matchbox-sized screen of my GPS unit and usually had no idea whether a route I'm about to follow was Olaffed until it crept onto my GPS screen. When it did I knew I wasn't going to get too lost because a fellow traveller has actually come this way in the last few years and track logged it with a GPS, rather than following some guessed-at trace by a cartographer in another country.

With an Olaf track you can zoom right in and follow a path accurately through a village instead of blundering around and frightening the mules. Sometimes though the track is out by several metres, which is odd, and other tracks finish up as dead ends – but that is all down to the quality and range of tracklogs sent in by contributors. Either way, stick Olaf in your GPS unit and you'll have an excellent and peer-proven map of many pistes in Morocco and pretty good highway information too.

## Google Maps

Even if it's free, used as a pre-planning reference map, Google Maps are misleading on southern Morocco compared to the more detailed paper maps reviewed on pp19-22. Click between 'map' to 'satellite' and you'll often see how inaccurate the highway overlay is compared to the true satellite image, although the terrain image can be illuminating. Pistes and roads are out-of-date, incomplete, not labelled with the standard Moroccan N- or R- road/track designations, inaccurate in hierarchy (closed piste and two-lane blacktop shown as the same – the same flaw as TPCs) or are non-existent, just like the worst paper maps reviewed. Furthermore, many town and village names are unrecognisable, presumably taken from non-standard US sources. Zoomed in, you can look at the Google map on Morocco a long time before you find a name you recognise and work out where you are.

## Google Earth

Now you're talking. Google Earth is particularly effective in vividly dramatising the arid topography of a place like southern Morocco, even if resolution on the 10-mile-square quadrants is rather hit and miss. Some undated sectors appear to have been shot through the bottom of a Coke bottle, while others (they are few) are just a few months old and appear as crisp as hanging out of a hot air balloon with a pair of binoculars. On Erg Chebbi you can even spot the tourist bivouacs in the dunes. Stripped of all the layers (although try 'Tracks4Africa' under 'More') and the often wildly-inaccurately positioned 'user-added' junk, at last you have a 'map' that cannot lie. With Google Earth you can preview your route or cook up new links between pistes, discover new areas and generally be amazed at the bird's eye view of your planet.

There are many Google Earth screen shots of the website's route pages showing the track of a given route.

# Recommended guidebooks

*Morocco Overland* covers southern Morocco off the beaten track and as such will be indispensable to ascertain the estimated depth of wells south of the Jebel Ouarkaziz, or whether camping atop the Col Belkassem is a good idea. By and large it leaves out the big towns, the listing of hotels and restaurants and accounts of 'Things to See and Do'.

For the big picture of mainstream Morocco, a conventional travel guidebook will greatly enhance your experience and background knowledge of the country. There are scores of specialist and regional titles covering the country, but for all their minor faults, only the *Rough Guide* or *Lonely Planet* editions do a reasonably comprehensive job while regularly releasing new editions. For practicality and ease of use, nothing else comes close. Both their 8th editions from 2007 were closely scrutinised while researching this book. LP published its 9th edition in 2009; you can expect the 9th Rough Guide in 2010.

## Doing Morocco

The average tourist to Morocco visits Fes or Marrakech and tries to shoot down to the desert for a night or two in the dunes; a version of the self-driver's 'Standard Morocco Tour' outlined on p11. The focal points along this route are regularly updated by LP or Rough Guide, but elsewhere in the south (and possibly in the north too) to cut costs, increasingly these books are getting shorter, so less visited places are skipped or appear not to have been updated for several editions. The former can be understandable – what's there to say about Akka Ighern – but the latter can be most frustrating when, exhausted and late at night, the hotel you were relying on differs markedly from the ageing review in your guidebook or a road that appeared sealed on a map is actually a track. The key word here is 'guide'; these books are not directories or tablets brought down from the mountain, and for what they cost, they repay the investment many times over.

Because *Morocco Overland* deals with the often overlooked 'places in between' down south, an effort has been made to provide information where accounts in the two guidebooks are either out of date or missing. Therefore, in this book you'll get a GPS point for the little-known hotel in a key town missed by both guidebooks, as well as fuller personal reviews of places I've actually stayed in; choices which are often based on Rough Guide or LP suggestions. Besides all the GPS stuff, you'll also get an impression of driving along a scenic highway, fuel stations and advice on car- and bike parking issues, subjects which the normal guidebooks seldom address.

Note that the following reviews relate both to the region and the type of travelling covered by this book. There is little doubt that accounts of the history of the Almoravids or the architecture of Fes are as good as it gets because once written, they don't change much. It's the practical details of accommodation, eating and getting around which can go out of date in any triennial publication, but are what most travellers depend on. In this respect the much more active LP online forum (see p26) is a bonus in keeping up to date.

When the term 'guidebooks' is used in this book's route guides, it refers to the 8th editions of these two titles, where they're not referred to by name. On this book's website there's also a selective compassion of relevant subjects and places in the south from the LP and Rough Guide to show in detail how they measure up against each other. Reviews of future editions or other useful titles will also appear there.

## Rough Guide Morocco

### 8th edition (October 2007) 820pp
Guidebook section 600pp; 140pp cover the south.

My impression was that this edition was an old, overweight dinosaur hampered by a drab format and much in need of the revamp which the parallel LP has already been through. The main towns are well covered including several which the LP skips altogether, but in between, like the LP, it suffers from patchy updates. Although it tries here and there, it's not especially useful for 'motoring' as they sometimes call it. Regional maps are mutually inconsistent as well as inaccurate (a common flaw with guidebooks), but this is only on the same 'road or track' level as the paper maps (see pp18-22). It's odd because, unlike the map publishers, the updaters are actually in the country.

Should you get sick or laid up with repairs, there's some great background material on Moroccan history, culture, books, music and language, but that changes little from edition to edition. When it comes to finite, precise practicalities and directions it can all get a bit woolly in places, although there is no escaping the fact that you've nearly **three times** as many pages in the south as the LP. For this reason it must be more useful. Make the most of it, the 9th edition will have a much reduced page count.

## Lonely Planet Morocco

**9th edition (February 2009), 536pp**
Guidebook section 320pp; 55pp cover the south.

Younger, snappier and less stodgy, the latest LP feels like it's long past its '7th-edition itch' and has been still further stripped down for the 9th edition. Now with just 55 pages covering the *Morocco Overland* area, the cutbacks on practicalities have gone a bit too far in places – for the same money in the south you get a little over a third of the coverage in the Rough Guide. Many accounts of not so out-of-the-way towns are so skimpy they seem merely index name checks while greatly easing the updating process by not being too specific. But you do get many well thought out boxes advising on the tours and other activities which tourists typically undertake, as well as whiter paper which gives a brighter look compared to a Rough Guide.

What they skip (see the website for a selective regional comparison with the current Rough Guide) *Morocco Overland* might well cover so it won't necessarily have you pulling your hair out – and if fewer pages means the remainder gets regularly updated then so much the better. However, it doesn't always seem so. The biggest gaffe in the south is *still* Imilchil. For such a well-known town someone really ought to make the effort to get up there and see how old the account is. This edition with the same cover is also published by LP in Spanish, French and German.

Lonely Planet guides are backed up by an excellent and long-established **website**, where you can buy selected chapters of their books as pdf files for a few pounds and visit the Thorn Tree users forum 🖥 www.lonelyplanet.com/thorntree. At the time of writing Rough Guide had no worthwhile equivalent.

# VEHICLE CHOICE & PREPARATION

Chances are you'll already know whether you want to tour the Moroccan outback with a motorcycle or a 4WD or a mountain bike; the appeal and practicality of each is quite distinct. It's worth noting that most of the routes in this book can also be managed in a regular car or van, as you'll discover when you get there. Only some well-watered and less rough routes are do-able on a mountain bike (see the list on p53) or even a regular touring motorcycle.

Realistically though, driving regular, road-oriented cars, motorcycles, scooters and bicycles on the piste is an unconventional choice – unless of course you live in Morocco. Most people are looking for a genuine reason to explore the off-road capabilities of their 4WDs or trail bikes and Morocco has plenty of great places to do just that.

In case it's not obvious, the motorcycle and bicycle travel addressed here is from an unsupported, self-sufficient point of view, carrying all your gear with the concomitant results in handling and effort when riding off-road. Both forms of two-wheel travel become much more light-hearted, as well as less risky with a load-carrying van or 4WD in support – see p92.

If you have a long-term overland journey in mind or lined up, particularly across Africa, for Western European-based travellers Morocco also happens to be a geographically-convenient location for testing both yourself, in a significantly alien culture, as well as your vehicle in an off-road setting.

## MOTORCYCLES

These days 'adventure bikes' – what used to be called big trail bikes (or 'dual sports' in North America) – are all the rage, with manufacturers jumping over each other to produce a machine which looks like it could take on the world. About time, one

might cry! It is in fact the second wave of a trend of potentially overland-ready motorcycles that kicked off in the early 1980s with Dakar Rally look-alikes such as Yamaha's recently re-launched Ténéré, a model which originally led to bikes like Honda's sadly defunct Africa Twin and now the most race-ready of the bunch, KTM's 640 (and a 690 Adventure one day soon). The ever-popular BMW GS series of flat twins, singles and now parallel twins are less obviously rally-derived, but you can be sure to see them all in Morocco.

## Little or large?

That is the question that can torment a Morocco-bound biker. Will the chore of riding the typical 3000-mile European leg from the UK on a 400cc single be worthwhile to have a responsive ride at the sharp end of the trip? Or does the smooth, cruising comfort of a big flat-, parallel- or V-twin add up to the nagging regret of doing less off-road exploring than you'd hoped?

Up to a point it depends on your attitude, your off-road-riding and overseas-biking background, as much as how committed you are to exploring off-road. Do you just want to get a feel for your abilities and your machine on a couple of routes and lap up the many other wonderful aspects of the Morocco experience? Riding the pistes doesn't have to be about nailing each berm in a shower of rocks and dust and getting some serious air. Older riders or those on heavier machines are satisfied to simply slow down – which you have to do off-road anyway – and find pleasure in gently exploring the back tracks on a capable machine.

The good thing is that sand – the bane of fully-loaded big bikes on *faux*-knobbly tyres – is rare or mostly easily avoidable in Morocco. What you get instead are **rocks** and stones that'll work your suspension into a lather and ask much more of your tyres' **toughness** than their tread pattern, but that otherwise make for reasonably predictable riding. Ridden with a steady and experienced hand it's amazing how far you can get with a machine that exceeds a quarter of a ton even before you get on it. That is until the going gets especially tough, muddy, sandy or the outfit falls over, at which point its '*bahn* storming virtues turn on you, bend over and pull down their pants.

Because the new-found popularity of big adventure bikes can exceed the abilities of many Moroccan novices, each route in this book addresses the suitability on such machines. All you have to do is pick the right route, take it easy and, if conditions become too much for you, have the wisdom to **turn back**.

It doesn't have to be about nailing each berm in a shower of rocks...

## Choosing a bike

Many trail bikes, not least the Ténéré I used to research this book, have seat heights not suited to inspire confidence to all. Choosing the right bike depends on your stature, or more particularly your strength and the ability of both your feet to touch the ground

## MOTORCYCLING IN MOROCCO

Moroccans have by and large inherited a continental attitude towards bikes, one that is positive and sees them as cool and exciting. Part of this is because swingeing import taxes mean that motorcycles of the type you'll be riding are unknown in the south of Morocco and are therefore exotic. Four-wheel drives are two a penny down there, but now that the Dakar Rally is finished with Morocco, anything much bigger or faster than a clapped out Mobylette is rarely seen.

### Road riding

It's probable that many riders of big 'adventure bikes' without experience in off-road riding come to Morocco with grand plans to carve through the pistes until they discover two things: how heavy a bike can feel when the tracks get tough; and what great roads there are for riding in the south.

Compared to the north, the riding here can be pure heaven. The weather is drier and warmer, the traffic is lighter, there are no big cities to deal with, the scenery's spectacular, the little-used tarmac is in great shape, the relief makes for some great mountain roads and basic, inexpensive accommodation is reasonably plentiful. Did I miss anything? So don't be disappointed if you find your well-meant plans to do your own mini-Dakar get a little truncated. You'll have learned about how your bike handles in the dirt which will be good for next time – and you'll have a great road ride.

### Spares and repairs

This exclusivity of riding a cool bike in Morocco backfires when it comes to needing parts or mechanical assistance. Down south you'll be pretty much on your own and even something as simple as an inner tube will be almost impossible to find. (There's a recommended parts list on p31.) Other riders can be a help and BMW dealers SMEIA in Casablanca can service or repair the very latest models, but at a fraction of UK prices.

If you need a part, often your best bet is to get something brought out to you by other tourists. Mechanics down south will only have a general moped- and car-based understanding of motorcycle engines and electrics, although steel welding can be done in any town or village with the gear.

In case you haven't discovered it yet, the Sahara Forum on the Horizons Unlimited website (direct link from 🖥 www.moroccooverland.com) is often used in this way, as well as for fault diagnosis on the marque-specific forums. Other than that, fly home yourself or get to Spain to get what you need; an option that will require some messing about with Customs as you'll be leaving your machine in Morocco unexported, but it can be done.

Bikershome Off Road Centre, ideally positioned on the south side of Ouarzazate is the sole beacon shining in the gloom and where, along with half-board accommodation, a well-equipped garage comes with the price of the room. The other UK bike tour operators in town have enough work maintaining their own big fleets of KTMs and Yamahas and are less likely to help or even sell parts which they themselves must import.

**VEHICLE CHOICE & PREPARATION**

at the same time while on the bike, as well as your confidence in handling a big machine.

Generally, shorter people may feel more comfortable on a single-cylinder trail bike like the old BMW 650 singles, and a lowered one at that.

You'll also learn, sooner or later, the right bike depends on how much you **load** it and the **tyres** it's shod with.

... of course it does!
© Jon Escombe

As long as it's in good shape a 15-year-old twin-lamp Ténéré ticks all the boxes.

Any of **Yamaha's** XT range, but particularly the old air-cooled 600s or the heavier fuel-injected 660s, including the new Ténéré, will manage just about all the pistes in this book. A TT250, especially the blue, post-2000 model makes a brilliant small machine; economical, very light and with great suspension. Something sporty like a WR450 is a bit wasted hauling baggage across Moroccan pistes, but will of course do it without getting into a sweat. Riding to Morocco on a 5-inch-wide seat and loading a slinky subframe with anything more than a toothbrush and a credit card is another matter. Even with its notoriously bad gearbox, the old Super Ténéré 750 twin would be a good alternative to a pricier Africa Twin or any of the weighty Triumph Tiger models. A new Super Ténéré with a bigger, parallel-twin engine might be out by 2010, but chances are it won't be as focussed as BMW's similar F800GS.

Any **Honda** with an 'X' as well as an 'R' or 'L' in the model name won't let you down in Morocco. The old Dominator and the Transalp, especially the new 700-cc model are the pick of the crop. A few years ago the much-loved but already-weighty Africa Twin became the 250-kilo XL1000V Varadero which may be a great bike but has never made an impact on overland travel – and the wrong sort of impact to off-roading. There must be something better in the pipeline unless the 220-kilo XL 700V Transalp is it. As long as you keep the payload on the skinny **subframes** sensible, Honda's larger XRs: 400, 600 and the water-cooled 650, as well as the Dominator-engined XR650L will all be up for some piste-bashing in Morocco.

**Suzuki** and especially **Kawasaki** are less popular on the European overland scene. The plucky Suzuki DRZ400 is the most widely used but their 650 V-Strom, now in various guises, is even more road-oriented than a Transalp, though has a great engine and is said to be lighter. With some decent tyres and

1200GS heading up to Jebel Sarhro, Route MH4.

under-body protection it can tackle the easier routes in this book while being a great road bike in between.

The long-established **BMW** GS series has had few lemons in its 30-year history, although the short-lived single-cylinder 650G- Xchallenge or Xcountry didn't catch on when something closer in form and function to KTM's Adventure certainly would have. So be it an older F650GS Dakar, the Boxers or the newer 800cc parallel twins, you'll have a bike that straddles the getting there and the being

# BASIC EQUIPMENT CHECKLIST

## Documents
- Passport
- Vehicle ownership document
- Cash, debit and credit cards
- Travel tickets
- European roadside recovery card
- Motor insurance
- D16 (see p68)
- Bike manual
- Maps
- Guidebook(s)

## Camping and cooking (optional)
- Tent
- Sleeping mat
- Sleeping bag
- Stove – plus fuel if not regular petrol
- Tea towel and pan scrubber
- Spoon and fork
- Cooking pot(s) and pot gripper
- Washing-up liquid
- Mug
- Water bag / bottle

## Sundry items and toiletries
- Swiss Army knife or multitool
- Head torch
- Lighters
- Ear plugs
- Soap (can be used as detergent)
- Toothbrush and toothpaste
- Toilet paper
- Universal basin plug

## Clothing
- Riding boots plus light shoes
- Fleece jacket
- Riding jacket
- Two pairs of gloves for highway and piste
- Socks and underpants

- Thermals and shirt
- Leather trousers or riding pants
- Cap or hat
- Crash helmet (and goggles)

## Bike spares and tools
- Spare key
- Wire, duct tape and cable ties
- Spare fuses, connectors and bulbs
- Spare nuts and bolts for rack fittings
- Two 2m-lengths of cable for jump starting
- Front and rear inner tubes
- Puncture repair kit: mini 12-volt compressor, handpump, tubeless plugs
- Clutch cable if not hydraulic
- Radiator sealant, epoxy & metal repair glue
- Diaphragm for CV carbs
- Hose clips
- Small tub of grease and small WD40
- Spark plug(s)
- Petrol pipe
- Spare bungees and straps
- Spanners, sockets and Allen keys
- Small adjustable spanner
- Cross- and flat-bladed screwdrivers
- Pliers with wire cutters (or multitool)
- Spoke key
- Junior hacksaw with spare blades
- Top-up oil, chain oil or lube, and rag

## Miscellaneous
- GPS unit with 12V power cable
- Camera, memory cards, charger
- Moroccan plug adaptor (same as Europe)
- Pen, notebook
- Spare batteries for electrical gadgets
- Mobile phone and charger
- PDA or iPod with contact list
- Waterproof bags
- String or rope

VEHICLE CHOICE & PREPARATION

# GEARING

The gearing on bigger, chain-driven road-oriented trail bikes is usually too high and too wide for off-roading with a self-sufficient payload. There's nothing you can do about wide ratios but you can easily **lower the gearing** by fitting a smaller engine sprocket, a job that with the right tools can take 10-15 minutes.

A front sprocket with 1 or 2 fewer teeth (12 is a minimum) gives better control at low speeds, such as doing U-turns, negotiating rough slopes and especially uphill hairpins.

With standard gearing you tend to slip the clutch which doesn't do it any good if you're carrying a heavy load or it's hot.

I calculated my 660 Ténéré did 8mph at tick over in first gear which was too fast for loose or rocky hairpin climbs and some descents. Five mph or less would be better.

Shaft-drive bikes are of course stuck with the gearing they're given, but while being at least 20kg heavier, BMW's 'Adventure' version of the 1200GS has lower gearing, making it more suited to slow, off-road riding.

Along with the less hardcore XR400, a KTM 450 is among the best of the lightweights.

there compromise as well as any bike of that size.

Out of Italy the manufacturers' selection of adventure bikes seems to be more about lamely trying to snare the odd 1200GS customer then producing something genuinely functional. The single-cylinder Rotax-engined Aprilia Pegaso seems as good as it gets. There is no such half-hearted pandering to market fashions over the border in Austria where KTM have cut out a solid niche of tough desert racers; a slick, corporate transformation from the ragged KTMs of the 1980s. The 450EXC would be the wrong sort of 'tough' for the ride down and is better rented or transported out there; once on the dirt nothing will stop it. The 640 Adventure is much better known as a long range, all-terrain load carrier. Fitted with quality components, out of the crate it's a post-2002 model more ready for Morocco than anything else here, you'll get a brilliant ride on any surface if not exactly the sort of comfort (if Japanese reliability) you can doze off to. The new 690 model ought to be out in 2010 and is said to have seen off the vibration issues; just don't count on an Electra Glide seat.

The above is merely the most obvious selection but what I've not listed should not be discounted. When you see step-thru mopeds older than you bimbling along the piste between desert towns you'll recognise anything can do it. Along with your biking budget, you just have to match up the needs of the European stage with the Moroccan routes to find what suits you.

## PREPARING A BIKE

For the whole nine yards on overland preparation to anywhere on anything, get a copy of the *Adventure Motorcycling Handbook*. There you'll find advice on everything from ways of carrying baggage to tyre choice. This section will focus just on Morocco because the good thing is that riding here requires comparatively little adaptation to most bikes and not that much in payload.

The problem is that at the very least you're taking on a road trip across Western Europe in probably a less than ideal season and following it with off-road riding in some remote desert and mountains. In a car these issues merely add up to more stuff in the back; on a bike bound for the piste any payload is the enemy of responsive handling and so off-road-riding confidence so you need to ascertain your priorities.

Much depends on what sort of trip you plan to have in Morocco. Is it primarily a road ride, two up, with the odd dabble along a piste just to say you've done it? In that case something like the two shortest MW routes, MS1 and maybe MS9 and the popular MH4 are good tasters with as little as 39km or 25 miles of piste (MW4) in a typical Moroccan setting. If you've never ridden off-road before or wonder whether your do-it-all adventure bike lives up to the hype, one of these routes in good weather would require nothing more than a

## CAMPING OR LODGING – AND EMERGENCY BIVOUACS

Most routes in this book start and end in towns with accommodation, although not all of it will necessarily feature in *Alastair Sawday's Special Places to Stay*. Camping gives you autonomy at the cost of payload and bulk which off-road on a bike is critical.

If you don't already own it all, then good quality, lightweight gear such as a tent, sleeping bag, mat and a stove will probably cost as much as you'd spend on lodging and eating in cheap south Moroccan hotels over a fortnight. Then again, with a few of you to share the load, camping can be fun and is all part of the adventure. Doing it this way you can save from about 150 dh (about £13 or euros) a day on the typical half-board hotel bill.

I set off on my Ténéré with all this gear because that's what I've always done; there was usually no accommodation option. After a while I realised I was in Morocco and not the Majabat al Koubra and so ended up spending just about every night in a hotel. Fun though it sounds back home, the reality of camping and cooking for yourself every night can be quite an effort after a hard day on the tracks. With the back up of a hotel, you can push yourself harder and later into the day – even on into the dark, knowing that on arrival all you have to do is haul your bags into a cosy room and wait for dinner. Many hotels without secure parking insist you wheel your bike inside for safe keeping, even though the chances of getting a bike stolen in Morocco are many times smaller than in Europe.

### Unplanned nights out

Even if you plan never to camp it's worth anticipating getting stranded out after dark should you get caught out. The knowledge that you've enough basic gear to spend a night out in reasonable, self-sufficient comfort is reassuring at all times.

Guess who's coming to dinner.

To this end stash some compact, ready-to-eat **snacks** such as chocolate, tinned fish or dried fruit, plus a few tea bags, sugar pellets or cup soups. Choose food you *like* rather than SAS survival rations and crusty energy bars. Don't bury it and wrap it in duct tape; it can be useful at any time should you miss lunch. A stove is not necessary but a small pot or metal cup to heat up some water over a **fire** doesn't take up much room as long as there's some combustible material around.

Depending on the terrain, lying down in all your clothes and a hat you can have a pretty comfortable night out tucked up alongside your bike with the seat or your boots as a pillow. However, the psychological comfort as well as the actual added warmth of a **bivi bag** or less expensive aluminium foil space blanket or plastic survival bag are worth the space, even if you never use them. A compact inflatable **sleeping mat** probably adds up to the same warmth not lost through the ground, as well as giving that extra comfort that may enable you to actually sleep rather than doze fitfully, watching the stars inch across the sky while praying for the dawn.

VEHICLE CHOICE & PREPARATION

carefully-ridden road tourer and the patience to take it easy while you get a feel for the machine.

Others will want nothing less than to pack each Moroccan day with dirt-track excursions on which a light, well-adapted machine with the right tyres and minimal payload will respond to the hammering much better.

## Essentials

With **tyres**, whether full knobbly, or trail tread-pattern such as a Tourance, **newer** covers will give you fewer problems with punctures. The best

Conti TKC80; a great tyre for road and dirt track, right up to the biggest 1200s.

compromise tyres are something like Pirelli's MT21, Michelin's T63 or Continental's TKC80. All these, and a few others besides, make both the ride across Europe and off-roading in Morocco fairly predictable by using a shallow and relatively dense pattern of knobs that gives a good footprint and profile on the tarmac with enough space in-between to get a bite on the dirt. Using these sorts of tyres also means you don't need to mess around dropping air pressures on the dirt to get the most out of them which means less risk of punctures when you inadvertently hit a rock step too hard. Unfortunately something like a TKC80 will probably be all but finished by the time you get back whereas an MT21 will still have some meat left.

**Chain and sprockets** will also wear faster with a full payload and on the dirt so make sure they have at least 5000 miles left in them.

Chances are your bike will fall over, most probably at speeds little greater than walking pace on mud or in sand. The best trail bikes are designed for this with foot controls that fold rather than bend as well as proper **hand guards** with a metal frame on the end of the handlebars. With the latter you can forget about the need for spare levers which can easily bend or snap, even in a simple fall.

The underside of the engine is also vulnerable and the rocky nature of most Moroccan tracks means some sort of protection is essential, whatever you ride. Many new trail or adventure bikes come with a skimpy plastic guard that alone will not be adequate; something like a full width **bashplate** of 2mm steel, or twice that in alloy, is what you want, curving up round the lower sides of the engine protecting water pumps and other vulnerable components. Crash bars of course are a good idea, especially if your bike's radiator protrudes, as well as a wider foot welded on the end of the side stand to stop it sinking on soft surfaces. And with a long ride in the cool season, any sort of **screen** is a good idea to reduce the blast of wind and rain.

Between them a proper bash plate and handguards are no-brainers for Morocco.

VEHICLE CHOICE & PREPARATION

# Fuel and water range

In my Sahara book I observe, 'water = time, fuel = distance'. In Morocco on a bike this pithy aphorism need not be pushed to the limit as it usually is in the central Sahara. With the exception of MW6 to Smara, the longest route in this book is MS8 at just over **300km** or nearly 200 miles – a good fuel range to aim for in Morocco. Two thirds of the off-road routes in this book are under 250km or 165 miles and many can be strung together in a near-continuous trail. A range of 300 kilometres should be possible on any bike with an 18-litre tank returning 17kpl or 48.5mpg (5.9l/100km). These days many fuel-injected bikes will struggle to return less than 21kpl (60mpg or 4.8l/100km) and so will need only a 14.2-litre tank to manage 300 kilometres. If that's a stretch or you want to try the longer routes, an inexpensive five litre plastic can from a motor factors gives you at least another 85-105km or 55-70 miles. In Morocco there should be no need for bulky and awkward jerricans.

Keeping close tabs on your fuel consumption rather than knowing 'it'll do 200 miles on a tenner' is an important aspect of overlanding. By becoming familiar with your bike's range of consumption figures you're able to predict how far you'll get in given conditions or how fast you can do so. Making these calculations these days can be tricky if you've been brought up to think in miles per gallon (mpg) because UK vehicles still come with mph speedos but we all buy fuel in litres.

One of the best features of my Ténéré's digital display (and doubtless many other bikes like this) was the ability to change the speed and distance read-out to kilometres. This meant a bit less brain work to convert a kpl figure to mpg which I can relate to. On page 86 (and also downloadable off the website) is a converter from mpg to kpl as well as an equation to calculate the more precise European-style l/100km. With this conversion UK riders with imperial instruments can quickly convert a fill-up in litres against the miles on the bike's odometre to get a comprehensible mpg figure.

## Water

Between spring and the early autumn **water** too can become an issue, particularly if you've bitten off more than you can chew and are falling off a lot, or the weather in the desert turns on you. Each route lists GPS points for all known **wells** and you should be prepared to use these; they're there particularly for motorcyclists and those mountain bikers who'll use this book to the full. At the warmer ends of the season at the very least carry **5 litres** on a day route, double that if you plan to overnight in the wilds.

## Carrying the load

People imagine the Sahara as a sea of dunes but in mountain or desert, Moroccan pistes are generally rough, stony tracks. In a car you sometimes have to crawl along for hours in first and second gear, on a bike you can fly along at twice the speed without any

The well at KM37 on Route MA9.

VEHICLE CHOICE & PREPARATION

If you choose alloy boxes go for easily detach-able mountings. It can enable you to push a bike into a hotel lobby or give you something to sit on while waiting for the AA.

VEHICLE CHOICE & PREPARATION

undue hardship to the bike or your backbone. However, the elegant often plastic, click-on baggage for the likes of European road touring which are often listed as a manufacturer's offi-cial accessory are in most cases not built to endure the hammering you'll get on Routes MS5 or MS7. Much of course depends on how you ride, how lightly you load them and the mount-ing mechanism. Such boxes will sur-vive much longer if you load heavy items across the back of the seat and also consider some added support such as strapping them up. BMW's expandable Vario cases seem to be an exception in this fragile but expensive category, as long as a bike doesn't come down on one in expanded mode.

It's one reason why **aluminium boxes** from the likes of Touratech are so pop-ular. For Morocco these boxes are often bigger than they need to be. While they're tough and will take crashing better than most plastic touring cases, the problem comes when you need to take a precautionary dab with your foot to steady your-self; something you'll learn to do less and less as your technique improves.

I used alloy boxes once for a long off-road desert trip which was much sandier than anything to be found in Morocco and all three of us grew to dread our shins getting caught under the box and snapped off as we dabbed inele-gantly across sandy oueds. Indeed the very fear of damaging our legs led to a loss of nerve and poor technique! Next time we agreed we'd all go for soft lug-gage or smaller boxes for off-roading.

For this book I used Touratech's little known, quickly-detachable fabric Zega Flex panniers and a waterproof Ortlieb bag. A detailed review of the Zega Flex appears on 🖥 www.adventure-motorcycling.com/xtz.

### Colour section (following pages)

- **C1 Top**: The High Atlas from the desert around Ouarzazate (© Eric De Nadai).
  **Bottom**: Heading north of Nekob on Route MH4.
- **C2 Top**: Mausoleum near Akka Igherm (Route MA11). **Bottom**: The climb out of Igmir (MA2).
- **C3 Top**: Crawling out of Igmir (Route MA2). **Middle left**: A day of locusts on the Desert High-way (Route MS10). **Middle right**: Tea break on ME4. **Bottom**: The Rekkam plateau (ME).
- **C4 Top**: Aït Benhaddou near Ouarzazate (© Waypoint Tours).
  **Bottom**: Spice market in Zagora (Routes MS1/2/5).
- **C5 Top**: Land Rover 101 stuck on Route MW6; see p253 (© David French).
  **Bottom**: Drying dates in Tadirhoust (MH11).
- **C6 Top**: High up on Route MH1 (© Waypoint Tours).
  **Bottom**: A storm rolls towards Route MH2 (© Manfred Schweda).
- **C7 Top**: Jebel Sarhro, Route MH4. **Bottom**: Tea break near Tizi n Tazazert, 2300m (MH4).
- **C8 Top**: Deep in the Anti Atlas. **Bottom**: The Ameln valley out of Tafraoute (MA8).
- **C9 Top**: Stand-off in Reguibat country, Route MW6 (© Daniel Hunter).
  **Bottom**: The palmerie north of Souk Tleta Tagmoute (MA11).
- **C10-11** At the viewpoint on Route MA10.
- **C12 Top**: Road riding along the Desert Highway: MS10 (© Raf Verleeben).
  **Middle**: Tree spotting on Route MS6 (© Raf Verleeben). **Bottom**: Cooling off on Jebel Sarhro.

# 4WD

As you'll find out for yourself, with care it's possible to do Morocco in a regular car but let's face it, you have a 4WD and you want to use it before some eco-terrorist sets fire to it. Morocco is a relatively undemanding destination in terms of payload and range, but in terms of all-terrain ruggedness it can be pretty challenging, not least because of the variety of conditions you can expect, from sub-alpine snow and mud to flooded tracks and Saharan dunes.

If you're new to genuine off-roading in 4WDs it's important to know how to operate your machine effectively so as to avoid both damaging your car as well as the inconvenience of getting stuck and unnecessarily chewing up the landscape. Modern, cutting edge 4WDs such as Land Rover's Discovery 3 have an impressive electronically-controlled array of suspension-, traction- and throttle-controlling systems to enable this, but in the real world driver input still requires more than turning a dial from 'grass' to 'sand'. Learning how to do this well is part of the satisfaction of driving on southern Morocco's pistes. There's more on off-roading in Morocco on p97. For a whole lot more on choosing, preparing and using 4WDs as well as the technology involved, see *Sahara Overland* or the forthcoming *Overlanders' Handbook*.

## WHICH 4WD

Petrol or diesel, long- or short-wheelbase, manual or auto and even models without 'Land' in the title will all work fine in Morocco where distances are relatively short and so vehicle recovery – and repatriation where necessary – is comparatively simple. You don't need the full-on, all-terrain ruggedness of a Land Cruiser or Defender but these are among the most common vehicles out there. Other popular models include the Toyota's Prado, the Land Rover Discovery, Mitsubishi Pajero, Nissan Patrol and Mercedes G-Wagen; all big, heavy 4WDs capable of carrying four people and their gear anywhere in Morocco.

Not all cars with 4WD capability will work on the mountain pistes of Morocco; a good way of distinguishing a potentially functional, all-terrain 4WD from the likes of a Honda CRV, Freelander or a Volvo XC90 is the presence of a separate low range gearbox. If the car of your choice has one you can be fairly sure that it's been built to handle genuine off-roading and not just look like it might. There's more on the efficacy of low range on pp97-98.

In Morocco the only thing that may limit a vehicle on some mountain

It's possible to get into a pickle choosing the right 4WD but in a low-risk environment like Morocco any machine in good shape will do.

VEHICLE CHOICE & PREPARATION

Double cab pickup; a good compromise.

tracks is its size. A small truck like a Unimog, MAN or an Iveco will struggle or even not fit on routes like MA1, -3, -6 and -7 and of course MH5. For them the pistes of the High Atlas, the desert and the east or far west will save too much inching around hairpins with wheels hanging over the edge.

Unusually in an overland setting, a short-wheelbase 4x4 with just two people would work very well on Moroccan pistes. Fuel stages are short and food stops frequent so there's no need to carry post-apocalyptic payloads. Camping gear can be for occasional use only as there's usually a hotel to be found. More significantly there'll be many occasions on washed-out pistes where a SWB's minimal body overhangs would help you get through without resorting to longer detours or mashing your bumpers. A Defender 90 fits the bill of course, as do the 73-series Land Cruisers common in France as well as the venerable Lada Niva. Any of the double cab pickups recently popular in the UK like the Mitsubishi L200, the Nissan Navara or Toyota Hilux will manage fine too. The Mazda B2500 I used to research this book gave me no lasting regrets (the full story is on the website: click 'Mercedes' then 'Mazda') – where it couldn't go I wasn't so keen to follow anyway. With a canopy on the back your gear can rattle around and suck in all the dust it likes while the cabin remains quiet and clean.

## Other factors

Although the available range in 4WDs can be limited, an **automatic gearbox** is a great choice for some of Morocco's steep, rocky tracks. Very often in the mountains it's difficult to be smooth with manual transmission as you lurch between first and second gears with the steering turning from lock to lock; on some routes you'll be driving like this for hours. Automatics make this sort of off-roading much smoother on the transmission and tyres as well as the vehicle occupants, allowing you to concentrate on positioning the car and its tyres carefully and even have a chance to look around.

A street-legal 4WD, 800cc V-twin automatic quad; about as agile as it gets off road but not so hot for the ride down through Europe.

Traditionalists often comment that it's impossible to push start an automatic with a flat battery, but for any overlander, manual or auto and especially if travelling alone, a second battery as well as a set of jump start cables are an inexpensive and very wise precaution (see p40). If the starter's gone and you're alone, you'd be lucky to bump start any car, manual or otherwise unless you happened to park on a nice, firm slope.

Within reason, **wheel and tyre size** and rim material are not critical.

## READ THIS FIRST: TRANSMISSION WIND-UP

Imagine having each limb twisted in a different direction. That's what's happening to your car's transmission components when you use locked-out four-wheel drive on a hard surface. On a loose surface such as sand, this tension (brought about by each wheel travelling a slightly varying distance) dissipates as undetectable wheel spin, but on a grippy surface such as bare rock found on hairpins, **wind-up** soon becomes apparent. Steering stiffens, your transmission clicks and groans, and then a suddenly spinning wheel unloads the tension, or something in the tortured transmission breaks.

Particularly on bare rocky hairpins such as Route MH4 for example, you should avoid driving a selectable 4WD in four-wheel drive, or a full-time 4WD with centre diff locked for long periods. In dry conditions with good traction it should not be necessary. Even on a wet road, driving locked-out in four-wheel drive is a bad idea. A wheel suddenly unloading the wind-up in a fast wet bend could bring on a disastrous skid. To release any wind up in the transmission only requires momentarily unlocking a central diff or releasing free-wheeling diffs or hubs. But note if there's a lot of tension in the system these actions may not work instantly; it may take a few bends and a minute or two.

Only engage selectable four-wheel drive or lock the central diff on loose surfaces where you think you'll need the extra traction. Away from the dunes in Morocco (what few there are) this only includes crossing steep, washed-out creek banks or muddy/sandy creek crossings; in other words no more than a few hundred metres on the average route in good conditions. Staying locked-out in four-wheel drive is fine though still not necessary on snow, mud and sand and gravel because any tension spins out before it builds up to damaging levels. It is only on bare rock or concrete (as well as the tarmac highway of course) that staying locked out can be bad for the transmission.

If you're now wringing your hands wondering if you can use your 4WD safely on the dirt, don't worry about it too much now. Whatever system your car runs, most of the time you can simply leave the road and follow a track without doing anything until the going gets tricky. Lock in the 4WD with the central diff or engage the front axle when you must, unlock it all when you can. After a few hours on the piste you'll get the feel for what is needed and within a few days you'll know exactly when to bring locked-in four-wheel drive into action.

This must be understood clearly. Full-time 4WD with the central diff locked provides near-optimum traction but will also wind up the transmission. Therefore the same limitations to driving on hard surfaces must be observed: lock the central diff only when you really need to and never engage it with the power on, with wheels possibly spinning; it won't like it.

There is more on off-road driving techniques on p97-8.

VEHICLE CHOICE & PREPARATION

The norm for 4WD rim sizes is either 15- or 16-inch and both tyre sizes will be found in Morocco, though not necessarily in your exact width or profile. What is important is a relatively tall tyre wall rather than a wide tread. Tall tyres give more ground clearance at the axle, maintain that clearance at lower pressures while creating a longer tyre print for better traction, and they add suspension (albeit undamped and so not ideal for road cornering). Tyres in the larger, 16-inch rim size as found on Defenders usually have these bouncy characteristics – i.e: oriented towards off-roading. These days alloy rims are the norm on modern vehicles including 4WDs because they're lighter than steel and so perform better. Dents in alloy rims (with the potential for losing the air seal) cannot be knocked out as easily as on steel, but short of some sort of crash, tall tyres, firm tyre pressures and moderate speeds all make such damage unlikely in Morocco.

The **suspension systems** on the types of vehicles listed will all work well in Morocco, be they leaf springs, coil or torsion bar on solid axles (as on

Defenders, older Discoverys and 80-series Land Cruisers) or with the now more prevalent independent front suspension (IFS) or even fully independent, cross-linked air suspension as on the latest Discovery. The reason modern 4WDs are adapting to independent suspension, that has been the norm on road cars for decades, is for the fairly obvious reason that it gives a much-improved ride and handling on the road where most of them stay. In my experience, providing one fits firmer springs, the ground clearance issues of IFS do not exist.

## 4WD PREPARATION AND EQUIPMENT

The great thing with driving off-road in Morocco is that, as long as the machine is basically in good shape and well-equipped you barely need more gear than going on a regular holiday. That's the way I approached one of the research trips for this book in my Mazda. I took a jerrican for fuel, an air bag

For this well-equipped Defender, Morocco was only the start.
© longroadtripsouth.com

jack, a shovel and some sand mats and didn't use any of them. But along with the air-con, I was certainly glad of the additions of a new clutch, a second battery, a compressor and, last but not least, uprated suspension. 'Camel Trophy' style accessories may give an appearance of rugged intent but are not essential. A first timer need only make sure the car is in good shape and take appropriate equipment.

Look in a 4WD magazine and you may be overwhelmed by the amount of preparation and gear your 4WD needs. The fact is, *it's only Morocco* where routes are short and help is never that far away. This is what you need:

- Five good tyres (or six old ones) and tyre-repairing equipment
- Uprated suspension
- Air compressor or foot pump
- Back-up battery
- Tow strap, a shovel, tall hydraulic jack and a base plate
- Thick pair of gloves for each person
- Secure, chassis-mounted towing points front and rear
- Tool kit and some spares
- 20-litre fuel can
- Jump starting cables

Unless you buy five new tyres, that lot above will cost well under £1000 for a car that'll be ready for anything in Morocco. Broadly speaking it can all be divided into improving some of your car's current systems (most notably tyres and suspension) and adding equipment to make it more effective off-road (including recoveries) and comfortable to live out of. There is plenty more on this subject in my *Desert Driving II* DVD. See the website.

VEHICLE CHOICE & PREPARATION

## SUMMERTIME IN THE MOROCCAN SAHARA

Although I could think of better ways of enjoying a holiday, within reason it's possible to do southern Morocco in summer (May to September) in a car without taking too many chances. You'll experience the same temperatures as the central Sahara at this time, but not the exposure in terms of distance.

Air-con helps of course, as does the ability to carry lots of water and setting off at dawn, although even then you'll probably regret it at times. Forty five degree days will also put a strain on your vehicle. Working hard in these conditions, any weakness in the cooling system can become apparent at a time when your safety margins are already slim.

According to the best information available (this incident was not reported in Morocco or elsewhere), in August 2008 a French couple suffered two punctures in a rental 4WD while on Route MS6. The man wandered off to try and, rather optimistically, get a mobile phone signal and eventually came upon a village. By the time he returned to his car later that day his wife had died from the heat. Although it's happened before, such a calamity won't befall everyone breaking down in the Moroccan Saharan summer; the mistake they were said to have made was travelling with less than a couple of litres of **water**, which outside of the air-conditioned car would have lasted less than an hour.

Sand dunes, where a 4WD will work hardest, are few in Morocco and easily avoided, but in soft sand in summer the temperature needle may get close to the red zone, especially when crawling along slowly in a tailwind. Because it's hard to know just how your vehicle will respond in such heat, play it safe and consider a new or reconditioned radiator (especially if it's ever been repaired), along with new or spare hoses and belts.

Old desert lore advises only fresh water should be used in the radiator in case of a survival situation (antifreeze being poisonous). It sounds prudent but overall you're much better off with the slightly higher boiling point and corrosion-inhibiting properties of antifreeze and putting another 20 litres of water in the back.

In my experience big, four-litre 4WDs are fitted with huge radiators and powerful fans that rarely overheat. Smaller engines work a bit harder and along with older engines, may benefit from a 'tropical' fan with extra blades (available for Land Rovers). Aftermarket intercoolers also raise engine bay temperatures; you'll feel it in the cab alongside the gearbox tunnel and the floor of the cubby box, though it won't necessarily register on the temperature gauge.

If your vehicle runs hot consider supplementary (as opposed to replacement) electric fans such as those made in the UK by Kenlowe or Pacet. Not built for off-road, the frames or feeble zip-tie mountings supplied can work loose on corrugations and damage the radiator, so make sure it's solid and that the retaining bolts are secured with locking compounds – and check them regularly.

Running thicker engine oil is another way of keeping things cool. In Europe 15W-40 has become the norm but 'old-fashioned' 20W-50 increases your cooling range at the upper end. If things get desperate, straight 40W can be used, but let the engine warm up gently on cold mornings.

One might suggest that summertime in southern Morocco may well be more suited to travellers from southern Europe than the British Isles. The former will at least be familiar with heatwaves of over 40 degrees and how their body and car may react. To a Brit the experience may literally take their breath away.

If the engine gets very hot point the car to the wind and open the lid. Always **leave the engine running** until the needle drops back to normal. Switching off a hot engine makes things temporarily worse – stopping the vital circulation of cooling oil and water can crack a cylinder head.

## General vehicle check

While it helps to have an aptitude and sympathy for mechanical things, you don't have to have an in-depth knowledge of your car's functions. Most car owners have little interest in how their machine works and increasingly complex and electronically-managed vehicles do not respond to roadside fault diagnosis by the owner. It's one reason why older and simpler vehicles are preferred for long-range overlanding. For Morocco, as long as it doesn't have a disastrous record for reliability, it's safe to take as complex and modern a vehicle as you like.

When checking over your vehicle, focus your efforts on what counts: the basics of engine, transmission and suspension. At times all will be working hard on Moroccan pistes so make sure they're in good shape **before** you start buying extra equipment. At the very least, the vehicle should be serviced well in advance of your departure with fresh oil, coolant and air-, oil- and fuel filters and with any serious faults addressed. You can save a lot of effort and time by either fitting new consumable items like tyres, fan belts and radiator hoses or taking them as spares and hoping for the best. They may well be available locally but getting hold of them may take a few days. Be warned though, simply buying these bits and throwing them in the back is not the same as fitting them and taking the partly-worn items as spares. That way you avoid the sinking feeling on discovering that your spare fan belt is the wrong size when you need it most. With show-stopping items like belts, it's a good idea to fit new and take the used but still usable item as a backup.

### Air filters

Raised air-intakes or 'snorkels' breathe at roof level where there are fewer airborne sand particles and also have the benefit of greatly increasing a vehicle's potential wading ability. They also look purposeful and up to a point can lengthen maintenance periods by keeping a filter cleaner for longer.

Most cars have air-intakes somewhere in the wing and some manage to pre-clean air better than others. I've found on 60- and 80-series Toyotas a raised air-intake makes little difference; whatever 'cyclone' arrangement they have to spin out the particles before they reach the air filter element works

Greasing the inside of the airbox keeps the element cleaner for longer.

well. My Mazda's pre-cleaning was not so good and the air filter element was relatively small, but for the cost of fitting a snorkel I could have bought 20 new air filter elements – enough for a quarter of a million miles.

Corrugated paper elements can be cleaned by carefully tapping out the dust or by using compressed air, but eventually they'll need replacing. Because you're probably only visiting Morocco rather than emigrating there, a new standard paper element will be sufficient for a typical month's trip. Use your air compressor to blow it

VEHICLE CHOICE & PREPARATION

clean after a particularly dusty run and consider taking a spare if you expect to be driving in convoy where rear vehicles can end up with bronchitis. Greasing the inside surfaces of an airbox is a useful dirt-biking practice which catches still more dust and sand before it clogs the filter.

## Transmission

Even with a lightly loaded vehicle your transmission will work hard in Morocco, crawling up steep, rocky slopes and out of creeks. If there's any undue slack in the drive or if gears jump out or are hard to engage (including low-range selection), you can be sure that a week in the Anti Atlas won't be a miracle cure. Prop shafts in particular have a hard time on rough tracks. Check there's grease in the telescoping section, fit a gaiter to keep out dust and also check for play in the four or more universal joints ('UJs'). They frequently wear unnoticed or lose retaining bolts so should be regreased or better still replaced on an older vehicle. They're not expensive.

With any manual 4WD, the many unseen components of the vehicle's transmission benefit most from a smooth, gentle driving style. Know the correct use of low range as well as the importance of not using locked diffs on grippy surfaces (see p39).

## Suspension

Along with good tyres, the single item that most Morocco-bound 4WDs will benefit from is uprated suspension. As is widely recognised, most 4WDs do not lead true 4WD lives and most are sprung at the factory accordingly. This is fine around town, but when bouncing along a track on a hot day with a full payload, original equipment ('OE') springs will show their limitations. Soft suspension means continuous bottoming out against the axle stops and having to slow down for the mildest bumps. It's harder on the tyres too which get compressed when the car bottoms out, and of course it reduces your ground clearance which leads to other problems.

On 4WDs with coil-sprung suspension like Defenders and Discoverys and 80-series Cruisers, firmer coils are widely available, relatively inexpensive and easy to fit. Resist the urge to go over the top with raising suspension; a vehicle's stability is greatly compromised by just an extra couple of inches above standard. Use the 'looks normal and level when fully loaded' rule as a guide.

Old-fashioned semi-elliptic leaf springs can be uprated, but are more expensive and harder to replace than coils. Adding a leaf or two to the pack and re-bending the current set (not such a bodge as it sounds) are some things you can do with leaves. Theoretically, a good leaf-spring manufacturer will be able to dial in exactly how much lift you want or the desired height when loaded.

The secondary leaf springs, ie: the ones which have loose ends and do not wrap around the mounting points,

Air Lift bags. The pressure can be modified for heavy payloads or even broken springs.

have a habit of cracking in tough conditions but this is no great drama compared to a main leaf breakage, and is one thing any Moroccan mechanic is familiar with. I fully expected this problem with the OE rear leaves on my Mazda in Morocco and sure enough I got it, although it took me days to notice as the Air Lift assister bags masked any sag.

Shock absorbers – more correctly described as dampers – are vulnerable to damage on some leaf-sprung vehicles, but work a lot harder with coil springs which lack the friction-damping element of leaves. If you're fitting new units take the old ones as spares; problems are common and even new ones can break, bend, seize, leak or get inadvertently crushed by rocks. A car is driveable with a missing damper but a spare front and rear unit takes up little space.

## TYRES

In Morocco, tyre choice is not as critical as it can be in other off-road environments, but because of the hammering they'll get, good-quality items are advisable. Remember that, along with suspension, your tyres will carry the brunt of the heavy shock loads over rough terrain for weeks on end, not just weekends away and if anything stops you on the piste, it will be a puncture. Don't take chances with tyres just because they'll wear out anyway. Save money elsewhere but replace old or inappropriate tyres with the best you can afford.

Ordinary drivers distinguish tyres by their tread pattern, today as much a factor of marketing as function. What matters much more is the integrity of the tyre design and the quality of the construction – something that is hard to see and is why people choose cheaper brands which look just as 'black and round' as more expensive tyres.

These days most 4WDs are fitted with tubeless tyres on 15-inch rims; 16s appear on more functional off-roaders like Defenders where the taller sidewall increases clearance. Because most piste surfaces are predominantly gravel or stone, in Morocco the finer points of tread design aren't that crucial.

In general choose AT (all terrain) designated tyres from quality manufacturers over cheap MT (mud terrain) or M&S (mud and snow) designated tyres (205 x 16 M&S tyres are particularly hopeless in sand). Providing they're a good brand in good shape, your current tyres might well be adequate and will certainly do in rocky Morocco.

As with many things, you get what you pay for. An expensive Michelin (who also own BF Goodrich) may last twice as long as other brands. There are no absolute rules; much depends on rim types, driving style, experience and engine power characteristics. One thing is certain though: drive a heavy car fast on any tyre in an under-inflated condition and you risk overheating which damages the structure of the tyre and will cause problems down the track.

### Pumps and compressors

For tyre repairs as well as for altering tyre pressures over varying terrain, some kind of pump is essential and a powerful air compressor is one of the most useful items you can fit to an off-roader. Besides saving time and effort, it means you're never reluctant to drop pressures (which means fewer boggings) or to re-inflate again – so avoiding premature tyre wear and damage.

Manual foot pumps take about 300 strokes to gain 1 bar (14.5 psi) and realistically are too slow for off-road use. Your engine generates electricity so it makes sense to utilise that energy to power an electric air compressor. Prices range from £20 for something not designed for the sustained loads of big 4WD tyres – to over £400. Plan to spend at least £100 for a model that will last the trip. What counts is not that they can inflate a bicycle tyre to 180psi, but how many cubic feet per minute (cfm) they can push out, espe-

Viair, 2.5cfm auto shut-off compressor located out of the way in the engine bay.

cially as pressure builds up. For something that pumps out at around 2 cfm or more, expect to pay £140. To avoid flattening the battery **keep the engine running** if re-inflating all four tyres.

## RECOVERY EQUIPMENT

In Morocco you could get stuck in sand, mud and snow in just one eventful day. In most cases simply backing up and finding another way round or turning back is the answer. There's always somewhere else to go in Morocco. Nevertheless, it's wise to be equipped against getting stuck.

Standard recovery items include a jack, a shovel, a compressor and a long recovery strap. This latter item, along with another car to pull you out is the single most useful item. Unless you're planning to play around on Erg Chebbi or Chegaga, **sand plates** or mats are not necessary in Morocco. In fact, outside of storm conditions, it's hard to imagine getting stuck on any of the desert routes in this book.

Your car's standard jack (ideally an extra-height hydraulic bottle-jack as opposed to inferior pillar- or scissor-jacks) will be good enough to make wheel repairs but not if you manage to get deeply bogged down.

Bottle-jacks are designed be placed directly under the axle or a wishbone, not on a chassis rail or a sill. This way the jack lifts the wheel directly off the ground and not the compressed weight on the suspension… and then the wheel. It's only this placement which makes them awkward to use off road and is why high-lift jacks or airbags are preferred.

### Hi-lift and airbag jacks

In Morocco the number of occasions when you actually need to jack the car right up are fewer than you think. Hi-lift jacks are well known to pukka off-roaders and though heavy and awkward to stow, and dangerous if used

An airbag jack can easily lift one side of a 2.5 ton 4WD to speed up recovery in sand.

VEHICLE CHOICE & PREPARATION

Whenever jacking up a car for anything more than a quick extraction or recovery, always chock the ground wheels and put something solid under the lifted wheels. Airbags tend to lose air over a few minutes.

VEHICLE CHOICE & PREPARATION

carelessly, their ability to lift a two-ton car quickly makes them very useful and they cost from just £45. The problem is a hi-lift needs a solid, chassis-mounted metal bumper, as on the front of a Defender, to lift up the weight of a car. Although adaptors may be available, most 4WDs these days have rounded plastic bumpers to limit injuries when hitting pedestrians and in the UK at least, bull bars rigid enough to take the weight of a car are no longer legal.

It's possible to get wheel adaptors to enable a hi-lift to quickly raise a wheel – either straps that hook into the spokes or clamps for the free-wheel drive housing (see the DVD). It's a useful facility when bogged down to perform a simple lift and recovery, but it's definitely not a stable way of lifting a car to get underneath – used alone a hi-lift jack never is.

Airbag jacks are tough vinyl balloons the size of a small dustbin which are inflated by the car's exhaust and can easily lift one side of a 4WD. For something like an older Hilux an air jack rated at two tons will do the trick; for a heavier Toyota 80-series four tons is a better bet. The 3-ton Draper example is the most easily available in the UK for just £50.

Air jacks are a rare sight but for effortless sand recovery or even righting overturned vehicles they're ideal, spreading the weight over a large area and requiring no strenuous or dangerous jacking. The bag needs less than 1 bar (14.5psi) to lift a car so no engine damage from the exhaust pressure can occur, although the exhaust system must be sound if it's to survive as well as fill the bag efficiently. They won't work on vehicles with twin exhaust pipes unless you seal one pipe (something like a potato works).

Under the car, choose the position carefully to spread the load; remember you'll be putting half the weight of the car on the lifting area. At the very least a thick piece of carpet should be used between the undercarriage and the bag – and something similar on the ground if thorns or rocks are present.

## TALL TYRES, NOT WIDE TYRES

A 'tall' tyre, that is one with a high sidewall is desirable off-road as it gives more protection to the rim and so a tubeless tyre's seal. You can tell this just by looking at a tyre size or aspect ratio, the second number in the tyre size moulded on the side. For example 185/75 15" decoded means 185 tread width in millimetres, '75' is the sidewall height as a

pecentage of width; so about 139mm – and 15" indicates the rim diametre.

A high aspect ratio of 65 or more is better for off-roading because, like a thick-soled boot, it provides added suspension over bumps and gives enough scope to partially deflate the tyre for traction in soft sand while still cushioning the rim.

## Shovels and tow straps

A shovel has many uses: burying waste as well as digging the car out. The best type to choose is one with not too large a blade – so anyone can use it without straining their back – and a full 'D' handle that you can grip and angle firmly rather than the cheaper 'T' handles as found on the ex-Army shovels available in the UK. The long-handled shovels recommended by some to dig sand away from under the car are in fact very awkward to use. If you're that stuck just get in there and scoop away with your hands.

Joining a rope and a strap with a rolled up magazine. It doesn't have to be the latest issue of LRO. © longroadtripsouth.com

Along with solid, chassis-mounted towing points, a tow strap (more compactly stored than a rope) is an essential part of any overlander's equipment. Nine metres is a standard length and the minimum necessary for towing or righting an overturned vehicle; 20 metres is much more useful for recovering a vehicle from deep sand, dune crests, a wet chott or mud. Two straps can easily be joined with nothing more than a tightly rolled-up magazine or a stick.

Both are less dangerous than shackles which are lethal if something breaks, although a couple of shackles rated at four tons or more are useful accessories if one car has closed towing rings, rather than more useful hooks which avoid the need for shackles altogether.

## Auxiliary batteries

Because the primary battery is such a vital component, especially with a diesel, a second battery is a good idea and essential if you're running things like fridges. For the cost involved, a spare car battery gives peace of mind, especially if you're travelling alone. I've heard of cheapo no-name batteries lasting for years and expensive sealed 'space shuttle' items mysteriously pack up in a few months. For any sort of remote driving where you can't readily flag down a passing car, a second battery can be considered as indispensable as a spare tyre.

When camping, a second battery also allows you to run electrical ancillaries with the engine turned off but, if correctly isolated, won't flatten the main battery on a freezing High Atlas morning when it provides a back-up should the main battery fail. Jump-starting from another car is the simple

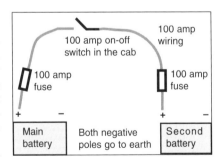

The simplest way to wire up a second battery is in series with a cut off switch in the cab. Starting on one flat and one good battery will instantly average out below 12 volts: it won't work. With the above set up, if the auxiliary battery goes flat through use, isolate it and start the car on the main battery. Then switch on the second battery to charge it up.

VEHICLE CHOICE & PREPARATION

answer (or tow-starting if no jump leads are available), but this assumes another vehicle is around.

Avoid expensive and specialised 'leisure' batteries as used by caravaners. These are designed for long, slow discharging and regular flattening, not to provide the short powerful burst of 'cranking' amps needed to start a cold engine and then quickly recover. In Morocco starting the engine is more important than keeping the milk from going off, so a second SLI ('starting, lighting, ignition) battery, either identical or a bit smaller, is best. There's more on running auxiliary batteries in the other two *Overland* books.

# 2WD

Just about all cars bound for the Moroccan pistes will be 4x4s; naturally enough as these vehicles can carry the load across rough terrain without complaint. But nearly all the pistes in this book can be done for much less cost but as much fun in a suitably prepared regular 2WD car or van. Morocco has very little sand (seasonal snow and mud may be another matter) and ground clearance rather than all-wheel drive is the critical issue and is something many 2WD cars have enough of.

## DO YOU NEED 4WD?

Many of the pistes in this book are regularly traversed by locals in 2WD vans or cars. Certainly they come from a limited selection with an often coincidental design, or with suspension modifications to provide better clearance, because with the good traction of dry conditions, four-wheel drive is hardly ever necessary on tracks. After all motorbikes manage fine and up to the point where Unimogs and the like come into their own, bikes can skip across gnarlier terrain with less discomfort than most regular 4WDs.

In all but the softest sand it's primarily **decent ground clearance** and not all-wheel drive, that enables a vehicle to keep moving; 99% of the time a car won't require all-wheel drive in Morocco. But it takes just one rock to crack a sump, one steep ascent or creek bank to fry a clutch, or a series of corrugations to have the engine fall out. That remaining one per cent can finish off an old machine.

Citroën C15 van. Up to 2-litre engine, great economy and ground clearance. © Citroën

Choosing to explore Morocco in a regular car is not as foolhardy as it sounds. It's commonly tried by experienced four-wheel drivers who've 'been there and done that', have nothing more to prove and so are looking for something new.

## Limitations of a regular car

Low ground clearance and long overhangs (the front or back of a car that sticks out beyond the wheels) are what initially limit a road car in an off-road setting, followed by a lack of a secondary 'low range' gearbox. In the thousands of kilometres I covered for this book in the Mazda pickup I usually engaged 4WD for less than a minute at a time and for a total distance of just a few kilometres. On most pistes I never engaged 4WD, but when I did it was almost always when in low range (which automatically selects 4WD) to crawl slowly over a ditch, rocks or through soft sand without straining the clutch or transmission.

Finally, not all regular cars have the **build quality** to take an off-road beating so breakdowns and other problems are simplified by choosing a model which is commonly found in Morocco – see p50.

## Road cars: what to look for

Part of the appeal of a road car is keeping it simple and doing it on a budget, as well as having a more pleasant vehicle to drive on normal roads (unless you can afford top of the range Land Cruisers and Rovers). Without the need to carry huge amounts of fuel and water, a hatchback or a small van makes an ideal choice for two people or less because of its relatively short wheelbase and limited body overhangs compared to a sedan (a car with a boot). When it comes to rear body overhangs many hatchbacks are in fact better than most 4WDs; it can take extreme angles before tailpipes, spare tyres and less commonly, fuel tanks, scrape. On the front end, spoilers, steering components and particularly the radiator's low position are the weak points.

Because most road cars feature independent suspension the underside is generally smooth, with no beam axle casings protruding, as on a 4WD. They therefore lend themselves well to the fitting of a long sump guard. Shorter cars also have a better ramp breakover angle which means they won't belly out so easily when driving over a hump or a sharp crest compared to a stretched limo. Saloons and estates generally have longer back-end overhangs and some have overhanging fronts too.

Try to anticipate what will ground out and whether it matters or not. Most importantly, consider the bottom edge of the **radiator** behind that spoiler. Will it get mashed and pushed into the fan following a nose dive into a narrow ditch?

**Larger wheels** are preferable as they roll over rough ground more smoothly while marginally increasing clearance on suspension components. Larger tyres (see box on p46) also produce a longer 'footprint' when deflated which helps traction in soft sand. Fifteen-inch rims are found on more modern Mercedes, bigger Peugeots and the like, but hatchback rims are usually fourteen inches or less.

Mercedes 190D on Route MA2
a few miles from Igmir.

VEHICLE CHOICE & PREPARATION

Recommending marques and models is trickier but naturally some have better reputations than others. Mercedes and the three main French marques of Peugeot, Citroën and Renault are most common on Moroccan roads, the former because of the superior build-quality of older models, while the French marques exist most probably because of long-established trade connections more than anything else.

With no 4WDs to speak of, French car manufacturers have long produced 2WD utilities to suit farmers; the 2CV being the original example. Many hatchbacks still fit in this category: Peugeot 106s and 205s, Citroen AXs and C15D vans, Renault Clios or Kangoo vans. French marques derived from the original 2CV concept are popular, even if they don't necessarily have the build-quality and reliability of German and Japanese equivalents. These models feature independent suspension with rear wheels attached on high-mounted arms offering excellent clearance as long as the payload is modest. During research trips, besides several old French and German hatchbacks, I saw many newer small, so-called 'car-derived' and 'high-cube' vans out in Morocco like the Citroen Berlingo/Peugeot Partner or the Renault Kangoo.

## Modifying a road car

Most Moroccan locals will not undertake any of these modifications; they'll just drive slowly and make repairs as necessary. This is really the best way to go as half the point of using a 2WD is not to spend extra money adapting it. As long as the general mechanical condition is good, particularly the tyres, you'll manage most of the time.

If you want to push a 2WD towards its limits, some under body protection of the engine and gearbox, as well as steering and suspension links, exhaust pipe, fuel and brake lines and fuel tanks, is a good idea.

The simplest way to achieve this is to fix on a big metal plate: 3mm steel might do or alloy twice as thick. This bash plate will earn its keep so it needs to be fixed on well. If you're doing this just as you're about to start a piste, wiring on an old oven door with a wire coat hanger is better than nothing, but a bash plate bolted solidly onto whatever points are available is best, as they often come adrift. Leave a small gap between the plate and whatever it's protecting; it may help to stuff in some thick, shock-absorbing material like a bit of old tyre, so a severe impact is not transmitted directly through the plate.

Raising ground clearance is most easily done on cars with coil suspension all round. The cheapest solution is a spacer above or beneath the coil: the car instantly sits higher. Mercedes offer these 'spring pads' in a variety of thicknesses (see the website) but anything will do. Extreme lifts will stress steering- and final-drive components, so don't go too far. It's another reason why buying a car with relatively good ground clearance in the first place is a good idea.

Remember too that the coil sits more or less halfway between the pivoting point of the wishbone and the tyre so a spacer or longer spring of 20mm will raise the car by 40mm at the wheel. It's not uncommon for coil springs to break but it's also usual not to notice this for months; another advantage of coil suspension.

Torsion bar suspension is also adjustable by repositioning the pivots in the spline. This increases the pre-tension (so raising the car) but on a hard hit can also twist it beyond the point it was designed to go which can lead to failure and a complicated repair.

It's worth reiterating that, just as with 4WDs, the easiest way of maintaining your car's ground clearance (and reducing stresses overall) is by **driving slowly and not overloading** it. Position any heavy loads centrally, between the axles.

Once you've made the best of your ground clearance and underbody protection, all that really remains is to ensure things like the exhaust pipe and fuel tank fittings are solid (they commonly come loose or fall off on corrugated pistes).

## OFF-ROADING IN A 2WD

You may have made the most of your ground clearance but in a 2WD you're still missing two 4WD attributes: all-wheel drive and a low-range gearbox. What this means is that when you hit rough ground you must rely on **momentum** – also known as 'speed' – to get you through. Knowing exactly when to accelerate and when to back off is crucial to successful off-roading in a 2WD, as are bringing a pair of **bridging planks** to smooth out the creases in the Moroccan landscape.

The problem is that sometimes you have to drive a 2WD fast across sandy creek beds or up the banks just to maintain that momentum to avoid getting stuck. Crawling carefully and in full control, as you can do with a 4WD in low range, won't always work and the faster you go the more the suspension compresses – and there goes your ground clearance. It's at times like this that a bash plate earns its keep.

**Reducing tyre pressures** to gain traction gives you a bit more leeway before you get stuck and is essential when you're stuck in sand. As with 4WDs, one bar or 14.5 psi is the optimum 'get-out-of-jail-free' pressure, but in stony Morocco it's best to leave tyres at road pressures until there's no choice.

Note that regular cars may not have **towing points** strong enough to withstand dragging a car out of mud or sand. The loops or rings you often see on the back are for locating a car on a car transporter. Pick attachment points carefully; close to a suspension pivot is a good idea, but certainly not bumpers. For more advice see p97.

An alloy sand plate cut long ways to make two thin ones will do near Erg Chebbi, but thick wooden planks have the added advantage of also bridging ditches.

VEHICLE CHOICE & PREPARATION

# Bicycle touring in Morocco

Setting off from Foum Zguid back to Agadir on a couple of inexpensive Decathlon bikes.

Within the limits of season and range Morocco offers self-sufficient off-road tourers some fantastic opportunities for adventuring. Distances are not too extreme, services (including transportation over dull stages) are close at hand and there's enough variety of landscape to find something you like.

I've not toured off-road on a bicycle in Morocco yet, but halfway through writing this book I rode from China over the Karakoram to the Hindu Kush of northern Pakistan on tracks for up to three days at a time and incredibly, I became an overnight expert on bicycle touring in Morocco! It helps that I was involved with editing Trailblazer's *Adventure Cycle Touring Handbook* ('ACTH') and their *Himalaya by Bike* which we used on the KKH. For the full story on long range bike touring it's all in the ACTH.

Linking the pistes of the south are also some great **road rides**, not least of which is Route MS10, the 1500-km 'Desert Highway' (see p196), nearly all of it on comparatively good surfaces and with very little traffic. If you're more into travel than off-road riding you may find the pistes give you and your bike simply too much of a beating. Take to the roads with the odd off-road excursion and you'll still have a great time in Morocco.

As it is, not all the off-road routes in this book are suitable for cycling. Some are simply too long, too rough, too arid and too remote. A selection have a combination of surfaces that won't shake your bike to bits all the time and have wells at regular intervals to avoid carrying masses of heavy water; the

The great thing with bikes is that you can sling them onto a car when you get tired or bored, and that you can get over rockfalls and other terrain which will stop everything bar a mule.

crux to making off-road riding fun.

This book assumes you're **self-sufficient**, but with a support vehicle, either following you or better still meeting you at the end of the day, all the *Morocco Overland* routes open up and riding becomes still more fun.

Whatever direction a route is described in, consider accessing the higher end by road where possible, so giving you a mostly downhill run. Don't worry about turning to flab or frying your brakes; in between there'll be plenty of uphill or loose stages where you'll be walking the bike.

Road riding most of the time will still give you a great time in the south of Morocco.
© Raf Verbeelen (and top of p54).

## Pick of the pistes

Cycling in Morocco doesn't have to mean heading south into the fringes of the Sahara, though this is often the initial motivation. Down here the sealed roads are quieter, the people can be less hassle and all in all it's what you've come here for. Taking the train from Tangier to Marrakech, or flying to these cities (or Ouarzazate) saves days cycling across the busier and less interesting north.

East of Marrakech picking up the two long trans-Atlas routes: MH1 and MH2 make a great way of getting down south without resorting to the obvious roads. Highway alternatives include the little-used R203 road over 2092-metre Tizi-n-Test south-west of Marrakech or the busier N9 Marrakech-Ouarzazate highway over the 2260m Tizi n Tichka pass. Turning west over the top at Aguim you can head down Routes MH6, MH8 in reverse or eventually MH7. Alternatively you can take the barely-used road from Demnate to Ouarzazate; Route MH12. All these high off-road routes will have their share of rough tracks or mud and even snow in the higher elevations from November to March. If you're exploring the routes in Jebel Sirwa and heading south-west, it's worth knowing that from Taliouine the R106 is a nice quiet road ride to Igherm and Tafraoute.

Once south of the High Atlas the Jebel Sarhro routes: MH4, MH5 and MH10 would be fun on a mountain bike; at worst you can carry it. The only self-sufficient MTBs I saw in Morocco were coming down MH4 to Nekob. Once down in the warmer Anti Atlas, early spring or late autumn would be best on the longer pistes. Just about all the routes in the 'MA' Anti Atlas region are do-able on a bike but they're stony and rough so better stick to the shorter ones like MA2, -4, and -5 which will tire you out less, as will MW4 and 5 and at a push MW3.

Over on the east side the riding is more Saharan, flatter and sandier but also bleaker in the ME region (ME1 is a great road into an area of short but fun routes). Routes MS1, -2 and -5 are all short but the latter especially will be rough, as will be MS7, even if it's only 163km. The longer routes have been done by bike but will require some commitment.

VEHICLE CHOICE & PREPARATION

## A bike for Morocco

While you could manage some of the *Morocco Overland* routes in an old 2WD car (as many locals do), with a fully-autonomous payload it's hard to imagine a cheap MTB not disintegrating fairly quickly after a couple of routes. For Morocco you'll have a better ride with fewer problems on a solid machine with quality front suspension and equipment to match: a mountain bike with tough wheels and tyres.

Down south what bike shops you'll find will cater for heavy Chinese clunkers or blinged-out 40lb MTBs. A five-star Shimano dealer will be a mirage so, as with motorbikes, expect to be self-sufficient for spares, special tools and repairs.

### Frames and other components

These days it doesn't really matter whether your frame is made from widely-used aluminium or less fashionable steel. Die-hard tourers prefer Cro-Mo steel's feel and small-town weldability, but aluminium frames have advanced enough to be reliable in the short term and suspension helps disguise alloy's inherent harshness. Your bike should have a **long rear triangle** so there's room enough to accommodate a rack and panniers that won't snag your heels. It's worth knowing that higher end MTBs may be spec'ed for climbing, with a short rear triangle, ie: the front of the back wheel is very close to the seat down tube. Aim for a handlebar set-up that doesn't put too much weight on your wrists; a common failing with MTBs – easily fixed by a more upright or adjustable stem. Select simple, solid, well-proven components which are easy to repair and use Loctite on all bolts that fix important components like racks.

Eight gears on the freewheel mean the chain can be wider and so stronger; don't expect to be cycling every last inch of the routes. In Pakistan I found my 24-speed gearing, composed of a 12–32 cassette with 22/32/44 chainrings, was

Schwalbe XR Marathons may be relatively heavy and expensive but will last for 1000s of kilometres with barely a puncture, as does their narrower and smoother City Jet, with less rolling resistance on the road. Right; spoke breakages on the cassette side require the removal of the cassette, something made much easier with this nifty gadget: a 'Next Best Thing' ('NBT') 2.

VEHICLE CHOICE & PREPARATION

ideally matched for my light payload of about 16kg on thin 26" tyres. By the time I was panting up steep tracks in 32–22 I could barely balance anyway. Walking is much less effort and only about half as slow.

## Tyres and wheels

Large 2" tyres will absorb the shocks and so spare your rims and spokes (the weak link on all bikes carrying a load off-road) – especially important if you're not running suspension on the front. They may slow you on the highway, especially if they're less than smooth like the XR Marathon, below left, but will give you more comfort on the tracks. Use robust touring tyres rather than lightweight off-road racing items: anything by Schwalbe is good as they seem immune to punctures; you can pretty much leave a spare tyre and even a spare inner tube at home.

Fat tyres make a suspension-less bike a bit less harsh on the dirt at the cost of swift downhill rolling on tar.

The Marathon series are the heavy tourers' choice; I ran skinny, three-year-old Schwalbe City Jets in Pakistan which rode with less effort and coasted faster down the hills compared to the fully-loaded Marathon-shod bike I travelled with, but they gave harsh riding on the dry tracks by the time the front fork had all but seized.

It may not look so off-road purposeful but I'd use such relatively slim and plain-treaded road tyres again because the highways in the south can easily be as satisfying as hammering along a piste for two or three days, focussed intently on a patch of dirt 15ft ahead. Only in mud (or at the speeds and agility only attainable without any baggage at all) would a knobbly tyre have a distinct advantage.

One thing that will need regular attention are your **spokes**. In the early days you can expect some loosening or even breakages (especially on the rear wheel) after which they should settle down as long as you keep on top of the dark art of spoke tensioning. The key I'm told is to turn a little at a time so you don't end up with Pringle-profiled rims. Carry spare spokes and the nifty gadget pictured opposite to remove the cassette. Biking lore states that the spokes always break on the cassette side where they cannot be replaced without removing it.

## Suspension

Prolonged riding over stones and corrugations with a full payload is extremely tiring. Add a headwind and you'll wonder if the Samaritans have an 0800 number. Along with fitness and a good attitude, up to a point fat tyres at medium pressures reduce the shock, but front suspension will relieve shocks from both your arms and the bike's components and improve traction on fast and loose downhill bends. Suspension forks are nowadays the norm, but as with so many trends, lower-end front forks are rather crude. You don't need the full 100mm or more found on better mountain bikes; 50-80mm will take the sting

VEHICLE CHOICE & PREPARATION

out of the trail but unfortunately these shorter-travel units tend to be less sophisticated and therefore far from plush. Whatever piece of crap I had on my Kashgar bike soon degraded into a centimetre of travel; about the same as my mate's bike running fatter tyres and a rigid Cro-mo steel fork.

The ability to **lock-out** the front fork (again, a high-end feature) is very useful, eliminating a bobbing, effort-sapping front end on long climbs. **Full suspension** bikes have drawbacks for carrying a touring load reliably, but without a load (ie: with a support vehicle) would of course make for a brilliant ride, especially downhill.

Old Man Emu rack. Aluminium but not cheap. The lower mount (unseen) is actually the wheel spindle, not a drop out – a longer skewer is supplied.

### Racks and panniers

It's only Morocco, even on a bike, so you could get by without a full touring set up on the front and thereby enjoy a lighter, more manageable bike on the dirt. I got by like this in Pakistan with everything on the back and between us had enough gear to sleep comfortably at 12,000ft without a tent. The trick is to plan your routes to make the most of the towns, villages, cafés and especially any streams or wells. Each route description details wells and other water sources.

As with motorbikes, the rattle of Moroccan tracks stresses a rack and its mountings – breakages are not unusual, especially on cheaper aluminium racks. A loaded rack will flex from side to side as well as take direct vertical shock loads, so quality racks in aluminium or steel from, among others, Blackburn, Old Man Mountain or Tubus are preferable.

Use chunky clip-on/easily detachable panniers such as Ortlieb Classics and something like a canoeing bag with a similar roll-up closure for light sleeping gear on the top of the rack. On the KKH I found this bag handy to quickly remove at rest stops giving something soft to sit on.

Avoid carrying anything more than a small rucksack on your back – it puts extra weight on your already stressed backside and makes you even sweatier. Something light with a hydrator of a couple of litres of water should be OK. Handlebar bags are very convenient for storing light, fragile and precious things such as a camera, tools, diary, maps, GPS and so on. They should have a quickly detachable fastener that allows you to detach them when away from the bike without even thinking about it.

### Water

It's essential to plan your routes wisely – both by season as well as time of day as your margin for error can be very slim. Depending on the weather and effort, a rider will require up to **six litres** of drinking water a day; if you're drinking much more than this it's really the wrong time of year or you have a leak. With the sustained physical effort of cycling, **clean drinking water** is all the more essential – you don't want to get too sick to cycle on to your next

VEHICLE CHOICE & PREPARATION

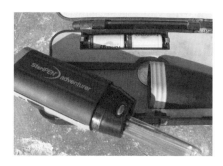

Battery-powered Steripen UV steriliser on the left; kills the micro-organisms but does not remove them or the sediment. The Katadyn Pocket filter does that and without batteries but costs over twice as much, weighs 550 grams and requires some effort.

VEHICLE CHOICE & PREPARATION

water supply, so be extra careful about local water. Fit two or more water bottle cages with at least one to take a large 1.5-litre soft drink bottle (fizzy drinks bottles are more robust).

Bottled water is easily bought in any village with a store, but quality filtration equipment greatly increases your autonomy and helps you avoid burying the planet in empty plastic bottles. In Morocco it's not essential to purify water from desert wells but sources near settlements are better treated. Some wells have a bucket and rope but take up to 40m of cord and a suitable container to enable you to draw up water anywhere. All the wells described in the routes in this book, with an estimated depth, have been visually checked, though not all may have water when you get there. On some sections you may be able to depend on passing vehicles, but this is a bad habit to get into.

Mixing in an **isotonic drink** powder like High5 makes sense in warm conditions, but also carry some pharmaceutical **rehydration sachets** like Dioralyte or Rehydrat and take pre-emptively as you feel yourself getting weak. You must be vigilant about your water consumption because the wind dries sweat so quickly you'll barely notice you're losing liquid.

## Clothing

Clothes have to be functional and comfortable, keeping you protected from the elements. Moroccans are used to European tourists walking about in skimpy clothing and can appreciate that cycling in a goat-hair chador gets itchy. But respecting local customs in the traditional south will pay off in the hospitality you'll encounter – something that's much more likely on a slow-moving bicycle. Man or woman, avoid body-hugging clothing as well as too much exposed skin.

Your face, hands, neck and eyes are permanently exposed to the sun so

Overall, a *cheche* works well on a bike. Easy to buy locally, make sure you get cotton, not brighter-coloured synthetics. If in doubt, light a corner; cotton burns, synthetics melt.

Cooling off; south of Alnif near Route MS4.
©Raf Verbeelen.

should be covered whenever possible. In Pakistan I found a baseball hat caught the wind on downhills, a hankie tied on my head was better but burned my face, while a wide-brimmed hat (lacking a neck strap) also caught the wind and obscured the mountain scenery all around while riding. A traditional *cheche* (turban) would have worked best, protecting you from sun, and dehydration as well as the cold, while not blowing away, but of course can't be worn with a helmet. I learned that you don't want the distraction of a hat that's about to blow off, especially when hammering down hill, but you definitely need to protect your head, neck and face with something.

## When to ride

Overall October to March is the most pleasant time as long as you avoid the High Atlas above 2000m in mid-winter. Here the desert will be as cool as it gets. At warmer times, set off in the early morning when the air is still cool, the wind is light and so water consumption is less. Have a long relaxing siesta or better still end the day's cycling by early afternoon and let the day cook away unnoticed. Riding at this pace, depending on your fitness and the wind, you could expect to cover up to 80km a day on the easiest tracks. On steeper routes with lots of pushing 30–50km a day may be all you can manage.

The wind not only slows you down, it also dehydrates you if you don't protect yourself properly, so will increase your water consumption. Remember, you're unlikely to be carrying more than a day's supply of water at any time so plan the route within your capabilities and around dependable watering points.

VEHICLE CHOICE & PREPARATION

If you leave the UK on a Friday night, by Monday afternoon you could be in Morocco and a day later south of the Atlas. Depending on where you start, you'll have covered nearly 2000 miles across four countries, taken two sea crossings and may well feel a bit frazzled. In bad weather a solo driver in a 25-year-old Patrol, or the rider of a DR-Z400 will feel very frazzled indeed.

## ACROSS THE CHANNEL OR THE BAY OF BISCAY

Most visits to Morocco will take place outside of summer, if not in the dead of winter, making for a possibly grim continental transit down to southern Spain. These short, cold and possibly wet days may not wrinkle the composure of a big BMW GS **motorcycle**, but they'll still add up to two very full days on the road with quite a bill for road tolls. You can halve this 1400-mile-plus stage from the Channel ports to southern Spain by ferrying from Portsmouth or Plymouth to northern Spain with P&O or Brittany Ferries.

With a car full of people sharing the driving as well as all the costs, **driving all the way** is less expensive. A similarly long crossing exists from Sète in France to either Nador or Tangier; for details see p65. It's not all about saving the pennies though and for a solo driver the three Biscay ferries (or the Sète – Morocco service) may be a more restful option in mid-winter.

The sample prices overleaf were taken from the operators' websites in early 2009 for an October–November trip. Not all the cross-Channel operators are listed and prices are bound to change so they only serve as a comparison.

Operators may offer promotional fares, as does membership of some organisations or reading the right magazine at the right time. Cars are assumed to be a typical 4WD less than 2m high (exact height tariffs vary) and 5m long, with two passengers. Cabins are two-berth, inside (ie, no windows). Exterior and 'club' class en-suite cabins are available on the longer routes at extra cost.

Bay of Biscay; you could see dolphins.

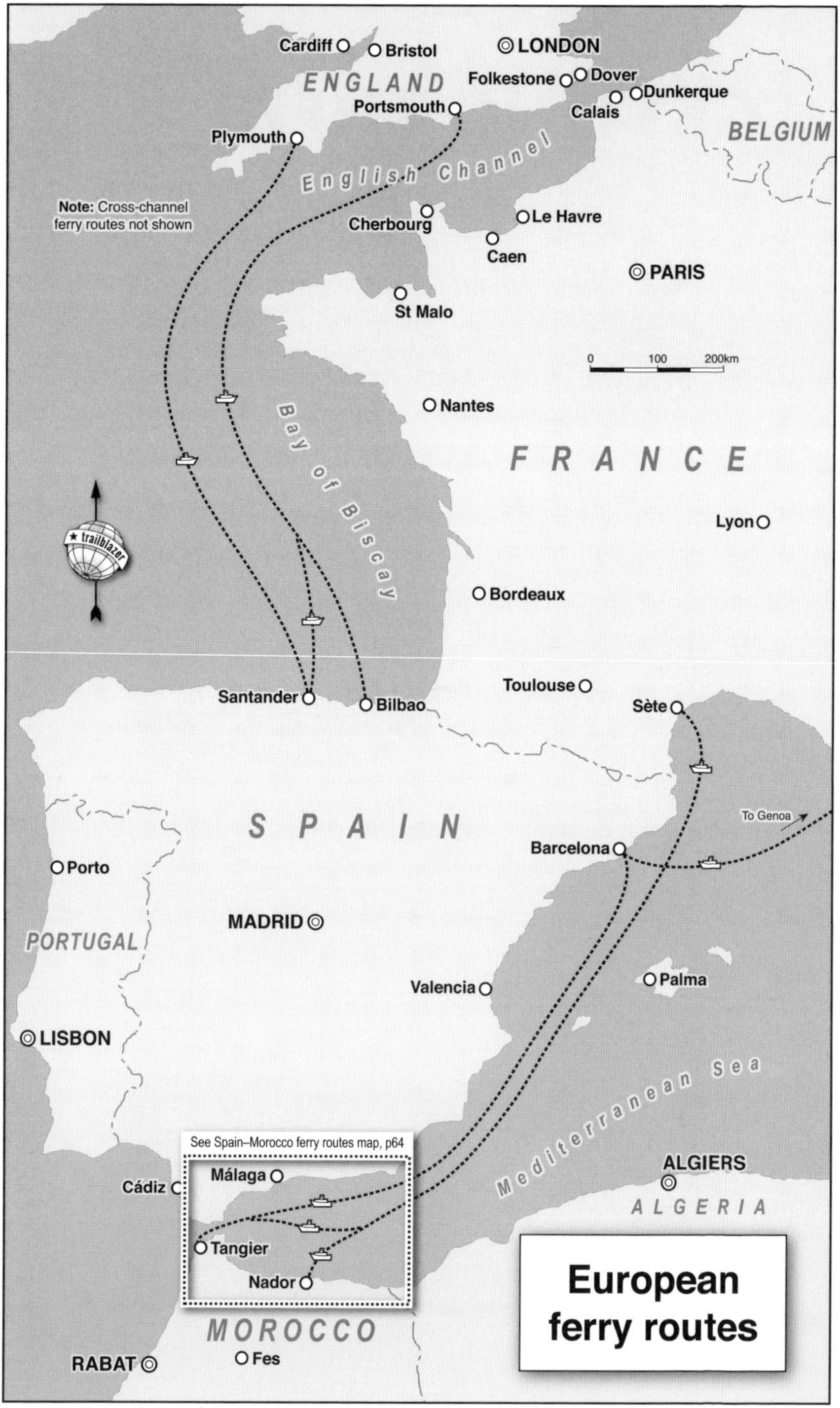

ENGLAND

Cardiff○  ○ Bristol  ◎ LONDON
Folkestone ○ ○ Dover
Portsmouth ○  ○ Dunkerque
Calais ○
BELGIUM

Plymouth ○

English Channel

Note: Cross-channel
ferry routes not shown

Cherbourg  ○ Le Havre
○ Caen
◎ PARIS

St Malo

Bay of Biscay

○ Nantes

FRANCE

Lyon ○

★ trailblazer

○ Bordeaux

Toulouse ○

Sète ○

Santander ○  ○ Bilbao

SPAIN

To Genoa

Barcelona ○

○ Porto

MADRID ◎

PORTUGAL

Valencia ○

○ Palma

◎ LISBON

Mediterranean Sea

See Spain–Morocco ferry routes map, p64

ALGIERS
◎
ALGERIA

Cádiz ○  Málaga ○

○ Tangier

Nador ○

European
ferry routes

MOROCCO

RABAT ◎  ○ Fes

GETTING THERE

| ROUTE | DURATION | FREQUENCY | PAX | 4WD | MOTO |
|---|---|---|---|---|---|

### Eurotunnel
**Folkestone – Calais**  40mins  Up to 4 per hour  Included  £98–£153 £48–£76
'Standard' non flexible fare. 'Flexiplus' fares are £398 for a car and £198 for a bike.

### Norfolk Line
**Dover – Dunkerque**  1hr 45m  Every 2 hours  Included  £33–£43 £33–£43
Lowest costs on early morning sailings given. Highest tariff listed at £57.

### LD Lines
**Portsmouth – Le Havre**  7 hours  One daily  Seat  £116  £52
4WD < 2.2m high. For an inside cabin add £24 pp each way

### Britanny Ferries
**Plymouth – Santander**  20 hours  Weekly*  Seat  £478  £205
**Portsmouth – Santander**  24 hours  Weekly*
*Both services mid-Mar to mid-Nov only. Inside cabin from £313 for a bike and £572 for two and a 4WD < 2m high

### P&O Ferries
**Portsmouth – Bilbao**  32 hours  Twice weekly  Cabin  £630  £326

On the overnight crossings such as those to Le Havre or Santander, a 'reclining seat' can be translated as 'sleeping on the floor' in much greater comfort. Bring a sleeping mat, sleeping bag or a blanket, blindfold and earplugs. For motorbikers, sleeping on the floor on the two, one-night Brittany Ferries services to Santander looks like a good deal compared to the ride down through western France, although I've found if you book late the 'free' reclining seats become mysteriously unavailable, forcing you to book a cabin with similar prices to the more frequent P&O service from Portsmouth.

## SOME FUEL PRICES AND EUROPEAN DISTANCES

### Fuel prices
These were the prices of fuel in Western Europe and Morocco in May 2009.

The highest and lowest European prices are in **bold** and all are given **in euros**:

| Country | unleaded | diesel |
|---|---|---|
| UK | 1.07 | **1.15** |
| Ireland | 1.03 | 0.95 |
| Netherlands | **1.37** | 1.03 |
| France | 1.19 | 1.07 |
| Andorra | 0.98 | **0.84** |
| Spain | **0.94** | 0.86 |
| Portugal | 1.16 | 0.98 |
| Morocco | 1.01 | 0.66 |
| Western Sahara | 0.62 | 0.39 |

Doubtless these fuel prices won't stay that way for long but one presumes their relationship to each other, based on the levels of state tax in each country, will broadly stay the same. See website: 'Updates'.

| Distances | miles | km |
|---|---|---|
| Dover – Almería | 1250 | 2010 |
| Dover – Algeciras | 1400 | 2256 |
| Le Havre – Almería | 1200 | 1930 |
| Le Havre – Algeciras | 1274 | 2050 |
| Bilbao – Almería | 596 | 960 |
| Bilbao – Algeciras | 665 | 1070 |
| Santander – Almería (via Madrid) | | |
| | 627 | 1010 |
| Santander – Algeciras (via Salamanca) | | |
| | 627 | 1010 |
| Dover – Sète | 704 | 1133 |
| Le Havre – Sète | 565 | 910 |
| Dover – Irun (Spanish frontier) | | |
| | 688 | 1108 |
| Le Havre – Irun | 562 | 904 |
| Irun – Algeciras | 715 | 1151 |
| Irun – Almería | 680 | 1094 |

The port of Tarifa is 14 miles or 22km south-west of Algeciras.

It's said the Bay of Biscay is notorious for occasionally rough ferry crossings. This may have been true once, but it would take quite a swell to disturb the composure of today's modern ferries. Having taken this route at least half a dozen times at all times of year, I've never experienced any significant discomfort in what were predicted as Force 8 gales. Catching that same storm on the road along the western flank of France would have been no picnic. P&O ferries have taken on the form of there-and-back 'mini cruises' with just a couple of hours on-shore in Bilbao but with plenty of activities on board from casinos, karaoke and cinemas to dolphin and whale spotting.

## CROSSING SPAIN
Even in a fairly gutless car and avoiding toll motorways, crossing Spain from north to south is possible in one long, 12-hour day, although circumnavigating Madrid at rush hour can cost you some time. Spain doesn't have the dense network of toll motorways (*autopistas*) as found in France (see box below) but what roads there are, are fast enough.

Almería may be a little nearer than Algeciras, but has less frequent services and longer crossings to Melilla or adjacent Nador. If you're in a blind rush, head for Algeciras any way you like because whatever time you arrive there, a ferry will be leaving for Ceuta or Tangier soon.

### Transporting a bike to southern Spain
Getting a bike transported to southern Spain and flying in after it is a time saving alternative if someone in your group has a van or trailer and the time. It must be Spain not Morocco because, to catch out European tour operators bringing in bikes for their clients who'd fly in, now the vehicle owner must be present at a Moroccan port of entry. There are ways round this (it helps if you do it regularly). Entering Morocco with say, a van and a bike *both in your name* can be done but don't do the TVIP online (see p68), do the triplicate version at the port and **put both vehicles on the one form**.

With Easyjet return flights from Stansted from £50, Málaga is the favoured option, just 140 sunny kilometres from Algeciras or 200 from Almería in the other direction. This inexpensive option can also work for car passengers wanting to miss out the European stage. Bikers can try and stash a van in Spain and ride to the ferry port and Morocco.

In the UK, specialised bike transportation services such as Bike Truck securely transport your bike and meet you in Málaga with return prices from

GETTING THERE

---

### FRENCH AND SPANISH TOLL ROADS

From somewhere like Dover, the French stage down to the Spanish border costs around €80 in tolls (*peage*), possibly more for a 4WD and about half that on a bike. Spain has a less dense network of toll roads or autopistas: (see 🖥 www.viat.es) but what there are are expensive. On a typical transit from northern Spain to Algeciras only about 20% of the road is tolled (*peaje*) and of course avoidable: they include autopista stages from the French border to Burgos; leaving Madrid for Toledo; and from Seville to Madrid; at a guess the cost is nearly as much as France.

On 🖥 www.mappy.co.uk you can enter your itinerary and it will calculate the fuel and French toll cost (cars only).

£500 per bike. Alternatively you could get a regular UK courier van service to do the run. Prices will have risen for sure, but in 2002 I got 7 bikes jammed in the back of a Mercedes Sprinter to Genoa and back a month later for under £2000. And with an economical average white van now available from around that price, it could even pay to buy a van especially for a Morocco trip and sell it afterwards. Although people consider it, **shipping** a vehicle into Morocco, by air or sea is way more hassle than it's worth. Short of riding down, combining vanning with an Easyjet flight to Málaga are your best options.

## CROSSING TO MOROCCO: MEDITERRANEAN FERRIES

Car ferries run across the Straits of Gibraltar as well as other ports on the south-east Spanish coast plus Sète, just west of Montpellier, and even Genoa (via Barcelona). If heading for Sète it's worth knowing the hilly *la Méridienne* A75 autoroute is free for 340km south of Clermont Ferrand to Montpellier (excepting the spectacular Millau Viaduct which you won't mind paying for). Driving from Le Havre via Orleans to Sète adds up to less than €40 in *peage*.

The quickest and most frequent service runs between Algeciras and the Spanish enclave of **Ceuta** on the North African coast; just a 35-minute crossing although official ferry operator prices are extremely high when you think of the tiny distance involved. Technically still in Spain and with the benefit of duty-free unleaded petrol (diesel costs about the same over the border) from Ceuta you can proceed a couple of kilometres to Fnideq (among other names); the Moroccan frontier. Though further, ferries to **Tangier** can actually be a little cheaper than Ceuta, presumably because they're Moroccan rather than Spanish operations.

**Algeciras** attracts touts who can intimidate some travellers, pulling scams like tricking you into paying 'parking fees' while legitimately queuing to board a boat, for example. Brace yourself; Morocco is coming to get you and this can lead for a tense few hours for a first-timer until you're well past Fnideq and wired up for action. Long before you approach the city you'll see countless places selling ferry tickets. The price is pretty much the same wherever you go and all will be kosher, but you've not much to lose driving right up to the port and wandering from office to office seeing what they offer. See the website 'Getting there' page for updates and – while it lasts – a link to an agency near Algeciras which has great deals on open returns to Ceuta.

There's something to be said for avoiding the scrum at Algeciras, Ceuta/Fnideq and even Tangier by taking crossings to the quieter ports of **Nador** or **Melilla** in the east. Sure, they cost more and take longer, but if you've just set a land speed record across France and Spain you'll be due for a spell of vacant contemplation. With negligible queues and barely two touts to rub together, at Nador you can be on your way in 30 minutes.

For many years I avoided Tangier for this very reason and still read stories about what might most generously be described as 'antics' befalling drivers unfamiliar to that city. But when my ferry was diverted there I found the port experience merely very slow. Although most find the procedure nowhere near as bad as they imagined, if you feel anxious about entering Morocco, it's not a bad idea to leave the perceived challenges of Tangier or Ceuta/Fnideq for the way back by which time you're more attuned to the Moroccan wavelength.

**Spain–Morocco ferry routes**

SPAIN

MOROCCO

Mediterranean Sea

To Barcelona & Genoa

To Sète

To Sète

Almería

Nador (Beni Enzar)

Melilla

Al Hoceima

Málaga

Marbella

Gibraltar

Algeciras

Ceuta

Tarifa

Tangier

0   25   50km

The list below gives available details at the time of writing. For some operators it's not possible to separate the price of the vehicle from a passenger, but where marked as 'included' it indicates two passengers. These prices will almost certainly go out of date so are best viewed as being comparative.

| ROUTE | DURATION | FREQUENCY | PAX | 4WD | MOTO |
|---|---|---|---|---|---|
| **Acconia Transmediterranea** | | | | | |
| Algeciras – Ceuta | 35m | Up to 15 daily | included | €189 | €70 |
| Algeciras – Tangier | 2½hr | 6–7 daily | included | €219 | €94 |
| Málaga – Melilla | 7–8hr | 2 daily | included | €257 | €90 |
| | | | Cabins from €36 | | |
| Almería – Melilla | 7–8hr | 2 daily | included | €257 | €90 |
| | | | Cabins from €36 | | |
| Almería – Nador | 4½–8hr | 4 daily | included | €297 | €124 |
| | | | Cabins from €26 | | |
| **Balearia** | | | | | |
| Algeciras – Ceuta | 30m | 5 daily | included | €198 | €75 |
| Algeciras – Tangier | 30m | 3 daily | included | €218 | €94 |
| **Comnav** | | | | | |
| Algeciras – Tangier | 2hr | 3–4 daily | €45 | €250* | €48 |
| | | * Half price if car under 1.8m. Cabins from €50 | | | |
| Almería – Nador | 6hr | up to 2 daily | €18 | €162 | €70 |
| | | | Cabins from €50 | | |
| Sète – Tangier | 36hr | 2 weekly | €40 | €245 | €100 |
| | | Meals included. Cabins from €110 | | | |
| Sète – Nador | 34hr | 1-2 a week | €35 | €210 | €100 |
| | | Meals included. Cabins from €110 | | | |
| Also **Genoa – Tangier** | 48hr | 1-2 weekly | | | |
| **Comarit** | | | | | |
| Algeciras – Tangier | 2½hr | 3-6 daily | €40 | €200 | €40 |
| Almería – Nador | 6–8hr | 4-8 weekly | €44 | €182 | €63 |
| Algeciras – Tangier | 30hr | 1-2 weekly | €57 | €273 | €233 |
| **FRS** | | | | | |
| Tarifa – Tangier | 35min | 8 daily | €39 | €120 | €35 |
| Gibraltar – Tangier | 1½hr | 1 a week | €32 | €110 | €30 |
| Algeciras – Ceuta | 30min | 6 daily | €42 | €162 | €32 |
| **Ferry Maroc** | | | | | |
| Almería – Nador | 7hr | 1–4 a day | €71 | €232 | €76 |
| **GNV** | | | | | |
| Barcelona – Tangier | 26hr | Weekly | €79 | €159 | €39 |
| (Service actually runs to and from Genoa via Barcelona to Tangier) | | | | | |

On night time crossings to Melilla or Nador a cabin might be desirable. Some sailings on these routes are also 'fast' which also means more expensive. Cabin prices are given at the cheapest available (usually interior, 4-berth, shared toilets). As with the longer ferry services from the UK, various configurations of exclusive, better-specified cabins are available. Getting a return price usually results in a 10% discount.

## ARRIVING BY AIR

At the moment, from the UK, Morocco is served by Easyjet, Ryanair, Royal Air Maroc (RAM), Air France via Paris and Iberia via Madrid. There are also charter operators such as Atlas Blue or Thompson Fly covering Casablanca, Fes, Rabat and Tangier from London; Agadir from London, Birmingham and Manchester; and Marrakech from London, Luton, Bristol and Manchester.

Marrakech is the cheapest place to get to from the UK and it's well positioned for getting beyond the High Atlas. Ouarzazate is even closer to the action but direct from the UK is not especially cheap; flying from or via Paris gives better options. The prices below are from early 2009 for an October 2009 flight with a November return.

| Carrier/Agent | from | to | Lowest fare |
|---|---|---|---|
| Easyjet | Gatwick | Marrakech | £96 |
| Ryanair | Luton | Marrakech | £90 |
| Iberia | Heathrow | Casablanca | £192 |
| RAM | Gatwick | Marrakech | £155 |
| RAM | Heathrow | Casablanca | £219 |
| Thompson Fly | Gatwick | Agadir | £155 |
| Atlas Blue | Gatwick | Marrakech | £181 |
| Unspecified | Heathrow | Ouarzazate | £249 |
| Unspecified | Heathrow | Tangier | £267 |

# AT THE BORDER 4

As has already been suggested, for most first-timers entry into Morocco can add up to a tense hour or two as their nose gets pushed right into the crack between Europe and Africa. Coming via Ceuta or less so Melilla merely prolongs it, but it's this moment that puts most people off driving to Morocco. Your xenophobia metre swings into the red as your vehicle becomes a conspicuous emblem of your separateness. At busier crossings like Fnideq or Tangier it's hard to tell who's in authority as guys wave you down to 'guide' you into a parking space 40 feet wide, or sell you an immigration card which you already have or are piled up just ahead.

This focus of attention can disorient you as you worry about wasting time in the wrong queue, having someone run off with your passport, or leaving without the correct papers. As always, at these sorts of borders it pays to be prepared, put on a brave face, keep your cool and be polite – but also to stand your ground. While there's nothing to pay for apart from motor insurance, it's not the end of the world to get a helper to submit your forms for you. He'll know where to go and what to do and even if you don't stick with him, he'll be back soon and all for a couple of euros tip.

The good thing is the border is much better than it used to be, if for no other reason than strict EU regulations to try and stem the northbound flow of migrants. Here in Africa these informal helpers are commonplace and are tolerated as merely trying to grab a few crumbs falling from the big cake. In some North African ports like Tunis these guys appear to work with the authorities to share the spoils of scamming you; in Morocco it's much more informal and small-time. Africa's reputation for bribery is much exaggerated and here it's unknown for a uniformed official to demand or expect a tip for a foreign tourist (locals passing through may be another matter).

## Joining the queue

If you arrive at Ceuta or Melilla from Spain you're still in Spain with no formalities to go through. In both cases the actual Moroccan border, Fnideq or Beni Enzar near Nador respectively, is a couple of miles down the road.

On the ferry you may find an A6-sized immigration card (see p71). They're in French and English. Under 'going to' write any big Moroccan town; for 'coming from' put the European port you've just arrived from (Algeciras, Almería, etc). For 'address in Morocco' make something up if you don't know: a *Hotel Fes* in Fes will do.

## YOUR CIN NUMBER

If you've been to Morocco recently you'll have a 'CIN' number (**national identity card number**) in your passport, as long as it hasn't been renewed. Composed of about 5 numbers and 2 letters (see right) it corresponds to your known details on the Moroccan immigration service database.

The CIN can be hard to find in your passport but should be next to your last Moroccan entry/exit stamps. It helps if you use this number on forms where it's requested. If you don't have one they'll allocate you one and stamp it in your passport on arrival.

## Temporary vehicle importation document: TVIP or 'D16'

Aboard the ferry (on longer crossings) or in the Moroccan port of arrival you need to find the Customs desk and get the triplicate white, green and yellow A5-sized 'TVIP' form titled in French: *Declaration D'Admission Temporaire de Moyens de Transport* ('Temporary Importation Declaration of [means of] Transport). This is a welcome alternative to the dreaded Carnet de Passage which Morocco does not require, and declares you'll re-export your vehicle once you leave Morocco. The TVIP form's valid for 6 months.

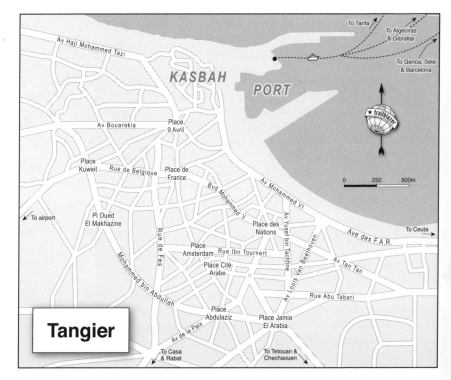

Tangier

Using the exact combination of a PC running Internet Explorer (as opposed to a PC running any other browser or any Mac) it's possible to fill out a version of the TVIP (also known as a 'D16') online before you leave the Moroccan Customs' website: ▱ www.douane.gov.ma/MRE.

On the above webpage several options are listed.
Click option three:
- *Admission temporaire des véhicules (D16TER)*
  then click the second option:
- *Saisie et Edition de la déclaration d'admission temporaire D16ter*
  Now fill out the following details:
- *Prénom et Nom*: Your forename and surname.
  *CIN*: If you have one from a previous visit enter it (see box opposite). If not click *Étrangers non résidant* or *autres* ('other').
- *Immatriculation*: Your vehicle's registration number with no spaces.
- *Marque*: Select from the menu. Along with many unknown marques, many bike marques are not listed so select '*autre*' at the end. For Land Rover select *Rover*.
- *Modèle*: For example 'Defender 300Tdi' or 'F800GS' followed by 'MOTO' if it's a bike.
- *Genre*: Select *Tourisme*.
- *Pays*: Select your country.
- *Date de 1ère mise en circulation*: Your vehicle's date of first registration written on your vehicle ownership document.
- *Châssis n°*: Your VIN (vehicle identity number) a long string of letters and numbers also on the ownership document.

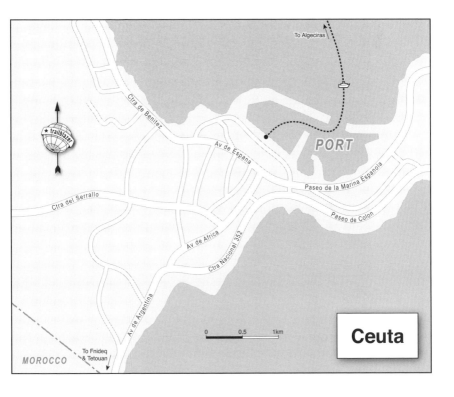

Then press *Imprimer* (print). Your D16 appears with all your information formatted in between French and Arabic translations, as well as a couple of bar codes. If it all looks correct (see opposite, on the left) then print the page. Although three copies come out you may as well print out an extra set. Don't forget to sign each in the bottom left-hand corner.

Whether you fill out a D16 in advance online, or the triplicate version while queuing in a Moroccan port doesn't matter, the former is one less thing to worry about, but do the latter if you have **two vehicles in your name**.

## Entry procedure at the port

If you're not sure where to go or what to do, hang back and follow someone. You'll need your **passport**, **vehicle ownership document** and a **pen**. A rudimentary knowledge of French helps. Ideally all your ducks will be in a row and you'll have filled out the immigration card on the ferry (having grabbed

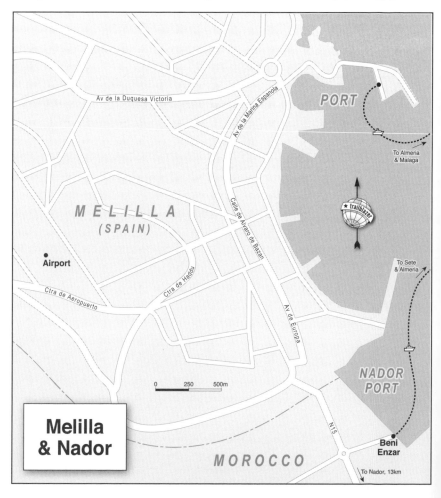

Melilla & Nador

Left: a printed out D16. You'll need three copies. Right: immigration card. Grab some spares.

a blank spare should you have made a mistake), your temporary vehicle importation permit ('TVIP') was printed off online back home (as above), and you may even have valid motor insurance for Morocco.

- Hand in your filled out immigration card to the police – they might come to your car in the big shed at Tangier East, or park up and hand it in at a booth at Fnideq or walk into the big embarkation hall in Nador. They will stamp your passport and if necessary issue a CIN too.
- If you haven't got the D16 ready to hand over to the Customs it's no drama; get the triplicate A5-sized form in white, green and yellow from them and fill it out. Then present it with your stamped passport and vehicle ownership documents back to the Customs to get a TVIP printed out. Whether a D16 or a TVIP (essentially the same thing), the guy will stamp and squiggle one or the other and hand two copies back. Don't lose these; you'll need to show them and get them stamped again when you leave the country.
- Possibly submit to a perfunctory search of your vehicle.
- Change money if possible, of find an ATM in town
- Buy motor insurance if available at the port (see p14).

To complete these few steps can take as little as 30 minutes at Nador, or up to two hours or more at the bigger ports when bigger ferries full of cars all arrive at once.

## Leaving the port

With all this done you can finally head out into the wilds of Morocco. Take it easy through towns, bored policemen sometimes look for a foreigner to pick on or check their documents.

Although diesel is at least 20% cheaper in Morocco than Europe, it's better not to arrive with the very dregs in a tank. All four major ports have fuel stations within a couple of miles of the port gates. With your papers all stamped and stashed and your tank and maybe a spare can full, one of the most stressful episodes; arrival in Morocco, is behind you now and you really feel you're ready to cut loose and see what Morocco has to offer.

# 5   ON THE ROAD

Various subjects are covered under this heading and add up to elements of driving or riding around Morocco that are not always well covered in the guidebooks recommended on p24.

### First days
Your first day or two in Morocco can be critical. After getting out of the port some travellers wonder what all the fuss was about, others get off on the wrong foot, get ripped off or intimidated in some way and flee back to Spain before they give the place a chance.

Experience, attitude and expectations add up to much of it, but so does your planning. Getting off the boat at somewhere like Tangier and blundering into the medina looking for a cheap hotel with secure parking and being taken in by the first 'good Samaritan' you meet can end in tears. On this side of Morocco (as opposed to Melilla/Nador), for your first night it's best to head for somewhere **specific**, **recommended** and **easy to get to**. Plan to arrive in Morocco early, factor in a couple of hours to get out of the port and have most of the rest of the day to get to somewhere more manageable such as Asilah or Chefchaouen well before dark, or an out-of-town campsite or motel with fewer parking issues. Knowing where you're going that first night is one less thing to worry about at a time when you've enough on your plate.

## DANGERS ON THE ROAD
Local **driving standards** in Morocco are no worse than in southern or eastern Europe, adding up to a certain macho flair that can sometimes be interpreted as aggression. In the east and south, traffic is very light with few big trucks and well-surfaced roads passing fantastic scenery, and with fuel, food and lodging never far away.

Along with beaten-up cars, you'll see many **pedestrians**, **cyclists** and **animals** on the rural roads, usually near towns and villages. Schoolchildren released from class seem to wander right across the road without a care in the world. **Slow right down** as you pass through these villages or any crowd.

On the road the most intimidating encounters will be with the **intercity coaches** which seem to run to a timetable that the driver can barely maintain but which will cost him his job. Give way to these coaches and other similarly pushy drivers. Don't be angered by flashing or hooting as they pass; this is a local custom for 'attention, coming through' rather then 'get out of my way', though edging right to let them know you know they're there is a good idea. Drivers will also flash you as they come towards you, day and night; it's hard to know why unless they want confirmation you're awake. The most dangerous places at **night** are rural towns, especially around dusk when a place can become mobilised by the evening *promenade*. A tractor or a bicycle with lights is as unknown as a moped rider with a helmet. The best advice is again, to slow down.

Bendy.

**Single-width roads** that vary from definitely one-car wide to two-cars-at-a-push can also be tense. Ideally, converging vehicles drive their nearside wheels off the asphalt onto the dirt as they pass each other, but such cooperation is rare. Usually, a game of chicken ensues with drivers waiting until the very last minute before edging slightly towards the shoulder, their mirrors whooshing just inches apart. In a right-hand drive car judging this distance can be tricky so it's best to just head for the dirt to be sure you won't get whacked; chances are you're in a rufty-tufty 4WD that can handle a few metres of rubble. Bikes have a better time of it; oncoming vehicles often pull to the right, but just as you get used to this there's always one who won't and gives you a fright. Always be ready to brake hard and take to the shoulder.

Next on the list are single-width **mountain roads** which, if sealed, have obviously a higher chance of traffic. Route MH12 is like this and, along with the landslides, roadside rubble and steep drops, you really must approach each bend with the possibility that someone is doing the same from the other side.

## Checkpoints and police

At most temporary checkpoints it's common for a tourist vehicle to be waved through, but don't always assume this. Slow down and watch the guy until he invariably gives you a signal to move on. Occasionally they may stop you (more so in the deep south), but chances are it'll only be for a chat. In the north it's rare to have to show your papers, but be ready and amenable to this. Despite many people's anxieties, unprompted **bribery** is unknown; that all starts from Mauritania onwards, but even then much less than is assumed. If you've broken a law such as overtaking on a solid line, that's another matter.

Only in **Western Sahara**, south of Tan-Tan, will the **permanent checkpoints**, very often on each side of a town, require full details right down to your mother's name. Here it speeds things up to hand over a home-made, pre-filled out form (*fiche* in French) with all your details in French. A Word template is available to download on the website at 🖥 **www.morocco-over land.com/fiche.doc**. This form can also be handed over at hotels which like to keep your passport to copy its details. It's always better to hand over a fiche than your passport and even the payment, if that's an issue. Down south many basic hotels rarely bother taking your details at all.

Police **speed traps** are common in the north, especially on the N1 along the Atlantic coast and even minor coastal routes. If the car ahead seems to be dawdling and isn't just a clapped-out Renault 4, chances are they know what could be around the bend. On the N1 and the parallel motorway, the legal limits are high enough to make good progress, but if you get caught fair and square you'll have to pay a heavy on-the-spot fine or try and talk your way out of it.

## Accidents and breakdowns

For most overland travellers, dealing with minor vehicle problems – or for bikers, minor injuries as well – will be as bad as things can get in Morocco. For a much smaller minority a road traffic accident or a heavy fall while riding may also involve injury.

If you've had an accident involving local drivers or pedestrians, it's best to get the police involved. Assuming you're not blatantly in the wrong and a minister's son is not involved, in Morocco there's little to fear from the police setting you up. If you are clearly in the wrong then hold on, it could be a rough ride. Amicably exchanging details, kicking your bumper straight and expecting the other party's insurance to eventually cover the costs of your damage is unlikely to happen. Because of this, in Morocco it's best to drive around as if you're effectively uninsured, in other words with great care. You may not be i.. ۔ie depths of sub-Saharan Africa, but you're certainly not in the EU out here. It is this lack of certainty in how things develop when they go wrong which puts people off visiting countries like Morocco with their own vehicle.

Many tourists feel nervous about accepting medical care in Africa, but while it may not always be reassuringly close at hand in the south, for regular injuries emergency healthcare in Morocco is reliable and efficient. All you have to do is reach it. Nevertheless, **travel insurance** which includes repatriation in the event of a medical emergency is worthwhile, inexpensive and can put your mind at rest. Ascertain that you're covered while driving or riding off sealed roads, familiarise yourself with the procedure to follow in the event of reporting a claim, and make note of the **emergency number** you'll need to call to get things moving.

### Breakdowns

Where an accident or breakdown happens and whether you're alone has a lot to do with how easily it gets resolved. On a sealed road and assuming no one else is involved, either your travel companion can tow you to somewhere useful or it won't be long before someone stops and offers to help. In southern Morocco, away from the tourist axis, chances are this'll be a genuine offer of assistance and not necessarily anything to be suspicious of. People may well become mobilised to help you, but any over-hasty claims of 'my brother has garage/is Rally mechanic' need some consideration. On the piste the same scenario may take a bit longer to solve but one thing is certain, **not travelling alone** certainly makes a tense situation easier and less expensive to fix.

It's most likely any spares for your vehicle will be miles away in a northern city or may not be available in Morocco at all. In this case many travellers have relied on others coming down to bring the needed part, as getting them sent by air courier can slow things down in Customs. In both cases, having

## ELEMENTARY VEHICLE TROUBLESHOOTING

If you don't know how engines work, try to solve problems logically: will it start; will it run; will it go, steer and stop? Engines won't start for two reasons: a lack of electrical power or fuel. More rarely some mechanical issue like a broken starter motor may be the problem or more commonly these days, a relatively insignificant electronic malfunction like a blown brake light fuse may disable your modern engine by default.

Should an error code appear somewhere on the dash, getting on the internet (for cars, for example, try ▯ www.obd-codes.com) to find out what it means may help track down the problem. Generally, they're classified with prefixes relating to 'P' (powertrain), 'B' (body), 'C' (chassis) and 'U' (network); hopefully you're a little wiser.

It's not uncommon for non-terminal error codes – to do with emissions, for example – to flash up even if the vehicle seems to be running fine. You can ignore these.

Once running, engines perform badly or intermittently usually due to the air/fuel 'mixture', though again on modern, electronically-managed engines, a loose connection, faulty battery, or some electronic sensor may be the cause.

Assuming the engine started and is running sweetly, only some element of the transmission can be a show stopper – brakes and steering usually leave you something to get by with. A clutch should not go without warning unless it's been flogged to death. In a car, if you're lucky, it's the master or slave cylinder seals (one is by the clutch pedal, the other by the clutch housing under the car) if you're not, it's the plate. With a bike it's usually the cable; wet clutches rarely just give out. On bikes or cars, gearboxes too give plenty of warning, often thousands of miles, before they pack up entirely. Which leaves only tyres; the most likely cause of a breakdown and the most easily fixed.

access to the **internet** and a **mobile phone** (see p18) speeds things up greatly. At the very worst, nip back to Europe to get what you need.

## Roadside recovery

When your vehicle is immobilised for any reason, it'll either be something you know how to fix sooner or later – or something you don't. Particularly on the piste, it can be a panic-inducing situation to suddenly have your Moroccan adventure stalled with a dead vehicle. It may sound glib advice, but don't worry and rely on your ingenuity. It's only Morocco and eventually it'll get fixed at the cost of some time and some money; your objective is to minimise both by thinking rationally so it's best get to a town with a hotel and phones.

In Morocco there's no national **roadside recovery service** as there is in Europe; certainly not in the south where roadside recovery is a local issue dealt with by a cut-down van or 4WD with a hook on the back. Just as back home, these freelance operators have you at their mercy and can charge whatever they can get away with. Some European nationals are able to cover these costs by being members of their national roadside organisations, but Brits are not so well supported. It's well worth asking your insurance company whether they offer an add-on to cover the cost of recovery and repair in Morocco. Chances are they won't, although certain UK motorhome specialist insurers like Comfort (who also insure cars) do offer this as long as you're insured with them. They'll farm out the recovery side of things to the RAC who then subcontract to a local Moroccan service. By the time this reaches you halfway between Foum el Hassan and Akka, you may well have sorted it out yourself, but with such cover, if you decide to sit it out you could get your costs repaid.

## Bush mechanics

'Knowing about engines' can help speed things up still further, but with mobile phones and internet, someone, somewhere will have an idea of what's wrong or what to do, even if you don't. Having a vehicle manual either in paper form or on a CD/laptop is useful. Even if it makes no sense to you, someone else may get it.

Relying on local mechanics is a lottery. In a simple case of an obvious mechanical fault that requires garage facilities, they can manage as well as any mechanic. Simple electrical and fuelling issues can also probably be dealt with, especially with older vehicles or models with which they are familiar. Remember, these guys have seen it all before and are familiar with problems caused by local conditions. Turning up at a dusty hole-in the-wall garage in a spluttering VW Touareg SE with error codes flashing across the dashboard will be less successful, as will any form of electronic diagnosis (see box on previous page). This is the gamble of using modern, electronically-managed machines south of the Atlas.

# DAY BY DAY

In most southern towns and villages you won't find supermarkets or clearly designated **shops** selling certain products. Instead, lots of small, general stores sell the same selection of items: tinned, dried, jarred or other preserved foods, soft drinks and juice, dried milk, processed cheese, sweets, fresh bread and some fruit and veg. With a bit of creativity there's everything you need here.

Bakers are usually pretty basic hole-in-the wall places rather than glittering *patisseries*. Moroccan bread is either a big flat brown bap or less commonly, a white baguette. The Arabic word for bread is something like *khobz*. The other place to shop is of course the **souk**, sometimes a weekly event and a big part of the fun of being in Morocco, even in a touristy town like Zagora. Fresh meat is another matter and not one I've ever bothered to investigate. It may be easier to track down a piece of lamb or chicken from a restaurant if you can't locate a butcher. There is advice on souvenir buying on p16.

## Dress codes

You may well range from sipping cocktails in sophisticated urban nightspots to slurping tea with desert nomads where the more conservative and traditional pace of life will require a more appropriate dress. Local values differ greatly between Casablanca's trendy Aïn Diab district and Labouirat, halfway to Smara. While Morocco is much less strict than other Islamic countries, it's good form and less crass to dress in long trousers or skirts down south. Women do not need to cover their hair or bare arms, but may feel less conspicuous in towns if they do the latter. There's more on Islamic customs on p12.

## Moroccan fuel

You can now easily get diesel as well as unleaded petrol everywhere. This fuel is as clean and reliable as anything you'll find in Europe. The two main service station chains you'll see down south are AFRIQUIA and ZIZ, identified at the start of many of this book's routes. These are spacious, modern-looking service stations often with a shop, restaurant, car wash and mechanic as well as toilets

## A CODE OF PRACTICE FOR OVERLAND TRAVELLERS

In 2003 a 78-page UNESCO report titled: *The Sahara of cultures and people. Towards a strategy for the sustainable development of tourism in the Sahara in the context of combating poverty* categorised Saharan tourists as 'excursionists', 'discoverers', or 'initiates'.

A final category, 'independents' was described as follows: *'These are essentially travellers who move around in complete autonomy, with their own 'super-equipped' vehicles, and make very little use of local personnel.... They consume lots of water and wood without necessarily realising what the consequences could be and make only minimal purchases in the countries they visit (food, fuel and craft products). As they are unsupervised, they often cause, through ignorance, irreparable damage to the environment and to neolithic sites. It would seem that their presence causes more damage than it might bring additional resources to those regions and their population. They are to be found in Tunisia, Morocco, Algeria and Niger, and less so in the Libya and Mauritania.'*

Some of the errors and exaggerations in the above are obvious; all that is missing are allegations of Satanic rituals and dolphin mutilation. Regrettably this is how overland travellers in the Sahara are being presented by certain parties with an agenda to promote.

The ability to travel freely but hopefully responsibly is now being restricted in many Saharan countries. In Morocco this freedom remains but even here the actions of a few are ruining it for the majority. Try to follow this code of practice for promote responsible tourism in the south of Morocco.

- Respect local laws and customs (see p13).

- Most travellers bring way too much food from home. Plan to buy food and other provisions in Morocco; there's more there than you'd expect.

- Always ask people first if you may take their photograph or film them.

- Cook on gas, and for camp fires consider easily found waste timber from home. Campfires are nice but there's no need for huge bonfires. If you're cold put on a hat!

- Burn what waste you can in a campfire or better still dispose of it all in town dumps.

- Bury all toilet waste at least a foot deep and burn toilet paper after use.

- If you need to change motor oil, do it in a town garage, not the desert.

- Think twice about making radical excursions off-piste that will leave clear and sometimes permanent tracks.

- Travel in small groups to lessen the impact on local resources.

In the end it all boils down to respect for the environment and the people who live there, as well as a desire to preserve the wilderness as you would wish to find it.

Adapted from *Sahara Overland*.

that won't give you nightmares. At these places the attendant fills you up, you pay him cash and he dispenses change from his satchel. I've never had a problem getting change (or short-changed), but I don't quibble over every last dirham because neither do they if it's a few dirhams over.

Smaller garages in the south (basic places, often under a *SHELL* banner) may still only serve two star leaded and diesel and have no other facilities. For modern petrol vehicles, using **leaded fuel** will coat the catalytic converter which may affect emissions, but it's not something you'll notice until your next emissions test and in my experience on the Yamaha did not affect performance. Overall, it's best to fill up with unleaded where possible. The availability of unleaded has much improved since this book was researched.

A few years ago near some tourist places like Tinerhir, a **scam** operated in some fuel stations where the numbers kept rolling on the bowser but no fuel was actually pumped. It's something that's easier to do to a car than a bike, but certainly in a car, if you bother to get out and open the cap you may find that these days the pump attendants will often point out the fuel bubbling up to the brim, presumably to prove you've not been tricked. It's another good reason to **always fill up a tank** rather than put in say, 100 dirhams worth.

For a **converter** to help re-calculate your fuel consumption into a system with which you're familiar, see p86.

## Roadside food

In Morocco it pays to learn the difference between a **café** and a **restaurant**. In towns the former serves coffee and tea, cakes, soft drinks and cigarettes; a place for young men to hang out. Out in the countryside a café will serve tea or instant black coffee, whatever preserved snacks they stock and at best, could do you an omelette and bread.

For a more substantial meal you'll need a restaurant, which besides the main roads in towns, are often found adjacent to AFRIQUIA and ZIZ fuel stations. At all these basic places it's best to ask what's available (in French: *qu'est qu'il y'a à manger?*) rather than wait politely for a menu and a napkin to be draped over your lap. In a town hotel or auberge, you'll simply be asked what time you want to eat which is fine if you're not fussy or a vegetarian.

Away from the posh, kasbah-hotels, authentic **Moroccan cuisine** is composed of a limited range of dishes. For starters there may be a soup (*shorba* is the Arabic word); a meat-based broth and rarely disappointing, or salad. A *salade marocaine* is a finely-chopped combination of tomatoes, onions, green pepper, olives, cucumber, seasoning and olive oil, all of which you can be sure won't have been flown in from Tanzania, but came into town on a cart.

For the main course **tajine** is a word you'll hear regularly, actually the name of the cooking vessel (much like the Indian 'balti'), in this case a thick ceramic plate with a conical top in which any number of stew-like dishes can be cooked, or even an omelette. In roadside restos they'll have half a dozen two-ring stoves round the back, all merrily bubbling away and waiting for the lunchtime rush. Tajines will vary from delicious, huge, overpriced and 'is that it?', but can be as good as authentic Moroccan cuisine gets down south.

Other more familiar staples include lamb *brochettes* served on a skewer with chips (*frites*), chicken (*poulette*) and chips, and of course **cous-cous**, which is commonly served as part of a bigger, communal meal and will be what you'll get fed by nomads or country folk. Cous-cous is a big bowl of fine-grained semolina, cooked by simply pouring on boiling water. Depending on what's piled on top, (a tajine of some sort), it can be a bit bland compared to the above dishes, but is easily prepared with only vegetables for vegetarians. Dessert will usually be an orange, possibly sliced and sprinkled with cinnamon, and a few dates. For some typical prices of meals see p17.

## Health and water

Intestinal fortitude varies from person to person, but Morocco has a good reputation for avoiding stomach upsets compared to somewhere like Egypt. There's more chance of a package tourist getting sick from an expensive hotel's stagnating buffet than by eating a brochette cooked before your eyes at a road-side restaurant. I'm comfortable eating in basic places like this or cheap hotels for weeks at a time and don't recall ever being ill in Morocco, although I'm by no means immune to getting sick from bad food.

**Bottled water** is widely available and its best to stick with it unless you're here long term or have good water filtration gear (see p57). Almost certainly tap water anywhere is fine, but on a short holiday it's not worth the risk. In a car, if you're reluctant to use **wells** and other natural sources, bring up to 60 litres from home and save on discarding 40 locally-bought plastic bottles.

## Stomach trouble strategy

Getting sick takes two forms. Most common but even then, rare in Morocco, is an onset of bowel activity requiring the need to be close to a toilet or a toilet roll. This could follow a meal you may not have felt good about anyway.

More severe but less common is full-on food poisoning when your whole body feels weak and sore and you need the toilet even when there's little to give. You're much more susceptible to the latter south of the Sahara or in the Moroccan summer at which time it's easy to get run down from the heat.

For both such ailments the best advice is to stop eating solids, drink plenty of clean water and most essentially, dose yourself with rehydrating powders like Dioralyte, as well as 'blockers' such as Imodium until normal alimentary service resumes. With proper food poisoning this may take a few days by which time you'll be feeling quite weak. Some say dairy products, rice, Coke or toast are OK to eat or drink while recovering. It's best just to manage with salty soups and sweet drinks.

ON THE ROAD

### WHEN GOOD HOLIDAYS TURN BAD: SURVIVAL STRATEGIES

Some readers may now be licking their lips at the prospect of learning cunning tips like pointing their watch's hour hands at the sun or rubbing Bear Grylls and Ray Mears together to make a fire. Within a week of writing this, both these presenters had prime-time shows on UK TV about desert survival and watching them made you wonder one thing: what have these guys got against lighters?

'Survival' in the wilderness sense has become a glamorous subject but one should ask, does chancing upon a dead camel and gutting it to sleep inside the cadaver, or more seriously, taking the time to arrange a solar still have any practical value? To a wilderness hiker possibly, but with a vehicle much less so because your bike or car, is carrying all the elements you need to survive and only when it – or possibly you – are incapacitated might you be in trouble.

The worst possible scenario might involve a lone biker in the middle of summer straying off a little-used piste or falling down a deep ravine and breaking a leg or more. Badly injured, unseen and dehydrating rapidly, the situation is indeed grave. The not-so-sensational advice is simply to avoid putting yourself in such a situation in the first place by adopting the following guidelines.

#### Choose your season
The shelter and carrying capacity of your car makes this less critical but even then, ill-equipped tourists have died in summer in the desert (see p41). Solo biking is much more perilous at this time, as it might also be in a mid-winter cold spell in the High Atlas.

#### Communications
Mobile phone coverage extends yearly across Morocco. It could be a lifeline. An inexpensively-rented satellite phone can fill the gaps.

#### Company
At any time of year, if you prefer to travel alone be prepared to face the consequences.

#### Equipment and provisions
Be sure you have the equipment to both recover and repair your vehicle and sustain yourself or again, be prepared to face the consequences and expense.

**Vaccinations** are no more necessary for Morocco than they are for Spain, and if you're a traveller you most probably have polio and tetanus. There may be mosquitoes in some oases in warmer months but there is no malaria.

## HASSLE

Behold the elephant in the room; the reason why many swear never to return to this country. Incessant and seemingly opportunistic begging, persistent hassle from touts which can turn nasty; being treated as a dumb, gullible tourist or worse still, the terrible feeling of discovering you've just acted like one.

Your mission is not to allow this notorious side of Morocco to get to you, and one of the best ways is to **head south** where, apart from a few well-known towns and places along the 'axis of tourism', people are more chilled and there's generally more space to relax. Then, when you feel you've got the hang of Morocco, you might be ready to march boldly across the Djemma el Fna or burrow deep into Fes' souk.

Some Moroccans involved with tourism – or even any sly individual encountering a tourist in need – have devised countless strategies of relieving you of your dirhams, and if you take the short stories of the late, Tangier-based Paul Bowels at face value, they've been practising among themselves for years and trust each other even less than a paranoid tourist. You don't necessarily have to be a worldly, streetwise traveller to be able to recognise whether a person is genuine because, just as back home, any stranger who approaches you, probably is not. The balance you then need to acquire is to be able to deal with these people on your terms, but also not to assume or treat every last Moroccan who says '*Salaam*' as a potential invader of your much prized personal space.

### More hassle

Broadly speaking, the hassle you get in Morocco falls into two categories: the harmless if at times irritating kids whose chants of *donnez moi*… bounce off the valley walls – and the more relentless and polished pestering from touts in the popular resorts and cities. In between, you may get taken in by your share of roadside chancers waving you down for a cigarette or a lift, even if they don't smoke or are going in the opposite direction.

#### *Donnez moi*… to give or not to give?

Chances are, over a stay of a few weeks, you'll be asked hundreds of times for *bon bons* or *stylos* (sweets, pens) or even just dirhams or cigarettes; whatever they see on your dashboard. Received opinion suggests that blindly handing out is wrong, however good your intentions. By doing so you further engender a begging mentality that stops people – if not whole African nations – from standing up on their own two feet.

An urban myth resurfaces now and again, claiming the origin of such widespread begging comes from successive rallies or expeditions who threw out branded pens and hats at the delirious throng, so to bask in an afterglow of a job well done. It's convenient and politically acceptable to blame big expeditions or rallies, but the reality is probably far more prosaic as it's easy enough to feel good by handing out whatever falls to hand. I've seen or heard of travellers becoming so intimidated by the kids that they think they must throw out a sacrifice or decoy lest they get stoned or torn limb from limb.

Detractors would say we have a lot of old junk we'd otherwise throw away so why not make someone's life a little better by passing on what you don't need? I've read accounts of travels in Morocco where the tourists unabashedly handed out expired domestic goods all over the country and saw it as a benevolent service. Locals hear of this and so equate 'tourist' with free goods. This is all very well as long as you accept that what you hand out may be taken swiftly to a souk and sold for something they actually want or need. And as anyone who's tried will know, you can never give away enough because in most cases it's not the need for the object so much as the desire to receive it. Of course one must distinguish between handouts and giving a tip in return for some service, however slight, or offering to cover the cost of genuine hospitality or a meal laid on by a poor peasant or desert dweller.

By African standards Morocco is not a poor country and these days begging is more of a genetic national reflex spawned from a long history of tourism rather than one of genuine need. But just as people claim to have travelled the world without paying a single bribe, so it's possible to get fixated on not giving anything ever under any circumstances whatsoever. This disregards the element of human compassion, especially when you pass through some bedraggled, windblown village with your mouth clamped around a succulent chicken, pesto and avocado bap.

One time we stopped in such a place on a baking hot day and a little girl came up to say hello. The lack of the usual clamour made the exchange much more equable and after we asked her name I gave her an orange that was lying around and which she took happily. 'Bad move' claimed my passenger. Now the little girl will associate car with free gift, just like the rest of Morocco and so the disease of indolence spreads. My only retort, other than being sympathetic for a poor child on a hot day in the desert, was when was the last time she may have seen a fresh orange? The injection of Vitamin 'C' will do her a world of good and was certainly better than some bubble gum or a *Morocco Overland* branded baseball cap. The debate continued for days.

Compassionate responses clearly vary with the manner in which you're approached. It's hard to respond warmly to a hoard of yelling schoolkids banging on your windows, but a peasant woman with babes in arms sitting quietly under a tree watching you eat is another. The rules are not black and white.

What it seems these kids crave above all is attention and this is easy to dish out in spades and takes up no room in your baggage. Ignoring people, be they Moroccan kids or the in-laws, is an excellent way of proffering disrespect and getting people's backs up. Crawling through a village at a safe speed, you can't outrun them so make eye contact, smile and wave. Sometimes approaching yet another such village you'll feel like the Bay City Rollers bracing themselves to head out for the nth time onto a stage drowned in teenybopper wails. Wave, nod, open your windows or lift your visor or goggles and have a few choice phrases like *rien ne va plus*. By doing so you're disarming the crowd (in some cases, literally).

## 'Hello my friend'

With these three chilling words you know your cover is blown and once again you'll have to Play the Game. Hustlers, *faux guides* (false guides), touts, plucky entrepreneurs, call them what you will, from their nests in doorways or on street corners they swoop down on their prey to see if they can get a bite. While far from unique to this country, these people are the bane of Morocco and are despised by honest, hardworking locals. They can be responsible for many miserable experiences and vows never to return.

While on the move, village kids are easy to deal with. Not so harmless in some tourist towns are the more malicious, misguiding and mischief-making touts, or the incessant pestering for any number of services from mechanics to guides, camel rides and accommodation. Some of course could be genuine, but with experience it's easy to read from the tone used, appearance or dress which ones are not, just as they too can probably spot a gullible target. Across the world these hustlers are attracted to places where tourists congregate and the best are extremely adept at persuading the credulous, in five major languages, that a carpet is an *ancienne*, a bargain and will probably fly itself home. Morocco is no different and, hard though you may think it to believe, twenty or thirty years ago was even worse. Attempts at outlawing the practice have worked to an extent, but with current levels of unemployment, working with- or on tourists is seen as a short cut to riches.

As bad as getting had can be, the drawback is of becoming suspicious of all encounters, so that you stomp about in a snarl in every town. When on foot, shuffling around slack jawed and purposelessly while clutching a map upside down is bound to attract the wrong sort of attention. Even if you don't quite know where you're going, look as if you do; adopt the same sort of advice given back home to lone women walking home at night.

My **advice** is this: engage beyond a quick smile, a shake of the head and a '*non merci*' at your peril. Don't even return a greeting, just smile and keep moving without provoking any antagonism. Leave them to focus on another target. Once you verbally engage in answering inane enquiries about your name or provenance, a relationship, however slight, has been established and it's much harder to break away – at worst requiring rudeness which is something you don't want to resort to. Ignoring them totally is mildly antagonistic – they will keep at you until you respond in some way – while gamely playing along eventually leads to a pitch.

Under pressure, or after too many instances of unremitting hassle, you might be tempted to shame or ridicule your tormentors. Don't waste your time; they've heard it all before and have skins as thick as the city walls of Taroudant. And even then, acting like this usually leaves a bad taste. Far better not to let things get that far, if possible. These hot spots are well known in Morocco and without trying to tell you where not to go, are alluded to in this book: in the south it's pretty much the line between Marrakech and Merzouga. If you find you don't have the temperament to deal with it, there's much to be said for avoiding these places and spending your money and time elsewhere. There's more chance of interacting with 'normal' people (see p229) which adds up to the vast mass of the population. Your memory of Morocco will be all the sweeter.

# Wild camping and safety

Wild camping is part of the appeal of overlanding in southern Morocco. In the north, if you're considering camping on arable land or in orchards, either ask permission first or be discreet. Even down south, wild camping in total solitude is not to be assumed. It's not uncommon to think you're alone under the stars only to have a nomad come out of nowhere to sit and watch you or hang around to see if anything's going spare. As often as not they'll also invite you back to the family tent to eat, which can end up in a night to remember.

For your own peace of mind it's good practice to camp **out of sight** of the highway or at least a kilometre from the tarmac, as well as a good distance from any settlement or encampment unless you're looking for interaction. This will dissuade chancers from stopping and coming over to nose around. Alone, your first night out off the road or out by the piste can be rather unnerving. It's common to feel vulnerable and exposed, but after a few nights you'll have the feel for finding a good spot (many are recommended in the route descriptions) and have organised your gear efficiently to make the whole process easier.

Desert lore suggests you should never **camp in a oued** or river bed for fear of flash floods. In fact the soft sand, vegetation, windbreaks and possible tree shade make oueds great places to camp compared to a stony plain. Just use your common sense if the weather looks stormy and you're close to, or in the mountains.

In the back of a car, in a roof tent or on the ground by your bike, it's good practice to tidy up and put things away; more against the possibility of a dust storm or rain shower than any chance of pilfering. And of course, in the morning don't leave anything other than tracks and footprints. **Burn** what will reduce to ash, throw out or bury organic matter and pack anything else like empty jars or tins to dispose of in the next town. This can be more easily said than done in some places, but at the very least it's better to centralise refuse in one place rather than leave it all over the desert.

When not using roadside lavatories, bury your toilet waste in sand or under a rock where it'll dry harmlessly and above all, get into the habit of **burning your toilet paper** (keep a lighter with the toilet paper). Many tourist sites in the Sahara have been despoiled by little white tufts of Andrex protruding from the sands.

## RENTING VEHICLES LOCALLY

In Morocco there are a few places offering motorcycles and many more offering 4WDs to rent, all of which are capable of doing most of the routes in this book. Combined with budget airline flights from under €100 (see p66), rental fees can work out low enough to make a week or two's exploring viable when compared to the time and expense of driving or riding down.

The drawbacks are that you don't quite know what you'll get and whatever it is, it'll have no camping gear, adequate tools or recovery equipment. Unless you know what you're getting into or are renting from the internationally-known rental agencies like Avis, Budget, Europcar, Hertz and National, it would be best not to plan too much of your holiday in Morocco around it.

All the prices on p84 were found in half an hour's Googling. The vehicles' condition of course is unknown. Smaller agencies often buy used fleets from bigger operators, but as far as the cars go, you should be fine with a Toyota Prado (a 3.5 TD that is also known as a 'Land Cruiser') and will be even better off with a 'real' Land Cruiser (a 4.2, six cylinder), especially if there are a few of you. Even with its standard suspension, a Land Cruiser will manage most of the routes in this book. Tellingly, no Land Rover Defenders were found to rent as self-drives, though plenty are used in Morocco for escorted tours. Freelanders and RAV4s will only manage easier pistes. Of the cities close to the routes in this book, cars are most commonly found in Agadir, Marrakech and Ouarzazate, with bikes in Agadir and Marrakech. See the box opposite for suggestions for short trips out of all three cities.

The prices given below are of course bound to change, but give an idea of what's available and where.

| Motorcycle | Location | Price per week |
|---|---|---|
| XR250R Tornado | Marrakech | 3500 dh |
| Yamaha XT 660/DR400Z | Marrakech | 5000 dh |
| Honda Transalp 600 | Agadir | €525 |
| Africa Twin | Agadir | €630 |
| BMW F650 GS (single) | Marrakech | €665 |
| **4WD** | | |
| Suzuki Grand Vitara | Various | €708 |
| Land Rover Defender with driver | Various | €770 |
| Daihatsu Terios | Various | £615 |
| Nissan Patrol/Land Cruiser | Agadir | €840 |
| Freelander/Jeep Cherokee | Various | £680 |
| Toyota Prado | Various | £695 |
| Toyota Rav4 | Various | £705 |
| Toyota Prado | Ouarzazate | £719 |
| Toyota Land Cruiser | Various | €910 |
| Toyota Land Cruiser | Marrakech | £767 |
| Toyota Land Cruiser | Essaouira | €1100 |
| Toyota Land Cruiser | Ouarzazate | £890 |
| Ford Ranger pickup | Various | €1190 |

## Using a rental

It must be understood that most rental agencies would not expect you to head off with a copy of *Morocco Overland* and a pick-axe to see how many routes you can knock out before handing the vehicle back. While out of the factory, some vehicles are better than others, the lack of off-road preparation and related equipment makes it clear that this is not encouraged. It's understandable as rentals are a hard-used commodity and only the toughest models withstand such use for long, let alone off-road in the hands of possibly inexperienced drivers or riders looking to get their money's worth.

Be aware of the expense that could be incurred if damaging a marginally -suitable vehicle while negotiating rocky tracks, and attempt to unravel the small print in the contract while reading between the lines. With a car at least, renting with one of the international agencies should come with some security. Ask what will happen if the vehicle breaks down and you can't fix it? Who pays for the repair?

With a car or bike, it may be best to come clean and fully explain your intentions and enquire about the state of the tyres (and on a bike, the chain as well). It might encourage the agent to check and renew such items. It's also worth noting that, as is the norm elsewhere in the world, insurance for damage and possibly even third parties is **not valid off sealed roads**, even if these tracks are designated as recognised rights of way (as most routes in this book are). The typically low speeds off road mean that the chances of having a **collision** or running someone down are small but if nothing else, this ought to be a reminder to keep speeds down, especially when passing through villages where throngs of kids will swarm towards you.

When collecting a car, don't leave the parking lot until you've checked the location and state of the **spare tyre** as well as all the tools with which to change

## TWO-DAY 4WD EXCURSIONS FROM THE MAIN MOROCCAN RESORTS

Renting a 4WD for a couple of days can add a bit of spice to a regular Moroccan holiday and is easily done from the three popular resort cities of Marrakech, Agadir and Ouarzazate. Below are some suggestions on how to make the most of a couple of days' car hire, whether you're an off-road novice or have some experience.

With all these routes it's best to clarify exactly what is permitted under your rental agreement as well as to be sure the car is in good shape.

### Marrakech
From this city the High Atlas MH routes are right on your southern doorstep. A good two days would add up to heading out of town via Asni and the Tizi-n Test pass towards Aoulouz. Here you can consider tackling routes MH6 or the more impressive MH7, taking the option to follow MH8 north at Askaoun. Or you can carry on to overnight in Taliouine at the many auberges there and then follow MH8 or the eastern half of MH7. Once you're down at Anezal turn north, Marrakech is about three hours away.

The 'Route of the Kasbahs' between Telouet and Aït Benhaddou is also a popular and easy to follow way of getting over the Atlas. See p162.

### Agadir
Out of Agadir you need to cover the 150km south-east to Tafraoute before you meet up with this book's opportunities. From here dropping down MA1 and coming back up MA2 will be a great day out, or with a bit more time you could work your way from Tafraoute along Route MA5 via the amazing agadirs at Amtoudi as far as Taghjijt and Timoulay on the N12 before turning back north via Tiznit on the N1.

For a **road drive** possible in any vehicle you could do a lot worse than heading out to Igherm and then taking either road south or south-east to Tata for an overnight stop. Next day come back up the way you didn't take, or hook up with one of the best stages of the Desert Highway (see p196): west via Akka and Foum el Hassan either for Assa and so Guelmim on the N1, or right for Aït Herbil, Bou Izakarn to pick up the NI north to Agadir. Or reverse Route MA11, another great desert drive.

### Ouarzazate
Ouarzazate sits among some of the best routes in this book. With the High Atlas to the north, Jebel Sirwa to the west and Jebel Sarhro to the east, it'll take some self-discipline to decide what to pack into two days of rental. If you want to get high, head east out to Dades and up the gorge. Don't spend time crawling along Route MH3. Instead head up MH1 in reverse over the highest track in this book to Agoudal for an overnight auberge, then come back down MH2 or even over to MH11 to get back on the N10 at Tinerhir or Goulmima for an easy drive back west to Ouarzazate.

Alternatively, at Dades or Tinerhir head up along MH10 (or MH4 from Tinerhir) and over the Jebel Sarhro for the amazing track over to Nekob or Alnif (both with good hotels and auberges). From there you can return via Agdz to Ouarzazate.

Besides the Jebel Sirwa routes outlined under Marrakech, above, the other good loop from Ouarzazate would be to head down towards Foum Zguid via Tazenacht, a great drive in itself, and then pick up MA7 to Issil and the N10 where you turn east back to Tazenacht for a spot of carpet shopping and so Ouarzazate. MA7 is slow and tough on cars – make sure your vehicle is up to it.

a wheel: jack with handle, wheel brace and crank (see below). Locals may have a fatalistic attitude towards punctures but you could easily waste the best part of a day when you find the spare is missing or the jack has no handle. (If you've never changed a tyre on the likes of a Land Cruiser before, the spare winches down on a chain from the back, using a rod as a crank slotted through a tiny hole near the rear number plate.) It's also important to be aware of the possible instability and inadequate lift of a standard supplied bottle-jack when lifting a car on soft ground (see p45).

Rental vehicles are unlikely to be supplied with any useful items for heading off-road, so the items listed below are recommended on a trip of a week or more of full-on piste bashing, either bought locally or brought from home.

- Portable compressor (see p44)
- Tow strap
- Multi-tool with flat and cross head screwdriver heads
- Combination of ring spanners adding up to at least 10, 12, 13, 14 and 17mm
- Adjustable spanner
- Zip ties and duct tape

Sand plates are barely needed in Morocco; a compressor and reading p97 on sand driving techniques is far more useful.

For a **rented motorcycle** check for a spanner to remove the wheels and bring the tools listed above plus tyre levers, a hand pump or mini compressor and a puncture repair kit, if not a spare tube. Hauling adequate **camping gear** on a plane or sourcing it locally is asking a bit much, so it's best to settle with using local lodgings which, with a bit of judicious route planning, are plentiful and inexpensive in the south.

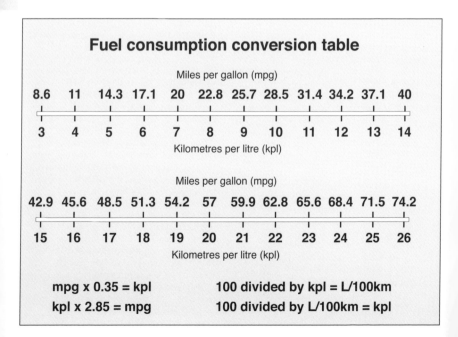

## Fuel consumption conversion table

Miles per gallon (mpg)

| 8.6 | 11 | 14.3 | 17.1 | 20 | 22.8 | 25.7 | 28.5 | 31.4 | 34.2 | 37.1 | 40 |
|---|---|---|---|---|---|---|---|---|---|---|---|
| 3 | 4 | 5 | 6 | 7 | 8 | 9 | 10 | 11 | 12 | 13 | 14 |

Kilometres per litre (kpl)

Miles per gallon (mpg)

| 42.9 | 45.6 | 48.5 | 51.3 | 54.2 | 57 | 59.9 | 62.8 | 65.6 | 68.4 | 71.5 | 74.2 |
|---|---|---|---|---|---|---|---|---|---|---|---|
| 15 | 16 | 17 | 18 | 19 | 20 | 21 | 22 | 23 | 24 | 25 | 26 |

Kilometres per litre (kpl)

mpg x 0.35 = kpl          100 divided by kpl = L/100km

kpl x 2.85 = mpg          100 divided by L/100km = kpl

# OFF THE ROAD 6

## Off-road riding

Many bikers dream of riding the desert sands but in Morocco tracks are predominantly **rocky** with sand filling some creek-crossings; for most riders that'll be more than enough sand. To an experienced dirt biker, rocky terrain doesn't hold too many surprises but to a beginner far from home on a loaded bike, inching off the blacktop for the first time can be unnerving.

In Morocco's mountains and desert it's not so much the actual riding as the relentless concentration demanded by riding and navigating that'll wear you out. Although you'll often be riding through spectacular scenery, the only chance you'll get to appreciate this splendour is by stopping, either by choice or by accident.

Your goal is to conserve energy, keep track of your position and preserve your machine from damage and yourself from injury; most biking trips to Morocco will include one and possibly the other. Having all this dropped in your lap after days of tranquil highway cruising can be quite daunting, especially if you're alone. Suddenly your sure-footed sled skitters about from rock to rock and feels as heavy as it really is.

Expect to fall off in the early days when you're still getting the feel for your machine off-road, and then later to fall off harder should you become over-confident. Only then will you have acquired the right balance of caution and confidence. In the inverse of a rodeo rider, your bike breaks you in after a few hard rides and within a week you finally loosen up. But push your luck and get too tired and you'll simply fall off through fatigue. You need to judge and pace it right.

Fifty miles an hour or **80kph** is the safe maximum speed on any dirt surface. Faster than that, it's not possible to react quickly enough to the ever-changing terrain and even half that speed will feel way too fast on some exposed mountain routes.

## Ride light

First-timers on the dirt tend to tense up and grip the bars. Try to relax your body because, as with suspension, when too rigid it has a detrimental effect on handling. On rough terrain try to hold the bars loosely, guiding the front end while allowing the bars to bounce around loosely in your palms.

By being relaxed and responding fluidly to the knocks, you'll preserve yourself and your bike from sudden and ultimately tiring shocks. Riding light includes weighting the footrests or standing up (see below) over any cross ridges or V-shaped dips, and using your body rather than the handlebars to steer.

You're body needs to relax, but the mind must be alert and at times ready to mobilise the body into assertive action. Anticipate and react to the changing surface just as you do with dozy car drivers and other hazards in a busy city. During the course of a long day on the dirt you'll find this kind of responsive riding saves both physical and mental energy. Alert, smooth riding is the key and learning to do so is part of the satisfaction of dirt riding in Morocco.

## Stand up on the footrests

One thing that transforms the control of a bike on rough or loose surfaces is standing up on the footrests. When you stand up and grip the bike between your knees:

- Suspension shocks are absorbed through your slightly-bent legs and not directly through your back.
- Your bike is much easier to control as the weight is borne lower through the footrests, not the seat.
- Your forward visibility is improved.

It's one reason why the more purposeful enduro bikes have such narrow seats and why trials bikes have no seat to speak of. You may never have stood up on your bike's footrests for long, but now is the time to try it and find out if it's a posture you can comfortably maintain for a while. Chances are taller riders may stoop so should consider taller bars or installing bar risers. When standing up for more than a few seconds – for example to get a good look ahead – it's OK to lock your knees out to save fatigue, but as you approach a hit, always **bend your knees**, just as you would when making a jump.

When standing up it also helps to press on the tank or seat lightly with your knees to brace the bike. With three points of contact – feet, knees and hands – the rigid bike is effectively triangulated to your flexible body and gives you much better control over rough surfaces. You may want to make sure your standing up knee-bike interface is comfortable. Inner kneepads may help. You may also find that non-motocross riding boots lacking a tough, steel shank are uncomfortable on your instep after a short period of standing, and that normal rubber footrests are fine until they get wet.

### Weighting the footrests

It's not always necessary to stand right up; sometimes just leaning forward, pulling on the bars and taking the weight from your backside and onto the footrests for a moment will be enough to lessen an impact. As you get the hang of riding on the dirt, standing up, just like sticking your leg out on a slithery

## BIG BIKES

Big heavy bikes have their own set of rules for off-roading. The mass and inertia that comes with all that weight means you're best off plodding along steadily and avoiding the need to make any sudden moves. Despite its daunting bulk the stability of something like a flat-twin GS responds amazingly well to this sort of riding. Just concentrate on the path of least resistance and allow the suspension to do its job while relieving it of excessive loads by keeping the speed down and standing up when necessary.

The high gearing and massive torque put out by such big-capacity machines (not helped by a Boxer's shaft drive characteristics) can be a bit of a liability on loose and rocky hairpins or deep gravel and sand. Trying to balance round a tight bend in first gear as the engine's power pulses thud away can be tricky without resorting to paddling. Slipping the clutch to raise the revs and so smooth out the pulses may help, but risks the back end stepping out as the clutch or traction alternate from grippy rock to gravel.

Any stylish motocross moves like sliding the back end while leaning forward, and sticking the inside leg forward to steady the machine takes some nerve on a machine over twice your weight.

In deep loose gravel or on sand it's easy to bury a heavy, powerful machine up to the crankcase until it can stand up by itself. A good trick to know in this situation (one that works on any bike) is to simply lay the bike on its side, fill in the hole excavated by the back wheel and then – the hard bit – pick the bike up again. With the engine off the deck, start the bike and walk it out under power to firm ground.

You can get a long way in Morocco on a big bike as long as you accept the off-road limitations which come at the cost of highway cruising panache. If a slope up or down looks gnarly and loose, get off and walk alongside the machine, assuming you want to continue at all. Or at least stop and have a think about your line over an obstacle. Not all the routes in this book are suitable to big bike pilots with limited off-roading experience. Give yourself a couple of weeks and all that could change.

bend, will soon become instinctive, as will briefly unloading the saddle to lessen an impact. In a nutshell: **stand when you must – sit down when you can**. The key is to preserve energy with smooth, efficient riding.

## ROCKY MOUNTAIN TRACKS

Some of the best routes in Morocco will be the mountain tracks in the High- and especially the Anti Atlas. In a car you plod along at little more than walking pace and watch the scenery inch by. A bike is faster and more fun on this sort of all-engrossing terrain, but too much speed on loose hairpin bends could all end badly.

Some of the routes in this book demand reduced speed for no other reason than uncertainty about what's around the next corner or over the brow of the hill. Keep your hands over the handlebar levers and be ready for anything: grazing goats, landslides, other vehicles.

Again, in the mountains as much as anywhere, you must ride within the limits of your visibility and the terrain. Read the ground constantly. A steep descent will probably end at a sandy creek or ditch, while a steep ascent rarely continues down the other side of the crest in the same direction.

On some very stony tracks, like the entry into the Cirque de Jaffar or the two MA routes over the Jebel Timkouka, or even coming down to Igmir (MA2) from the north, excessively wide alloy panniers will be a liability. With the wall of rock rising to one side of the track you'll be forced to take the more exposed drop-side rut where putting a wheel wrong does not bear thinking about. On a bike some of these ascents and descents are very challenging, requiring clearing rocks or even walking the bike up. On all these kinds of routes keep tyre pressures firm and check your rims and spokes (if you have them), sometimes nightly.

## Riding in sand

Morocco has very few sandy pistes but occasionally you can't avoid riding in a sandy rut, usually across a dry riverbed. Here you must be ready to stand up and gas it to maintain front end stability. Momentum and acceleration are often the only things that will get you through a particularly soft stretch of sand, so don't be afraid to stand up and accelerate hard at the right time, revving your engine as hard as necessary. A quick snap of the throttle gives the drive and stability to blast assuredly across a short, sandy oued. No matter how much your bike weaves and bucks around, keep the power on and your backside off the seat for as long as it takes. So long as the front wheel remains on course (or even if it doesn't) you're moving and so remain mostly in control. Decelerate, and sand builds up in front of the front wheel, the geometry of the front end's self-centring 'castor effect' is lost and down you go. Keep off the brakes, especially the front. Reduce speed through the gears not the brakes – or lock the brakes hard, stick your best leg out and hope for the best.

Sand-riding can be hair-raising and you'll often come close to falling off, so much so that at times it'll feel like a relief to actually fall off and get the inevitable over with. The techniques described here are the only way to get through soft sand, short of paddling along at 2kph. As often as not, this is the safest if not so elegant solution.

### Knobbly tyres

Trail tyres like Tourances are essentially road tyres with an off-roady appearance and will compromise your off-road experience. The extra grip, control and directional stability of proper knobbly tyres or even just Pirelli MT21s and Continental TKC 80s makes dirt riding less unpredictable and so more fun. Unlike on a car where tread block is immaterial to cornering, a motorbike needs knobs to lean over securely on the dirt. With knobbly tyres you can also leave the pressures almost at road levels while still benefiting from the knobbly tread pattern for good grip in the dirt.

### Low tyre pressures

Dropping tyre pressures to as little as 0.6 bar (10 psi) lengthens the contact patch with the ground, dramatically increasing traction and reducing wheelspin. It works even with a regular trail or road tyre, but in rocky Morocco is not such a good idea, unless you're spending a day in soft sand. In this underinflated state, even a tubeless tyre gets much hotter, while a conventional tyre can pinch a tube on a sharp-edged hit that can result in a puncture. Ride light, keep your speed down and your tyre pressures as high as possible.

## Dune riding

Arriving at Erg Chebbi the temptation may be to dump your baggage and head out for a quick blast. On my solo biking trips in the central Sahara the idea of thrashing about in the dunes was always far too risky and, nearly 30 years later, passing Erg Chebbi I feel no different. Motorcycle accidents are most common in dunes where riding anything heavier than a 250cc dirt bike is just too dangerous. If it's part of a piste like MS6, commit yourself to the task single-mindedly. The sand may appear cushion-soft, but a cartwheeling bike landing across your backbone is not.

Dunes can be a maze of varying, similarly-coloured slopes, sometimes hard to distinguish and Erg Chebbi is particularly complex. Most accidents

### CROSSING FLOODED TRACKS

Flash floods often peak a few hours after a storm, after which time the flow quickly recedes. Waiting overnight or even just a few hours can see a violent, impassable torrent drop to just a trickle of mud and debris. All running fords or faster flash floods should be given at least a moment's thought before diving in. It only takes rushing water a foot deep to push a bike onto some unseen rubble and down it goes.

If in doubt the simplest answer is to **walk** across. By walking you can pick a good line, get a feel of the surface which can include rocks, holes or broken cement, all waiting to deflect a front wheel and ruin your day. Getting your feet wet is the only sure way of knowing the depth and what lies below the surface. Better wet feet than soaked baggage or a water-logged bike. If it can be walked it can probably be ridden and can certainly be crossed by walking alongside the bike under power. If it's too dangerous to walk then chances are walking alongside a running bike will be risky too.

It's said that a rider should walk with a bike on the downstream side so that if the bike falls or the rider stumbles he'll fall on the bike rather than be possibly pinned under it. This may be true at the extreme end of the scale with water rushing over your knees, but in less severe conditions it can be easier to lean onto the downstream side of the bike which is being pushed against you by the flow (as below), so making a stable combination. It's also easier to walk a bike on the left side with your right hand resting naturally on the throttle and front brake and your left easing the clutch in and out to stop the engine stalling, something you'd rather not do on a kickstart-only XR400.

Otherwise, pick your spot. Generally where the flow is wider it's less deep and the current less strong; it may look a long way across but it will be shallower. As you ride across, keep your feet ready to drop in and steady yourself, and keep the speed down to give you more time to correct a hit. Except of course, when taking action shots!

OFF THE ROAD

Hamada du Guir. Better wet boots than wet boots and everything else too. © Eric De Nadai

happen when the speed you're compelled to maintain sends you over a drop. If you're lucky it'll just be a harmless tumble; if not it's the end of your trip and the beginning of a stressful evacuation.

Approaching dune crests on a bike is tricky compared to a 4WD as you don't have the stability or the traction of a 4WD. It can often be easier to plan to fall over on a crest rather than go over the edge and fall down with your bike behind you. Having fallen on a crest, pick the bike up and walk it down if necessary. In the dunes, never let your concentration drop while riding, attack very soft sections standing up on the footrests and with the power on. Cross other deep tracks as close to right angles as possible and with a short burst of acceleration. You can expect your engine to get very hot in the dunes as you'll be revving it to the limit in the lower gears. Keep an eye out for the temperature and stop to cool it down if necessary, but keep the engine running. There's more on Erg Chebbi (or probably the same advice repeated) on pp 174-5.

# Day trips for motorcycles

Give your bags the day off and it's like having a whole new bike.

Even if you're not lugging around full camping gear (is it even worth it? See p33) you'll still have brought a certain amount of baggage that you don't need every minute of the day. While these bags may not weigh much, alloy boxes and in particular hard road-touring cases can be a liability off-road, either getting in the way on narrow tracks, getting damaged in a fall, or simply breaking their mounts and falling off (the weak spot with many touring cases).

If you want to dabble on some pistes but don't want to mash your Givis, the routes in this book can be chopped up and re-arranged into 25 day trips of varying length and difficulty. These route ideas are also handy if one of your party wants a day off, but you're keen to keep riding. Leave most of your gear in a hotel or auberge and enjoy a fun day out on a lighter, slimmer bike with the knowledge of what awaits you at the end of the day. For recommended places to base yourself see the website link or your guidebook.

Distances opposite include figures taken from maps along non-GPS'd stages (usually highways) so may vary from your readings. Distances in brackets indicate approximately how much of the total distance is tarmac. An 'r' after the route indicates it follows this book's route description in reverse. Many southern loops include a stage along Route MS10; The Desert Highway, (see p196) but as it's all road it's not indicated opposite.

**L1      Alnif – Tizi n Ouli Ousir – Alnif**
**(MH5, MH10)                    100km (includes 7km tarmac)**

A hundred kilometres of off-road action up to the heights and back down. On a good day the scenery here is something special and if you and your bike survive unscathed – or even if you don't – you'll roll back into Alnif very satisfied. A 600cc trail bike would be on the limit up on the Ousir, while big adventure bikes will see as much, if not a whole lot more, by doing the route below.

**L2      Alnif – Iknioun – Nekob – Alnif**
**(MH10r, MH4)                              228km (97km)**

Using a track only opened in 2008 and incorporating most of the route above, but without the extremes. At twice as long it's pretty much twice as good too because any reasonably fit bike can manage it. With the back up of fuel in Nekob and no backtracking, it's among the best loops in the land.

**L3      Assa – Aouinet Torkoz – Tadalt – El Borj –Torkoz – Assa**
**(MW4r, MW5)                               227km (98km)**

A very satisfying day's ride out from Assa up into the hills and canyons, and back again for an Orangina at the roadhouse. With little sand and little chance of mud, a big bike will manage fine.

**L4      Bouanane – Beni Tajite – Korima Pass – Bouanane**
**(ME4, ME5)                                182km (88km)**

An easy way of getting the best out of Route ME4 and all of ME5 in a day. There could be some tricky riverbed crossings on a big bike so give yourself plenty of time. Can be strung out into a very full day on a lighter machine by riding along the N10 to the Guir Bridge and reversing the piste section of ME7 over the Col Belkassem up to Beni Tajite (fuel) and then getting stuck into ME4 and ME5. You may want to check that the ultra-basic hotel in Bouanane town square is still there and is a place you'd be happy to spend two nights.

**L5      Dades – Tinerhir – Agoudal – Dades**
**(MH2, MH1)                                265km (167km)**

Up to the motorable crest of the High Atlas and back down again, with a lunch in Agoudal or maybe the upper Dades's restos if you're pressing on. Could be a stretch on the fuel, but you can coast on the downhills and on a warm, sunny day in dry conditions it's as good as a loop gets in the High Atlas. In the conditions I drove it, it would be fine on a big bike with TKCs or the like.

**L6      Foum Zguid – Issil – Agmour – Foum Zguid**
**(MA7, MA6, MA9)                           213km (20km)**

On a well-shod and light bike in good hands, this rocky canyon and valley ride with virtually no tarmac will be a blast that will leave you worn out but buzzing for hours. The MA9 stage is an easy ride just when you'll need it and can have an easy ending too. It would be too much in one day on a big bike.

**L7      Foum Zguid – Mrimina – Dakar piste – Lac Iriki – Foum Zguid**
**(MS8, MS7r)                               237km (78km)**

A full day out of Foum Zguid with a possibility of making your own tracks back to town from around KM170. Otherwise it may be a bit of a reach on fuel and anyway it's best not done alone.

### L8 Igmir – Ouafka – Amtoudi – Aït Herbil – Igmir
### (MA2, MA5, MA2) 182km (includes 111km tarmac)

One of two routes out of the Igmir guest house midway up Route MA2 and which, accessed from north or south, can be a tricky ride on a big bike looking to shed its load for a day out. This loop incorporates a visit to Amtoudi's adagir and a refuel in Aït Herbil. The MA5 section of piste is easier and you could string it out by doing the short but enjoyable dirt stage of Route MA10 from before Aït Herbil to Foum el Hassan and back.

### L9 Igmir – Izerbi – Tasserirt – Tizerkine – Afella – Izerbi – Igmir
### (MA2, MA1, MA2) 139km (66km)

A shorter day but with great scenery and quite a lot of river bed shingle at the end which may be tricky on big, wide bikes. Head north out of Igmir past Izerbi and down the lovely Tizerkine Gorge and south to Afella. Here you follow the river bed piste towards Aït Herbil (a short diversion to refuel is possible) before heading back up to Igmir, an amazing ride in itself.

© Eric De Nadai's XR4 prepares for lift off.

### L10 Mhamid – Erg Chebbi – Lac Iriki – Mhamid

Let your tyres down, check your water and head west out of Mhamid to have a blast in the dunes and on the pan-flat lake bed until it's time to go home. It may be a good idea to keep track of where you go with a GPS, not go alone and take it easy in the dunes where fuel consumption will rise. Most suited to lighter, 400cc bikes on knobblies as even a 600 will be hard work.

### L11 Midelt – Cirque de Jaffar – Midelt
### (MH1) about 90km

The classic short, spectacular, all-piste run out of Midelt. The way back to Midelt from KM48.5 is unlogged but will get you back one way or another. Allow three hours on a bike and a big bike will manage OK if the weather's been good.

### L12 Ouarzazate – Anezal – Ouarzazate
### (MS9) 116km (62km)

This adds up to a fun half-day out of Ouarzazate to get the measure of your abilities and your bike. It can be strung out with lunch at a resto in Tazenacht or Amerzgane, both nice towns, or of course you could simply ride the same route back to Ouarzazate to make a good day out on the piste.

### L13 Ouarzazate – Anezal – Askaoun – Aguim – Ouarzazate
### (MS9, MH7r, MH8) 321km (144km)

Could be a bit much in a day on a big machine so not a good idea in mid-winter's short days and possibly freezing conditions as much of it's over 1500m. The last 100km or so are on tarmac and on the way back there's fuel from Aguim onwards. You'll get back to Ouarzazate dazed but satisfied.

**L14     Tafraoute – Tizerkine Gorge – Timkyet – Tazalarhite – Tafraoute**
**(MA1, MA3r, MA8r)                                    114km (79km)**

A satisfying excursion along the back roads and tracks east of Tafraoute. The loose climb after Timkyet may require some thought on a big machine, but after that, it's an easy ride over the plateau and down the other ride. Although not long, this will take more than half a day.

**L15     Taliouine – Aoulouz – Askaoun – Anezal – Tazenacht – Taliouine**
**(MH7)                                                 289km (196km)**

This is Route MH7 made into a loop, a great ride in good weather and well worth dumping the baggage for. It adds up to a long day and could get snowed under or muddy in winter around Jebel Sirwa, but on the way back there's fuel in Aoulouz and Tazenacht and a couple more places west of there before you return to Taliouine.

**L16     Taliouine –Askaoun – Assarag – Aoulouz – Taliouine**
**(MH8, MH6)                                           223km (117km)**

If the weather is good, this is a brilliant ride up towards the southern flanks of Jebel Toubkal, North Africa's highest peak, and then an easy but possibly muddy 'Transit' route back down through the villages to Aoulouz (fuel). If you have the fuel range you can make it all a bit sportier by turning off at MH6/KM79 or so to pick up MH7 heading back up to the heights of Askaoun and the mountain road back down to Taliouine.

Overall, this way is about the same distance. A big bike and a confident rider on TKCs or the like should manage this in good weather. Allow a full day.

**L17     Taliouine – Askaoun – Aoulouz – Taliouine**
**(MH8, MH7r)                                          158km (119km)**

This is a shorter version of the route above, adding up to a two-hour piste with some impressive switchbacks from Askaoun down to the valley floor, the dam, and so the tarmac to Aoulouz.

**L18     Tata – Akka Ighern – Foum Zguid – Tata**
**(MA9)                                                296km (184km)**

A fun blast along a 'Dakar' stage for a late lunch in Foum Zguid and a nice sunset ride back along the Desert Highway to Tata. The rough start out of Akka Iguirn can be avoided by turning off near Kasba ej Joua – and the rough last few kilometres can also be got round too. All in all, a great outing between the ranges and easily done in a day.

**L19     Tata – Imitek – Tazegzaoute – Timkyet – Afella – Tata**
**(MA3)                                                240km (120km)**

On road and trail, another great day out in the Anti Atlas, riding through this book's cover picture up onto the plateau and down towards Afella. Includes shingly riverbed stages, steep ascents and descents so could be hard work on a big bike and not recommended two-up. Just before Afella you take an unlogged but easy track back east towards Imitek (see MA3/KM140). Allow a full day.

### L20     Tazenacht – Zagmouzere – Askaoun – Anezal – Tazenacht
### (MH9, MH8, MH7)                    219km (includes 88km tarmac)

A great day out from Tazenacht, adding a full circuit of Jebel Sirwa broken by short but impressive road stages. Route MH9 may get muddy; at KM59 take the unlogged track north-west about 20km to Zagmouzere and pick up the mountain road up to Askaoun. From here east it's a great ride below Sirwa summit over high passes (may be snowy in winter) before dropping down to Anezal and a great road ride back to Tazenacht. Give yourself a full day on this one.

### L21     Tazzarine – Oum Jrane – Alnif – Tazzarine
### (MS3, MS4)                                     177km (58km)

One of the few logged loops you can take out into the Sahara zone in a day, giving over 100km of piste and a good impression of the desert tracks out here. Some short sandy stages. Also possible from Alnif which may have the edge on good, if basic hotels.

### L22     Tighmert – Fask – Tadalt – Aouinet Torkoz – Tadalt – Tighmert
### (MW5, MW4r)                                    217km (134km)

If you find yourself near Guelmim and fancy an easy day out from a quiet hotel, this will tick the boxes. A rocky run between the desert ranges that's possible on a big machine.

### L23     Tinerhir – Iknioun – Nekob – Alnif – Tinerhir
### (MH4)                                          254km (100km)

A classic run over Jebel Sarhro that's been done two-up on a 1150GS running Tourances. The rise up to Iknioun can get muddy, but beyond that it's just the rock-step descent and the distracting views that will need concentration. From Alnif a track by the radio mast leads north and soon turns to tarmac before it gets to the N10.

### L24     Tinerhir – Gorge to Gorge – Todra – Tinerhir
### (MH1r, MH3, MH2r)                              207km (162km)

Even though it's mostly a road and a great ride up the Dades gorge, you'd still want to leave a full day to include MH3 and even Todra can have its moments after heavy rain. It can just as easily be started from a hotel in Dades. Even without luggage a beginner on a big bike may struggle on the gorge link track. A lot depends on recent weather.

### L25     Zagora – Agdz – Jebel Rhart – Zagora
### (MS1)                                          160km (97km)

An easy and scenic run up the kasbah-lined valley to the Draa bridge and back down a flat piste that's manageable on a big bike, even two-up. Do-able in half a day.

# Off-road driving

In a comfortable four-wheeler with the air-con humming and the Psychedelic Furs on the stereo, it's possible to feel immune to the hammering your vehicle is getting. There is a tendency to assume that 4WDs are indestructible and worse still, for a minority to drive them as if they are.

Unlike bikes, the risk of personal injury in a car is small, but the risk of damaging your 2-ton wagon while off-roading is not, and it's this which ought to limit your speed on the tracks of southern Morocco. On many rocky mountain routes you may drive for hours at little more than walking pace; any faster and something may break.

Along with punctures, suspension commonly fails in Moroccan conditions, even when driving at a moderate pace. Flood damaged tracks apart, the need for good axle articulation or 'twisting' is rarely needed, except on routes like MH3 and MH5. Most other routes are passable in a 2WD with care.

## Ditches and creeks

What you will be in for is a lot of crawling in and out of ditches and oueds, such as on Route ME3. Here, long body overhangs (usually the rear) combined with low suspension can be a liability. All such obstacles should be taken slowly to avoid compressing the suspension and so reducing ground clearance. Use the low range gearbox to maintain control rather than relying on momentum, as a 2WD or a bike must do. If it looks like the back might dig in and lift the weight off the rear wheels, crawl up or down the bank at an angle very slowly in low first. Know too when to use a central diff lock, if you have this feature; avoid locking it unless stuck in soft sand or mud (more on p39).

If you have to inch around a fallen boulder or **rockfall**, get someone ahead to guide you with clearly agreed hand signals to spare unnecessary contact with the vulnerable tyre sidewalls or undercarriage.

## Getting stuck

At a sensible pace it's all very easy in a 4WD until you become stuck, and in Morocco it could be snow, mud, a landslide, rockfall, flooded creek or sand that brings your wheels spinning to a halt. Unless you're dying to put various items of recovery equipment and techniques into use, the trick is to avoid getting stuck in the first place by knowing **when to turn back**. Along with not damaging their vehicle, it's something a solo driver or a single vehicle will address frequently. With more than one vehicle and the equipment outlined on p45 you can be a bit more adventurous and explore your car's abilities. Initially, there can be a thrill about cracking out the unused hi-lift, shackles or sand plates and early on, until you get a feel for how your machine responds, they may actually be needed.

The skill you want to master is to look ahead and assess the risks, primarily to reduce impacts to the car but at times also to avoid getting stuck. If you're unsure, get out and have a look around on foot. Are there other recent

This tyre is at around 40% of road pressure in preparation to cross a river. Contrary to the impression and the bulging sidewall, the contact area does not become wider but, in this condition, about twice as long, imitating a tracked vehicle. The need to optimise traction by altering tyre pressures is one reason why a powerful compressor is a useful accessory. The tyre is a BFG All Terrain ('A/T'), a good choice for Morocco.
© longroadtripsouth.com

tracks or an alternative route to one side? If you do get stuck will it be an easy recovery? One reason people tend to push their luck and even play around on dunes is that getting unstuck is relatively easy (though so too is rolling a vehicle). Dry sand doesn't stick like mud or waterlogged sand, and doesn't soak like water, hurt like rocks or freeze like snow. Scooping away with your hands is actually quite pleasant as long as it's not 40°C.

Particularly in sand, the knack is to **stop before you get bogged**. Recognise that the vehicle is losing speed and soon you'll be going down quicker than you're going forward. If you do this in time simply reversing out and trying elsewhere will do the trick.

Whatever loose surface you're stuck in, **reducing tyre pressures** is the first step, if it's not been done already. It doesn't have to be much; 70% of normal road pressure is a start and will enlongate the tyre's footprint enough to improve traction in all the above scenarios. If you're not being towed out (or if you are because you're deeply bogged) take the time to **clear the wheels** in whichever direction you're going. Now is the time to engage low range. In most vehicles this automatically engages the front axle or locks the central diff, though on bare rock it's not a state you want to be in for long (more on p39).

### Flooded tracks

Briefly powerful torrents following storms are more dangerous than regular rivers and in Morocco many locals have paid with their lives under-estimating their force. At a flooded road ford there'll often be a queue of regular cars and vans waiting on either side and in your big off-roader there can be pressure to plough in bravely. Resist this and firstly see if others are crossing. Otherwise, walking is advisable, but if the current is flowing hard and rises much above your knees it's too risky even to do that. In a car, that mass quickly builds up on the car's flank and remorselessly pushes it sideways, possibly over an unseen edge and onto its side. Aiming slightly upstream deflects this force and can help 'ferry' the car across as the current pushes you forward as well as sideways, but this sort of practice is marginal. It's better to wait a few hours for a raging torrent to recede. If you do this, place a stick or a stone at the flow's edge to see more easily if it's dropping.

The aftermath of flooding in the desert is another matter. In the autumn of 2008 (and again in April 2009) the Oued Rheris closed Route MS6 for weeks at Remlia. Elsewhere, on clay pans such as the normally dry Lake Iriki along Route MS7, the surface can appear dry and cracked, but beneath is a soggy mush which a heavy 4WD will readily sink into and require towing out.

There's more on off-roading in the two other *Overland* books and the DVD.

# Introduction to the routes

Understandably, wanting to make the most of their holiday, many visitors take on too much in Morocco, misjudge the distances involved and the appeal of actually slowing down. Accept that in a typical fortnight's break you won't see it all. It's not all about ticking off routes; they're merely an effective means of unveiling the essence of southern Morocco which doesn't lie between two waypoints. It's not a bad idea to view your first trip as an exploratory tour to see what you'd like to see or do more of next time.

## Route descriptions

The '*Description*' introduces the route but will be influenced on whether I rode or drove it and the weather that day. Even then it's well worth reading the entire route description to get a full feel of what lies ahead. '*Off-road*' is a summary of track conditions for vehicles other than a 4WD which can manage anything, namely 2WDs or 'road cars', heavy 'adventure motorcycles' and mountain bikes. Recognise that these conditions **are very reliant on decent weather**. '*Route finding*' assumes that you may not have a GPS or 'Olaf' (see p23) and adds to the route description. If you don't have a metric odometer to record distance, to convert kilometres to miles 'halve it and add a quarter'; 40km = 25 miles.

'*Fuel and Water*'; with the exception of ME5, MH3 and MO2, each route begins and ends at a fuel point. Known water sources are described along the way, but not all may be dependable and others may exist. The '*Suggested Duration*' is based on which vehicle was used to log the route; it's probable the MTB estimates are a bit optimistic.

An attempt is made to use cardinal points ('north', 'south-east', etc) rather than 'turn left at...' so that the description needs less interpreting in reverse. Frequently 'the Rains' are referred to, a catastrophic few weeks of rainfall that befell Morocco's north coast and eastern provinces between the two main research trips in 2008. Some tracks logged before the Rains may not be in the same condition, while others logged in the aftermath are bound to be repaired or improved. To help clarity the **route maps** only show the main settlements.

## Additional online content

Each route has a corresponding online folder with additional content to print off or download onto a laptop, a hand-held image reader or a GPS unit. It varies from route to route but includes a stripped-down list of key waypoints in a .gpx file format to import into any GPS, track logs depicted on small-scale maps and from various angles on Google Earth, photos, corrections and clarifications and anything else that might be useful. Don't get over-excited about the .gpx files – you'll soon learn that most routes are navigable without a GPS, it's merely a good back up when things go awry and can save time if the way ahead is not clear. The website address is on the back cover.

# ROUTE INDEX

## Outline of the East region

Arriving from Spain or France at the ports Melilla or Nador (see p70), this corner of Morocco lacks the imperial cities or palm-fringed kasbahs found elsewhere so travellers usually head south-west for Fes or directly south towards Erfoud. Between the coast and the Oued Guir, which parallels the Algerian border, sprawls the **Rekkam Plateau** where the High Atlas ranges spill out eastward into a barely populated tableland cut by river courses and littered with uncultivatable scrub.

The tracks of the northern Rekkam such as Route M1 in *Sahara Overland*, have little going for them; the few sealed roads around here are quiet enough and every southward mile will get warmer and drier. It's at the southern edge that the Rekkam begins to crumple into lateral ranges and where things can get a little more interesting for exploring off-road.

This region may not be top of the list for first-timers in Morocco looking for the sand, seas and dates but, as in the far west, tourist infrastructure is minimal if non-existent here. This can mean the negative effects of tourism are limited which you may find is reason enough to spend some time exploring the Moroccan east.

## ME Routes

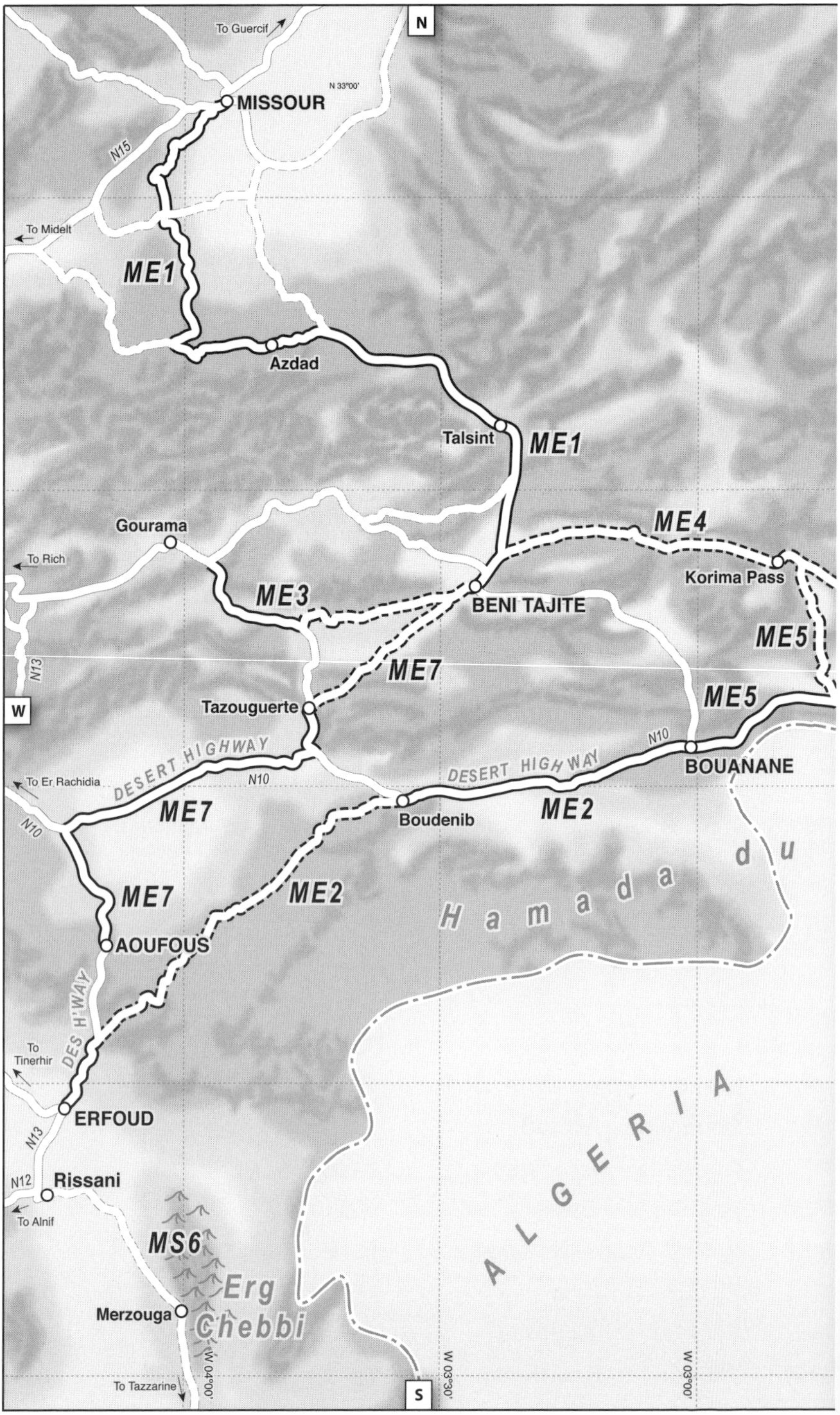
N
To Guercif
N 33°00'
MISSOUR
N15
To Midelt
ME1
Azdad
Talsint
ME1
Gourama
To Rich
ME4
Korima Pass
BENI TAJITE
ME3
ME5
N13
ME7
Tazouguerte
ME5
W
DESERT HIGHWAY
N10
BOUANANE
To Er Rachidia
N10
DESERT HIGHWAY
Boudenib
ME7
ME2
N10
ME7
ME2
Hamada du
AOUFOUS
DES H'WAY
To Tinerhir
ERFOUD
N13
ALGERIA
N12
Rissani
To Alnif
MS6
Erg Chebbi
Merzouga
W 04°00'
W 03°30'
W 03°00'
To Tazzarine
S

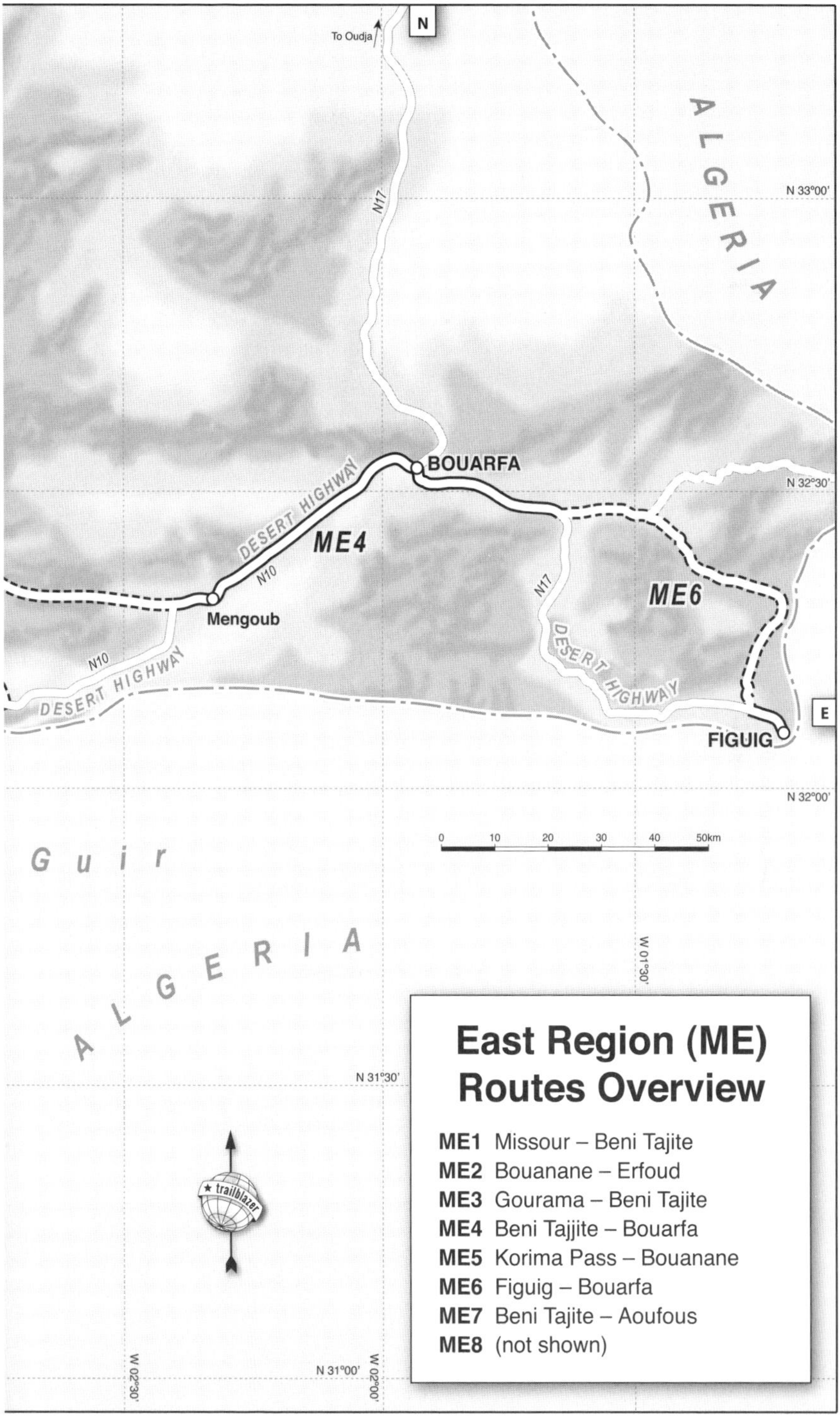

**ME – MOROCCO EAST**

N

To Oudja

ALGERIA

N 33°00'

N17

BOUARFA

N 32°30'

DESERT HIGHWAY

ME4

N10

N17

ME6

Mengoub

N10

DESERT HIGHWAY

DESERT HIGHWAY

E

FIGUIG

N 32°00'

0    10    20    30    40    50km

G u i r

W 01°30'

A L G E R I A

N 31°30'

★ trailblazer

N 31°00'

W 02°30'

W 02°00'

# East Region (ME)
# Routes Overview

**ME1** Missour – Beni Tajite
**ME2** Bouanane – Erfoud
**ME3** Gourama – Beni Tajite
**ME4** Beni Tajjite – Bouarfa
**ME5** Korima Pass – Bouanane
**ME6** Figuig – Bouarfa
**ME7** Beni Tajite – Aoufous
**ME8** (not shown)

# ME1    MISSOUR – BENI TAJITE                    163KM
October 2008 ~ Yamaha Ténéré

While the Rekkam Plateau may not be immediately inspiring, coming down from the ferry ports this satisfying
back-road drive brings you to the heart of the ME collection of tracks. Once at Beni Tajite road-bound vehicles need not fear; they can continue on tarmac south-
east to Bouanane, or west to Gourrama from where
sealed roads lead west to Rich on the N13, or cut back
south-east via Tazouguerte to the Guir Bridge on the N10.
South of Guercif, Missour is the biggest town along the
N15 before it gets to the Midelt junction, but the guidebooks don't cover it.
There are signs for at least two **hotels** in town, a gîte as well as plenty of cafés
and restaurants, including one nameless joint on a corner, 150m east of the
town centre fuel station offering just about the best brochettes in the east. The
*motel* at the AFRIQUIA roadhouse on the south end of town costs around 200dh.

## Broken bridges
Looking at a map you may think the route to Talsint would go directly south-
east via **Taoura**. However, if you follow the sign at the north end of Missour
indicating 'Talsint 98km' you'll soon come across a big space where a bridge
once spanned the substantial **Oued Moulouya**. Its source is just south of El
Kebab 150km to the west (the end of Route MH2) and the Moulouya might be
described as the geographical boundary between the High- and the Middle
Atlas. Whether correct or not, even with the dam in between, the river can pick
up quite a head of water by the time it gets to Missour. The steel bridge is present on a crystal-clear segment of Google Earth dated 'February 2005', as are
the deep green waters, but by late October 2008 only the concrete abutments
remained. The steel trellis was nowhere to be seen and people were wading
across up to their waists to get to their side of town. Even then, this route on
to Taoura remains a piste, while the less-direct road south of Missour which
you're about to follow was already sealed in 2005, possibly because it useful-
ly connects several villages along the way to Talsint.

This road, which becomes the R601, crosses the Oued Moulouya at a stout
bridge around KM26, but at the village of **Ouizret** at KM36, a feeder stream
had knocked out the bridge and the short but fast-flowing crossing was only
possible in a 4WD, on a mule and with a bit of desperate paddling, on a motorbike too. Mercedes vans and the like were not trying it, but diggers were at
work and barring repeats of The Rains, this important link is bound to be
repaired by now.

The next bridge out was at KM47 with banks ten feet high freshly-cut on
both sides of the same river. Unlike at Ouizret, the new fording point a short
way upstream was wide but shallow and crossable by Mercedes vans and so
it's unlikely this bridge will get a priority repair. The access track to this crossing and continuing on the far side where it rejoins the road was also a bit
rough, but is bound to improve. Beyond here there was one off-road detour
around a creek at about KM63, eight kilometres after a pass.

All these transient obstacles mean that larger vehicles with low, long over-hangs such as campervans might want to ask around at Missour or be pre-pared to turn back.

## Route description

At the **fuel station** in **Missour** town centre head south-west out of town. In a kilometre or so, just before the AFRIQUIA with the motel, turn left at the lights and soon cross a concrete ford of a usually-dry tributary of the main oued. You enter an outlying garden suburb and wind along treelined lanes; what might be the original villages of Missour.

At KM4 bear left in the village. Soon you emerge from the greenery into the scrub and at KM5.5 turn left at the T-junction (also accessible had you gone straight at the lights and turned left off the N15 a few kilometres from town). The road winds along a shallow, arid valley, even veering west at times and passing small villages.You return to a feeder of the Oued Moulouya at KM36 just before **Ouizret**. By now the crossing should be manageable to all vehicles. Heading through Ouizret you'll pass the old mud-brick ksar; once the core of every Moroccan town was like this.

There could be another riverbed to ford at KM47 if the bridge is still out just by the village of Tadmaia and 8km later you cross a 1400m pass. On the far side, tracks lead south-east to **Tagouast** village but the road then curves west, south then back east to get around an escarpment and a canyon. Note that this is not the sharp turn or crossroads indicated on many paper maps. At KM62, about a kilometre before what may still be a small diversion around a washed-out oued, a track heads off south-west through a gap in the range to possibly make a link with Route ME8. This would be suitable for off-road vehicles only.

Around here you begin the eastward traverse along the base of the Jebel Asdad. Just north of **Tagentatcha** village you cross a big bridge, which man-aged to survive The Rains, and **Boumeryema** village (a name not found on maps) at KM92 is at the crossroads with the track coming down from **Taoura**. Carry on eastwards and at KM109 crest a 1700m **pass** on the Jebel Tioudersine. A few kilometres later the road turns south and takes a sinuous passage through the Jebel Skindis. South of this pass, the vegetation suddenly changes as the land takes on a much more arid appearance.

Soon after passing a village with a pink mosque you arrive in **Talsint** (KM133) with a ZIZ fuel station, a restaurant and a shop or two. Once through town the road curves south again through a gap and at KM142 a thin track runs off south-east to pick up Route ME4 coming up from Beni Tajite. The main turning left for ME4 is at KM159 as you bend to the right, and 2.5km after this point you pass an AFRIQUIA at the junction for the road to Gourama.

KM163 is the ZIZ fuel station at the north end of **Beni Tajite**. This appears to be a garrison and maybe a former mining town with little for the visitor. For a basic **café** in the town centre, head south from the ZIZ a couple of hundred metres, turn left and immediately right; it's on the right. Tracks lead from Beni Tajite in all directions and the **tarmac road** continues east and then south to **Bouanane** on the N10 'Desert Highway', about 60km away and where there may still be a basic **hotel** in the town square.

# ME2    BOUANANE – BOUDENIB – ERFOUD          155km

April 2008 ~ Mazda pickup

## Description

This is a nifty short cut from the east down to Erfoud, though it won't actually save you any time. After crossing the possibly flowing Oued Guir you traverse a rubbly limestone plateau, crossing several lesser oueds on the way.

Southbound, heading away from the mountains it's not exactly on the shortlist for designation as an Area of Outstanding Natural Beauty, a bleak plain occupied in places by hardy nomads on the western limit of the Hamada du Guir. But it's always fun to be off the road, travelling at your own pace and dealing with each oued as it comes. At KM124 you pass the junction for an interesting descent to Erg Chebbi arcing very close to the Algerian border before arriving at the sand sea from the north.

## Off road

The oued crossings can get washed out and we found a few muddy spots with big puddles. The Oued Guir out of Boudenib was six inches deep but has a firm surface below. If it's much deeper, read the suggestion at KM66 on p107. On the limestone plateau a car will get a hammering if you go too fast, and rainfall will always affect this route's northern end. **Bikes** large and small will manage fine; **road cars**, what have you got to lose? On a **bicycle** it's at least pretty flat and oued crossings over your knees can be waded. With good suspension or fat tyres and the wind behind you it could be a nice if undramatic excursion. It's unlikely you'll encounter any traffic.

There are many splits in the track on the northern half that can get confusing, but as long as you keep going south and west you'll get to the Erg Chebbi route junction at KM124 from where the way to the Erfoud highway is clear.

Having failed to find the start in 2004, in 2008, we actually drove this track from Erfoud to Boudenib. The route description has been reversed as it's more useful for those coming off the ferries at Nador or Melilla and heading into the desert. Because of this, some obvious landmarks when heading southbound may not have been recorded.

## Route finding

As mentioned there are several tracks on this route, sometimes they merely fork and rejoin, at other times they may lead off to nomad camps so keep alert. The **map** for this route is on pp110-11.

## Fuel and water

There is fuel at Bouanane and Erfoud. The Ziz at Boudenib still looked abandoned, though there is fuel in town; ask around. There are a few wells and water in the oueds as well as some big puddles.

## Suggested duration

Three or four hours will do you if the oueds are on form. Mountain bikers will need to plan a night out in the wilds.

**0km** **N32' 02.2'  W03' 03.1'**
**Bouanane** fuel station. Head west on the N10 for Boudenib.

**57 (96)** **N31° 57.02'  W03° 36.10'**
**Boudenib** town centre, such as it is. On maps it's marked as a bigger town than Bouanane but it's not really. Seven hundred metres up the road is the old *ZIZ* fuel station looking no more active than it was in 2004.

**61.5 (93.5)** **N31° 57.11'  W03° 37.85'**
**Leave the tarmac** to the south at kilometre post 'Boudenib 1' near a white bollard. Within a few hundred metres fork left.

**63 (92)** **N31° 56.86'  W03° 38.75'**
You pass a modern *khettara* underground irrigation system.

**64 (91)** **N31° 56.67'  W03° 39.12'**
Cross a small oued.

**65 (90)** **N31° 56.39'  W03° 39.57'**
A track joins from the left as you turn south-west.

**66 (89)** **N31° 56.04'  W03° 40.03'**
Drop into the wide Oued Guir here which may be running a few inches deep. If it's running too fast or deep to cross but you still want to try your chances on the rest of this route, return to the road and carry on west a few kilometres to the **Oued Guir** bridge on the N10 where the river comes out from the north and turns east just after the bridge back towards Boudenib. Once over the bridge you're effectively 'south' of the river. From this point head south, cross country to KM77.5, below. Or better still, give up and take the road south!

**66.5 (88.5)** **N31° 55.94'  W03° 40.18'**
Exit the oued, turn right and continue west and slightly uphill.

**71.5 (83.5)** **N31' 55.6'  W03° 43.3'**
At this point the track turns south.

**75.5 (79.5)** **N31° 54.28'  W03° 44.65'**
The track curves to the west gradually and then again, after another sharp turn south of here. In 1500m cross a oued.

**78 (77)** **N31° 53.09'  W03° 45.13'**
As the track turns to the south-west Olaf (see p23) forks off to the left, you can keep right on the more direct line.

**80.5 (74.5)** **N31° 52.28'  W03° 46.54'**
Various tracks diverge.

**84 (71)**
Rejoin Olaf.

**91 (64)** **N31° 48.11'  W03° 50.76'**
Approach a oued from the north-east, possibly with water.

**94.5 (60.5)** **N31° 47.17'  W03° 52.51'**
A track comes in directly from the left opposite a cairn on a hillock on the right, and in 500m a track joins from the right.

**100 (55)** **N31° 45.90'  W03° 55.27'**
Cross a small oued and another soon after.

**102.5 (52.5)**
The track turns south beneath a small mesa to the north.

**103 (51)** **N31° 45.07'  W03° 56.94'**
Fork right.

**112 (43)** **N31° 41.99'  W04° 00.13'**
Fork right, but these are possibly parallel tracks. Isolated small dunes appear as you cross the stony limestone plain.

**115 (40)** **N31° 40.93'  W04° 01.32'**
Key point. Find a way to cross the big Oued Rahmoun, possibly running and with a **well** on the far bank. The old cobbled ford is badly damaged. Five hundred metres after the oued a track joins from the left, probably an alternative crossing for the oued.

**119 (36)** **N31° 39.20'  W04° 02.38'**
Cross the smaller Oued Arid with a washed-away cobbled ford.

**120 (35)** **N31° 38.92'  W04° 02.67'**
Fork right. Left is a triangle on the Erg Chebbi junction.

**124 (31)** **N31° 37.04'  W04° 03.13'**
Key junction marked with cairns for the

route east down to Erg Chebbi. It goes east, right up to the Algerian border before swinging south around the Bine el Korbine escarpment and then back west below the ridge and along the Oued Talrhemt leading south to Erg Chebbi.

For Erfoud turn west here and drive down over limestone slabs into the Oued Zerzel valley.

**125.5 (29.5)     N31° 37.24'   W04° 03.95'**
As you cross a small creek there's a mysterious memorial hidden on the right to Marius-Louis de Bouche ('1898-1933'?) from his friends at Citroën. A spell of Googling didn't come up with anything.

**126 (29)       N31° 37.33'   W04° 04.23'**
Pass a well on the left (30m). The piste

then does a loop round a bend in the valley before continuing south-west.

**131.5 (23.5)     N31° 36.54'   W04° 05.61'**
Another well on the left of the piste.

**136 (19)       N31° 34.69'   W04° 08.61'**
Fork right near some buildings where people may have fossils for sale.

**141 (14)       N31° 32.92'   W04° 11.08'**
**Join the N13 highway** and turn south for Erfoud. In about 7km you'll come to an *Afriquia* fuel station.

**155         N31° 26.23'   W04° 13.95'**
*Total* fuel in the centre of Erfoud. Erfoud is not as touristy as Rissani, so may be an easier place to spend time.

# ME3   GOURAMA – BENI TAJITE                    74KM
April 2008 ~ Mazda pickup

## Description
With tarmac roads to the north and a good piste from the south, this little-used track across the Plain of Snab gets harder year by year as the Jebel Bou Arouss washes away the pistes and carves at the banks of the oueds. It's eastern Morocco's equivalent of Russia's Kolyma Highway only it doesn't hit -70°C in January.

Scenically, there's not much drama here, most of your time will be spent focusing on the ground ahead and wondering what the next ditch holds.

## Off road
How not to get snagged on the **Plain of Snab**, that is the question. As anywhere in the desert, a track which runs below a ridge gets cut up by the runoff. Old road builders got round this by constructing fords and culverts, but tracks still  require maintenance, something which ME3 no longer gets unless you're in the mood. A **short 4WD** or a lightly-loaded **trail bike** will manage it all, but big bikes will need to launch rather than finesse over obstacles. **Road cars** will need 'bridging planks' to lay across the deeper gullies.

## Route finding
East by east it is and fully Olaffed too, although the outdated paper maps can portray a false sense of ease. Expect to make regular deviations to find easier creek crossings. You probably won't see any traffic. The route **map** is on p120.

## Fuel and water
Gourama and Beni Tajite. No wells were seen on the piste.

## Suggested duration
A 4WD or dirt bike will take an hour or two, anything less will take longer, although a portable mountain bike is relatively immune to the creek banks.

**0km**      **N32° 20.28' W04° 04.27'**
Gourama ZIZ fuel station. Leave town to the east.

**5.5 (68.5)**
Tarmac junction: turn right for Boudenib towards a distinctive cone hill. Left leads to Beni Tajite from the north; the route normal people take.

**17.5 (56.5)**
Pass mud-brick ruins on the edge of Mehalla.

**29 (45)**
A pylon piste heads off to the left, possibly to meet this route later.

**31 (43)**      **N32° 13.27' W03° 49.33'**
**Leave the road** to the left just after a oued crossing. 'Boudenib' is written on the ground in stones just as you start the piste. Head north towards the ridge and village there.

The ruins on the south side of the tarmac are **Atchana fort**, built just before WWI. This valley saw several battles with renegade tribes in the last century right up till 1931. There's not that much of interest left at the fort apart from the stone pentagram emblem of the *goumiers* (native troops engaged by the French) set with stones and which now features in the Moroccan flag.

**33 (41)**      **N32° 14.18' W03° 48.90'**
A track joins from left and then another, possibly the pylon piste from KM29. Soon you come to a big oued just south of a village. The bank opposite may be too much for 2WDs or big bikes, but get used to it, this is how things will continue. In this case head north up the oued into the village and find a way back to the next waypoint.

**35 (39)**      **N32° 14.53' W03° 47.81'**
A track joins from the north, possibly a regular piste from the village.

**37 (37)**      **N32° 14.57' W03° 46.73'**
The track ahead splits off in three directions; straight ahead or left may be best (we took a diversion to the south) but expect washed-out oued crossings.

**39 (35)**      **N32° 14.21' W03° 45.51'**
However you got here, continue directly east. In the next 11km or so there are half a dozen gully and oued crossings which may take some negotiating in a 2WD.

**50 (24)**      **N32° 14.95' W03° 39.12'**
A few hundred metres after a view of the Snab Plain ahead, you drop down into a oued, drive along it for a bit and exit on the left where you can.

**52.5 (21.5)**      **N32° 15.14' W03° 37.61'**
Cross a wide, stony oued (as opposed to the gullies you've encountered so far). and work your way round to the main piste visible ahead.

**54.5 (19.5)**      **N32° 15.29' W03° 36.51'**
A track joins from the left near a few cairns, possibly an easier way round a oued.

**58.5 (15.5)**      **N32° 15.78' W03° 34.10'**
A big line of cairns heads directly south. There are no more tricky creek crossings from here on.

**65 (9)**
Pass three white-painted cairns to the north and an old milepost on the right saying 'Beni Tajite'. The hills to the left have receded and in 1.5km you easily cross a wide, possibly flowing, oued.

**68 (6)**      **N32° 16.23' W03° 31.04'**
At a **concrete block** the Tazouguerte track (Route ME7) joins from the south-west. Turn left (north-east) for Beni Tajite.

**70 (4)**      **N32° 16.90' W03° 30.03'**
A local track joins from the left.

**73.5 (500m)**    **N32° 17.59' W03° 28.12'**
Drive among some trees by a wall then turn right **onto a road** to the south-east, passing **Beni Tajite** barracks on your right. After a couple of hundred metres turn left (north-east) for the ZIZ.

**74**      **N32° 17.59' W03° 27.91'**
ZIZ fuel. For the café go back to the main road, turn left then right; it's on the right. There is no hotel here. From Beni Tajite roads and tracks lead off in all directions.

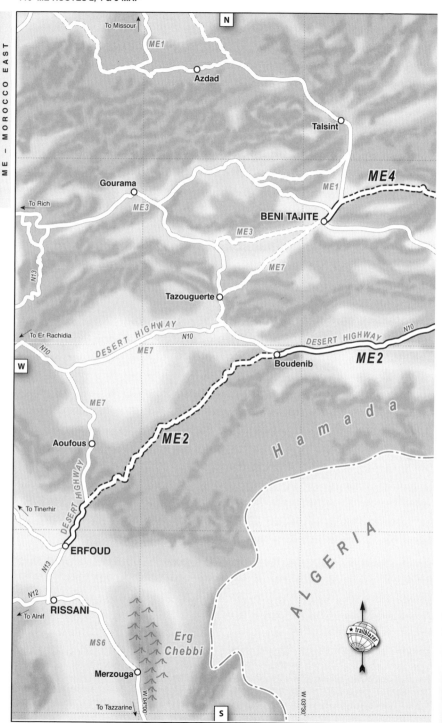

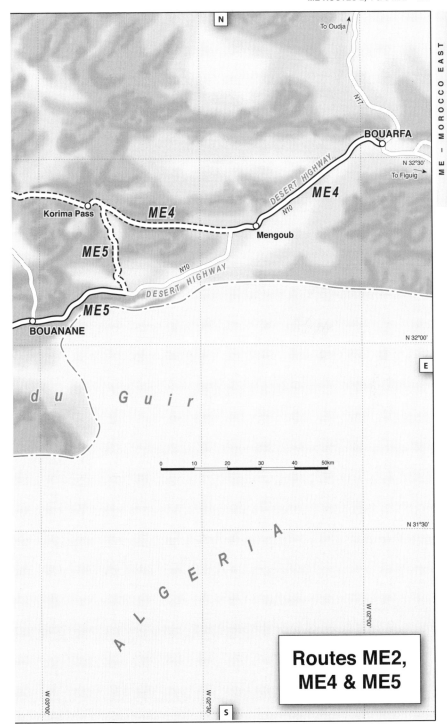

# ME4    BENI TAJITE – BOUARFA                    165KM
May 2008 ~ Mazda pickup

## Description

Whether you've got here via Route ME1, ME3, or along a shell-lined tunnel from the Fiji Islands, this is a satisfying run eastwards between the jebels, dodging washed-out creek crossings. The highlights might be a break or a camp at the KM36 oued crossing, and the 'Korima Pass' (as I have named it). Soon after this point you can take the branch that is Route ME5, back down to the N10 highway and west to Bouanane, or continue on right though to Bouarfa. You'll see a couple of nomad tents along the route, especially in the east, but no villages to speak off, just some areas of cultivation.

This being the far east of Morocco the scenery won't set your hair ablaze but it's as good as it gets. As always, the jebels guide you eastwards and some of the broad oueds offer a break from the drab, scrubby plains, giving a sense of openness but interest.

This is another route we tried in 2004 with a Merc (M2 in *Sahara Overland* in the opposite direction) getting as far as KM70 just before the Korima Pass. I now know it would have led to challenging conditions which may well have folded the car in two. Back then we headed south (Route ME5). Nothing much has changed for better or worse since M2 was logged.

## Off-road

The original piste built up over oueds with small bridges, culverts and fords has disappeared in places, with some concrete fords also mashed by flash floods. As everywhere in the Moroccan East, crossing these places adds a challenge and a 4WD will often resort to low range to climb up the steep banks.

**Regular cars** should manage most of these oued banks; elsewhere they'll need to look around for an easier crossing. In many places these diversions have developed from the original route (and since Olaf was logged) into the current way through. At KM42 a 2WD wants to be ready to blast across 100m or so of soft sand as it comes out of a big oued crossing and 2.5km later the same sandy oued crossing goes over some rocks and may pose problems for 2WDs looking to maintain momentum along with an intact sump.

These short sandy sections won't cause a **big trail bike** too much concern and they'll manage the ups and downs of this route just fine. The relatively smooth track rolling along between the successive oued crossings makes appreciating it all the easier and so makes a good, if long, route for a **mountain bike**. As always in Morocco the caveat is the weather. If it's raining or been raining recently, things could get a whole lot more interesting.

## Route finding

Straightforward enough, notwithstanding keeping track of the long deviations around the washed-out original piste. Olaf often follows this original route which suggests the track log data may be quite a few years old (a guess backed up by other Olaffed tracks in the 'ME' area which were probably submitted by the same person).

On the bright side, the orientations given on the RKH, Michelin and GeoCenter maps are reasonably accurate, except that the RKH has again jumped the gun and wrongly predicted this route's tarmacing. With no villages of substance along the way, it's not likely to happen.

No **traffic** was seen and with tar roads to the south and no villages en route one wouldn't expect any excepting nomad servicing at each end of the route. This route's **map** is on pp110-11.

## Fuel and water
Beni Tajite and Bouarfa have fuel stations. Wells as indicated and with a few of the bigger oueds running in May.

## Suggested duration
Allow half a day for a 4WD, a 2WD may require longer to deal with the oueds and a slick motorbike might blast through in 3 or 4 hours. As always, overnighting out here with a near certainty of privacy would be worthwhile.

**0km          N32° 17.58'   W03° 27.91'**
ZIZ fuel at the north end of **Beni Tajite**. In case you miss it, in 1500m you get to an AFRIQUIA by the junction west to Gourama where a sign reads 'Talsint 28, Missour 156km' (near enough; see Route ME1).

**4 (161)          N32° 19.39'   W03° 26.36'**
Buildings and pylons as the road bends to the left. You leave the road to the right and carry straight on, onto the piste alongside cultivation. In 3 or 4km you cross a flood-damaged oued, the first of many.

**11 (154)          N32° 21.06'   W03° 22.94'**
Go straight, not right which leads to old zinc and lead mines on the jebel. There'll be other tracks leading off south later, also to be ignored.

**13 (152)          N32° 21.43'   W03° 21.73'**
Well on the right near a bridge and a field.

**26 (139)          N32° 22.62'   W03° 13.47'**
Fork. Keep left.

**30 (135)          N32° 22.35'   W03° 11.06'**
Keep straight, not right (which goes to some buildings on the valley side).

**31 (134)          N32° 22.37'   W03° 10.37'**
Fork left. Straight ahead goes to more buildings on hill and the old route (Olaffed).

**33.5 (131.5)    N32° 22.84'   W03° 09.32'**
Track splits. Go left to get over and around the Oued Safsaf, the easiest way

via N32° 22.96' W03° 09.13', 400m further on. Or go right and try the original crossing point to the south at N32° 22.66' W03° 08.75'. From this point cross the oued with relative ease and continue to KM36.

**35 (130)          N32° 23.05'   W03° 08.79'**
Back on the northern Oued Safsaf crossing, you pass a **well** (15m) at this waypoint. Soon after the well, fork right and head south-west back towards the original track over the oued.

**36 (129)          N32° 22.67'   W03° 08.60'**
You're on the east side of the Oued Safsaf. Whichever route you tried, Oued Safsaf is a nice place for a break. On the far western bank there are some rubbish-free ruins by a **well** and shady trees where the steep western bank drops into the oued (if coming from the opposite direction 2WDs may struggle up this bank).

In the oued, apart from water running over the remains of the ford, you may see tiny fish and frogs in the pools and pink oleander on the banks. All in all it's a great spot for a lunch break or even a camp.

**39.5 (125.5)    N32° 22.02'   W03° 06.19'**
Oued crossing by a broken ford.

**41 (124)          N32° 21.77'   W03° 05.34'**
Pass a pump house on the right from where a small concrete canal follows the track to the village. In less than a kilometre (N32° 21.62' W03° 04.83') at a stone building turn left and cross the wide, shingle bed of the possibly running Oued

Hallouf just before it joins the Oued Remila. As soon as you exit this oued there's a patch of soft sand worth being ready for, as well as some buildings. Out of the oued head north-east.

**43 (122)          N32° 21.78'  W03° 04.50'**
You're on your way out from the settlement and on a parallel track north of the main washed-out track – it rejoins from right in about 400m.

**44 (121)          N32° 21.98'  W03° 03.42'**
You recross the now wide and sandy Oued Remila but with blue-grey rocks to get over on the far side. Once out of this oued there's a tricky crossing of a small side oued. It's worth recce-ing this whole section in a 2WD so you get it right first time. Within a kilometre you'll join other tracks looking for a way over these oueds.

**50 (115)**
Cross W03° as you head east towards a pass – useful to orientate yourself on a gridded paper map. In 700m you cross a stony oued and in 1.5km (N32° 22.07' W02° 59.10') take the northern route alongside the oued.

**54.5 (110.5)    N32° 21.81'  W02° 57.75'**
Arrive at a ruined village and possibly a nomad encampment near a broken bridge on the old route on the south side of the oued. Cross the Oued Safsaf easily here and rejoin Olaf following the original piste eastwards. There are some small plots and well pump nearby.

**56 (109)          N32° 21.48'  W02° 56.79'**
After a nicely cobbled ford take the track to the left by the tree. Right (straight) goes to a washout.

**62 (103)          N32° 20.49'  W02° 53.54'**
Go over a damaged ford.

**62.5 (102.5)    N32° 20.44'  W02° 53.19'**
A minor track splits off to the right. We headed left into hills via a tricky oued crossing which may be hard for 2WDs. The track from the right rejoins soon after.

**63.5 (101.5)    N32° 20.44'  W02° 52.63'**
Cross the wide Oued Safsaf to the south

side over the remains of a broken ford. You're now heading into the Korima Pass gorge on a wide, red-earth track which rises above the oued below.

**66 (99)            N32° 20.82'  W02° 51.29'**
**Korima Pass** with thick oleanders in the Oued Safsaf and palm trees with ruins on the north bank. Another nice spot for a break or a camp.

**69.5 (95.5)      N32° 20.29'  W02° 49.55'**
Fork left.

**70 (95)            N32° 20.21'  W02° 49.27'**
Enter the Oued Safsaf here, cross it and drive along the north-eastern bank to the south-east.

**70 (93.5)        N32° 19.73'  W02° 48.62'**
Broken ford. (KM88 of Route M2 in *Sahara Overland*). Cross the ford and in 500m you get to a junction at N32° 19.67' W02° 48.39' where Route ME5 goes south to the N10 and Bouanane. For Bouarfa cross the oued on a ford and on the far side take track to the right (south-east). Left leads up into the hills and possibly some old mines.

**79 (89)            N32° 17.56'  W02° 44.79'**
A piste joins from the right.

**83.5 (81.5)      N32° 16.90'  W02° 42.17'**
An old track joins from the right.

**94 (71)            N32° 16.39'  W02° 34.78'**
**Well** (20m) on the north side of the track.

**109 (56)          N32° 15.57'  W02° 26.25'**
Two kilometres before you reach the N10 highway the piste **becomes old tarmac** with buildings and cultivation nearby. At the highway turn left for Bouarfa.

**165                N32° 31.89'  W01° 57.71'**
AFRIQUIA fuel in **Bouarfa** town centre. There's another bigger fuel station on the northern outskirts of town; to get there turn left (north) at the roundabout.
    Since 2004 Bouarfa has transformed itself into a thriving town complete with local versions of Starbucks, promenading students and a couple of **hotels** which at the time of writing only the *LP* had noted.

# ME5   KORIMA PASS – BOUANANE                    53KM
March 2004 ~ Mercedes 190D

## Description
This route was blundered through in 2004 while looking for a way to the **Korima Pass** and now adds up to just a way of getting off Route ME4 and 22km to the N10 highway to head back south and west. There are no markers but tracks are clear with little chance of straying into the jebels. You can be in Bouanane (fuel and basic hotel) in less than two hours. The **map** is on p111.

**0km**               **N32° 19.7'   W02° 48.3'**
At KM72 on Route ME4 before the big oued with a concrete ford, head south-west, passing a few buildings until the track leads south.

**3 (50)**            **N32° 18.1'   W02° 48.5'**
Cross the oued with a broken concrete bridge. Half a kilometre later (N32° 17.6' W02° 48.5') the track splits. Take the right fork, an easy track across a flat valley of gravel with jebels on either side.

**5 (48)**
There's a distinctive cone hill 8km to the west as you continue along the valley, soon diverting to the left around what can only be described as a washed-out oued.

**11 (42)**
On the horizon you can see a radio mast on top of Jebel Zelmou. This ridge marks the border with Algeria. A little while later, a track leads off to the right; you continue south.

**13 (40)**
Cross another oued and carry on south until you come across a track heading to the south-east. Follow this track via N32° 11.8' W02° 49.7' towards a mine.

**16 (37)**            **N32° 11.7'   W02° 48.2'**
Mine buildings. Take care not to end up in the crusher. Drive out south along the mine access road to the highway.

**22 (31)**            **N32° 08.7'   W02° 46.6'**
**Rejoin the N10 highway**. A sign here points back to 'Ksar Anbag', possibly the name of the mine.

**53**                 **N32° 02.2'   W03° 03.1'**
**Bouanane** fuel station. You'll find a basic hotel (at least in 2004, the guidebooks skip this town now), cafés and shops in the town square. There's certainly more going on here than in Boudenib, even though it appears bigger on all the paper maps.

  Although I've not driven it and the maps don't show it, there is now a sealed road north and west to **Beni Tajite**.

# ME6   FIGUIG – BOUARFA                          110KM
April 2008 ~ Mazda pickup

## Description
To some travellers Figuig has a curious 'Land's End' appeal, stuck as it is in Morocco's south-easternmost corner and within sight of Beni Ounif in Algeria whose different-coloured street lighting at night highlight its exotic proximity. For trans-Sahara travellers using the short Spanish-Moroccan ferry links, up to 1994 this border had been a convenient way of getting into Algeria and so onto the 'easy' Tanezrouft piste to Mali. Then the border closed. Which country instigated the restriction is not clear, but in 2008 Moroccan overtures to re-open borders were rebuffed by Algeria citing the unresolved issue of the Western Sahara (over which Algeria fought Morocco in the 1980s and lost). In

the current climate of people smuggling and with Al Qaeda of the Maghreb operating in the region, it's even less likely to happen.

Some guidebooks suggest wistfully that **Figuig** slipped into decline following the closure, but the town's wealth was always in its palmeries, not cross-border trade (which continues semi-officially with the smuggling of fuel and other commodities). In the early 1980s Figuig looked much as it does now if not poorer; it was never a caravan terminus like the southernmost Moroccan oases further west.

Having made the effort of getting here, many travellers choose to spend a a day or two relaxing and wandering around. A major contributing factor in this is the appeal of the *Hotel Figuig*, the town's only worthwhile hotel and camping spot, while in town the *El Meliasse* by the SHELL works through its own malaise. Situated on a bluff overlooking the palmeries below, the *Figuig* is no pimped-up faux-kasbah pitched to receive tour groups by the coachload. Nor is it a no-star roach palace, but seems to occupy a category all of its own.

Up in town there's broadband, a garage for repairs as well as all the usual shops. Only **petrol** (as opposed to diesel) may be in short supply, probably connected with the smuggling activities. On a bike it's something to think about when you take the 110-km ride out from Bouarfa (the tarmac or this route are about the same distance). And of course if you're set on knocking out every last mile of the Grand Moroccan Traverse stringing this book's off-road routes together, or are setting off to follow the **Desert Highway** (see p196), you don't get the badge unless you start or end in Figuig.

Especially late in the day, the N17 highway down from Bouarfa is no eyesore as it snakes its way through the ranges. Scenically this track is no better; it's merely a novel way or arriving or leaving Figuig. It sets off right along the Algerian border along which it's said trained mules of undefined nationality undertake smuggling sorties, but there's usually no problem with tourists driving this route. You set off into a pass between the Jebel Maïz and the Jebel Amour (noting the geological disparity between the two ranges) and then curve along a valley behind the Maïz to continue north-west up the Oued Safsaf. By the time you emerge into the broad, *raïma*-dotted plain and the sealed road running east to Iche (or Ich), much of the close-range drama is over. Once back on the N17 you should know the way back to Bouarfa and by now ought to be suitably psyched up for the beginning or the end of your Moroccan adventure.

## Off-road

In fair weather at least there are no problems to be had on the way back, whatever your vehicle. The effort of **pedalling** ME6 may not be that worthwhile considering the pleasing and quiet N17 desert highway running nearby.

## Route finding

All the paper maps and of course Olaf show the orientation of this piste accurately, but these days the route cuts corners here and there, such as the point where the piste meets the Iche road at KM68 (worth knowing if you're reversing this route). You'll see many side routes so keep an eye out for the key waypoints. Although many maps seem to show **Iche** as just over the border in

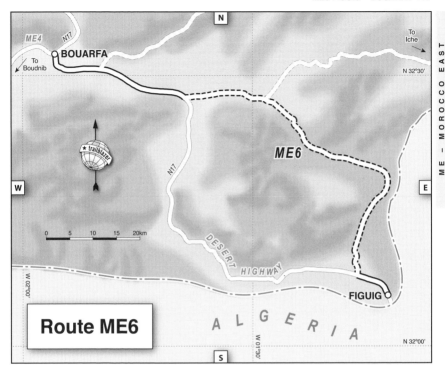

Algeria, the small oasis is actually in Morocco. You won't see much through-traffic on this route; the **map** is above.

## Fuel and water

Bouarfa and Figuig. Petrol may be in short supply in Figuig. Diesel seems OK. There are a couple of wells on the piste.

## Suggested duration

Allow three hours to do the trip with a car or a motorbike.

**0km          N32° 07.20'  W01° 13.93'**
*SHELL* in **Figuig** town centre (see opposite). Head north out of town for Bouarfa.

**8.2 (101.8)     N32° 09.15'  W01° 18.19'**
A couple of kilometres after the checkpoint (where it's worth checking the status of this route) by a post indicating 'Bouarfa 99' turn right **onto the piste** and head north towards the jebel. In a kilometre and a half cross a wide, shingle oued.

**20 (90)         N32° 15.08'  W01° 16.11'**
Pass a small fort on the right and head into the pass between the Jebel Maïz and the Jebel Amour.

**25 (85)         N32° 17.42'  W01° 14.77'**
Head past another bigger fort on the right. About 2km later you pass a marabout (shrine) on the right of the piste.

**31.5 (78.5)**
You'll notice buildings and a water tower right of piste with a big fort and some greenery a kilometre to the north-east.

**36.5 (73.5)     N32° 19.46'  W01° 20.29'**
Cross a wide oued with a broken ford towards a site of some diggings. By the excavation, 800m after the oued, fork right then head north for a pass.

**39 (71)          N32° 20.36'  W01° 21.15'**
Having passed some palms in a oued, fork left here (although you can keep right and meet up at KM41.5). In a kilometre or so you pass some weathered granite boulders which have their uses.

**41.5 (68.5)**
The split from KM39 rejoins from the right just before a oued crossing.

**42.5 (67.5)      N32° 20.81'  W01° 22.46'**
Fork left. In 600m a track joins from the left at N32° 20.95'  W01° 22.87'.

**44.5 (65.5)      N32° 21.48'  W01° 23.30'**
Another track joins from the left. Then, as you cross a ditch-oued where the track splits again, keep right and then 300m on cross a wide, stony oued.

**50 (60)          N32° 24.15'  W01° 24.76'**
Cross the Oued Moulay El Harrane; the left fork is better. Soon a rough track joins from the right.

**52 (58)          N32° 25.08'  W01° 25.24'**
Olaf rejoins from the left and soon another track joins from the left just before a high-banked oued crossing. In 1500m a track joins from the right.

**57 (53)          N32° 26.97'  W01° 27.17'**
Fork right. Soon after there's a small oued crossing with a shady tree and 400m later a track joins from the left, having taken an easier way across the oued.

**58 (52)          N32° 27.42'  W01° 27.65'**
Pass a **well** on the left and some buildings just before another crossing of the Oued Safsaf. Leave Olaf here and strike out to the north-west.

**63 (47)          N32° 28.54'  W01° 30.00'**
Cross a ford. Various tracks go left and right but the main route north-west is obvious and the road is not far. There are a few nomads' tents hereabouts.

**68 (42)          N32° 29.45'  W01° 32.87'**
**Join the tarmac** running to Iche and turn left (west).

**82 (28)          N32° 27.45'  W01° 40.91'**
Rejoin the N17 near a radio tower and turn right (north-west) for Bouarfa.

**110               N32° 31.91'  W01° 57.70'**
*AFRIQUIA* fuel in **Bouarfa** town centre. There is another fuel station on the Oujda road, north out of town. For more details on Bouarfa see the end of Route ME4.

## ME7    BENI TAJITE – AOUFOUS                    119KM
October 2008 ~ Yamaha Ténéré

### Description
While not a route you'd cross continents to tick off, ME7 is a moderately amusing way of getting down towards Erg Chebbi. Apart from a few flood-carved ditches, the **Col de Belkassem** is the off-roading crux. The view up there was nice enough when I paddled over it at dusk, as were the crumbling ruins of Tazouguerte's old ksar. Back on the N10 'Desert Highway' you follow the road to the N13 Er Rachidia junction and turn south, passing the many oases lining the Ziz valley. As an extension to Route ME1, this route can be a handy and undemanding taster for an off-road novice.

### Off-road
The only tricky bit is getting over the rocky Col Belkassem pass which can't get much worse than when I came through and christened my sump guard. Between there and Tazouguerte there were several wash-outs. A **regular car** without planks may find the Col and these creeks a bit of a struggle.

If you've come down ME1 on a **mountain bike**, this route is a fun way to get south onto the N10. But from there on at pedalling speeds things can get a bit dull and windy, so stick your thumb out or have a plan.

To spice things up on the way down south, you could cross the Guir bridge at the N10, turn left onto the sands and work your way cross-country towards KM75 on Route ME2 and then follow that route down to Erfoud or even turn south-east at ME2/KM124 and head all the way to Erg Chebbi.

## Route finding

The trickiest part can be finding the way out of Beni Tajite and getting on course for the Col. At worst, once clear of town just make the Col a 'Go to' and follow the GPS arrow; the tracks are there. After the Col the deviations around wash-outs won't boggle your mind too much and soon you're on the road and will wonder what all the fuss was about. The route **map** is on p120.

## Fuel and water

Beni Tajite and Aoufous for fuel, plus station about 16km west of the N10-N13 junction on the way to Er Rachidia. Away from the towns and villages no wells were noted on the short off-road section but there's always the Oued Guir.

## Suggested duration

The 30-km off-road section to Tazouguerte can be done in an hour or so.

**0km**                 **N32° 17.59' W03° 27.91'**
Ziz fuel station at the north end of **Beni Tajite**. Head south along the road on the east side of the Ziz for 250m and at the main road, turn right. Head up this road north-west for 350m past the barracks on the left and at around N32° 17.60' W03° 28.15' turn south-west down an avenue of trees and curve west out **on a piste** into the desert.

**6 (113)                 N32° 16.22' W03° 31.05'**
Arrive at the junction marked by a concrete block where Route ME3 comes in from Gourama to the west. You continue south-west towards the Col which sits across the Jebel Hajiba. The piste is clear with the occasional parallel track as it follows a shallow valley.

**21 (98)                 N32° 10.17' W03° 39.14'**
Crest a low pass with a cairn.

**26 (93)                 N32° 08.62' W03° 41.48'**
Summit of the 1236m **Col Belkassem** with enough space to camp should you want a pitch with a view. Getting down the far side can be rough, but was in bad shape following The Rains.

**34 (85)                 N32° 04.79' W03° 47.13'**
**Join the tarmac** just south of Tazouguerte and turn left. Soon to your left will be the ruins of old **Tazouguerte** and to your right the palmerie down in the Oued Guir canyon.

**43 (76)                 N32° 00.81' W03° 46.35'**
Junction with the main N10 at the Guir bridge where the river runs more often that you'd expect. There's usually a small café here. Turn right or west.

**95 (24)                 N31° 51.68' W04° 16.13'**
Arrive at the junction with the N13 **Er Rachidia** road, turn left and head down to follow the scenic Ziz valley past the so-called *Oases du Ziz*.

A kilometre west of the junction the long-established *Meski Source Bleu* campsite keeps going with good shade, a spring-fed swimming pool and a resto, but with partly-dormant ablutions.

**119                 N30° 41.9' W04°10.8'**
The Afriquia fuel station in the palmerie on the south end of **Aoufous**. Erfoud is around another 20km further on.

ME – MOROCCO EAST

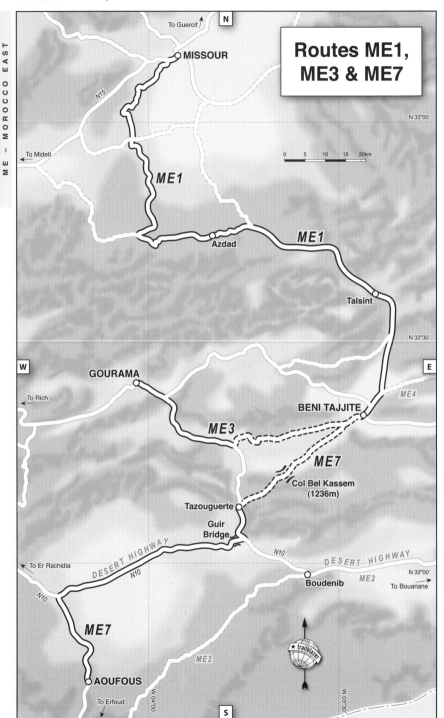

To Guercif
N
MISSOUR
N15
N 33°00'
To Midelt
ME1
0  5  10  15  20km
ME1
Azdad
ME1
Talsint

W
GOURAMA
E
To Rich
ME4
BENI TAJJITE
ME3
ME7
Col Bel Kassem
(1236m)
Tazouguerte
Guir
Bridge
To Er Rachidia
DESERT HIGHWAY
N10
N10
DESERT HIGHWAY
N 32°00'
Boudenib
ME2
To Bouanane
N10
ME7
ME2
AOUFOUS
To Erfoud

S

# Routes ME1, ME3 & ME7

# ME8  The road to Bou Redine

May 2008 ~ Mazda pickup

**80KM** RETURN

Between Midelt and Rich all the paper maps show a fairly prominent track leading east from Nzala (on some maps) via Aït Alla to Bou Redine (on some maps) where the track takes an intriguingly winding route through the ranges to Gourama. As we were heading for Gourama it could prove an interesting deviation, or so we thought. We were not the only ones tempted to try this intriguing mountain track; some friends on a BMW motorbike tour slipped away from the group on their big GSs, but being there in the midst of The Rains, didn't even get 20km.

The unsigned track starts 40km south of Midelt by a building and two radio masts at a snow gate (N32° 32.20' W04° 29.09') barring the 1900m **Tizi-n Tairhemt** to the north. It winds east eastwards easily enough, north of the Jebel Aouja taking the odd deviation around wash-outs and passes through the oued south of what one presumes is the village of **Aït Alla**, 10km from the asphalt.

Here at N32° 32.22' W04° 23.50' head for N32° 32.17' W04° 23.26' and at N32° 32.11' W04° 22.61' stay in the oued where the track squeezes past the bushes hard against a bank and then go up a slippery, broken culvert. The track continues in and out of the oued and over rolling hills, and 27km from the road slips north to a parallel valley and a settlement soon after. You continue oued skipping for 3km until N32° 33.76' W04° 11.65' on the outskirts of Bou Redine (or 'Boudin' as it was signed). Here the main track turns north and on some maps makes a link with Aït Alou Kchamene about 8km to the north along a canyon to pick up a piste labelled variously as: 'R604'; 'R601'; 'P5121'; '4987' depending on which map you're using.

A few months later I came through, logging Route ME1 from Missour and realised later that the track which leaves this scenic drive at N32° 39.46' W04° 04.46', about 62km from Missour, may lead west through Bou Sellam and then, at a crossroads turn south towards Aït Alou Kchamene and Bou Redine via Jebel Yhoudi ('Mountain of Jews', as it happens, one of many like-named features in Morocco), a distance of about 22km. See the map on the website.

At Bou Redine (the welcome here was not so warm, it must be said) the track southwards depicted so confidently on current paper maps is not evident, although a 2350-metre high jebel is. Old French maps show a more plausible thin black line continuing east along the valley for 20km or more before turning south through a gap and cutting back west and south to Gourama. We were told at Bou Redine a piste did indeed continue to Gourama but that it was 'up and down'. As one cannot be sure what locals categorise as difficult, we continued down the oued (past a little 'roadblock' the kids had set up for us in the meantime) for another 4 or 5km up to N32° 34.13' W04° 09.23' as far as an abandoned mine on the north side of the valley set below another high ridge.

By now the track was barely visible and seemed to continue in the creek bed to the right. I walked on a kilometre or two towards a pass, but while the ground was passable to a lithe 4WD or a light bike, the moderately more used route seemed to follow a narrow creek full of recent rockfall from the adjacent slope. Looking on Google Earth (see images on the website) the village of Ksar Almou Abtour (about 11km after this point) looks like it's probably accessed along a canyon from the north via Tagentatcha (KM65 on Route ME1) which features on Google Earth and some paper maps.

As it was, according to the old French maps, from the abandoned mine it was still at least another 17km of possibly similar 'walking-pace' terrain before the track turned south through the jebel to head back south-west for 25km to Tiouzaguine (on the paper maps) from where it drops another 15km through various villages leading to Gourama.

This last 15km may well be a good access track out of Gourama to these villages, but north of Tiouzaguine and east of Bou Redine it does not seem a normal route as depicted on the paper maps. Barging onward off-piste (as opposed to off-road) is not really in the spirit of this book, but the canyon route north of Bou Redine must almost certainly lead by and by to ME1.

# Outline of the High Atlas region

Stretching from Midelt south-west to Aoulouz, 'MH' is the biggest region in this book. It includes the geologically separate Jebel Sirwa and Jebel Sarhro massifs south of the High Atlas which are neither technically the Sahara or the Anti Atlas.

Along with the 'MS' Sahara zone, parts of this area are where most tourists go in southern Morocco, where the landscapes and Berber culture sum up the appeal of the south. Certainly if your vehicle is up to it, you'd want to attempt either **Trans Atlas Routes** MH1 or -2, as well as one of the road crossings to either side.

Visually the High Atlas itself is not as dramatic as it sounds and compared to further south, some villages can have a gloomy, sodden feel. Add the fact that **bad weather** here is not so unusual and with winter closing many routes, you'll need to get lucky on the heights. The lower elevations of the Sirwa- and noticeably more arid Sarhro massifs are more reliable destinations in mid-winter.

# MH Routes

# TRANS ATLAS: MH1  MIDELT – AGOUDAL – DADES    317km
May 2008 ~ Mazda pickup

## Description

For those looking for the meatier crossing of the High Atlas, this two-day run won't leave you disappointed. Providing rivers, mud or snow don't block the way, it gets off to a great start following the popular **Cirque du Jaffar** out of Midelt, a traverse under the snow-bound slopes of the 3700-metre Jebel Ayachi. The 'cirque' refers to the amphitheatre-like valley head you drop into and climb out of; others interpret it as the half-day 80km 'circuit' most off-roaders take out of Midelt. Either way the Cirque is just one highlight on this route. You rejoin the tarmac at KM37 for about 40 kilometres, passing through mountain villages which continue once you're back on the piste and on the way to Imilchil.

Near here you join the Imilchil-Rich road, but only for a short while. Soon you're back on the piste heading for Agoudal and the main crossing of the range. Even in the good conditions we had, it'll be slow progress to the 2906m Tizi-n Ouano, the highest route in this book. Here the descent commences alongside the gorge of the upper Dades to Msemrir and the resumption of tarmac down the Dades Gorge, bedecked with all the rich fruits of tour-bus tourism. If you've enjoyed the wilds, Boumalne du Dades is not a particularly propitious spot to end up. Ideally you'll have got here early enough to head on to Ouarzazate or get up into the Jebel Sarhro massif directly ahead.

MH1 is a 300-km run over the High Atlas with only about 80km of tarmac. If you don't see something you like, demand a full refund at the kiosk by the Dades roundabout. On MH1 it's hard to think of a dull stretch.

## Off road

Plenty to make you think over a couple of days. When we did it in May the descent into the Oued Jaffar was the roughest section of the route which wasn't saying much. However, any of the piste stages are prone to flood damage, mud or snow and in winter over the top from Agoudal to Tilmi won't be a snow-clearance priority. Here, MH2 from Agoudal to Tinerhir may be in better shape and more used; the locals will know. Mud and snow will make things exhausting on a heavy **motorcycle** without knobbly tyres and in such conditions it'll turn into an epic for sure.

Setting off in a **regular car** at any time is bound to be an adventure too; the best chance of completing the full crossing is from spring onwards. On a **mountain bike** it will be a fair old trek too, and if you don't want to camp you'll have to plan your days quite closely.

## Route finding

As is so often the case, we found the hardest part was finding the start of the route out of Midelt town, as well as the odd distracting new road on the way to Imilchil. Once out of Agoudal there's only really one way down to Msemrir and this whole route is Olaffed just about all the way.

Traffic will amount to other off-road recreationists in the Cirque and local traffic including road-building on the way to Imilchil. Over the Tizi you're back in the domain of adventure tourists again. The **map** is on pp132-3.

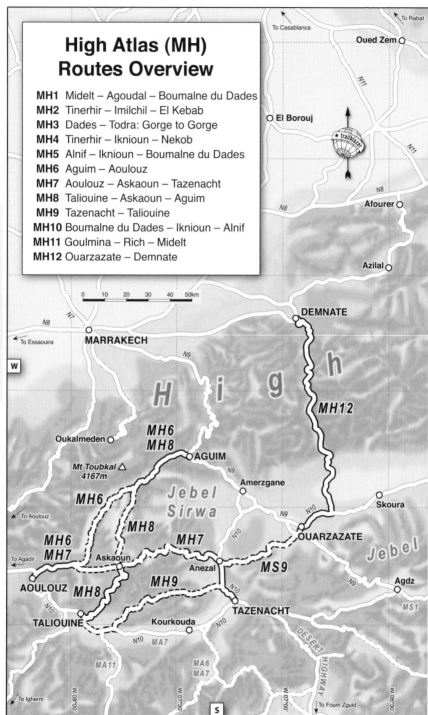

# High Atlas (MH)
# Routes Overview

**MH1** Midelt – Agoudal – Boumalne du Dades
**MH2** Tinerhir – Imilchil – El Kebab
**MH3** Dades – Todra: Gorge to Gorge
**MH4** Tinerhir – Iknioun – Nekob
**MH5** Alnif – Iknioun – Boumalne du Dades
**MH6** Aguim – Aoulouz
**MH7** Aoulouz – Askaoun – Tazenacht
**MH8** Taliouine – Askaoun – Aguim
**MH9** Tazenacht – Taliouine
**MH10** Boumalne du Dades – Iknioun – Alnif
**MH11** Goulmina – Rich – Midelt
**MH12** Ouarzazate – Demnate

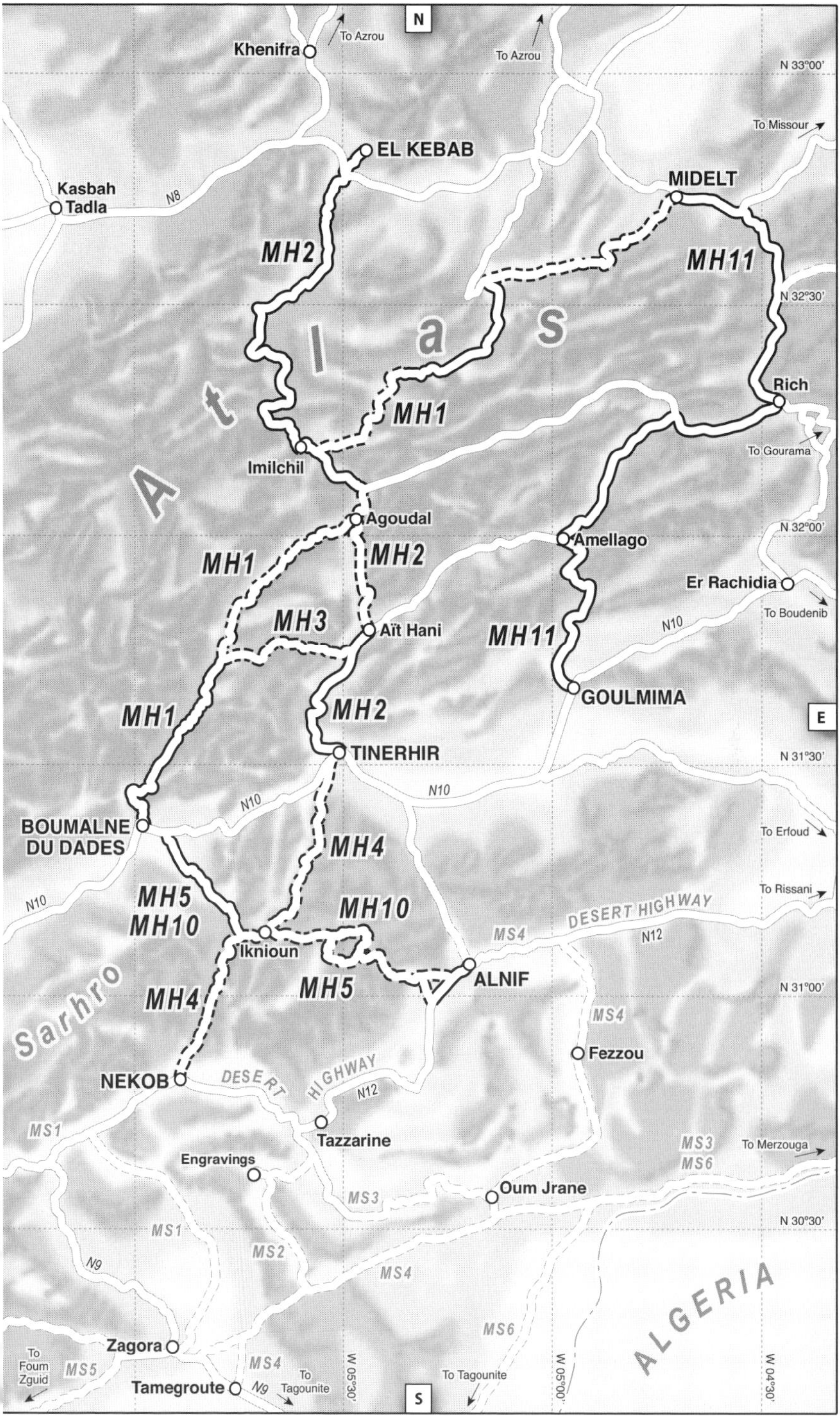
N
To Azrou
Khenifra
To Azrou
N 33°00'
To Missour
EL KEBAB
Kasbah Tadla
N8
MIDELT
MH2
MH11
N 32°30'
A t l a s
MH1
Rich
Imilchil
To Gourama
Agoudal
MH1
MH2
N 32°00'
Amellago
Er Rachidia
To Boudenib
MH3
Aït Hani
N10
MH11
GOULMIMA
MH1
MH2
E
TINERHIR
N 31°30'
N10
N10
BOUMALNE DU DADES
MH4
To Erfoud
To Rissani
MH5
MH10
N10
MH10
DESERT HIGHWAY
MS4
N12
Iknioun
MH5
ALNIF
N 31°00'
MH4
Sarhro
MS4
Fezzou
NEKOB
DESERT HIGHWAY
N12
MS1
Tazzarine
MS3
MS6
To Merzouga
Engravings
Oum Jrane
MS3
N 30°30'
MS1
MS2
N9
MS4
ALGERIA
MS6
Zagora
To Foum Zguid
MS5
MS4
To Tagounite
To Tagounite
Tamegroute
N9
W 05°30'
S
W 05°00'
W 04°30'

## Fuel and water

Only at each end for sure though there may be some in the bigger villages at a price. There is plenty of water running in the creeks, in the village wells and from stores. [May 2009: there is now an *Inov* fuel station north of Imilchil].

## Suggested duration

Of all the routes in this book MH1 can get quite a beating from the elements, so give yourself two full days if the weather and road conditions are on your side. If they're not, bring a fat book and some M&S hibernating pyjamas. In good conditions a mountain biker could cover this route in 4 or 5 tough days and end up with quite a sense of achievement.

**0km          N32° 41.07'   W04° 44.60'**
**Midelt** town centre roundabout with *Shell* and *Total* fuel stations. One way of getting to the start is to head north past a red and white bollard in the road and over a bridge with red and white posts.
   In 600m (N32° 41.31' W04° 44.80') turn left onto a minor road. If you're coming from the north you'll see a brown sign indicating 'Circuit Touristique Jaffar' pointing right.

**1.3 (315.7)      N32° 40.93'   W04° 44.89'**
Turn right below some ruins. The general direction is south-west below the snow dappled north face of Jebel Ayachi.

**6 (311)          N32° 38.53'   W04° 45.88'**
The **tarmac ends** so carry on straight past minor junctions to the left and right. The way ahead is clear.

**13 (304)         N32° 36.25'   W04° 49.07'**
Fork left here. In 4km you'll find yourself turning south through the cedar trees towards the mountains and at KM21 you pass between barbed wire fences.

**25.5 (291.5)     N32° 33.77'   W04° 54.09'**
Fork with an arrow on a rock. Curve left, south, up into the pass where the track becomes rubbly. The other track to the right turns north then west.

**26.5 (290.5)     N32° 33.20'   W04° 53.68'**
Come over the pass (2262m with enough flat space to camp) and enter the **Cirque**. Start a loose descent, in a car inching round a huge fallen boulder on the off-side. Down below there are flat-roofed dwellings at the bottom of the valley.

**29 (288)**
Turn sharp right as you cross a oued and begin climbing round a spur.

**30 (287)          N32° 32.47'   W04° 53.74'**
Junction. Left is washed-out so descend right to the valley floor whichever way and meet the kids who've already heard you coming and may have prepared their traps!

**30.5 (286.5)     N32° 32.35'   W04° 53.81'**
Cross a oued prior to climbing back out of the cirque. For us the kids half-heartedly blocked the way here with stones. There are no real options to go wrong but once you're ascending to the north-west past fence posts through cedar woods to either side, you're on the right track.

**34.5 (282.5)**
The cirque is behind you now as the ground opens out onto a good earth road.

**38 (279)**
A nice camp spot as you cross a small oued.

**44.5 (272.5)     N32° 32.29'   W04° 58.49'**
Pass a settlement in the meadows with a view to the northern plains and the snowy peaks to the south. A rutted, dried-mud section may follow.

**48.5 (268.5)     N32° 31.77'   W04° 59.49'**
About two-and-a-half hours driving from Midelt you get to the key junction where a sign says: 'Tiz-n Zou 10; Tounfite 30; Imilchil 130'. Turn right here if you're just doing the loop back towards Midelt otherwise, those heading over the Atlas con-

tinue straight ahead on an unusually good forestry track for a few kilometres.

**52 (265)**
Villages, meadows, poppies, wheat. All very scenic – in spring at least.

**60 (257)       N32° 31.06'  W05° 03.46'**
Go straight down towards the villages making up **Tizi-n Zou** (the wide track to the right goes to a dam). The village track may get muddy.

**61 (256)**
Leave one village over a damaged ford on a hard mud track. A kilometre later, at another village you pass by a yellow building on a rise on one of two tracks that soon converge.

**63 (254)       N32° 31.04'  W05° 05.07'**
Cross a very narrow bridge with railed sides. Or dive through the river if you're feeling sporty or are in a wide Humvee. All around are cypress and cedar trees dotting the barren, ashen slopes.

**73 (244)       N32° 29.91'  W05° 10.53'**
**Join the tarmac** and turn left for Imilchil.

**91.5 (2255)       N32° 23.49'  W05° 09.97'**
A *gîte d'étape* in Tayoudit village.

**93 (224)       N32° 23.04'  W05° 10.61'**
Turn left at a sign 'Imilchil 85km' on a road which bypasses **Agoudim** village.

**97 (220)       N32° 21.56'  W05° 11.05'**
*Oudadn Auberge* by an apple orchard, a lovely place for a lunch break, overnight or simply just to get snowed in. Half board is 120dh per person.

**110 (207)       N32° 19.46'  W05° 16.09'**
**The tarmac ends** at the end of Anemzi village but may have progressed a bit further by now. It's a hard-packed earth road from here on.

**120 (197)       N32° 18.75'  W05° 20.58'**
Start of a three kilometre-long canyon full of mature trees and from where things could get messy after heavy rains.

**127 (190)       N32° 18.64'  W05° 23.48'**
*Gîte d'étape Ouyide* in a rocky gorge.

**128 (189)       N32° 18.45'  W05° 24.29'**
Track to the right; you go straight on.

**132 (185)       N32° 17.40'  W05° 23.83'**
Junction at the edge of **Anefgou** village to the left. 'Imilchil 47'. In 500m there's another junction, keep left as the valley opens out. In a couple of kilometres you pass the tiny 'Hotel Fezaz', which looks like more of a basic auberge.

**136 (181)       N32° 15.84'  W05° 25.59'**
Tighiste village. Willows, grass and a National Park Forestry centre.

**147 (170)  N32° 12.45'  W05° 27.31'**
The track tops out at 2649m. On the far side are pastures with horses; it looks a good spot for camping.

**151 (166)       N32° 10.90'  W05° 28.18'**
Tilhri or Tabanast village.

**154 (163)**
A wide cultivated valley with mountains to north and south, front and back.

**163 (154)       N32° 09.14'  W05° 34.46'**
Reach **the tarmac road**. Left is for Agoudal and Dades. Right is for **Imilchil** (9km, **fuel**) on Route MH2.

**174 (143)       N32° 05.99'  W05° 30.62'**
**Leave the tarmac** to the right for the village of **Almaghou**.

**179 (138)       N32° 04.54'  W05° 28.69'**
Akdim village with *La Kasba* camping and café. Just after the village the track turns right to cross the oued around N32° 04.16' W05° 28.33'.

**183 (134)       N32° 02.78'  W05° 27.93'**
**Timaryne** village. Just after the village there may be a muddy or dried mud section alongside riverbed plots.

**190 (127)       N32° 00.53'  W05° 29.39'**
**Agoudal** town centre at 2350m. MH2 goes south-east over the oued to Todra. You turn right before the oued along the south side of town, passing between the town and fields.

Among other auberges in town *Auberge Agoudal* has half-board in a cosy en-suite room for just 110dh per person.

**190.5 (126.5)   N32° 00.31'   W05° 29.67'**
Turn right here and in 500m turn left to join the main route out of town. Head south for the hills.

**197 (120)        N31° 58.70'   W05° 32.72"**
Go straight not left at the 'Grotte Akhiam' sign. Drive in the oued.

**198 (119)        N31° 58.94'   W05° 33.23'**
Pass some buildings on the right with possible diversions after the village around the mud. There are signs and blue arrows on the rocks to show the route.

About 1500m later there's a **cistern** on the left and soon after a narrow passage above a gully. There could be yellow and purple flowers on hillsides and lots of washed-out gullies. In a kilometre or so the grassy pastures could make nice wild camps.

**202 (115)**
Orchard on the left, houses on the right.

**204 (113)        N31° 57.25'   W05° 36.09'**
Short cut directly uphill for 4WDs and bikes, otherwise go left.

**213 (104)        N31° 54.70'   W05° 39.73'**
**Tizi-n Ouano** highpoint at 2906m. Some buildings and a bit of rubbish. Good views to the south over what might be called the upper Dades gorge.

**219 (98)**
Tilmi village far below with the deep gorge below left. In about 3km the big descent begins with occasional steep short cuts and a possibly washed-out bend 4km further on (N31° 51.53'  W05° 43.50').

**229 (88)        N31° 50.93'   W05° 44.05'**
A junction to the valley to the west. You carry on straight and in 500m cross a oued back on the valley floor with the orange *Gîte d'étape Ighounta* on the far bank. Crops and cultivation resume with flowery meadows all around in spring.

**233 (84)**
Aït Moussa out Ichou village.

**235 (82)        N31° 50.02'   W05° 45.70'**
Cross a bridge in Aït Ali Ouikkou.

**237 (80)**
Izmaguene village.

**240 (77)        N31° 48.03'   W05° 46.59'**
Take the left track and in 500m cross a bridge over a oued. Soon there's a sign: '**Tilmi Centre**', a track joins from the left and you pass an old kasbah. All this is within one kilometre.

**247 (70)        N31° 47.73'   W05° 46.65'**
Sign: right to Asaka restaurant and Aït Mohamed. An Olaf loop rejoins from right (a split from around KM240). In a kilometre there's a café.

**251 (66)        N31° 43.11'   W05° 48.17'**
Reach the upper turn-off for MH3 just before Msemrir.

**255 (62)        N31° 41.77'   W05° 49.05'**
**Msemrir** town centre (about three hours driving in good conditions from Agoudal) with a pharmacy, small shops and some auberges. As you leave town the river flows alongside the road for a bit, then you climb out above the gorge.

**285 (32)        N31° 31.74'   W05° 55.49'**
From around KM280 the hotels begin and at this point, by a cliff-edge hotel, is the much-photographed '**Dades Gorge hairpins'** viewpoint.

Now the gorgeside **hotels and restos** multiply and in about 5km on the left is the posh *Chez Pierre* restaurant and auberge (featured in all the guidebooks). For around 200dh per person it's as good a meal as you'll eat in Morocco and it won't have to be a tajine, cous-cous or an omelette.

**298 (19)        N31° 26.87'   W05° 58.39'**
Unusual rock formations on the far side of the valley with auberges, shops and even fake camels and nomads to pose by.

**315 (2)        N31° 22.49'   W05° 59.55'**
**Dades** central roundabout on the N10 highway. Turn left for fuel and Tinerhir or right for Ouarzazate.

**317        N31° 22.07'   W05° 58.87'**
*SHELL* fuel station on south side of Dades.

# TRANS ATLAS: MH2 TINERHIR – IMILCHIL – EL KEBAB 241KM

May 2008 ~ Mazda pickup

## Description

This is the easier of the two trans-Atlas routes with 'only' 49km of piste from Aït Hani to just before Imilchil. Of course that 49km is about as high as you can drive in Morocco. It kicks off with a run through the 'Costa Todra', a development bearing little relation to the impressive but not exactly mind-blowing spectacle of the actual chasm itself. Once you've explored some of the other out-of-the-way places in this book you may think so too, but the Gorge is well and truly on the tourist axis on the road south to Zagora or Erg Chebbi.

With that behind you, you pass through Tamtatoucht where one presumes they're now happy to earn an honest dirham running numerous auberges instead of misguiding travellers heading for the Gorge to Gorge track (Route MH3). You may slip past the kids in Tamtatoucht, but they're all waiting for you at the series of villages starting with Aït Hani, although only with their hands out or looking for a distraction. You shake them off – in some cases literally if they're swinging from your roof rack – and set off into the barren ranges of the High Atlas. At KM63 the track mysteriously improves as if tarmacing is imminent, only to return to a string of puddles on an upland plateau that at least offers some good flat spots for **wild camps**. Agoudal and the following string of villages up to the tarmac at KM101 see more stylo-stampedes, but both Agoudal and Imilchil make good places to stay.

When we arrived at Imilchil the kids must have been away on a day trip, or maybe they've all just got over it (it does happen). From here it's an unchallenging and increasingly pastoral descent down to the lowlands, or at least as low as they get before the land rises again to become the Middle Atlas.

El Kebab is but one place to end the crossing though there's now fuel at Imilchil and in Aghbala at KM196. El Kebab has a nice 'Friday night in South London' ring to it and anyway, the people at the town's ZIZMO seem game.

You may learn that the evocatively-named High Atlas are not exactly the Torres del Paine, at least as seen at drivable elevations, and that the southern massifs of Sirwa and Sarhro have more colour. This transit lacks the greater drama of Route MH1 which intersects it, but chances are it'll be crossable when MH1 is not.

## Off road

**Regular cars** have the highest chance of making this trans-Atlas route as opposed to MH1, and on a **big motorbike** there's not much to stop you that won't stop everything else. The short off-road stage makes this a manageable **MTB** route. There are no particularly precipitous stages clinging to the mountainsides as there are on MH1 though in winter there's a good chance this area will be snowy. We were told that snow is never more than a couple of feet deep and the ploughs come through within a day or two, however one would think the 27km village-less stage between Aït Hani and Agoudal would not be a snow-clearing priority. Unfortunately they've not invented the 'mud plough' yet and in the cooler season it's much more likely **rain** will make a mess of things, especially south of Agoudal if not right up to the tarmac at KM101.

MH – HIGH ATLAS

## Route finding

No problem providing the track is not mist-bound or under a couple of feet of snow. Traffic is thinnest between Aït Hani and Agoudal but is not exactly bumper-to-bumper from Imilchil towards El Kebab. For the route **map** see pp132-3.

## Fuel and water

Apart from at each end and at Aghbala (KM196) and Imilchil (KM121) it's possible to get fuel in the intermediate towns at a price. With its several villages and high elevation a shortage of water is likely to be the least of your problems.

## Suggested duration

Possible in a day but two days could be twice the fun. There are auberges in just about every village up to Imilchil; beyond that we saw nothing.

**0km          N31° 31.23'  W05° 31.99'**
**Tinerhir** TOTAL fuel. Head into the town centre and after a kilometre at the lights on the east side of town turn left, west, for Todra. As the road winds towards the gorge you will pass an endless succession of gîtes and auberges.

**14.5 (226.5)    N31° 35.00'  W05° 35.48'**
Arrive at **Todra Gorge** and pay 5dh to pass through (it's official; an old guy with a hat and a satchel). The tall, narrow chasm is especially dramatic when the overhead sun lights up the walls. There may be rock climbers here and almost certainly the all-day tourist souk selling brightly-coloured head scarves, boxed sets of trilobites and magic slippers.

Beyond here the road may be under repair from flash floods with diversions along the oued. Soon the road emerges out onto the Aït Hani plains.

**36 (205)      N31° 40.85'  W05° 32.25'**
**Tamtatoucht** village at a sign for the track that heads north-west to meet Route MH3. There are several auberges and cafés here.

**45 (196)      N31° 44.22'  W05° 29.71'**
Pass the point where Route MH3 rejoins the road, more or less halfway between Tamtatoucht and Aït Hani.

**52 (189)      N31° 46.89'  W05° 27.14'**
**Aït Hani** village. Cross the oued possibly filled with green crops and at the junction turn left; the **tarmac ends**. Right leads to

Amellago and Goulmima or Rich (Route MH11). Drive north-west through a village alongside the crop-filled oued.

Aït Hani runs into a string of villages and unless the Pied Piper has been through recently, you'll have a chance to meet the lively village kids.

**58 (183)      N31° 49.64'  W05° 28.25'**
You pass a couple of auberges and at the *Auberge Carrefour* ('crossroads') you go straight, north. In 500m you get to a junction with white stones. Go straight again – north-north-west (left goes to a gîte). Soon you're out in the open on a gravel piste.

**61 (180)      N31° 50.99'  W05° 27.29'**
Fork. Left is a steep and loose ascent, fine for a 4WD. The right fork is a longer, less steep ascent better for 2WDs or big bikes with road tyres.

**63 (178)      N31° 51.79'  W05° 27.33'**
The two tracks rejoin and the surface suddenly improves, but only for a few kilometres. After 4 or 5km you pass the 2650m **Tizi-n Tiherhouzine** high point.

**79 (162)      N31° 57.30'  W05° 28.67'**
There are many flat camp spots hereabouts as well as some water crossings. This area would also become a very muddy trap after heavy rains.

**83 (158)**
Cultivation resumes as you near Agoudal. In 2km you pass the *Auberge Arfoud* on the southern outskirts of the village.

**85 (156)      N32° 00.50'   W05° 29.37'**
**Agoudal** village centre where Route MH1 turns south for Dades. Carry on through the village with a couple of stores. In 500m you get to the *Auberge Ibrahim* which seems a popular spot. We carried on for nearly another kilometre and stayed at the *Auberge Agoudal*, a more secluded spot beyond the north end of town at 2350m. It's run by Hassan, a nice old guy who knows just what tourists want. Half-board here with an en-suite room with piles of blankets was 110dh per person.

**92 (149)      N32° 02.78'   W05° 27.93'**
**Timaryne** village. Just before the village there may be a muddy or dried-mud section alongside riverbed plots.

**95 (146)      N32° 04.16'   W05° 28.33'**
Just before a village the track turns down right to cross over a cultivated riverbed.

**96 (145)**
**Akdim** village with camping and a café.

**97 (144)      N32° 04.87'   W05° 29.08'**
**Aït Amer**, go straight at an Arabic sign pointing right somewhere 18km away (probably Outerbate on the road to Rich).

**101 (140)      N32° 05.99'   W05° 30.62'**
Just after a ZIZ fuel sign in the village of **Almaghou** you **join the tarmac road**. Left leads 20km to Imilchil, right goes on to Rich (about 118km) or back down through Amellago and the Rheris Gorge to Goulmima (MH11).

**112 (129)      N32° 09.14'   W05° 34.46'**
At this point Route MH1 from Midelt joins the Imilchil road. If conditions are good and you want to end up in Midelt, turning off here is a great way of stringing out your trans-Atlas crossing.

**121 (120)      N32° 09.39'   W05° 37.86'**
**Imilchil** town centre, famed for its September *moussems* or marriage/match-making festivals. There are up to a dozen auberges and hotels in town but surprisingly the guidebooks weren't much help at the time, so until they catch up it may pay to do some research in advance if you'd like to stay in a recommended place. For such a well-known place the town gave no hassle from touts. There is an *INOV* fuel station just north of town.

**126 (115)      N32° 11.78'   W05° 38.53'**
*Auberge Tislite* in a quiet location overlooking Lake Tislit. We stayed here as parking was less exposed than in town. It was a great location and a warm welcome but comparatively pricey at 220dh per person half-board with an en-suite room. There's a big heater and also a big tent by the lake for camping. There's another lake, Isli, further east, also with an auberge.

From here the tarmac road sets off north, winding through a limestone gorge after 8km which opens out into a valley of tawny pastures and poppy fields (or maybe just snow and mist…). The trees get thicker as you descend past a few mud-brick villages.

**183 (58)      N32° 26.83'   W05° 45.71'**
Out of the mountains and heading into the hills, you turn right for Aghbala along a wide red-earth valley. Look back onto the Atlas to the south as you head east.

**196 (45)      N32° 28.59'   W05° 38.91'**
There is **fuel** on the west side of **Aghbala**, a big farming town as well as plenty of shops and cafés, but no obvious hotel. As you leave town the valley widens into the rolling plains of the northern High Atlas.

**231 (10)      N32° 41.13'   W05° 33.82'**
Having passed the town of Sidi Yakia Oussad down to the left you get to the junction with the R503 by a couple of roadhouses. Right is for Midelt, left is for Khenifra.

Turn left and if you're seeing it through all the way to El Kebab, fork right in 200 metres up an unsigned minor road (the actual road sign is back a bit). Follow this windy road over the hill and drop down the other side into the valley of the Oued Srou and El Kebab.

**241      N32° 44.51'   W05° 31.54'**
The road drops right into **El Kebab's** *ZIZMO* in the town centre. A slap-up plate of brochettes is surely in order while you mull over where to go next.

MH – HIGH ATLAS

# Routes MH1, MH2, MH3, MH11 & MH12 (Trans Atlas)

To Oued Zem

Kasbah
Tadla

El Ksiba

N8

N11

0 5 10 15 20 25km

Beni Mellal

N8

Afourer

To Marrakech

N8

Azilal

To Marrakech

H i g h

W

DEMNATE

To Marrakech

Msemrir

MH1

Dades Gorge

MH12

★ trailblazer

BOUMALNE
DU DADES

N10

MH5
MH10

N10

J e b e l

Skoura

To Marrakech

MH4

OUARZAZATE

W 07°00'

N9

To Agdz

W 06°30'

S

To Agdz

W 06°00'

Nekob

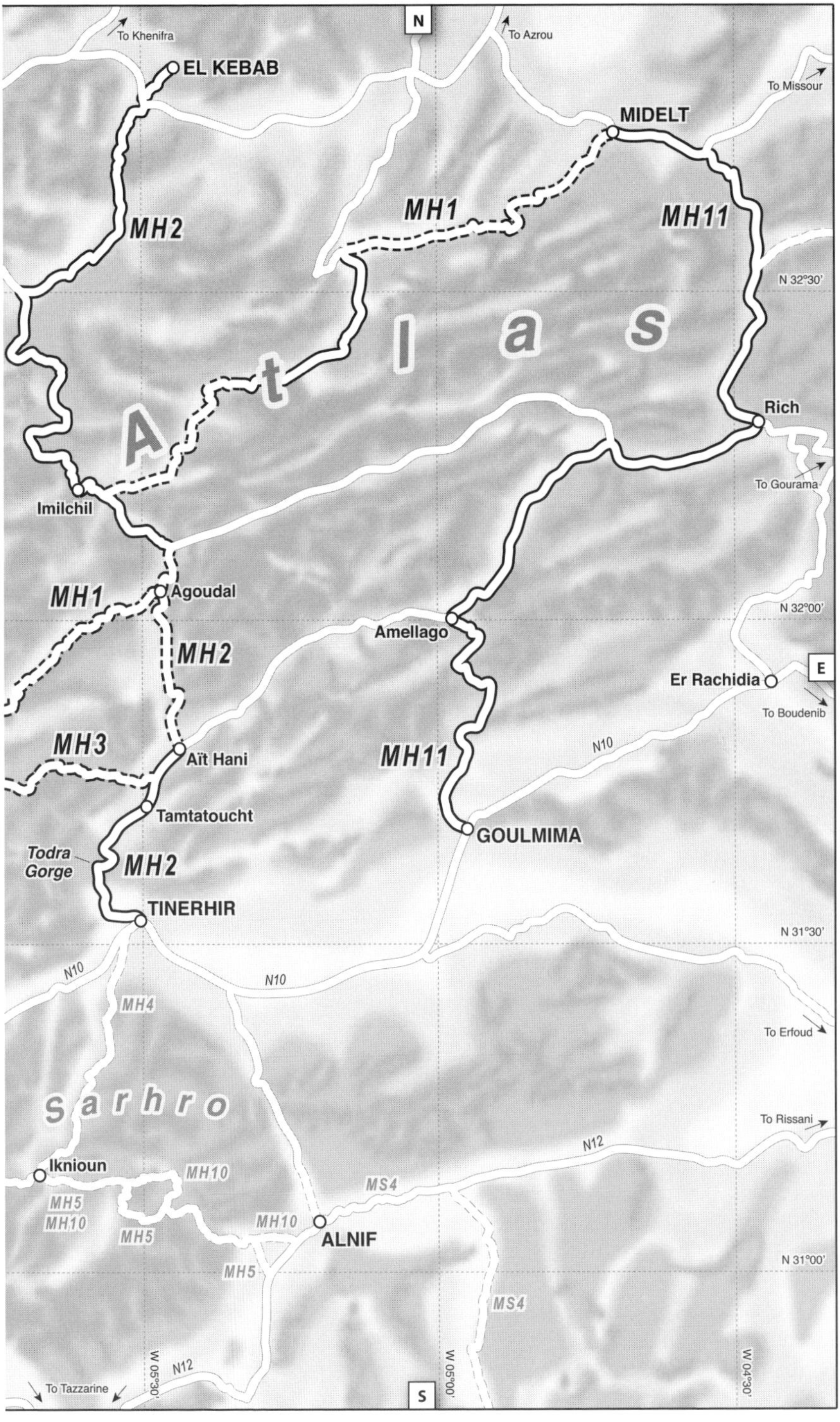

N

To Khenifra

EL KEBAB

To Azrou

To Missour

MIDELT

MH2

MH1

MH11

N 32°30'

Rich

To Gourama

Imilchil

MH1

Agoudal

MH2

Amellago

N 32°00'

E

Er Rachidia

To Boudenib

MH3

Aït Hani

MH11

N10

Todra
Gorge

Tamtatoucht

MH2

GOULMIMA

TINERHIR

N 31°30'

N10

N10

To Erfoud

MH4

To Rissani

Sarhro

N12

Iknioun

MH10

MS4

MH5
MH10

MH10

N 31°00'

MH5

ALNIF

MH5

MS4

To Tazzarine

N12

S

MH – HIGH ATLAS

## MH3   DADES – TODRA 'GORGE TO GORGE'    45KM
May 2008 ~ Mazda pickup

### Description

Situated astride the two well-touristed gorges, this is a popular high-clearance, off-road challenge between the two villages of Msemrir and Tamtatoucht. Such is its popularity that it appears on maps when other far more useful routes do not, and even the two main guidebooks attempt brief accounts, although only the LP reads like the writer has actually done it.

This route description takes the option to end at the tarmac 7km north of Tamtatoucht, a village once notorious for misguiding travellers attempting to access the link from that end. I tried it this way myself in the late 90s, before the tarmac reached Tamtatoucht, but in the end could not be bothered to out-wit the hostile attempts at misguiding. A few years later a contributor's yarn in one of my other books even had the rider pulling a knife on a *faux guide* who'd led him up a dead end! It may sound like an over-reaction but if you've never been to Africa before, when you don't know where you are or where you're going or are yet to tune in to local sensibilities, it can quickly get quite intimidating and make you paranoid.

The tarmac road to Aït Hani now makes all this less of a problem and an explosion of auberges and associated tourist services in Tamtatoucht presumably gives them something else to do. Msemrir by comparison is close enough to the start of the clear route to make effective misguiding (or warnings that only a guide knows the way) all the more difficult, but at KM2.3 they will try!

These hassles only exist at either end; once on the route you're unlikely to encounter any confusion or tricks; only Berber shepherds inhabit this bleak valley to beg or to sell trinkets. It was here we first encountered kids earnestly 'sweeping away' pebbles from the track as we approached. It's better than blocking the way with full-sized stones or throwing them of course, but seemed a particularly demeaning, ineffectual and initially perplexing form of attracting attention. You can see why some Moroccans regard tourism as a curse and are ashamed of how it has affected their kids.

We did this route on an overcast day so the scrubby hills were not exactly in a blaze of glory but even then, by Moroccan standards it's comparatively dull once you have a chance to relax out of the limestone gorge at the start. The scenery gets better at the eastern end as you emerge high above the Aït Hani plains, but MH3 has neither the barren purity of the desert or the lushness of the best oasis routes.

### Off road

You'll hear many yarns from the *faux guides* about the horrors of this route and one guidebook claimed the crossing was easier east to west. If anything the opposite is true, it could just be Tamtatoucht spin to encourage travellers to start there and invest in local guiding services.

Nevertheless, after MH5, this is technically the second **toughest route** in this book (though way easier and infinitely more popular than MH5) and following The Rains became briefly impassable. At this time *Morocco Overland* contributor Tim Cullis took over 12 hours to drag a group of bikes through, though within a week or two the popularity of the route saw 4WDs scraping by and now it's probably back to normal. The tough sections are at either end, though inching your way through the narrow limestone gorge right at the start may alarm you as to what lies ahead. Stuck inside a car here, the exact route is not easy to see; hopping out for a quick foot recce can save backing up or vehicle damage. Doing so I found a bike's broken lever which told its own story…

This gnarly section ends at KM10 and in good weather, no matter what you're told, what lies ahead is straightforward both technically and especially navigationally. With that behind you, only the slabbery at the far end as you descend to the Aït Hani plains requires more low ranging in a 4WD or on a bike, riding gently to protect the rims while keeping your balance and watching where you're going.

Of course all this does not account for mud, running water, ripped out riverbanks and even snow. The crossing tops out at a not-insubstantial 2639m which is sure to be snowbound (and of course not cleared by machines) in mid-winter, a time when many visit Morocco.

Although I've made hasty assumptions before, I'm confident you will not see a Mercedes 310D minibus on this route; it's strictly for **4WDs**, **trail bikes** and **MTBs** and even they get stuck or must turn back in bad conditions. I've heard of big GSs doing this route (not too difficult in the conditions we met in May) but later on the day we did it, I came across a pair of novice Ténéré riders who chose to give Gorge to Gorge a miss.

There is **frequent traffic** in the main season. We saw at least 15 Toyotas either carrying groups or self-drive rentals piloted by somewhat bemused occupants a little out of their comfort zone, plus a bunch of mountain bikers supported by a Land Rover and a few motorbikers. Up to that point it was more tourists than I'd seen after three weeks in Morocco. Our thought was they could have picked so many more interesting routes in Morocco but what do I know! Gorge to Gorge remains a classic, convenient, short and intense mini-adventure.

## Route finding

Can be tricky with locals out to mislead you but thanks to Olaf, GPS, the internet and books like this you're one step ahead of them. They like to spin the yarn that, like the shifting dunes of the Sahara, the route changes from year to year and all your space-age gadgetry and route descriptions are to no avail.

The truth is once you've covered the kilometre and a half from the blue sign where they can wait, you're on your way in. Beyond that, until the descent begins around KM35 the route might shift by a few metres here and there, but basically it goes up one valley to the **Tizi-n Uguent Zegsaoun** pass at KM17.8 and more or less down the next, using the original track where it still exists, or the riverbeds where the track has been washed away. There is no ambiguity here, but as you look down over the Aït Hani plains many routes lead into the gorge link route which is one reason why it's easier to find the start from Msemrir, even if it's possible to avoid Tamtatoucht doing this route in reverse. If doing that or trying via Tamtatoucht, the key point if heading to Msemrir is KM38.5; from here westwards all is clear – in a route-finding sense at least. The **map** for this route is on pp132-3.

## Fuel and water

Boumalne Dades is 62km from the start at Msemrir and Tinerhir is 45km from where this route joins the tarmac so that adds up to a **152-km fuel range**. The next fuel north is at Imilchil, or Midelt or Rich to the east. No wells were seen but the creeks flowed at the far end (in May) or there may be snow to melt.

## Suggested duration

We took three hours plodding steadily in a 4WD and let a few other cars past. A sprightly moto could do it in less than two hours. On a mountain bike it can be done in a short day but would require overnighting in Msemrir, a fairly stiff haul up from Dades. It would of course be more fun without full luggage.

**0km          N31° 41.77'  W05° 49.05'**
**Msemrir** village where the tarmac ends. Wind your way north through town with several auberges and cafés, but no noticeable hassle.

**2.3 (42.7)     N31° 42.74'  W05° 48.23'**
Key point: junction at a blue sign and a spring with a **well** nearby and maybe a *faux guide* chancer or two. Three tracks diverge here. The clear track going uphill to the right seems the obvious route but it isn't (it soon curves back south).

Straight ahead is one of the Olaf tracks but in spring it may be overgrown, ploughed over or unclear. However, that is the original way into the limestone gorge, passing along the right side of a cultivated patch of land – it meets the route below at around KM4.

**3.1 (41.9)     N31° 43.12'  W05° 48.18'**
With the above route from the blue sign unclear, we carried on round to the northwest on the main track (the route over the Atlas to Agoudal) for a kilometre and with the help of Olaf turned right off the piste at this point and down into the field. Very soon another track joins from right.

**3.5 (41.5)     N31° 43.15'  W05° 48.01'**
Head east on a rutted track across the field.

**3.9 (41.1)     N31° 43.10'  W05° 47.75'**
Cross the field and head for red earth track heading east. Both Olaf routes have now converged.

**4.4 (40.6)     N31° 43.16'  W05° 47.45'**
Another track joins from the left. You're now right on track to continue the crossing. Head into the narrow limestone gorge where the track goes in and out of the stony oued. There is no single clear way, just follow the most-used route or one which your vehicle has least trouble on. In a car it can be tortuous, low range stuff for a while and bikers may find it easier to walk their machines under power over some bits. You can imagine that after heavy rain this narrow gorge would get quite a rinse out.

**10.2 (34.8)    N31° 43.59'  W05° 44.50'**
Emerge with some relief from the limestone gorge. The track eases right up and either follows the original piste or dips in and out of the oued.

**18 (27)        N31° 44.58'  W05° 41.30'**
You're at the high point, 2639m on the **Tizi n Uguent Zegsaoun** watershed. Depending on the condition of the track you can take the direct route steeply down to the left.

**21.5 (23.5)    N31° 45.21'  W05° 40.42'**
After several switchbacks on the way down from the pass you drop into a oued, but are still at 2450m.

**23.6 (21.4)    N31° 45.28'  W05° 39.21'**
Still in the oued you pass through a red rock defile.

**26 (19)        N31° 44.98'  W05° 38.09'**
Leave the oued.

**26.5 (18.5)    N31° 45.06'  W05° 37.76'**
At this junction cross a oued and go steeply uphill, or take the alternative track

which goes to the left for an easier crossing and which joins this route 200m later.

**32.2 (12.8)    N31° 44.57'  W05° 35.04'**
Pass a cave on the left and enter a stream. In 500m you drive out on the north side of a oued. An exposed low range ascent follows.

**33.8 (11.2)**
Pass caves occupied by shepherds on the left high above the valley floor.

**35.2 (9.8)    N31° 44.35'  W05° 33.61'**
A couple of kilometres of nasty low range slabs begin here. In a couple of hundred metres at N31° 44.26'  W05° 33.56' head left steeply downhill on slabs.

In 500m head round the north side of a rounded hill. A short cut steeply down to the left looked a bit washed-out to us but was probably fine.

**37.3 (7.7)    N31° 44.10'  W05° 33.03'**
The steep short cut above rejoins your track from the left above *Auberge Taghrot* at N31° 44.15' W05° 33.02'. Another track here leads steeply uphill and links up somewhere above.

**38.5 (6.5)    N31° 43.91'  W05° 32.74'**
Key junction. Turn south here for Tamtatoucht about 8km away, (making a

total crossing distance of around 47km). We went left towards the tarmac road. In 500m take the left track at N31° 43.84' W05° 32.64' and continue winding your way westwards. Around here there may be deviations to get round sometimes muddy sections.

**41 (4)    N31° 43.71'  W05° 31.47'**
Fork left; a more direct if rougher route on to the tarmac.

**43 (2)    N31° 44.08'  W05° 30.52'**
Pass over some stones presumably blocking the way from where you've just come but we had no problem getting here. This looked like a genuine 'road ahead washed out' warning rather than a false block to misguide you, as there was no one around for miles. Pylons are visible ahead alongside the tarmac road.

**44 (1)    N31° 44.08'  W05° 30.06'**
Cross a small oued.

**45    N31° 44.22'  W05° 29.71'**
**Join the tarmac** at a non-descript point about 7 or 8km north of **Tamtatoucht** and about the same distance south of **Aït Hani**. There are several auberges in Tamtatoucht now, and that's even before you've got to the **Todra Gorge** and Tinerhir.

MH – HIGH ATLAS

## MH4   TINERHIR – IKNIOUN – NEKOB    112KM
November 2008 ~ Yamaha Ténéré, BMW 1200GS & BMW GS1150

### Description
Situated between the desert and the High Atlas, the distinctive **Jebel Sarhro** massif is considered separate from the Atlas. However it's similarly mountainous and may experience the same weather over 2000m and so, like the Jebel Sirwa, gets grouped in the MH zone.

Crossing the basalt massif of the Jebel Sarhro, this piste makes a direct and spectacular link between the ever-popular locales of the Todra Gorge and Zagora in the south. It rises gradually over the high plains north of Iknioun and then turns west and south up to the 2316m Tizi n Tazazert pass.

From here the vegetation as well as the scenery takes a dramatic turn as a series of basalt ridges, flat-topped mesas and ravines of twisted black rock unrolls ahead of you. It's a fabulous descent and you'll want to stop again and again to marvel at, and photograph, your surroundings.

In 2008 this route was covered twice in the opposite direction as far as KM53 and the Tinerhir end was checked up to KM3.5. Nevertheless, having covered the southern half northbound, I still think it's best done heading southwards as described below, allowing the drama of the Sarhro ranges to unfold before you in the late afternoon light.

## Off road

The track gets rough once over the top but despite this fact, old Mercedes vans still manage it and anyway, coming down is less of a strain on a **2WD**; you just have to ease gently over the bigger rock steps. Being bare rock as opposed to loose stones and earth there's nothing for any heavy rain to wash out, though there may be some puddles and creek crossings further down as you pass the cultivated area after the *Auberge Tazlout* at KM84. Apart from these possibly muddy patches and of course allowing for the weather, **motorcycles** as large as they come running road tyres manage this route fine, and I even saw a pair of loaded up MTB-ers nearing Nekob one time.

With an easy asphalt link coming up from Dades to Iknioun, the northern half of this route gets less traffic than it used to, but it all meets up on the impressive south side of Sarhro. Besides the self-contained **mountain bikers** we saw at least a dozen self-drive or local 4WD tours, a few motorbikers and a couple of local Mercedes vans.

## Route finding

Assuming nothing has changed too radically from the account between KM3 and -53 (the bikes I did it with in 2008 carried on this way) it's all a straight forward up one side–down the other. The **map** is on pp142-3.

## Fuel and water

Tinerhir and Nekob for fuel. There can be snow on the pass, run-off on the north side and water at the auberges and villages plus the odd well as indicated.

## Suggested duration

It's a slow descent in a car so allow a short day to cover the 112km.

**0km**          **N31° 31.24'  W05° 32.00'**
*TOTAL* fuel station on the north side of the main road in **Tinerhir**. Leave to the west through the town but after around 220m, close to a *Banque Populaire*, turn south at the lights at the sign for the *Hotel Timbuktu*. Continue down this road, past shops and then houses to the very end of this road, right through a possibly new housing development (foundations in April 2008).

**3 (109)**
The road ends near a sewage outlet and low bridge. Turn right, or south-west for a few hundred metres to the very corner of the plots / finished apartments.

**3.5 (107.5)     N31° 29.60'  W05° 32.04'**
**Leave the asphalt** at the corner and follow the gravel track heading south-south-west past a low walled enclosure on your left with a hill with a turret on top visible not far to the right. Radio masts are visible on the horizon. From here to KM53 the exact details are several years old.

**8 (104)**
Cross a oued and enter a village with a palmerie. Continue south-south-west through the village passing a pink mosque on the right as you leave.

**10 (102)**
Pass an access track to the radio mast on the right. Keep left. The track becomes

stony. In 2km cross a oued after which the track turns towards the south-south-west, aiming for the hills.

**14 (98)**
The track heads up a river bed for 500m and soon you start climbing into the hills. Then, after a kilometre or so the track flattens out and snakes along a valley.

**22 (90)**
Cross a oued and continue along its western bank. The heading is generally southwest as you sometimes drive along the creek bed.

**24 (88)**
Leave the oued and start climbing sharply into the hills above. Within a kilometre you get to a distinctive extruded fin of black rock after which the track twists upwards again for the next few kilometres.

**28 (84)          N31° 19.6'  W05° 35.4'**
A track joins from the right, with buildings visible below.

**30 (82)**
Elevation 1850m. The track flattens out to give a view of the possibly snow-topped mountains to the east. Half a kilometre later you begin descending with a village visible in the valley below.

**32 (80)**
Near some cultivated land on the left a track goes off to the right. Take the left track. In a few hundred metres you pass some houses on the left. Then the track curves upwards again through a landscape of boulders and grassy tussocks.

**34 (78)          N31° 17.8'  W05° 35.6'**
Having flattened out, the track forks. Take the right fork, bearing south-south-west. A kilometre later you pass a **well** on the left of the piste and nearly two kilometres later (KM37.6) a thin flat sandy oued, resembling a track, crosses the piste.

**40 (72)**
After you've passed a few buildings on the left and stone ruins on the right, a couple of tracks join from the right.

**43 (69)**
Pass a few more buildings up to this point where a track joins from the left.

**44 (68)          N31° 13.1'  W05° 37.3'**
Junction with the Agoultine mine track leading off to the east. Soon you begin heading south-west and pass a small village.

**49 (63)**
A large **well** on the right. In a kilometre you cross a oued with some houses on the right.

**53 (59)          N31° 10.56'  W05° 40.06'**
Junction. Left is Route MH5 coming from Alnif and the less gruelling MH10 going to Alnif. Turn right for Iknioun.

**54 (58)          N31° 10.24'  W05° 40.46'**
**Iknioun**. A busy little town with a couple of cafés and an auberge right in the centre. Seems to be the place for Yamaha 50s. The **tarmac starts here**; follow it out of town along the valley to the west, past a copse with the 2712m Sarhro high point of Amaloun n Mansour to your left.

**59 (53)          N31° 10.22'  W05° 43.58'**
The tarmac to Dades runs off to the north-west; you leave it here to the west **along a piste**.

**60 (52)**
**Aït Moraid** village. Your chance to buy locally-made cedar wood cups with attractive brass trim. They sure smell nice.

**63 (49)          N31° 09.56'  W05° 45.75'**
Junction. Right goes to Tiourit. You keep left going south, descending for a few hundred metres at which point the track begins to climb again. Over the next couple of kilometres there are a number of false passes followed by further ascents.

**66 (46)          N31° 08.34'  W05° 46.11'**
**Tizi n Tazazert Pass** (2316m). Over the next 6km or so you pass the *Café Tizi* entrenched at 2299m among the outcrops (omelette 12dh; half-board in plain stone cabins 110dh) and the spectacularly situated and even more basic *Hotel Café Tiza*.

MH – HIGH ATLAS

From here on, the rock-step descent sets in with great views all around.

**84 (28)          N31° 03.24'   W05° 47.27'**
With the major part of the descent over, the *Auberge Tazlout Bab n Ali* (40dh in dorms, 110dh half board) is a nice spot to end up if you don't want to push on to Nekob. There's another similar auberge a kilometre later.

Cultivation resumes as the track passes dry stone walls. In a while you cross a oued and continue along its western bank with fields to your left

**95 (17)          N30° 58.55'   W05° 48.99'**
Fork: left is down to village of Tirhremt n Oudrar, you curve right and uphill around the village and palmerie below. Soon after here, around some sharp bends you may find your route splits from Olaf for a kilometre or so.

**100 (12)          N30° 56.62'   W05° 49.67'**
A track branches off to the left and joins the highway about 5km east of Nekob. Keep right for the regular way to Nekob.

**107.5 (4.5)      N30° 53.86'   W05° 52.09'**
A track and pylons join from the right which lead to a village. In less than a kilometre another track joins from the right at N30° 53.38'  W05° 52.03'.

**109 (3)          N30° 52.99'   W05° 52.24'**
Arrive at the oued and cross it, coming out by a blue sign near some radio masts (N30° 52.99'  W05° 52.23'; a handy point to aim for if doing this route in reverse and taking the track north-west from the side of the ZIZMO). From here follow tracks to the south-east and enter Nekob.

**110              N30° 52.16'   W05° 52.68'**
ZIZMO fuel station on the south-west edge of **Nekob**.

We stayed at the *Auberge Ennakil* just out past the east end of town, a handy place with great views from the terrace north over the palmerie and the Sarhro massif beyond. There's secure parking inside the compound and small rooms for 160dh or bigger en suites upstairs for 250dh – both half board. The food was OK but for me the stay was spoiled by the tiresome high spirits of the teenagers who'd been left to run the joint.

# MH5    ALNIF – IKNIOUN – DADES                    116KM

April and November 2008 ~ Mazda pickup, Yamaha Ténéré

## Description

Over the top from Alnif is a lot harder than anything else in this book, following a track up onto the Sarhro massif that suddenly deteriorates and is destined to be ever less used by vehicles between KM42 and KM55 following the completion of a new route in 2008 (Route MH11). Depending on who's been through and made repairs to the road since the last rains, the route may be impassable and so that task may fall to you. The only people to travel it seem to be some bikes and 4WD drivers looking for a challenge. On this route they'll surely get it.

As on so many pistes of this type in Morocco, it's interesting to observe the change in the villagers as the altitude and remoteness sets in. Up high the peasants are poorer and reserved and behave conservatively. Just 20 kilometres away and 1000 metres lower down in sat dish country, the kids are riding bikes and whoop hyperactively as you pass by in your space ship. As elsewhere, many appear to be in urgent need of writing instruments or confectionery, but at least are light-hearted in their demands.

While it might be comparable with the Jebel Sirwa massif, geologically-distinctive Jebel Sarhro's south side is a lot drier. Where Sirwa feels alpine in places, fed by Toubkal's rains, Sarhro has a Mediterranean, or given the gradients maybe even a Corsican feel in its foliage, colouring, scents and wildlife. The drama of Sarhro's volcanic ranges is most evident looking down or across from 2000m or so, over a vista of conical peaks and ragged ridges of twisted, igneous rock. All you have to do is manage to reach that height! The day I first tried it in the Mazda the weather had cleared after a week in the desert with scorching sand winds and orange skies so I could have been overdosing on ozone. I wasn't the only one; I saw a pair of lizards whose back halves were no less blue than the sky.

## Off road

In the right hands a Jeep or a Defender 90 would walk up this route with little more than a shrug; an agile LWB Defender or any moderately lifted, full-size **4WD** on tall tyres might make light work of it too. A locking rear diff won't do any harm in some spots. Otherwise, unless your axles can flex like Olga Korbut after an olive oil sauna, at the cost of some axle clearance it may help to **reduce tyre pressures** to get more traction over some boulders and rock steps.

In the state I first encountered the track, any longer or lower vehicle on less tall tyres would not have scraped through; it depends on how much work you want to put into it and how confident you feel. Alone and already with one broken rear spring and driving more of a load carrier than a rock crawler, these qualities ran out for me at KM49. From here I walked up to about KM51.5, a pass facing the **Tizi n Ouli Ousir** next to a 2211m peak; KM54. On the way, I passed enough additional axle-wrenching sections to make me glad I'd spared the car.

A few days later I approached the track from the Iknioun end and easily drove to within a kilometre of the Tizi n Ouli Ousir. And a few months later I managed to ride and push my laden **motorbike** up to the pass but this small victory was soured by the oil dripping from a cracked crankcase, collapsed forks, a dented rim, flat tyre and a sore head! Either way I'm sure glad I wasn't on a 1200GSA with a metre-wide profile of shin-snapping, rock-snagging alloy boxes. It may well have been done like this, but on a bike MH5 is one route worth doing as a loop (see p93) with all the clobber left at a hotel.

Slung over a shoulder, **mountain bikes** make short work of ruined tracks but carrying a load will be tough on the rims, rack and legs. MTBers will also enjoy this track combined in a loop with MH11 without full baggage.

## Route finding

This route is fully Olaffed. It's hard to get lost driving up the valley but at the sharp end it can get hard to follow the actual track in some washed-out creeks. Here it pays to get out and walk so you don't end up having to back out awkwardly or get yourself hung up on a rock. The only local traffic to be found on the high ground will be donkeys; beyond the villages you're on your own for the meaty part of the route. Finally I can say with some confidence that you will not encounter any Transit or Merc vans traversing the full length of MH5.

# Routes MH4, MH5 & MH10 (Jebel Sarhro)

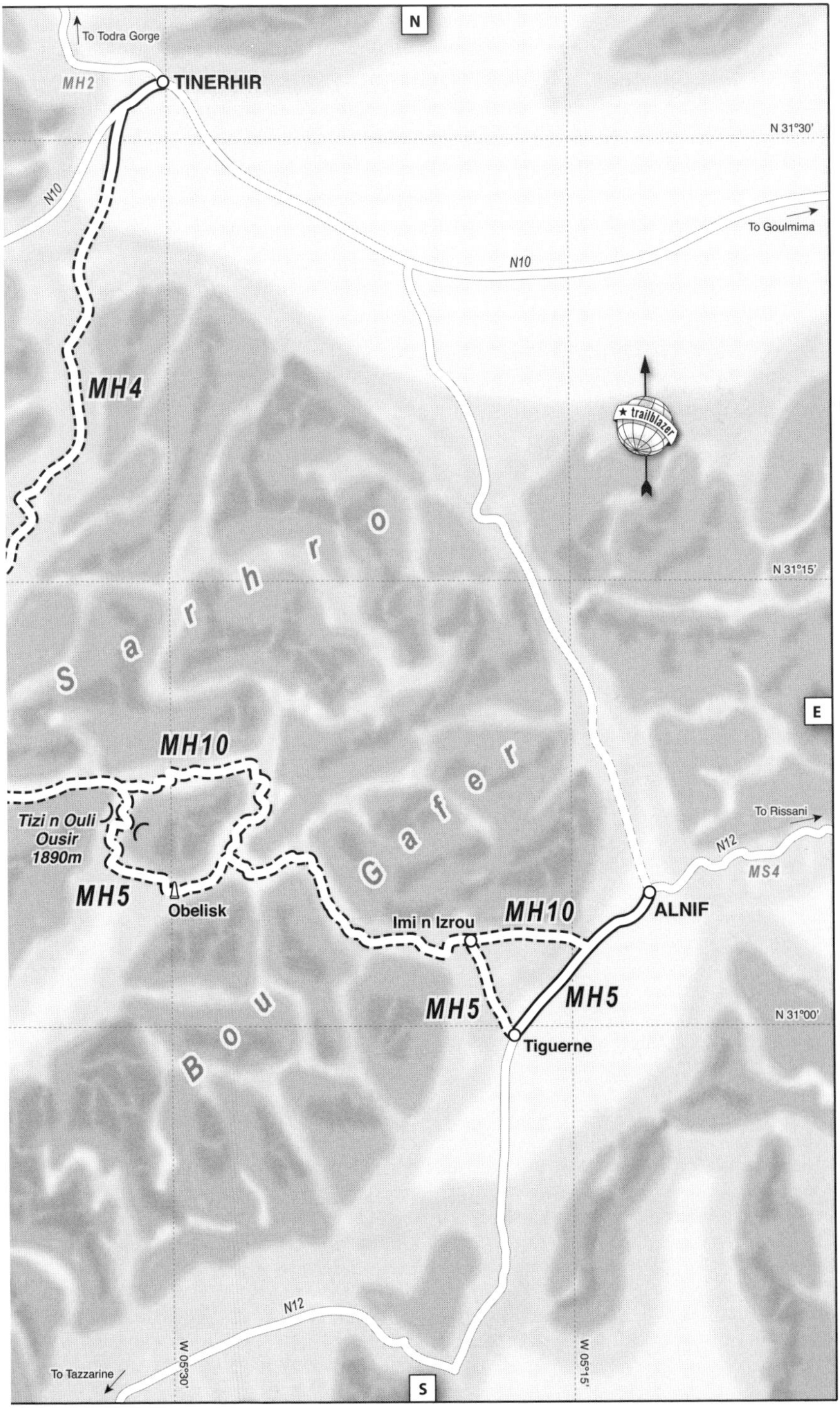
N
To Todra Gorge
MH2
TINERHIR
N 31°30'
N10
To Goulmima
N10
MH4
trailblazer
Sarhro
N 31°15'
E
MH10
Bou Gafer
Tizi n Ouli Ousir 1890m
To Rissani
N12
MS4
MH5
Obelisk
Imi n Izrou
MH10
ALNIF
MH5
MH5
N 31°00'
Tiguerne
N12
To Tazzarine
W 05°30'
S
W 05°15'

At KM55, but not a moment earlier, the difficulties dissolve as you join the improved Iknioun-Alnif track. The **map** for this route is on pp142-3.

Incidentally, the old Route M4 from *Sahara Overland* starts just west of the **Hotel Bougafer** and bus stop in Alnif and goes past the red and white radio tower where it curves north. The first 15km are a wide corrugated track; from there on the next 30km over the pass to the N10 are sealed.

## Fuel and water

Alnif and Dades for fuel. Several wells as indicated. What running water there was was barely an inch deep in late spring but was more evident after The Rains in November 2008.

## Suggested duration

In a 4WD leave Alnif early to give yourself a full day to make it across, turn back and reverse MH11 or just plain turn back. You'll need about 4–5 hours out of Alnif to get past the worst of it, possibly including some time for rock clearing, recce-ing and road building.

Motorbikes will have fewer delays but need some skill to keep upright while mountain bikes will want to make two fun days of it.

**0km**            **N31° 06.75'   W05° 10.34'**
**Alnif** Ziz on the east side of town with a resto (brochettes, salad, chips, 2 coffees 70dh) and internet over the road. For details of the **hotels** here see the end of Route MS4.

Drive west through town, past the other Ziz at the west end of town and past the Olaffed turn-off (N31° 05.35'   W05° 12.63) about 5km after the Ziz. At the time of logging, the Olaf route was rough and neglected so the more-used route from Tiguerne to Imi-n Izrou below was chosen, but Olaf's been re-graded since.

**11 (105)          N31° 02.67'   W05° 15.41'**
Turn north off the highway just before Tiguerne village **onto a graded track** to Imi-n Izrou village.

**17 (99)           N31° 05.56'   W05° 17.27'**
The Olaf route mentioned above (now also graded) joins from the right by the Oued Tazlaft below **Imi-n Izrou**.

Within a kilometre you cross the oued (with a well on the right) and drive steeply up through town, passing a building on the left with coloured balcony balustrades. There's no need to follow the Olaf detour around to the left unless you're very shy.

**19 (97)           N31° 05.22'   W05° 17.97'**
Leave town to the west and pass through the gap in the range along the south side of the Oued Tazlaft. Tazlaft village is directly ahead. Follow the track up the valley, initially along the oued and passing some finely made dry stone buildings.

**31 (85)           N31° 07.10'   W05° 23.20'**
The track turns west up the valley towards the peaks.

**38 (78)           N31° 08.01'   W05° 26.43'**
This junction appeared a few months after this route was initially logged; the point where Route MH11 at KM81.5 comes in from the north (on your right). This is a new and easier way to Iknioun, avoiding the Tizi n Ouli Ousir pass.

**39 (77)           N31° 07.44'   W05° 27.06'**
Pass by a **well** (25m) with a rope on the left of the piste.

**42 (74)           N31° 07.11'   W05° 28.76'**
Come over a rise and you see what lies ahead...

**44 (72)           N31° 07.43'   W05° 28.94'**
Cross a oued and a steep, loose climb commences.

**47 (69)      N31° 07.68'  W05° 30.51'**
You reach an ominous obelisk indicating
'1710m' which is about right. It commem-
orates one of the last battles for French
colonial dominance here in 1933 over the
Aït Atta Berbers. The truly gnarly section
now begins.

**48 (68)      N31° 08.32'  W05° 30.71'**
Cross a stream in a small gorge.
Depending on your ground clearance and
presence of recent tracks, the best way
ahead may require a short walk to work
out.

**49 (67)      N31° 08.63'  W05° 31.04'**
After more marginal, diff-scraping
manoeuvres I parked up at this point,
close to a seemingly abandoned hamlet
(although there were some peasants
around).

From here I walked 2.5km up the track
to about N31° 08.94' W05° 30.91', a saddle
west of a cone hill. From this pass the
track dropped into a bowl (photo below
right) and climbed up again to a higher
pass, the Tizi n Ouli Ousir about 2km
away. Tizi n Ouli Ousir is marked on some
paper maps and is unmarked but alongside peak '2211' on the French 250k maps.

A few days later I walked over the
Ousir pass from the north side (leaving
the car about 500m before the pass – it
was quicker to walk) and dropped
halfway down into the bowl, and a few
months later also rode from the north to
this point.

Nothing in the bowl and up to the cone
hill to the south looked any harder than
the 2.5km section I'd walked up from the
south side. Therefore, from where I left
the car on the south side to where I rode
with the bike from the north side just over
the Tizi n Ouli Ousir is a little over 4km,
with about one kilometre unwalked.

**54 (62)      N31° 09.65'  W05° 30.59'**
**Tizi n Ouli Ousir** pass, 1890m. From here
a very stony few hundred metres leads
down to the new Iknioun-Alnif track. On
a bike or in a car you'll have to inch down
to avoid possible damage to the undercarriage.

**55 (61)      N31° 10.17'  W05° 30.58'**
Join the much better track and turn left or

west for Iknioun and Dades. Turning right
here follows a new track to Alnif (Route
MH11), something you might wish you'd
known about if getting this far has cost
you.

**59 (57)      N31° 10.20'  W05° 32.35'**
A **well** on the right and cultivation all
around. Soon another **well** appears on the
left.

**64 (52)      N31° 09.94'  W05° 34.94'**
Crest a 1957m pass with a view of the
Iknioun valley ahead. As you continue
down, tracks join from left and right, with
several **wells** in the next few kilometres.

**72 (44)      N31° 10.56'  W05° 40.06'**
The track from Tinerhir (Route MH4) joins
from right with a red and white radio
tower on the left.

**73 (43)      N31° 10.27'  W05° 40.44'**
**Iknioun** centre with an auberge, lots of
Yamaha 50s and a couple of cafés. **Start of
the tarmac**. A kilometre out of town
there's a shady copse on the right.

**78 (48)      N31° 10.22'  W05° 43.58'**
Route MH4 over the Tizi n Tazazert Pass
leaves the tarmac to the left and heads
west as the tar turns north-west.

**111 (5)      N31° 21.84'  W05° 54.85'**
Join the N10 highway. Turn left for Dades
or right for Tinerhir.

**116 (0)      N31° 22.01'  W05° 58.05'**
*INOV* fuel station on the eastern edge of
**Boumalne du Dades**.

Looking south from the Tizi n Ouli Ousir to
the cone hill at KM52. Is there a problem?

## MH6   AGUIM – AOULOUZ                                   125KM
April 2008 ~ Mazda pickup

### Description
If you've just come from Marrakech over the Tizi n Tichka and are looking to
get yourself west, this route will take you there over the southern side of the
High Atlas. After you turn off the N9 the tarmac ends beneath the slopes of
**Jebel Toubkal** where a rough track drops down past cascades and through a
string of villages to the valley floor, bringing to mind the Hunza valley of
northern Pakistan, although Moroccan towns are actually more picturesque.
You re-emerge at Aoulouz, midway between Taroudant and Taliouine.

### Off road
The road out of Aguim is sealed but twisting and narrow and once the asphalt
ends at KM37 it's initially a rough and possibly muddy descent into what
might be called the upper Souss valley. But incredibly, **Transit vans** possibly
older than you and with a full load, manage it daily; at times you may need to
back up for them. In rain this would become a messy run but at least you'll be
slithering downhill.

### Route finding
Nothing to tax the brain here; ride up the hill and down the other side. If you
get in a muddle there are plenty of people to ask. Not all the branches and
forks appearing on Olaf were evident, possibly due to roadworks and the fact
that it got dark around me.

There are plenty of **other routes** criss-crossing this region; broadly speaking the **Jebel Sirwa** massif. You could make a great couple of days of it by linking parts of Routes MH7 and MH8. If coming up from Ouarzazate you could
start this route by taking the initially sealed road to Bou Tazoult about 40km
before Aguim, joining this route at KM17 near Sour. The **map** for this route is
on pp152-3.

### Fuel and water
Fuel at Aguim and Aoulouz and plenty of water running off the slopes, out of
springs and in the villages.

### Suggested duration
This can be done in half a day, or in a day out of Marrakech or Ouarzazate. The
off-road stage is fairly congested or steep, with comparatively few opportunities for a secluded overnight stop. Neither Aguim nor Aoulouz look such great
places to stay, but at the far end Taliouine or Taroudant will have plenty of
what you want.

| | |
|---|---|
| **0km**          **N31° 09.50'  W07° 27.78'**<br>TOTAL fuel station at the south end of<br>**Aguim**. Head north for 500m and turn to<br>the north-west. Soon the snowfields of<br>Toubkal appear as you pass through a<br>string of villages. | **17 (108)         N31° 07.83'  W07° 35.65'**<br>There's no clear sign of the route back<br>south-east to Bou Tazoult, but look care-<br>fully and it crosses the oued just after a<br>hairpin before Sour. It joins the main N9<br>highway at N31° 05.42' W07° 17.84'. |

**22 (103)    N31° 05.67'  W07° 37.19'**
Village of **Sour** (not that any sign tells you so).

**37 (88)    N31° 02.16'  W07° 42.36'**
At a wide saddle below Toubkal and with a red radio mast 500m to the north-east, Route MH8 leaves the tar to the south for Askaoun. **The tarmac ends** a couple of hundred metres further west at N31° 02.17' W07° 42.55'.

Here the challenging driving or riding begins (allow up to 3 hours to Aoulouz) as you drop down from the pass past possibly running water, red rock shelves, grassy green meadows and several villages. Or it could be a foot of snow over a muddy quagmire.

**53 (72)    N30° 59.60'  W07° 48.89'**
After a long and at times tortuous descent you pass a **hotel-café**, probably in or near the village of **Assarag** which appears on some maps and signs.

A right turn here leads up a tortuous route about 12km to a viewpoint over **Lac Ifni** right below the summit of Toubkal. Allow up to half a day there and back, depending on the track conditions.

**60 (65)    N30° 57.34'  W07° 49.58'**
You turn down some sharp hairpins and the worst of the descent is behind you.

Around here a track possibly leads out south-east to points on Route MH8.

**64 (61)    N30° 56.11'  W07° 51.43'**
Cross a river and the track improves. Two kilometres later you pass a rockslide area and then the track improves still further.

**79 (46)    N30° 50.58'  W07° 54.00'**
Junction with a track that presumably leads east to Timgdal, or possibly to KM30 on Route MH7.

**101 (24)    N30° 44.35'  W07° 58.91'**
**Rejoin the tarmac** near a reservoir on the south side of the road. Within a kilometre you pass the turn-off left which passes below the dam wall and leads back up east to Askaoun; Route MH7 to Tazenacht.

**119 (6)    N30° 42.44'  W08° 08.48'**
A tarmac road joins from the left and the road becomes wider.

**121 (4)    N30° 42.04'  W08° 09.17'**
Roundabout on the main N10 Taroudant –Taliouine road. Turn left or south.

**125    N30° 40.41'  W08° 10.54'**
**Aoulouz** town centre *MOBIL*, with a *SHELL* serving unleaded a few hundred metres further on.

# MH7    AOULOUZ – ASKAOUN – TAZENACHT    166KM
April and November 2008 ~ Mazda pickup and Yamaha Ténéré.

## Description
A thrilling traversal up and over the highest drivable point of the **Jebel Sirwa** massif over the sub-alpine meadows with grass green enough to induce travel sickness. Out of Aoulouz you follow a tar road as far as the reservoir and then branch off around KM24 for the valley drive up to the heights of Askaoun, the crossroads of the Sirwa, and where route MH8 comes up from Taliouine on the way up to Aguim. Your route lies east where you rattle your way over two 2500m-plus passes, Tizi n Tleta and Tizi n Melloul, surrounded by patches of either snow or dazzling emerald pastures. You round the north side of Jebel Sirwa itself, 3304m high, which at one point is just a few kilometres away and gives a good chance to stretch the legs. From here the track improves with more spectacular views across the valleys and plains as you wind down to Tachakoucht, with a particularly good-looking old town, to meet the ever-encroaching tarmac sooner rather than later.

At Anezal on the N10 highway, Tazenacht is only 26km to the south over an impressive pass and viewpoint, but alphaphiles can take the road north to Amerzgane and Aguim to pick up Route MH6 back to Aoulouz via Assarag and Aouzioua, so completing one of the few tours in Morocco composed of towns and villages only beginning with 'A'.

In April at least, while Taliouine and points south were cooking oppressively, up in the Sirwa babbling brooks trickled off the passes, purple and yellow flowers shimmered in the restfully cool breeze and birds twittered about their business. The greenery and views were a real tonic for the eyes and anywhere up near the two passes it's worth turning off your engine to listen to birds flying and the flowers pollinating. In winter, or the pouring rain the scene may not be so bucolic but it's still worth the excursion to see how far you can get. If you get stuck it'll probably be quite soon after Askaoun from where you can drop down the steep, bendy tarmac road (reversing Route MH8) to the auberges in Taliouine.

## Off road

I rode the Aoulouz to Askaoun section on a bike soon after the October 2008 rains and, all things considered it was in good shape, taking me just over an hour from the reservoir turn-off to the top. This is 'Transit country' though and the road is only a little wider than those vans; something to bear in mind on the hairpin section after KM37.

The last few kilometres up near the top before Askaoun the track can get gnarly, as it can do even in good weather over the two high passes east of Askaoun. But then again, just as I was filming myself saying this is 'true 4WD country' and that even the Transits can't bash their way across here, an old Golf came wobbling nonchalantly down the Tizi n Tleta. As I was reminded elsewhere, tracks in Morocco exist primarily for local people to get around in **normal cars**.

A **light bike** will make light work of the rock steps and even on a heavy GS and the like, it would be a great ride as the very rough sections are quite short and the rewards worthwhile. With its copious water points and sheltered spots, this route, or versions of it, would also make a great mountain bike ride. You can carry an **MTB** over the worst of the snow or the mud and enjoy a great descent to Anezal and beyond.

## Route finding

Straightforward, it's fully Olaffed and for once reasonably accurate on the Michelin and RKH maps, although there isn't much traffic on the piste sections. For this route's **map** see pp152-3.

## Fuel and water

Aoulouz and Tazenacht, as well as a ZIZ the eastern point of the N10/N9 triangle of roads near Aït Benhaddou. There is plenty of water tickling down off the mountain as fresh as a daisy. You pass a well as you approach Askaoun.

## Suggested duration

A full day as described but it would be a shame not to spend a night out, ideally over 8000ft.

**0km**          **N30° 40.27'  W08° 10.71'**
**Aoulouz** main street *SHELL* with unleaded
super, which the *MOBIL* up the road does
not have. Head north-east out of town on
the road to Taroudant.

**5 (161)**          **N30° 42.03'  W08° 09.20'**
Cross the bridge over the Oued Souss and
at the roundabout turn right for
Aouzioua.

**6.5 (159.5)**     **N30° 42.44'  W08° 08.48'**
A road leads off to the right; you carry on
straight, north-east.

**18 (148)**          **N30° 43.89'  W08° 01.91'**
**Aouzioua** town with a few stores.

**23.5 (142.5)**     **N30° 44.18'  W07° 59.34'**
**Leave the tarmac** and turn right to pass
through gardens right below the dam
wall and head up the other side.

**25 (141)**          **N30° 44.01'  W07° 59.10'**
Turn sharp left here and continue uphill to
follow the south edge of the reservoir
eastwards.

**30 (136)**          **N30° 42.47'  W07° 57.10'**
Cross a big bridge and turn right. Turning
left here probably brings you to KM79 on
Route MH6.

**33 (133)**          **N30° 42.09'  W07° 55.75'**
After a brief downhill stretch turn left off
the track and soon cross a concrete bridge
to the north side of the river.

**35 (131)**
Tizzouguine village.

**37 (129)**          **N30° 42.12'  W07° 53.53'**
Around here you leave the river and get
stuck into the steep climb up to Askaoun
which barely relents for a metre.

**64 (102)**          **N30° 44.27'  W07° 46.65'**
Arrive at Route MH8 just south of
**Askaoun**, just after a **well**. At this point if
you can get to KM65 without crushing
someone's prize marrows then give it a
go. Otherwise turn north along the pine
avenue for 300m to the flag stand in front
of an official-looking building (N30°
44.43'  W07° 46.65'). Here turn back south-

east through the trees for 350m toward the
minibus park (N30° 44.30'  W07° 46.50')
by the arches. Drive on east into the market place and turn right, south, out of the
square and then turn left (N30° 44.29'
W07° 46.46'). Then, after 200m (KM65)
fork left at N30° 44.22'  W07° 46.39'.

**66 (100)**          **N30° 44.27'  W07° 45.80'**
Fork right and follow a rocky washed-out
track with ground squirrels dashing about
and cairns on the track side.

**71 (95)**          **N30° 44.46'  W07° 43.35'**
Start of a rough, first-gear ascent. Soon
you enter a narrow pass, cross a small
concrete bridge where the pass opens out
and reach some ruins and flat grassy
meadows suitable for camping.

**76 (91)**          **N30° 45.26'  W07° 40.63'**
At this point, as you inch over rocks and
turn a hairpin over a stream and head
uphill, it's only 8km south-east and just
under 1000m of ascent to the summit of
**Jebel Sirwa** (3304m). There are flat grassy
camp spots around and this looks like the
easier access point off this route with
(according to the old maps) a track leading to within 2km of the summit.
   Note that getting to the actual summit
of Jebel Sirwa involves some exposed
scrambling; many trekkers don't take the
risk. If you're fired up by the idea of
trekking in the Moroccan Atlas you'll
want Trailblazer's 2009 edition of
*Moroccan Atlas – The Trekking Guide*.

**79 (87)**          **N30° 46.24'  W07° 40.53'**
At 2437m the track is better now.

**81 (85)**          **N30° 46.54'  W07° 39.95'**
Hard to tell, but this could be the **Tizi n
Tleta** (2448m), a flat pass by some outcrops with stone sheep folds and goat
holders. It's clearly used as a camping
spot, but remains clean.

**83 (83)**          **N30° 47.49'  W07° 39.66'**
The track rises still further to 2514m as a
valley opens out to the east with a tran-
shumance hamlet visible below.

**85 (81)**          **N30° 47.40'  W07° 38.77'**
Junction with a track leading down to the

MH – HIGH ATLAS

hamlet, and maybe on to other villages to the north. In a kilometre there's a sharp bend in the piste over a stream. It's another idyllic grassy camping spot and a good base for a trek towards Jebel Sirwa summit; just 9km away at 166° (but see KM76).

**88 (78)        N30° 46.97'  W07° 37.76'**
**Tizi n Melloul** at 2518m; high point on this route and now on a good track.

**90 (76)        N30° 46.89'  W07° 36.82'**
The descent begins and after a couple of hairpins another track leads down to a hamlet to the north as you come to a vista of the parched Ouarzazate plain far to the east. Tachakoucht is also visible about 15km away along the track.

**104 (62)        N30° 48.83'  W07° 33.09'**
Four tracks meet at a sign. You carry on east. Soon there's a sign for Tourtit, a village just north of the piste. The track became wide here and sealing may be imminent although it's unlikely they'll ever seal the track to Askaoun.

**107 (59)        N30° 48.19'  W07° 32.37'**
A confusing sign for Ouarzazate/ Tazenacht; carry straight on. In about a kilometre or more you come round a bend and see the pretty colours of Tachakoucht and the tarmac ahead (if you're not on it already).

**110 (56)        N30° 47.95'  W07° 31.54'**
**Join the asphalt** right by **Tachakoucht**, still at just under 2000 metres.

**126 (40)**
Tamazight village just off to the southwest as the road swings sharply east.

**140 (26)        N30° 45.46'  W07° 17.37'**
Join the N10 highway at **Anezal**: a few cafés, shops and an auberge. Tazenacht is a particularly great drive over the **Tizi-n Bachkoum** to another nice town with mellow people and great carpets.

Otherwise north leads past the seemingly abandoned **Gas Haven** 'roadhouse' – a mirage of South-west Americana but actually a film set from a 2006 remake of Wes Craven's 1977 desert mutant-psycho slasher *The Hills Have Eyes*.

A short distance later, after the Oued Iriri, the road forks: left or north for **Amerzgane** (fuel, 41km from Anezal), a nice small town with cafés and a couple of roadside **B&Bs** a few kilometres to the north on the Marrakech road. Splitting right leads to Ouarzazate which is 62km from Anezal with a ZIZ at the point of the triangle of roads where the N10 meets the N9.

Note that the N10 between Tazenacht and the ZIZ at the triangle is barely two cars wide and full of bends and climbs so whichever way you go, keep your wits about you **after dark**, especially on a bike.

**166        N30° 34.69'  W07° 12.34'**
**Tazenacht** SHELL on the north side of town with an AFRIQUIA on the west exit to Taliouine, a ZIZ on the south exit to Foum Zguid and a no-name fuel station in town just in case the other three all run out. Right opposite this town centre fuel station is a string of cafés, restaurants and a couple of cheap hotels.

For impression of the roads south of Tazenacht which go east to Agdz and south to Foum Zguid see The Desert Highway: Route MS10. For more on Tazenacht see Route MA6.

# MH8  TALIOUINE – ASKAOUN – AGUIM        133KM
April 2008 ~ Mazda pickup

## Description
This is a great route up from the Anti Atlas of Taliouine onto the sub-alpine ranges of Jebel Sirwa and the High Atlas itself. You pass from the domain of goat and palm to that of sheep, golfing-calibre grass and even cattle and horses, to rejoin the tarmac close to Jebel Toubkal's summit whose northern slopes

you'll have been watching all day, most clearly on cloud-free mornings.

The scenery is wonderfully refreshing if, like me, you've come up from the baking desert. You'll see why in Islam green is the colour of paradise, and alpine scenes on thick laminated posters adorn many cafés and roadhouse walls.

As you cross through the pass at KM71.5 the land changes from wild Mediterranean to pastoral. Here shepherds tend their flocks and herd with dogs, streams trickle to feed bright green grass and crossing a limestone basin you can't help being reminded of England's majestic Yorkshire Dales.

## Off road

This route takes a sporty direct route from KM58 to 68 after which the track hugs the very edge of the flower-speckled mountainside up to the pass. Beyond here the water which gives this route such a verdant feel could also turn it into a mud bath, so be ready for anything in rainy times, especially in mid-winter.

In good, dry conditions a **regular car** could manage this (though not from KM58 – an Olaf diversion may exist to the west) and **big bikes** too will have a great ride. On a **mountain bike** most of the height is gained along the tarmac to Askaoun. Here you might want to spend the night to give yourself a full day to get back to the tarmac and maybe even Aguim.

## Route finding

It can get a bit complicated with the mass of tracks in this region so pay close attention to the description. The route is mostly Olaffed. Minibuses trundle up to Askaoun, but you won't see much beyond that. At the top end, the narrow tarmac road is relatively busy with Transits, Bedfords and mules running between Aoulouz and Aguim and is not something to leave for the dark with weary reflexes. The **map** for this route is on pp152-3.

## Fuel and water

Taliouine and Aguim for fuel with plenty of water in the villages and streams.

## Suggested duration

This route can easily be done in a day as long as conditions are good, but Aguim is no Shangri La, so either plan to head on over to Marrakech, back down to Ouarzazate (see KM133) or camp out in the recommended spots from around KM61.5.

**0km         N30° 31.91'  W07° 55.31'**
**Taliouine** town centre fuel. Head east on the road to Tazenacht past a couple of auberges: for more see Route MA7. There is an old ksar to the south of the road which may be worth a wander.

**1.5 (131.5)     N30° 31.77'  W07° 54.44'**
Turn north off the main road for Askaoun, a twisty but asphalted scenic drive. At around KM40 you pass a nice mountain village with a rounded, castle-like ksar of dark stone beneath which might lie a thick shaggy carpet of ripening corn. In the spring all is bright green and babbling brooks; it could be the Alps.

**48 (85)       N30° 43.71'  W07° 46.53'**
A piste heads off left by a well, signed for 'Houzioua' (Route MH7 coming from Aoulouz). Soon you pass the *Auberge Noussounfou* on the right, but it may be defunct.

MH – HIGH ATLAS

Routes MH6, MH7, MH8, MH9 & MS9 (Jebel Sirwa)

N
To Marrakech
N9
MH12
0 5 10 15 20km
Tizi-n-Tichka
2260m
Telouet
N9
AGUIM
N9
trailblazer
Amerzgane
Aït Benhaddou
N 31°00'
N10
To Boumalne du Dades
N9
MH12
N10
OUARZAZATE
E
N10
N9
To Agdz
MS9
Tachakoucht
MH7
Anezal
MS9
MH9
N10
MH7, MH8
MH9
TAZENACHT
DESERT HIGHWAY
To Agdz
N10
DESERT HIGHWAY
N 30°30'
MA6, MA7
W 07°30'
W 07°00'
S
To Foum Zguid

**49.5 (83.5)  N30° 44.43'  W07° 46.65'**
**Askaoun**. A line of trees leads to a square with a flag ahead of a building with a radio mast. (The market square is to the south-east.) **Tarmac ends**. Head round the left of this building, heading north-west. Soon you cross over a pass towards the pylons at N30° 46.52'  W07° 46.82'.

**55 (78)  N30° 46.92'  W07° 46.59'**
Arabic sign for somewhere to the right.

**56.5 (76.5)**
Taouyaot ahead and a place in Arabic signed to the right. In 500m or so at N30° 48.14'  W07° 46.05' you cross a concrete bridge over a stream.

**58 (75)  N30° 48.11'  W07° 46.10'**
The palms and gardens of **Anrouz** village. Soon after this point you get to a fork where you turn right to the north: N30° 48.41'  W07° 46.05'. You're leaving Olaf which may come round to the waypoint listed at KM68, below. Soon you pass a sign pointing to the right going down to a bridge and a river. You carry on north.

**60 (73)  N30° 48.91'  W07° 45.97'**
Junction to the left, keep right and head to a village. Within 500m pass a red-walled compound on the right with glass on the wall tops. Half a kilometre later a promising sign proclaims 'Aguim' in English.

**61.5 (71.5)  N30° 49.89'  W07° 45.85'**
Here a track leads down right to a village. Keep left. Although the way ahead gets a bit thin, work your way around to N30° 49.88'  W07° 46.03', about 500m further on, then take lesser tracks up the hill to reach N30° 49.97'  W07° 46.26', another half a kilometre on (KM62.5). Struggle along a washed-out track for a bit; don't worry, it's the right way – or one of them. There are nice and quiet camping spots from here up to the pass, 10km away.

**68 (65)  N30° 51.15'  W07° 46.86'**
Just after some weathered boulders hanging over the track and an axle-flexing section is a **junction** with a fork leading downhill (west) to what looks like a more promising-looking track. If you followed Olaf at KM58 or so, it may well have come

along this main track down below to N30° 50.95'  W07° 47.46'. Down at this point a white sign indicates 'Aguim' is a right turn, back up hill to where you are now. So the route you've just taken is a less used but more direct version. Ahead at the white sign below may lead to **Assarag**; KM60 on Route MH6.

There now begins a precipitous section along the valley side to a pass – not a good place to be texting at the wheel or 'bars – although there are enough flat spaces here for scenic camps. The sunny southern aspect is popular with Mediterranean-looking plants.

**71.5 (61.5)  N30° 52.28'  W07° 46.18'**
Head through the pass (2342m) and past some old buildings. The scenery and vegetation suddenly change into a duller upland plain. In 500m or so another sign indicates Aguim.

**73 (60)  N30° 53.07'  W07° 46.18'**
A sign says Assarag is left, probably only around 10km away. Right is for Aguim. The landscape here is bleaker, with fewer flowers but with grass pasture and a smoother track.

**79 (54)  N30° 55.49'  W07° 44.97'**
With a view of **Jebel Toubkal** to the north-west, you top out at **2521m**.

**82 (51)  N30° 56.81'  W07° 44.30'**
You drop down into a grassy limestone basin with horses, sheep and dogs, and streams and karst outcrops. Pass around the east side of the basin which looks like it could get muddy in heavy rain.

**90 (43)  N31° 00.54'  W07° 42.79'**
**Limestone Pass**. Drop down and soon you'll see the red and white radio tower just beyond the tarmac road.

**92 (41)  N31° 01.39'  W07° 42.52'**
The seemingly little-used or abandoned short cut you passed earlier joins from the left.

**96 (37)  N31° 02.17'  W07° 42.36'**
**Join the asphalt** with the red radio mast about 500m to the north-east. Turn right, east, for Aguim, about an hour away

along a narrow, twisting road through a string of mountain villages.

**111 (22)**
**Sour** is the name of this village.

**116 (17)**       **N31° 07.83'   W07° 35.65'**
There's no clear sign of the alternative route south-east to **Bou Tazoult**, but look carefully and it crosses the oued just after a hairpin. It joins the main N9 highway at N31° 05.42'  W07° 17.84'.

**132 (1)**        **N31° 09.76'   W07° 27.95'**
Junction with the N9 Marrakech-Ouarzazate road in **Aguim**. Turn right, south, for the fuel station.

**133**        **N31° 09.50'   W07° 27.78'**
TOTAL fuel in Aguim. For somewhere to stay there are a couple of *chambre d'hotes* (B&Bs) by the roadside between here and Amerzgane, to the south on the road to Ouarzazate.

# MH9   TAZENACHT – TALIOUINE          94KM
November 2008 ~ Yamaha Ténéré

## Description
This track links a string of villages drained by the run-off from Jebel Sirwa to the north. You follow a track rising towards the route's 1804m high point soon after which you bounce off southwards. Despite the muddy finale I experienced, it's a fun and undemanding route if you feel you've been up and down the N10 to the south one time too many.

## Off road
Only the few poorly-drained miles of mud around KM67 might give even a 4WD something to think about, but this was following very heavy rains. Here is a rare instance where knobbly or aggressive off-road tyres would be worthwhile. Other than that, the route should be easy, even in a **2WD**.

## Route finding
The way is Olaffed up to the point where this route leaves to head south-west. I saw only one or two cars and vans on this route serving the villages. Note that the villages named on most maps and those names found locally rarely match. The map for this route is on pp152-3.

## Fuel and water
Fuel in Tazenacht and also Tinfat (no unleaded), a few kilometres after you rejoin the N10. There are plenty of villages and streams for water

## Suggested duration
Half a day will get you through, or a good day out can be had out of Ouarzazate by doing this after Route MS9 and a lunch in Tazenacht. Coming through on MS9 you get a good view of the Jebel Sirwa summit turret which at KM42 is just 12km to the north.

**0km**       **N30° 34.70'  W07° 12.34'**
**Tazenacht** SHELL on the north side of town. Take the road north towards Ouarzazate and Marrakech.

**8 (86)**
Pass a sign for Taghdoute village visible to the west.

MH – HIGH ATLAS

**9 (85)    N30° 37.91'  W07° 15.92'**
Turn off to the west by a yellow sign, possibly onto a new tarmac road which was completed but still barred at the time. This new road only lasts a few kilometres as far as the reservoirs to your south. Beyond that point there was no evidence that **the piste** would be sealed further west.

**17.5 (76.5)**
Signs indicate Emdgher Tahtani village with Emdgher Foukani a couple of kilometres further on.

**23.5 (70.5)    N30° 36.10'  W07° 23.64'**
Cross a oued and go straight, not northwest for Mouidat village. A few kilometres on pass through **Nekob** village from where, according to some paper maps, a track leads directly south to the N10.

**30.5 (63.5)    N30° 36.54'  W07° 27.46'**
Skirt around **Tamejecht** village in a loop to the north.

**35 (59)    N30° 36.22'  W07° 30.12'**
Drive through what could be **Tafrent** village and in a little more than 500m keep left, not right for Taouzoute. This way was a bit washed-out but joins up with the track coming north from town in a kilometre or two.

**38 (56)    N30° 35.78'  W07° 31.70'**
Aflan Oussir to the north. Continue west, passing the 1804m high point on this route

**41 (53)    N30° 35.08'  W07° 33.11'**
**Aït ou Almane** (or some such) followed by another village in 1500m. A couple of hundred metres after that place, keep left in case it isn't obvious. When I came through a stream had washed away the track and following it north, upstream, was a mistake. It's at times like these that Olaf saves you exacerbating errors.

**46 (48)    N30° 35.34'  W07° 35.39'**
Reach a main junction and a sign, still only just below 1800m, and turn southwest. Right or north-east leads to Aït Amrane and Tizgui and probably trekking access to the summit of Jebel Sirwa which is 12km to the north.

**48.5 (45.5)**
Pass round Assaïs village to the south after which follow a few more villages and switchbacks.

**55.5 (38.5)    N30° 32.84'  W07° 39.21'**
The top of a 1536m pass with a view to **Azgour** village ahead.

**57 (37)**
Drop down to cross a river, rise out steeply on the far side and head right and then west.

**59 (35)    N30° 32.77'  W07° 40.74'**
T–junction. Leave Olaf here and turn south and west for Tinfat and the highway. On the way you pass a couple of **wells**. Right is signed for an auberge in 4km and comes in around 20km from this junction at **Zagmouzere** (archway where the track meets the road: N30° 34.13' W07° 51.34') on Route MH8 and a few kilometres north of Taliouine.

**67 (27)**
Around here, just a short distance from salvation at Tamassine, it got very muddy and instead of Transits, tractors shouldering piles of passengers were serving the villages – but this was a week after exceptional storms in the region. If it looks bad for you too, turn back and try the Olaf route to Zagmouzere.

**69 (25)    N30° 29.37'  W07° 44.12'**
Pass by **Tamassine**'s custard and olive mosque.

**71 (23)    N30° 28.44'  W07° 44.45'**
Arrive at **Tinfat** on the N10 highway by the basic *Café de Siroura* and turn west for Taliouine.

**75 (19)    N30° 28.14'  W07° 46.54'**
A basic SHELL fuel station but no unleaded, nor much else around to make a worthy end to this route. Carry on west towards Taliouine, crossing a dramatic pass after which the scenery changes noticeably.

**94    N30° 31.49'  W07° 53.22'**
ZIZMO **Taliouine** westside, a few kilometres before the town centre. For accommodation options here see the end of Route MA7 or your guidebook.

# MH10  DADES – IKNIOUN – ALNIF                    113KM
November 2008 ~ Yamaha Ténéré

## Description

Stuffed in between the Alnif and Boumalne du Dades (or just 'Dades') roads, the **Jebel Sarhro** massif is a geologically-distinctive area and I'd not be surprised to learn it possessed its own unique biosphere too. At their heights the ranges claw at the sky in jagged ranks unique to Morocco, evoking southern Algeria's Hoggar at Assekrem. The rock may not all be volcanic but it sure looks igneous, and doing this route six months after logging Route MH5 I again had visions of Corsica in mind, even though I've never been there.

As you inch away from Iknioun this route takes you as deep into those ranges as you can get on anything with wheels. The track rises up to look out over the gnarliest peaks looming over valleys from which there seems no exit; in moody light calling it all Wagnerian would not be going too far. And best of all it's a lot easier on your vehicle than its ugly sister MH5, and no less dramatic at the right time of day.

This is a new link between Iknioun and Alnif, completed in mid-2008 between the two main research trips. When I set off I didn't know where it would end up other than Alnif, or maybe somewhere to the north along the near-completed tar road linking the town to the N10 Dades highway. Only when the track started turning south and even west at around KM75 did it transpire that it would come down to join Route MH5 somewhere before that track turned nasty. When the road building machinery pulled out it's probable they re-cut the eroded track from Imi-n Izrou village (KM101) back to Alnif as well as south to Tiguerne on the N12, which is why MH5 has a slightly different start via Tiguerne.

## Off road

Unlike adjacent MH5, you won't have to do so much as a foot recce on this route unless it's to work out a good angle for an action shot. **Four-wheel drives**, although maybe not plain old cars, will take it all in their stride and even a big **motorbike** will manage it with a bit of ungainly paddling through the short sections of sand and gravel (just make sure no one's watching). Some climbs and hairpins were awkward, but my bike felt particularly overloaded when I wobbled through. I boldly predict **mountain bikers** will have a great time on this route; a gradual tarmac ascent from Dades up to Iknioun and then mostly level or downhill dirt and good wild camping around KM71, just a short distance after a handy well.

## Route finding

The only mistake you might make if you don't have Olaf is possibly taking a wrong turning to a village or farmstead between Iknioun and KM62, but this error will soon become evident when you're entangled in someone's washing line and fluttering chickens. Beyond KM62 the crutch that has been Olaf is kicked away until you rejoin MH5 at KM81.5, but there are only a couple of alternative turn-offs until you get to the Oued Tazlaft and the regular piste back to Izrou and the highway. The only traffic I saw after Iknioun was a couple of Transits as I neared Izrou. For the **map** see pp142-3.

## Fuel and water

Alnif and Dades for fuel. Several wells as indicated. There was running water here and there, but this was soon after The Rains.

## Suggested duration

I took three and a half hours on a bike going slowly and stopping frequently so a car could manage it in about the same time, while hotshot motards could shave off the minutes at the cost of having a good look around. Cyclists would have more fun making two days of it, but with the undemanding climb or a lift to Iknioun you could blast through in a long day.

**0km**      **N31° 22.06' W05° 58.88'**
*SHELL* fuel on **Boumalne du Dades'** eastern outskirts. A *tajine Marocaine* and a coffee here was just 35dh and somehow my bike registered a mind-boggling 86mpg after a fill up. I can't wait to come back here.

**6.5 (106.5)**      **N31° 21.85' W05° 54.85'**
Turn south off the highway and follow a narrow tarmac road up to Iknioun.

**35.5 (77.5)**      **N31° 10.24' W05° 43.62'**
Already at over 2000m, Route MH4 heads off north towards the Tizi n Tazazert pass and Nekob.

**44 (69)**      **N31° 10.29' W05° 40.43'**
**Iknioun**; the **tarmac ends**. Pass through town where the track may diverge; if you take the lower left fork, fork right a little later where the tracks soon join up.
    After about 1km at N31° 10.56' W05° 40.06' Route MH4 comes up from Tinerhir. You fork right here and follow a narrow track past hamlets below the looming 2712m mass of Amaloun n Mansour mountain, unmistakably the **highest point** in the Jebel Sarhro massif.

**56 (57)**      **N31° 09.86' W05° 34.81'**
At this hairpin go left, back off the pass.

**62.5 (50.5)**      **N31° 10.17' W05° 30.58'**
Just by some rounded rocks Route MH5 comes in from the south-east via the **Tizi n Ouli Ousir**; you don't want to go there.

**68.5 (44.5)**      **N31° 10.59' W05° 27.65'**
**Well** (4m) on the right.

**71 (42)**      **N31° 10.67' W05° 26.34'**
Viewpoint to the north after a loose climb to a flat area with space to camp at 1700m.

**73.5 (39.5)**
Another great viewpoint to the south-west this time over successive jagged ranges. In about 500m fork right.

**76 (37)**      **N31° 09.65' W05° 25.15'**
Cross a oued with a lone palm by a stone farmstead. After the climb ignore the two tracks to the left, both lead to a distant building.

**80 (33)**      **N31° 08.36' W05° 26.25'**
Gardens and buildings. You now cross the upper Oued Tazlaft which can be sandy and gravelly and which you'll parallel nearly all the way back to the highway.

**81.5 (31.5)**      **N31° 08.01' W05° 26.43'**
Join Route MH5 at around KM38 and turn left or east for Alnif. The route from here onwards is straightforward: on to Imi-n Izrou village and out the other side to the road.

**101 (12)**      **N31° 05.56' W05° 17.23'**
Just after the oued on the east side of **Imi-n Izrou** the track forks: left is the direct route east to the highway just west of Alnif. Right is Route MH5 in reverse via Tiguerne, handy if you're giving Alnif a miss and are heading south-east towards Tazzarine or Nekob.

**108 (5)**      **N31° 05.35' W05° 12.63'**
**Reach the tarmac** and turn left, east, for Alnif.

**113**      **N31° 06.75' W05° 10.34'**
*ZIZ* fuel, **Alnif** west side about a kilometre from town. For accommodation options here see the end of Route MS4.

# TRANS ATLAS: MH11  GOULMIMA – RICH – MIDELT    182KM
November 2008 ~ Yamaha Ténéré

Particularly for desert-bound arrivals out of Nador or Melilla, here at the eastern end of the High Atlas the usual transit across the mountains follows the N13 via Rich to Er Rachidia and so to Rissani and Erg Chebbi. It passes through the Tunnel du Légionnaire which, while not quite as exciting as it sounds, is at the head of the impressive **Gorges du Ziz** where the river soon gets caught up in a reservoir. Route ME1 is another way of getting south and east on quiet sealed backroads, while this route adds up to an equally intimate return to the north.

Initially it follows the course of the **Oued Rheris**, the 'other' big oued of the Tafilalt region besides the Ziz. Soon after breaking out of **Goulmima's** enveloping palmerie you find yourself crossing and re-crossing the Rheris over fords before entering its deep canyon, an easterly equivalent of the Todra Gorge but without roadside *checheries*. Instead you'll meet the real thing, nomads padding silently along the road, leading their flocks or mule caravans down from the heights to the markets of Goulmima.

The gorge opens out and the road rises up to lonely Amellago where you leave the Rheris and set off east along a broad lateral valley which typifies the High Atlas ranges. Near Rich and the road, you join up with the near-parallel course of the Oued Ziz and once through town pick up the N13 for the Nzala Pass and Midelt. The map for this route is on pp132-3.

## Description
Start off at the ZIZ fuel station on the south side of **Goulmima** and drive northeast up through town with plenty of shops, cafés and a hotel or two. At the far end of the main road, pass under the arch and get to a roundabout (KM2.5). The sign here for 'Amellago 53' is easy to miss from your direction, but turn sharp left here by going nearly right round the roundabout and then right, north-west up a backstreet. Continue along this road until you suddenly burst out of the rustling green shade into the dazzling desert. You soon cross a branch of the Oued Rheris; continue north across the desert to the village of

---

### THE ZIZ AND THE RHERIS

Interestingly, both rivers rise up within a few kilometres of each other just east of Agoudal in the High Atlas, but like twins separated at birth, the Rheris heads off down one valley and Ziz along the next one up. A couple of hundred kilometres later, near Rissani they glance by just a few kilometres apart before again heading off in separate directions. Finally, over 400km from their sources and close to the Algerian border the two rivers become one and flee the country as if in some

incestuous pact, destined only to evaporate in the desert where the *simoon* disperses their combined outwash over the sands of the Grand Erg Occidental.

For a few weeks in November 2008 and April 2009 both were flowing along their full length right through to the border and maybe beyond, cutting off Route MS6 and making the Ziz fit for kayaking as it rushed past Erg Chebbi.

**Tadirhoust** at around KM20. If it's already past your bedtime there are signs here for *Gîte Pauline*, while at the north end of the village are the mud-brick ruins of a ksar. Beyond the village is a ford, one of many you may cross as the gorge walls rise around you at KM36. At the right time of day with the sun shining on red cliffs above and the Rheris flowing below, it's a grand place.

Soon you rise above the gorge and are out in the open again, but now the desert has given way to a scrubby upland plateau. The tiny hamlet of **Amellago** rolls up at KM52 where the road splits west or left for Aït Hani on Trans Atlas Route MH2 – or right for Rich. There's a café here and signs for a *gîte* 3km down the Aït Hani road.

You set off north-east along the broad plain between parallel ranges. At KM74 a road shown on some maps as sealed is just a track, although at Mzizel junction, KM92, an asphalt road does indeed lead north-west and then west towards KM101 on Route MH2 and continues as tarmac on to Imilchil (fuel) and if you like, El Kebab. At this point you've crossed the watershed separating the course of the Oued Rheris from the Ziz and will pass by the gardens and villages alongside the Ziz as you near **Rich**.

Appropriately, at KM114 there's a ZIZ fuel station as you cross the river and enter the back of town. On the far side of the bridge turn left, follow the road round to the right and then turn left into a main backstreet and then immediately right into the main square or boulevard with cafés and restaurants. The basic **hotels** in town, along with possible car parking issues, put us off staying here one time. Carry on east along the boulevard out of town to an *AFRIQUIA* at the junction of the N13. Turn left or north here, cresting the 1894m **Nzala Pass** at KM166, so leaving the High Atlas ranges behind you. Several vendors hang out on this pass, selling either two-stroke premix or argan oil – I've never stopped to find out. At KM184 the N15 turns off north-east for Missour, Guercif and so Nador (for more see Route ME1) while **Midelt** and its good range of **hotels** and restos is just 16km up the road. We arrived late one night and settled with uncharacteristic extravagance on the *Hotel Kasbah Asmaa* (420dh for two with breakfast buffet, plus parking guardian tip) just before the town and which is summed up well in the two guidebooks.

## TRANS ATLAS: MH12   OUARZAZATE – DEMNATE   158KM
November 2008 ~ Yamaha Ténéré

The main Trans-Atlas road crossing is the N9 over the 2260m **Tizi n Tichka**, linking Marrakech and Ouarzazate. Just to the west is the reputedly much more interesting but less used R203 route over the 2092m **Tizi-n Test**, also running from Marrakech but to nowhere in particular on the N10 between Taroudant and Taliouine. If you're an off-roader the Tichka has the benefit of setting you up for the very popular Telouet – Aït Benhaddou 'Route of the Kasbahs' (see * p162) paralleling the road to Ouarzazate, or Route MH6 out of Aguim. Taking the Test will suit motards and lines you up for MH7 from Aoulouz over Jebel Sirwa, a great route.

Chances are, if you're coming from Ceuta you're going to cross one of these passes, so when you've been there and done that, MH12 to Demnate makes an alternative way of getting back north. The R307 (as it's designated) is a very **narrow mountain road** and on the southern stage of the climb you'll be able to count the traffic on the fingers of one hand and may wonder why they bothered going to all the effort to seal it all. Possibly a tarmac capping resists the relentless weathering better. There are precious few sweeping vistas over rolling hills such as you'll see when crossing the highest stages of Trans Atlas Route MH1 south of Agoudal. The nature of MH12 is climbing and dropping over two near 2200m crests, separated mid-route by a trough. The first crest up from the Ouarzazate plain follows a series of narrow valleys, bleak, arid and barely populated and so barely used.

Up here blockages from **landslides** are frequent, closures of the 307 are not uncommon and road repairs near continuous. You can see why. The road is merely a platform cut into steep scree slopes that drop straight down to the valley floor. Any rain or snowmelt loosens this debris which smothers the narrow carriageway while bigger rocks mash the asphalt. The rubble on the road is never fully cleared and, with no Armco or parapet, on a motorbike you may find yourself edging around the rubble-strewn hairpins in one of two, foot-wide ruts of tarmac, ready to correct a front wheel slide. It's not always the rhythmic, bend swinging jaunt you'll get into on the Tizi n Tichka or Test. Following the mid-route drop, you climb to nearly the same height as before, followed by the long descent to the tree line and Demnate.

I took three and a half hours on a bike trying to beat the sunset. The only **accommodation** spotted was a sign for a gîte in Tourfine and possibly a café or two, although the villages from here onwards have small shops. Any road vehicle including a normal-sized campervan could manage this route as long as the rockfalls aren't too bad. On a loaded bicycle it would be quite a two-day work-out, much quieter than the Tichka but maybe not as satisfying as MH1 and MH2 combined as a run from Dades to Imilchil and El Kebab. The map for this route is on pp132-3.

## Description

If you want the following distances to line up, start at the top-of-the-hill SHELL in **Ouarzazate's** town centre. Head east out of town on the N10 to Skoura and Boumalne du Dades; after 2km bear right past the flashier eastside hotels. Soon you pass the huge reservoir which is now the head of the **Oued Draa**, which once flowed right to the Atlantic (near KM142 on Route MO1). At KM18 turn north off the N10 onto the R307 and head for the hills. For about 25km you traverse the arid peneplain at the foot of the Atlas which rises abruptly ahead, right across your horizon. At KM45 just after a village the road turns west and gets stuck into the slopes. Soon you're swinging left and right as the narrow road claws up the hillside. After a brief drop you attain this route's **2190m high point** at KM73, high above the sun-blighted village of **Tamzerit**. There's no sign to announce you've reached the **Tizi-n Fedrhate**, nor any feeling of having topped out.

From here you drop down just as steeply, possibly fording a shallow river at KM80 where the more temperate vegetation and trees become evident. By

Coming down to Demnate.

the time you reach *Toufrine* village (KM101 at 1625m, *gîte d'étape*) across the upper reaches of the Oued Tessout valley, you're at the bottom of the 'trough' running between the two high points. Traffic becomes marginally more frequent and as a result the road is in better shape.

Soon after **Aït Tamlil** village you'll have a view east to the brick-red slopes of what is probably Jebel Rhat, while directly to the south the north slope of the Jebel Anghomar (3610m) could be covered in thick snow. The 2059m **Tizi–n Outfi** crops up at KM119, only this time you get a sense of a pass. Beyond this point things become a bit lusher and busier; cypress and other pine trees appear, along with more vans serving the villages. The road drops away steeply, and by and by you pass the flashy new **hotel** situated by the natural limestone arch of **Imi n Ifri**, a local tourist attraction.

While it has some basic **hotels** as well as ATMs, fuel and restaurants, **Demnate** at KM158 is not necessarily a place you might want to stop for the night. If you've not done so yet, now could be the time to visit Marrakech, less than two hours to the west.

* Why no 'Route of the Kasbahs' in *Morocco Overland*, the most popular track in the land? We drove it in 1999 and it was indeed a great route, passing the roof-top stork nests in **Aït Benhaddou**, the gorgeous mud-brick kasbahs as you rise up the valley and the fabulous ruins at **Telouet**.

Sadly, it seems its position alongside the 'Axis of Tourism' has made it a victim of its accessibility. It's said big groups of inconsiderate 4WD tours have ruined the track surface and intimidated the locals, creating a hostility manifested by stone-throwing kids. Or maybe it was the other way round. Either way, if you do go this way, try to spread some good will, and wherever you drive or ride on the tracks of Morocco, remember this is where people live. Follow the guidelines outlined on p77.

# SAHARA

## Outline of the Sahara region

For off-roaders the Moroccan Sahara is understandably the main draw. Though only occupying a slither of the world's largest desert, the chance to ride or drive in an environment so close and yet so alien to Europe is all you could ask of a great adventure holiday. Distances are still relatively short and only a few routes demand an overnight stop, but a night out in the desert is part of the reason you've come here; if you don't know that yet, you will the morning after.

Another attraction here is that the routes are **less rocky** than elsewhere, with small dunes in between the two main sand seas of Chebbi and Chegaga. At its best this open terrain is much more exhilarating than following a stone-bound track through the hills, although real dunes are another thing altogether: see p175.

In the high season outside of summer you won't be alone out here. Land Rovers shuffle tour groups daily between Zagora and Merzouga so it's worth remembering that the Anti Atlas is also largely Saharan, as of course is the Moroccan West.

## MS Routes

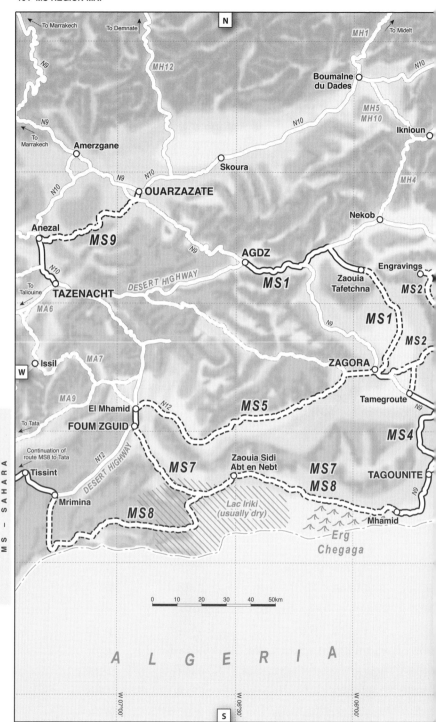

# Sahara (MS)
# Routes Overview

**MS1** Agdz – Jebel – Zagora
**MS2** Zagora – Engravings – Tazzarine
**MS3** Tazzarine – Oum Jrane – Rissani
**MS4** Tagounite – Oum Jrane – Alnif
**MS5** Zagora – Foum Zguid
**MS6** Tagounite – Erg Chebbi – Rissani
**MS7** Foum Zguid – Mhamid – Tagounite
**MS8** Tata – Tissint – Tagounite
**MS9** Ouarzazate – Tazenacht (shown on pp152-3 map)

# MS1   AGDZ – ZAGORA                    121KM

April 2008 ~ Mazda pickup

## Description

The 'Vallée des Kasbahs' N9 road down to Zagora is no eyesore for sure, passing many palm-shrouded villages backed by dramatic jebels and each with their own crumbling ruins. MS1 is an alternative, crossing the Draa about 35km east of Agdz and soon enough getting on the piste which uses the **Jebel Rhart** (or 'Beni' on some maps) as a big berm to swing you into Zagora from the desert side.

The scenery is dramatic but not too varied and once you near Zagora the pace speeds up as you draw into town via a series of irrigation canals.

## Off road

A couple of rocky oued crossings may give a **2WD**'s exhaust a fright, but other than that it's plain sailing. **Bikes** have nothing much to fear from MS1 except fear itself. A mountain biker will find this route easy enough, but at **cycling** speeds it's well worth the scoot down the N9 road sooner or later.

## Route finding

Straightforward; there aren't too many wrong directions you can wander off in, but you won't see that much traffic. The **map** for this route is opposite.

## Fuel and water

Agdz and Zagora for fuel; water from the villages. No wells were noted but there must be some out there.

## Suggested duration

A couple of hours with an engine; cycling will take at least a full day.

**0km**          N30° 41.52'  W06° 26.83'
ZIZ fuel station on the south side of **Agdz**. Head south for Zagora.

**28.5 (92.5)**
Turn left over the Draa and take the N12.

**45 (76)**          N30° 45.43'  W06° 03.59'
Turn right onto a tar road leading down to the town of Zaouia Tafetchna. Climb over a 1178m pass and enter a basin.

**59 (62)**          N30° 41.08'  W05° 57.18'
The **tarmac ends** by a red tower in **Zaouia Tafetchna**. Follow a track through town.

**60 (61)**          N30° 40.77'  W05° 56.61'
Drive in and out of the oued on the edge of town and then at N30° 40.69'  W05° 56.54' leave the oued to follow a grey, graded track passing dry stone walls and heading for a pass.

**66 (55)**          N30° 40.65'  W05° 53.42'
Crest a 1041m pass.

**67 (54)**          N30° 40.52'  W05° 52.98'
A track joins from the left. Possibly an angle on the route heading east to Tazzarine shown on some maps, though at the time it didn't seem so obvious.

**70 (51)**
The grading ends and the track gets a bit rougher.

**73 (48)**          N30° 38.43'  W05° 50.45'
Junction, turn left and cross a stony oued with a water tower and village ahead.

**75 (46)**
Pass by the water tower on your right.

**76 (45)**          N30° 37.35'  W05° 49.31'
Fork, keep right (straight), the long

escarpment of the **Jebel Rhart** is to the east.

**80 (41)**      **N30° 35.64'  W05° 47.77'**
Top of a 924m pass with a rocky descent and a village far ahead.

**85 (36)**      **N30° 33.67'  W05° 46.29'**
Cross a sandy oued with the old kasbah nearby.

**85.5 (35.5)**
Pass the kasbah of Anoui on the right but keep heading directly south.

**93.5 (27.5)**      **N30° 30.40'  W05° 43.59'**
Pass some gardens and a palmerie on the left.

**96 (25)**
Various tracks come and go as you approach a village, but keep heading south.

**97 (24)**      **N30° 28.56'  W05° 43.23'**
Fork, go left to avoid the kids or head through the village if you have no fear.

**98 (23)**      **N30° 28.02'  W05° 43.17'**
Rejoin the other track by the water tower.

**100 (21)**
Over to the east the Jebel Rhart range ends as you pass a water tower and palmerie to the right.

**101 (20)**      **N30° 26.82'  W05° 43.81'**
Fork left here with buildings on the right and a palmerie soon after; continue west-south-west.

**102 (19)**
A track joins from the right; continue south-west. If you happen to be driving in the dark the lights of Zagora are visible ahead. The piste gets fast and dusty.

**110 (11)**      **N30° 22.59'  W05° 46.96'**
Pass a water tower on the right.

**111 (10)**      **N30° 22.23'  W05° 47.26'**
Cross an irrigation canal.

**112 (9)**      **N30° 21.96'  W05° 47.37'**
Pass under some pylons and then cross

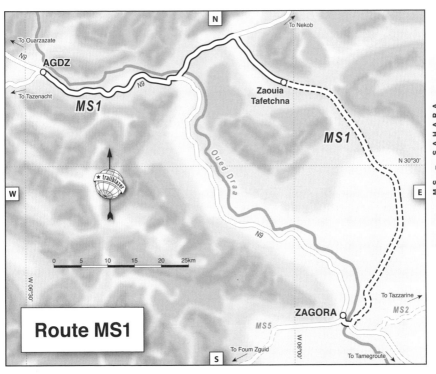

three fords. At N30° 21.21' W05° 47.31' pass some gardens and more pylons, cross the sanded-in canal again and pass between walls and palmeries. At N30° 20.93' W05° 47.32' continue straight.

**115 (6)          N30° 20.31' W05° 47.88'**
Recross the canal and follow the track past the garden walls.

**116 (5)          N30° 20.03' W05° 48.45'**
Cross tracks and pass a sign for a kasbah hotel, then recross the canal and keep going straight. At this waypoint you **join the tarmac**. Turn right and head into Zagora. At a junction with the Mhamid

road turn right, passing the kasbah hotels popular with tour groups. By now you'll have probably attracted a moped posse of touts eager to offer a full range of Zagora's many services and products.

**119 (2)**
Cross the oued and go up the hill towards the town centre. You level off by some sort of palace on your left and drive up the main road.

**121          N30° 19.70' W05° 50.30'**
**Zagora** town centre; CMH fuel station on the main road.

# MS2   ZAGORA – AÏT OUAZIK – TAZZARINE          100KM
May 2008 ~ Mazda pickup

## Description
This is a great way of getting to the Tazzarine area and is about half the distance of the road though probably no quicker. It starts with a rubbly approach to the pass at KM32 from where the rubble continues until you turn north up along the back side of the Jebel Rhart escarpment and a parallel ridge to the east.

You continue up the Ouazik valley until you reach the village of that name. This route then takes you on an excursion to see some prehistoric **rock engravings** a couple of kilometres west of the village, but be warned, unless we missed something, they're not of the calibre you can see in Fezzan, Tassili N'Ajjer or the Gilf Kebir and are about as basic as genuine prehistoric engravings get, no matter what the guidebooks tell you.

With those ticked off, you head back and up a valley east of Aït Ouazik and pick up the sealed Tarhbalt road in time for lunch in Tazzarine. You can easily do this route in half a day.

## Off road
Nothing too difficult here apart from the shaking you get from the initial rubble track up to the pass and the turn-off north, as well as some oued stages further up. High clearance **2WDs** and **big bikes** won't have kittens.

## Route finding
All the current paper maps copy each others' mistake and depict an old French road cutting directly north-north-west up to Tazzarine avoiding Aït Ouazik (where it's even marked). This is not the route you follow and is so old now it's hard to see any trace of it where it once headed over the escarpment at around N30° 34.3' (according to old French maps) or possibly at N30° 33.0' (on Google Earth).

Despite that, there are no route-finding dramas to be had here. This route can also be an alternative start to Routes MS3 / MS5 and MS4 if you find your-self in Zagora.

Plenty of tourist 4WDs shoot through this way, linking Erg Chebbi with Zagora, but on the northern stage up to Aït Ouazik traffic is less common, despite a few nomad tents. The **map** for this route is on pp176-7.

## Fuel and water
Fuel at each end and in a couple of wells and villages along the way.

## Suggested duration
Allow yourself a morning's drive or ride if you go via the engravings. It's a long and rough route for an **MTB rider** who'll find it tough to do in a day.

**0km**          N30° 19.71' W05° 50.29'
**Zagora** CMH fuel station. Head south down the main road and after 700m turn downhill to the left. Wind down and cross the oued and pass through the flashy kas-bah resorts and Amerzrou suburb.

**2.5 (97.5)**    N30° 19.09' W05° 49.71'
Pass the junction leading left for Route MS1 up to Agdz and carry on straight through Amerzrou.

**8 (92)**        N30° 18.26' W05° 46.99'
At a sign indicating 'Tazzarine 90km' turn left onto a stony track.

**11 (89)**
The piste descends to the desert floor as it turns south-east.

**12 (88)**       N30° 19.26' W05° 45.50'
Cross a small oued and turn east.

**22.5 (77.5)**   N30° 21.95' W05° 39.90'
Route MS4 comes up on the right from Tagounite. There is a **well** 200m away with a bucket and rope.

**24 (76)**
Another track joins from the right as your track turns north-east.

**31.5 (68.5)**   N30° 25.25' W05° 36.21'
Tracks join from the left as you approach the **Taflalet pass**. 2WDs will want to pick their way carefully up the pass.

**33.5 (66.5)**   N30° 25.50' W05° 34.98'
A piste splits to the right – a parallel, pos-sibly less rough route. Soon there's anoth-er split to the right for the parallel piste. In a car it's best to just boldly plod ahead at 10 mph.

**41 (59)**       N30° 27.96' W05° 31.39'
Turn north along either a 'white-painted' track or this route.

**42 (58)**       N30° 28.52' W05° 31.55'
Cross a bouldery oued.

**43 (57)**       N30° 28.92' W05° 31.81'
The 'white-painted' track joins from the left. There's a nice sandy creek on the right for a break.

**44.5 (55.5)**
You pass a graveyard on the left. The track is hard sand and smooth.

**47.5 (25.5)**   N30° 31.11' W05° 32.44'
Pass a **well** about 200m to the left.

**52 (48)**       N30° 32.99' W05° 33.80'
Another **well** to the left of the piste and some nomad tents.

**55 (35)**
The piste gets rougher here with many washed-out gullies.

**58 (42)**
You're close to the backside of **Jebel Rhart**.

**60 (40)**       N30° 35.87' W05° 37.12'
Cross the oued.

**63 (37)**
Some palms on left and maybe pink ole-anders in the oued.

**65 (35)**
Leave the oued; the track becomes smoother.

**68 (32)**          N30° 39.74'   W05° 37.38'
A nice spot on the right for a camp.

**69 (31)**          N30° 40.38'   W05° 37.37'
Junction. Turn right for a direct route to Tazzarine. Head straight on for the engravings.

**70 (30)**
Pass a football field on the left.

**70.5 (19.5)**      N30° 41.01'   W05° 37.79'
Join a track by a wall near a 'Stop' sign in Arabic. Turn left.

**71.5 (28.5)**      N30° 41.06'   W05° 38.26'
Junction. Go right (although left possibly leads directly to engravings without even needing to leave your vehicle).

**73.5 (26.5)**      N30° 41.66'   W05° 39.28'
Turn south off the piste towards the next waypoint. We parked up at N30° 41.59' W05° 39.32' just before a ditch-oued and took a 2km round-trip walk to the **engrav-**

ings at around N30° 41.19'  W05° 39.49'.

**79 (21)**          N30° 40.00'   W05° 37.59'
Heading back past the 'Stop' sign, you meet the piste coming up from KM69. Continue through village past some solar panels and pass an interesting-looking old ksar.

**80 (20)**          N30° 41.28'   W05° 37.25'
Cross a oued, leave the village and head into the valley.

**84 (16)**          N30° 40.65'   W05° 35.14'
Turn to the north-east on a blue-grey corrugated track with a **well** on right and pylons nearby.

**91.5 (8.5)**       N30° 43.42'   W05° 32.13'
Fork right towards a building.

**92 (80)**          N30° 43.77   W05° 31.73'
**Join the tarmac**. Turn left for Tazzarine. Right leads to Taghbalt: Route MS3.

**100**              N30° 46.92'   W05° 33.80'
The ZIZMO in **Tazzarine** town centre with an omelette café opposite.

# MS3   TAZZARINE – OUM JRANE – RISSANI          266KM
May 2008 ~ Mazda pickup

## Description
A low swing eastwards to Erg Chebbi, at the tarmac's end in Taghbalt you follow the banks of the large **Oued Taghbalt**, fringed by many gardens and palmeries until you cross the oued at KM48 and head out into the barren, stony desert. This track eventually brings you back to the oued and presently round to the fabled settlement of Oum Jrane from where you drop down to the white sign at KM76.5 and head directly east to pick up Route MS6 coming up from Tagounite. Here both routes follow the same path though chotts (salt pans) as well as a string of auberges through to Taouz, Merzouga and finally fuel in Rissani.

You'll see it all along this route, the customary oueds and jebels are joined out here by wide open and sandy stages culminating with the well-earned spectacle of Erg Chebbi.

## Off road
As far as Oum Jrane and on to the junction with Route MS6 at KM104 there's no great difficulty for **2WDs** or **bikes**. The nastiest section by far is the couple

of kilometres before Remlia where you cross the **Oued Rheris** just as it prepares to disgorge its spoor all over Oued Ziz (see box on p159).

This time round I was rather lazy watching my orientation and followed tracks to the south which turned from manageable small sand dunes into deep ruts of fine, dusty *feche-feche* – an often misused word and not one I use lightly! I scraped through (on hard tyres admittedly) and as I left Remlia still choking on the dust I had to hold myself back from warning a trio of **loaded bikers** heading into the mire.

Looking at the old French map it seems keeping as far north as possible, even to the point of missing out Remlia will shorten this nasty section; it's certainly not worth trying on a fully-armoured BMW Adventure unless you're carrying some spare collarbones. The people of Tafraoute (KM118) don't use this route in 2WDs and go directly north along easier tracks to meet the Rissani-Alnif highway; something other 2WDs will need to do too unless they're on stilts.

Beyond Remlia the track is merely washed-out and rough in places, crossing chotts by turns smooth and bumpy, possibly all the more so following The Rains when this part of the route would have been under water. At Taouz you rejoin the tarmac to Merzouga at the foot of Erg Chebbi and proceed to Rissani, for whose desert guides – both real and *faux* – the now easily-followed tarmac to Erg Chebbi heralded the end of an era. This route feels too long and arid to attempt on an unsupported **mountain bike** so if you try it, have a good plan. At the very worst, it won't be too hard to get a lift out.

### Route finding
It took a bit of trial and error to get from Taghbalt to the Oued Taghbalt crossing at KM48 but now we're all the wiser. From there onwards, out in the desert untrammelled by confusing tracks, it's all much less confusing.

This is one of several satisfyingly long Saharan routes in this area which can be mixed and matched with each other to make your own itinerary starting or ending at places like Tagounite, Tamegroute, Zagora to the south, or Agdz and Timerzif near Alnif to the north.

This region is popular with other off-road tourists, and 4WD tour groups, especially beyond Oum Jrane where you're bound to meet other traffic. The route **map** is on pp176-7.

### Fuel and water
At Tazzarine and Rissani there are fuel stations and whatever they can get away with at Oum Jrane and possibly Tafraoute. Water from wells and villages along the route as marked.

### Suggested duration
This route is do-able in one long day but why wear yourself out? There's a Sunset Strip of auberges from about KM105 onwards and plenty of deserted spaces in between.

Once you get to Merzouga (KM223) there's a solid bank of auberges facing Erg Chebbi. Experiencing a sunset or a sunrise here is what many people remember best from Morocco, so don't miss out.

**0km**        **N30° 46.92'**   **W05° 33.82'**
ZIZ fuel in **Tazzarine** centre. Head south-east out of town for Taghbalt, not right for Nekob and Ouarzazate. Follow the **tarmac to its end** at Taghbalt.

**36 (230)**
Cross the oued and enter **Taghbalt**.

**37 (229)**    **N30° 37.75'**   **W05° 21.08'**
At the water tower follow the track around to the left.

**37.5 (228.5)**   **N30° 37.76'**   **W05° 20.93'**
Fork, head south-east. There is a sandy oued to the right.

**38 (228)**    **N30° 37.55'**   **W05° 20.66'**
Turn left steeply down into the palm-filled oued and drive across it.

**39 (227)**    **N30° 37.47'**   **W05° 20.20'**
Cross the oued again. On far side turn left at N30° 37.40' W05° 19.96' below the cliff with a mosque on top.

**40 (226)**    **N30° 37.56'**   **W05° 19.71'**
The track climbs out of the oued to a T-junction. Turn left here and follow the banks of the major Oued Taghbalt below a rubble hill.

**48.5 (217.5)**   **N30° 38.33'**   **W05° 15.21'**
Having followed the oued bank winding in and out through various fields and gardens, just after a school drop down into the wide oued and cross it to the north.

**49 (217)**    **N30° 38.53'**   **W05° 15.15'**
Drive steeply out of the oued and at this junction go straight, away from the oued into the hamada on a graded earth track, not right. Right from this junction they may be building a direct route along the north side of the oued to KM62.5.

**52.5 (213.5)**   **N30° 39.86'**   **W05° 15.47'**
T-junction, turn right. A nice descent into a oued soon follows.

**57 (209)**    **N30° 40.78'**   **W05° 13.60'**
Fork right.

**61 (205)**    **N30° 39.50'**   **W05° 11.77'**
A track joins from the left. Soon you arrive at a village and palmerie.

**62.5 (203.5)**   **N30° 39.40'**   **W05° 11.02'**
This is possibly a junction heading south to Oued Taghbalt (the direct route from KM49). You continue east over a sandy oued towards telegraph poles.

**63 (203)**    **N30° 39.35'**   **W05° 10.56'**
Drive through the village of **Taksha**: pylons, a palmerie and new buildings.

**64 (202)** N30° 39.06'   W05° 10.33'
Pass a school on the right with a blue and yellow map of Morocco on the wall. Soon you come to a junction. Turn left for Oum Jrane. The piste runs just above the wide Oued Taghbalt which you follow more or less all the way to Oum Jrane.

**66.5 (199.5)**   **N30° 38.70'**   **W05° 09.25'**
The western outskirts of Oum Jrane.

**68 (198)**    **N30° 39.13'**   **W05° 08.39'**
Leave the oued via slabs. In 500m a track joins from the left.

**69.5 (196.5)**   **N30° 39.08'**   **W05° 07.85'**
A track heads off south. Take it and head for KM76.5 if you don't want to experience Oum Jrane. Otherwise continue south-east towards some buildings.

**71.5 (194.5)**   **N30° 38.39'**   **W05° 06.75'**
Oum Jrane west end. From here you have a chance again to head south to KM76.5 to avoid the town, or even freestyle south-east towards KM83.

**72 (194)**    **N30° 38.53'**   **W05° 06.41'**
**Oum Jrane** town centre; Morocco's 'Timbuktu' and now a shadow of its former glory. There are a couple of shops and offers of **fuel** and **water**. To pick up Route MS4 to Alnif go to the school at the east end of town and turn north over the oued. Otherwise this route heads south-east out of town, following any track heading towards KM76.5, below.

**76.5 (189.5)**   **N30° 36.40'**   **W05° 05.62'**
Crossroads. White sign indicating 'Auberge 5km' pointing to Oum Jrane. It's possible a route cuts south from here to pick up MS6 on its way to Tagounite.
   You turn east and follow any eastbound track. Fast, smooth going; not something you often get in Morocco.

**83 (183)        N30° 36.92'  W05° 01.92'**
A track joins from the left and from here on it occasionally gets sandy.

**97 (169)        N30° 37.79'  W04° 52.58'**
Another track comes in from the left. There are low hills to east and the track gets a bit rough following the fast stage. North of a hillock you cross a sandy oued.

**100 (166)       N30° 37.92'  W04° 51.97'**
Another sandy oued beside a hill with trees to north. Any track east is good here.

**104 (162)       N30° 38.15'  W04° 49.37'**
Route MS6 joins from the south-west by a three-stone cairn. There is a long, low sand dune ahead.

**105 (161)       N30° 38.23'  W04° 48.71'**
Cross this dune easily. *Auberge Dinosaur Kem Kem* lies just to the south. Kem Kem is the local name for this vicinity and from here on east there are at least half a dozen **auberges** out in the desert before you get to Taouz.

**110 (56)        N30° 38.58'  W04° 45.45'**
A **marabout** (shrine) is just to the north of the piste and *Auberge Marabout* to the south, beside the sand dune.

**112 (154)       N30° 38.48'  W04° 43.91'**
Pass another auberge and blue-grey hills to the south-east: Jebel Zireg with a radio mast on top. On the far side is Algeria. Start crossing the chott of Lake Maider.

**117 (49)        N30° 39.98'  W04° 41.48'**
Signs point to **Tafraoute** auberges nearby; the piste goes straight ahead over a pass. We popped into the *Auberge Hammada Kem Kem* where two tajine-baked omelettes, a water plus a cinnamon-sprinkled orange cost 100dh. From here we were told a 2WD piste leads north to the Rissani road.

**119 (147)       N30° 40.16'  W04° 40.18'**
You're over the pass and entering a valley with a crenellated ridge to the north and dunes to the south.

**130 (136)       N30° 40.58'  W04° 33.43'**
A sandy section starts around here.

**134 (132)       N30° 40.18'  W04° 30.89'**
A track and a sign point north which could be interesting. You continue east on a bumpy piste.

**139 (127)       N30° 40.51'  W04° 28.36'**
Sign: 'Auberge Oasis Ramlia 7km'. Low dunes appear ahead. Brace yourself for many winding tracks around small dunes and bushes and nastier **feche-feche** powder. For big, heavy bikes it's the worst sort of terrain. In a car I wandered along tracks too far south where the oued becomes wider and only just scraped through. Consider lowering your tyre pressures and stay well north where the oued is narrower. Head up to N30° 41.5' or so, bypassing **Remlia** altogether.

**145 (121)       N30° 41.14'  W04° 25.00'**
*Auberge Ramlia* where a piste goes north. Head north-east on a stony track.

**147 (119)       N30° 41.97'  W04° 23.81'**
Junction of pistes.

**149 (117)       N30° 42.39'  W04° 22.98'**
*Aghbalou Ramlia Auberge* to the left with its name in stones on the hill behind. Soon there's a sandy descent towards a chott. Cross it following occasional cairns on either side. From this point you're following the course of **Oued Ziz** upstream, but the route may not be exactly as described, following The Rains when the Ziz down here was flowing briskly.

**162 (104)       N30° 43.05'  W04° 19.10'**
Cross various chotts or salt pans in between stretches of hamada.

**166 (100)       N30° 44.68'  W04° 12.74'**
Having just passed an auberge you now pass the duneside *Auberge Ouzima Rimal* which looks better than most. In 2km you pass *Kasbah Ouzima Desert Hotel* and a kilometre later the *Erg Ouizima Auberge*.

**171 (95)        N30° 45.87'  W04° 10.39'**
*Auberge Porte de Sahara*. Here, white-painted cairns lead right, down and across the Oued Ziz to rejoin the track at KM176 via a village, but it's actually simpler to go straight ahead about 2km and cross the oued around N30° 46.7'  W04° 09.6'.

## ERG CHEBBI

The good thing about the dunes of Erg Chebbi near Merzouga is that they look like something right out of the movies; the problem with this pint-sized sand sea is there's nowhere else like it in Morocco so it has been well and truly discovered. It is indeed the grand terminus of Morocco's Axis of Tourism.

For many people Chebbi exemplifies the Sahara and they come here in their droves to walk, camel and even to ride and drive over the sands. Moroccans have a saying 'See Ouarzazate and die' but many tourists would settle with seeing the dunes of Chebbi before giving up the ghost. The only other option, Erg Chegaga south of Zagora, lacks Chebbi's rosy hue and supine forms which sees it glow so evocatively at sunset.

Erg Chebbi is actually one of the tiniest 'ergs' or sand seas in the Sahara, just seven kilometres wide by 30-odd from north to south. Just over the border the Grand Erg Occidental in north-west Algeria runs for hundreds of kilometres in all directions – check out the comparative scale on Google Earth. Despite the estimates and gross exaggerations you'll read or hear about, the highest dune here is just 150 metres above the desert floor. At Chegaga it's 100 metres.

### On the Erg

Arriving at the Erg and never having driven in desert dunes before, for many off-roaders and particularly bikers, riding to the top of the tallest dune is their goal. On a light, unloaded bike it's do-able and easiest coming up from the east side. Many try blasting up any old way before getting bogged down, exhausted from falls or getting injured.

The nature of Erg Chebbi with its **small dune formations** makes it extremely challenging to drive on. Like the northern Grand Erg Oriental in north-eastern Algeria and Tunisia (Route A1 in *Sahara Overland*), these small dunes have no pattern and are like trying to jet-ski up and down over a stormy swell. Huge dunes and the pattern of corridors which readily form between them are actually much easier to negotiate.

Erg Chebbi may be small but in my experience it's not the type of terrain any normal Saharan piste would cross unless there was no choice, so be warned. To take a rental 105 into the dunes with no sand mats or means of re-inflating the tyres is asking for a recovery which may cost you dearly; the Merzougans know all about that.

Driving or riding over virgin sand dunes is an invigorating and amazing experience,

**176 (90)      N30° 46.70'  W04° 08.65'**
A sign indicates 'Auberge Hassi Ouzima 2km'. The 'white-cairn/village' route joins from the right. Head north.

**180 (86)      N30° 48.66'  W04° 08.23'**
Two tracks lead over a oued. Occasionally, twin cairns feature alongside the track hereabouts.

**183 (83)      N30° 50.15'  W04° 08.44'**
A track seems to join from left and soon the track forks, but either fork will do.

**184 (82)      N30° 50.62'  W04° 08.16'**
Signs for various auberges. Another track joins from the left. Head along the edge of a dried-mud oued.

**185 (81)      N30° 50.69'  W04° 07.35'**
Junction. Turn left down into the oued among gravel hillocks.

**194 (72)      N30° 52.42'  W04° 02.58'**
Pass along a sunken section of track. Black hamada follows.

**198 (68)      N30° 54.22'  W03° 59.69'**
Crest a rise with a radio tower installation on the left. The tarmac is visible ahead.

**200 (66)      N30° 54.53'  W03° 59.58'**
**Join the tarmac** at a sign: 'Centre Taouz' (to the left). Turn right for Merzouga and Rissani.

**223 (43)      N31° 06.02'  W04° 01.08'**
**Merzouga** junction. Turn sharp right for the village (post office, some shops and a grubby souk). The auberge turn-offs are all to the north.

**266      N31° 16.9'  W04° 16.3'**
**Rissani** fuel station on the western end of town, near the arches.

but is also one of the most dangerous. While the sand may look soft to fall on, a bike cartwheeling behind you or the insides of your rolling car are not. Take your time and think about what you're doing and the consequences of getting stuck, particularly in a bowl or 'vortex'. Once a car has dropped into even the shallowest one, even with plates there's no room to get enough momentum to drive yourself out.

As many know, the key to improving traction on soft sand is **reducing tyre pressures** to 1 bar (14.5psi) or less. It's quite amazing to see where a car can go at these pressures – the tread pattern is comparatively immaterial. A light bike can manage with 0.7 bar or 10psi. As with a car, pressures this low transform a bike's handling and make dune riding **safer** and more predictable because you're able to go slower without getting stuck and so have more time to think.

On dunes **momentum** is required to stop yourself sinking but caution is also essential to not shoot off a crest. Then there are challenges with perspective in the featureless glare of high sun angles or with the sun behind you. In these conditions it's quite easy to ride off the crest without even seeing it. There's also the unpredictable hazard of

No one in their right mind would drive over dunes like these, but many try. © P. Hartleb

other users: quads, bikes and 4x4s bombing around on a busy day. Some lose their heads here and end up rolling or mashing their vehicles. And with all these users comes the rubbish left by the irresponsible.

And finally there's also the conflict of tearing about while other tourists attempt to commune less conspicuously with the sands. Give them some space and confine your dune-bashing away from the popular mid-western flanks of the Erg, head south to the lower dunes or even go round the other side.

## MS4 TAGOUNITE – OUM JRANE – ALNIF 237KM
March 2008 ~ Mazda pickup

### Description
One of the better routes in this region, taking a less-used axis towards the north-east. Once the road section is knocked out, in a car it's a rough, rubbly start until you're well past the Tizi n Taflalet Pass. Here the terrain smoothes out and opens out as you turn for the north at KM128 towards Oum Jrane situated along the south banks of the Oued Taghbalt. You strike off to the north-east here following increasingly thin tracks which rise up to a pass, cross a sandy oued and then the Jebel Atchana before picking up a more-used piste to Fezzou. Here a wide track or possibly even tarmac lead to the main Alnif highway.

The conditions I did it in were rather windblown but there's no doubt on a clear day the scenery here is as impressive as anything in the Moroccan Sahara; the valleys, some dunes, the villages, a ruined ksar at KM177 and as always, a ring of jebels surrounding you.

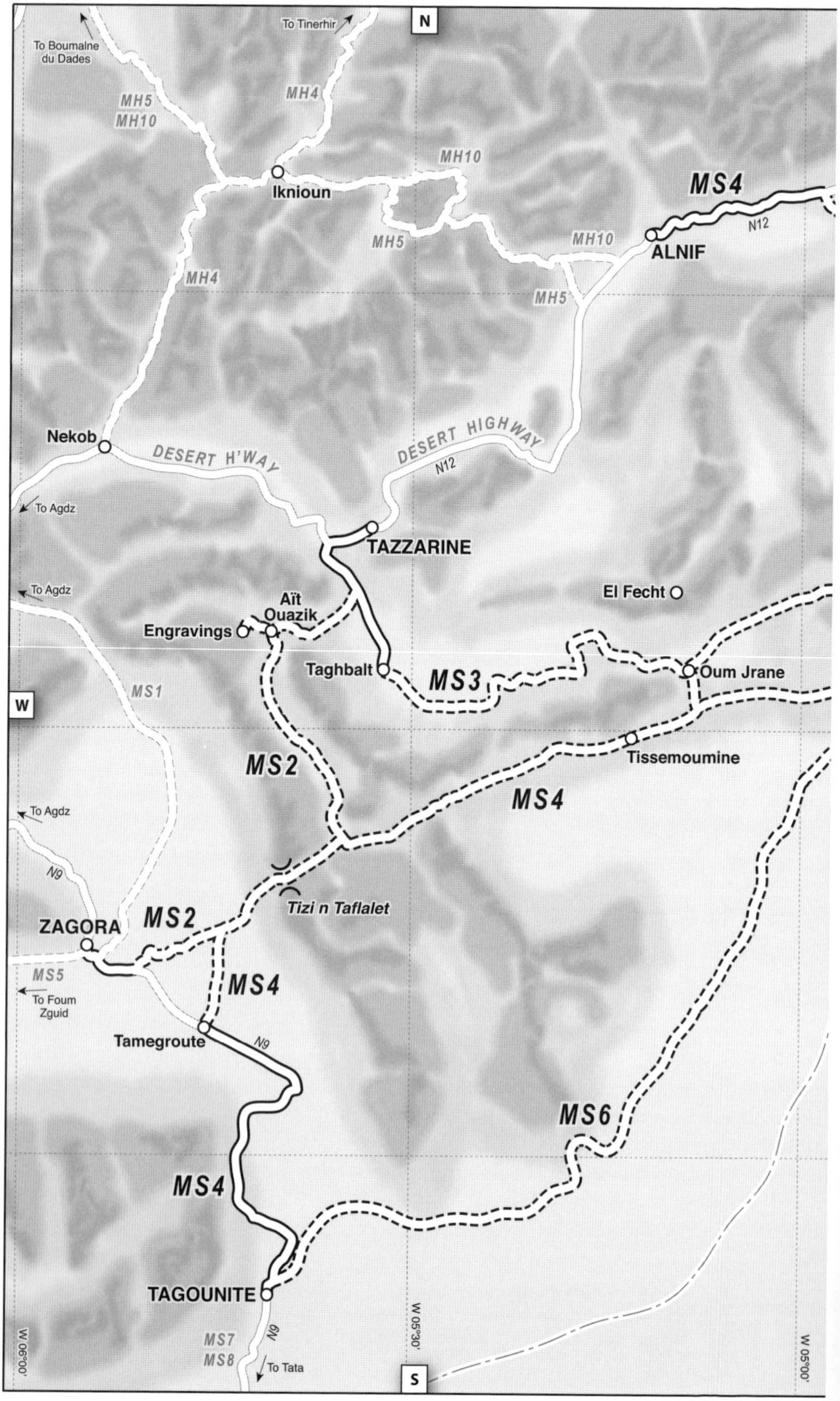

N

To Boumalne du Dades

To Tinerhir

MH5 MH10

MH4

MH10

Iknioun

MH10

MH5

MH5

MS4

ALNIF

N12

Nekob

DESERT H'WAY

DESERT HIGHWAY

N12

To Agdz

TAZZARINE

To Agdz

Aït Ouazik

El Fecht

Engravings

Taghbalt

MS3

Oum Jrane

W

MS1

MS2

Tissemoumine

MS4

To Agdz

N9

Tizi n Taflalet

ZAGORA

MS2

MS4

MS5

To Foum Zguid

Tamegroute

N9

MS6

MS4

TAGOUNITE

W 06°00'

W 05°30'

MS7 MS8

To Tata

N9

S

M S – S A H A R A

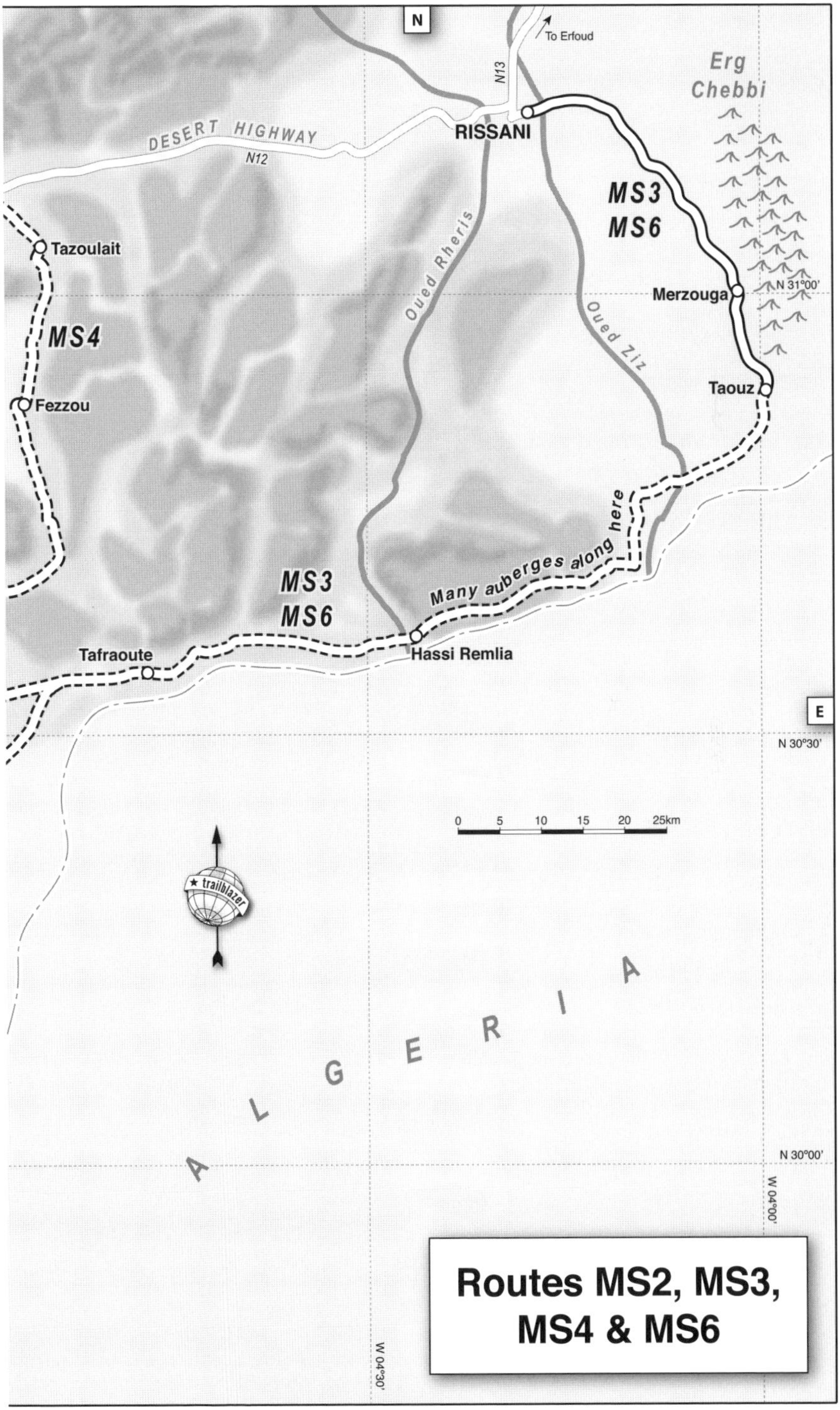

**N**

To Erfoud

N13

*Erg Chebbi*

DESERT HIGHWAY
N12

**RISSANI**

*MS3 MS6*

Tazoulait

*MS4*

Oued Rheris

Merzouga

N 31°00'

Fezzou

Oued Ziz

Taouz

*MS3 MS6*

Many auberges along here

Tafraoute

Hassi Remlia

**E**

N 30°30'

0  5  10  15  20  25km

trailblazer

N 30°00'

A L G E R I A

M S – S A H A R A

W 04°30'

W 04°00'

**Routes MS2, MS3, MS4 & MS6**

## Off road

No great hardships lie in store for **big bikes** and only the sandy oued crossing at KM152 will take some gumption in a **2WD**. If you can get past that, then the rest of the piste is do-able, but there are many other alternative ways north. Again, this route is a bit of a stretch for a **bicycle**.

## Route finding

This route uses a popular zone for tour group convoys passing between Zagora and Erg Chebbi, but once you leave Oum Jrane it thins right out to local mopeders or even pushbikers. Compared to what's normal in Morocco, the track gets a bit 'thin' until you rejoin it on the north-north-west-bound stretch to Fezzou village. The map is on pp176-7.

## Fuel and water

Fuel at each end or in Oum Jrane at a price. Reaching the N12 at KM214, if you're wanting to head east, Rissani is about 70km away. There's water from only a couple of wells and of course the villages.

## Suggested duration

Even with the highway start and end, it could be a long day to Alnif so consider a desert camp after Oum Jrane if you have the means.

**0km          N30° 00.29'   W05° 34.55'**
**Tagounite** ZIZ fuel at the north end of town. Follow the highway north towards Zagora, over a pass in the Jebel Bani with great views over the arid desert marked by the splash of the Oued Draa and its gardens. Come down off the pass, cross the Draa and head into Tamegroute.

**49 (188)          N30° 15.58'   W05° 41.02'**
On account of its Koranic library **Tamegroute** is a tourist town with all that that entails. Turn right at a market area where the back road soon becomes an unsealed road. At the end of this road, after 400m turn left for 150m and at the end turn right for 100m. You reach a canal running along the middle of the road. Turn right again and then cross the canal doing a U-turn and drive back north-west to get to…

**50 (187)          N30° 15.83'   W05° 40.81'**
… this point where a **wide stony track** runs north-east near the arch of a market-place on the right. Carry on north-east. When you pass a…

**50.5 (186.5)    N30° 15.94'   W05° 40.75'**
…blue door on the corner you know

you're on the right track out of town. For those not on a light bike with great suspension, what follows can feel very rough as it crosses over rocks embedded in the black, stony hamada.

**62 (175)          N30° 21.63'   W05° 40.07'**
One of the junctions with Route MS2 coming over from Zagora. Soon you get to a good **well** (25m) with buckets and a rope. Another Zagora junction is just ahead (KM22.5 of MS2) before you cross a oued and head for the Taflalet Pass. There are old camel caravan trails on the right and soon cleared salt licks on the left.

**66 (171)          N30° 22.54'   W05° 38.52'**
Junction with a track coming up from the south.

**70 (167)**
You're now turning into the pass.

**72 (165) N30° 25.24'   W05° 36.21'**
Join another track from Zagora as you head into the **Tizi n Taflalet**.

**74 (163)          N30° 25.49'   W05° 34.99'**
Junction to the south with red painted rocks to probably a better track which

meets up at KM83. There is another junction 750m later doing the same thing; your last chance. Great ranges all around.

### 78 (159)
You start wishing you took that parallel track to the south. In 500m at N30° 27.05' W05° 32.67' a track goes off to the south.

### 79.5 (157.5)    N30° 27.24'  W05° 32.40'
Go past a thin cross track.

### 81 (156)    N30° 27.91'  W05° 31.49'
Junction where MS2 goes up to Tazzarine. There's another cross roads in 500m.

### 82 (155)    N30° 28.04'  W05° 31.19'
Muddy **well** (15m) near some blue-grey rock slabs. You turn south-east soon after.

### 83 (154)    N30° 27.75'  W05° 30.78'
Near a basic tourist camp with a **well** and tank you meet the alternative track you wish you'd taken at KM74. Turn left to the east and within 500m (N30° 27.77'  W05° 30.49') at red-marked rock, fork right.

### 87 (150)    N30° 28.22'  W05° 28.37'
Tracks join from the right.

### 88.5 (148.5)    N30° 28.37'  W05° 27.48'
You pass a village on the right as the track curves north-east through a low pass and joins tracks you may have split from earlier. The trees have been stripped to stumps around here for firewood. In a couple of kilometres you may pass a drinks hut.

### 94 (143)    N30° 30.16'  W05° 24.59'
You pass the sanded-up mud block garden wall of the village Imi-n-Ou Assit. A kilometre after the village fork left at N30° 30.51' W05° 23.81' (though the tracks may well join up later).

### 96 (141)    N30° 30.85'  W05° 23.43'
Fork right; left heads for the hills and, according to the paper maps, may reach KM38 on Route MS3. For once they may be right; Google Earth shows the piste as an interesting-looking track following a canyon winding through the jebel about 18km to **Tarhbalt**.

### 98 (139)    N30° 31.26'  W05° 22.40'
You've just crossed a oued by a couple of

buildings and a palmerie. At around KM100 the track speeds up for a bit before the valley narrows through a grassy oued – possibly a good lunch spot. Then the valley opens out again and you can speed up. This route continues directly east-north-east to the waypoint below.

### 112 (125)    N30° 34.56'  W05° 14.90'
Sign for Oum Jrane auberge 15km. Continue east-north-east. If you're following Olaf, in about 3km it heads north-east for Oum Jrane, probably via a more direct route. If you go this way, aim for KM132.5, the school on the east side of Oum Jrane. Back on this route, you'll notice a lone water tower on the hill to the south. You continue east-north-east, enjoying a fast smooth track.

### 121 (116)    N30° 35.42'  W05° 09.56'
The white mosque of **Tissemoumine** is visible directly to the north as you zip along a smooth sand sheet, not a common feature in Morocco.

### 128 (109)    N30° 36.40'  W05° 05.62'
White sign for 'Auberge Restaurant Camping Aumjrane, 5km' pointing north. Turn to the north here. Straight ahead are Routes MS3 and soon MS6, both leading to Erg Chebbi and Rissani.

### 131.5 (105.5)  N30° 38.33'  W05° 06.18'
The southern outskirts of **Oum Jrane**. For the centre of town head 500m to the north-west where you'll find a few stores offering water and fuel and the auberge somewhere, but no café to speak of.

Despite the kids stampeding towards you, Oum Jrane could be worth a bit of a wander. Just to the north-west of the town centre the old town sits on a cliff, overlooking the broad **Oued Taghbalt** you're about to cross.

Otherwise head 500m northwards (KM132.5, N30° 38.62'  W05° 06.25') for the pink and yellow school at the east end of town. Pass the school and turn north to cross the oued. Look back left and you can see the old town above the oued.

### 133 (104)    N30° 38.96'  W05° 06.35
A thin track leads off to the north-east. Directly north goes to the more used route to **Rzou** or **El Fecht** and **Aït Sadane**, close

to the N12 highway between Alnif and Tazzarine.

Carrying on north-east, in a kilometre and just before a grassy oued crossing, you'll see the symbol used to define Berber or Amazigh identity marked out on the hill alongside an Arabic word. Continue north-east for 2km to pass over a low saddle between two sand-swept hills.

**139 (98)          N30° 41.48'   W05° 03.91'**
Keep heading north-east even though tracks head off to the east-north-east.

**141 (96)          N30° 42.17'   W05° 03.16'**
A track joins from the west as you cross a once-cobbled oued.

**142 (95)**
There are some dunes hereabouts to the west and east with tamarisk tree mounds. The track is corrugated but can be difficult to follow in sweeping sand.

**145 (92)          N30° 43.23'   W05° 00.99'**
Approach some abandoned buildings.

**146 (91)          N30° 43.31'   W05° 00.65'**
Pass a couple more sanded-over ruins with several smooth broken rock cores lying around.

The landscape improves and soon you get to a junction with a track near 5°W that runs between **El Fecht** (about 11km to the west) and **Tafraoute**, KM134 on Route MS6 and about 32km to the east.

**149 (88)**
Head north-east on thin tracks.

**151 (86)          N30° 44.55'   W04° 57.97'**
Pass a cairn and head east-north-east towards a ridge.

**152 (85)          N30° 44.89'   W04° 56.96'**
Tracks converge on a white pile of rocks to mark the crossing point over a sandy oued. 2WDs will struggle here. Carry on east-north-east for the pass, passing blue grey marble outcrops.

**154.5 (82.5)    N30° 45.37'   W04° 55.50'**
Sandy pass; nice spot.

**157 (80)          N30° 45.55'   W04° 54.37'**
A junction just after the dune, take the left

fork to the north-east. Right presumably heads down to Tafraoute (see above).

**158 (79)          N30° 45.89'   W04° 53.50'**
Fork left with another fork soon. You'll see broad bands of camel tracks.

**162 (75)          N30° 47.05'   W04° 51.63'**
Bear left here to the north-east.

**164 (73)          N30° 48.00'   W04° 50.71'**
Join a northbound track on dark grey hamada. In 3km you'll see dunes to the east with trees and greenery. It could be a good camping spot.

**173 (64)**
You're on a well-formed corrugated track.

**174 (63)          N30° 52.99'   W04° 52.61'**
A track leads off to the north-west to follow the Oued Dahmane to a not very obvious passage through the Jebel Tiberguent at N30° 55.2' W05° 04.7' towards **Ait Sadane**, among other places (marked on the Michelin map). You continue north.

**177 (60)          N30° 54.21'   W04° 52.98'**
The ruins of Tamgannt kasbah are east of the track. Soon you pass an old graveyard and see the radio tower of Fezzou ahead.

**180 (57)          N30° 55.62'   W04° 53.87'**
Southern outskirts of Fezzou; a water tank under a tree.

**181 (56)          N30° 55.85'   W04° 53.90'**
Join a well graded track which looked like it was due for a damn good sealing.

**182 (55)          N30° 56.49'   W04° 54.14'**
**Fezzou** village centre.

**184 (53)          N30° 57.41'   W04° 54.39'**
Junction. Follow the new track north-east out of town. It **may be sealed now**. The track or road may also wind westwards to the Jebel Tiberguent pass speculated on above.

It's a straight run up to the N12 now, even if the track never gets sealed. You pass through the village of Bou Dib, cross a pass where a track leads to Azerkour (or Achbarou) 9km before Alnif, and just after the pass the village of Ihandar which is followed by an unusually long ford.

**214 (23)      N31° 11.20'   W04° 57.20'**
**Join the N12 highway** near **Timerzit**, just
off the highway to the north-west. At the
time of writing the 10-mile square Google
Earth quadrant covering this village and
Azerkour was just a few months old and
sharp enough to slice ripe tomatoes; each
villager would easily be able to make out
their house.

**237            N31° 06.97'   W05° 09.72'**
*Afriquia* fuel on the east side of **Alnif**.
Two hotels, the *Bougafer* and the *Gazelle du
Sud* face each other at the other end of
town. Having tried both I prefer the
*Gazelle du Sud* offering more-than-you-
can-eat half board with an en-suite room
for around 170dh and bike parking in the
lobby. There are several cafés in town as
well as internet and numerous fossil
emporia.

The old Route M4 from *Sahara
Overland* starts just west of the **Hotel
Bougafer** and the adjacent bus stop. It
heads off past the red and white radio
tower where it curves north. The first
15km are a wide corrugated track; from
there the last 30km over the pass to the
N10 east of Tinerhir are now sealed.

# MS5   ZAGORA – FOUM ZGUID                    130KM
March 2004 ~ Mercedes 190D

## Description
This is a valley-bound alternative to Route MS7, following the north slopes of
Jebel Bani between these two desert towns. Like MS7 it's quite stony and
scenically you get less of a view and feeling of being out in the desert.

Initially it passes through pastoral allotments and gardens supplying
Zagora's hotels, and then becomes more remote with only a few nomadic
encampments to either side.

## Off road
Obviously we managed in a **2WD** adding a few dents to the Merc's bash plate
on the way. Anything else including **big bikes** will have no problems. This
route is mostly stony, at its worst from KM56 as the route squeezes between
two parallel ranges, until KM88 after which the piste improves. Because of this
**mountain bikes** would not have much fun on this route, although in March
2009 I read it had been **graded** from KM79 westwards. Asphalt may follow.

## Route finding
Leaving Zagora is now easy for the first 8km to the aerodrome. As you move
further west you follow one clear stony track across the hamada, with an occasional branch here and there. And of course looking at the big picture, you
have the Jebel to the south as a guide almost all the way. We saw no traffic on
our traverse in 2004. The **map** for this route is on p189.

## Fuel and water
Zagora and Foum Zguid. There is one known well at KM31 and several gardens in the western half.

## Suggested duration
Less than half a day will do you on this one.

**0km**                    **N30° 19.7'  W05° 50.3'**
Zagora *CMH* fuel station. Head south down the main road and as you pass the *Hotel de la Palmerie* on the right (N30° 19.4'  W05° 50.4') turn right where you'll see the new position and version of the famed *'Timbuktu 52 jours'* sign). Follow a wide **gravel track** and enjoy it while it lasts.

**8 (122)**                **N30°16.45'  W5°53.66'**
The gravel track ends at the aerodrome. This is as far as I checked in 2008. The account which follows up to KM127 dates from 2004. It may all be graded.

**11 (119)**               **N30° 16.7'  W05° 56.3'**
Pass some gardens to your north, just after crossing a oued. The track runs through a settlement (Tagourt).

**15 (115)**               **N30° 16.0'  W05° 58.2'**
A lone acacia to the right with gardens behind it. The piste heads south-west for a while.

**20 (110)**
The track heads south directly towards Jebel Bani.

**23 (107)**
The track now swings south-west with buildings visible among the trees at the base of the Jebel. Soon the track heads directly west.

**25 (105)**               **N30° 12.2'  W06° 01.2'**
Pass a small oasis garden to the south with a few buildings. There is another oasis 5km further on with rammed earth ruins (N30° 11.7'  W06° 03.8').

**31 (99)**                **N30° 11.4'  W06° 04.8'**
More rammed earth ruins and gardens and a **well** (8m). Leave the abandoned village with a well on your left.

**35 (95)**                **N30° 10.8'  W06° 06.8'**
Cross a oued, a mixture of sand and stones.

**37 (93)**
There's a large pink house north of the track by a fenced-off field, with a walled palmerie and orchards a kilometre later.

**42 (88)**                **N30° 08.8'  W06° 10.7'**
Cross a big oued – again rocky and sandy. Within 500m you cross the oued again and pass partially-walled fields and buildings to the south.

**50 (80)**                **N30° 07.0'  W06° 14.2'**
Another collection of buildings with fields. The track now heads north-west, away from the Jebel.

**56 (74)**
The piste becomes stony as it heads towards a oued line and the pink town of Bou Rbia at the base of distant cliffs to the north-west.

**60 (70)**                **N30° 08.4'  W06° 20.5'**
The stony piste splits. Take the left fork to the west towards Bou Rbia.

**61 (69)**                **N30° 08.4'  W06° 21.4'**
Pass a white concrete bollard by the track and cross a stony oued. **Bou Rbia** is now to the north.
    A few hundred metres later the track splits again; continue just south of west. In another kilometre there's another white bollard by the piste (N30° 08.1'  W06° 22.0').

**64 (66)**                **N30° 07.9'  W06° 22.7'**
The track splits. Going straight ahead is more direct but stonier. Taking the southern branch south-west towards the Jebel is sandier with a sandy oued crossing at KM66 (on the far side of the oued take the track to the right) and is a relief from the stones.

**73 (57)**                **N30° 05.4'  W06° 26.9'**
The direct stonier route rejoins the piste from the north and the now stony track continues south-west towards the Jebel.

**75 (55)**
Cross a narrow stony oued, and again 300m later. Heading south-west.

**79 (51)**                **N30° 03.7'  W06° 30.0'**
Cross the 6° 30' line right by a 'stranded' concrete ford to the north of the track. Reports from 2009 suggest that from this point a new fast, wide track now leads to El Mhamid. Say a prayer to St Koni.

**85 (45)          N30° 02.3'  W06° 33.1'**
The track splits; take the left (southern) fork. This is another divergence as at KM64; you can take the right fork if you like but you may find it stonier. They converge after a concrete ford in around a kilometre. A kilometre later (KM87) there's a stony oued crossing. How many times have I used 'stony' so far?

Soon after you find yourself heading for a village alongside a long lone dune and the track becomes less… stony.

**90 (40)          N30° 01.5'  W06° 35.9'**
The valley opens out again to the north-west as you pass south of the village with the lone dune to the north-west. Within a kilometre or two the track starts swinging to the north-west passing a white bollard at KM92 (N30° 01.4'  W06° 37.3').

**104 (26)          N30° 05.5'  W06° 42.3'**
The track now turns north across a big oued – and again a kilometre later.

**106 (24)          N30° 06.8'  W06° 41.9'**
Join a wide, smooth track heading north-

west. A couple of times it might still revert to the old stony piste as it crosses unfinished bridges (in 2004 at least).

**116 (14)          N30° 08.9'  W06° 47.7'**
Back on the smooth surface, you arrive at Smira village. From here in 2004 we drove alongside pylons through a oued alongside an unfinished road.

**124 (6)          N30° 07.5'  W06° 52.4'**
Arrive at the eastern outskirts of El Mhamid. Cross the oued and drive through the dense palmerie.

**127 (3)          N30° 07.5'  W06° 52.8'**
**Reach the tarmac** road in **El Mhamid**. If reversing this route, the piste begins opposite a pink building with a white sign on the oued side in three languages asking you to keep the desert clean.

**130          N30° 05.40'  W06° 52.66'**
**Foum Zguid** fuel with unleaded at the north end of town. For more on Foum Zguid see the end of Route MA9.

# MS6  TAGOUNITE – RISSANI                    283KM
October 2003 ~ MTB (Raf Verbeelen). Part updated 2008 ~ Mazda pickup

## Description
Along with rarely undertaken Route MW6, this route, which also runs close to the border, gives a taste of the true Sahara a thousand kilometres further south. It's also remarkably smooth underwheel compared to other Moroccan pistes. Along with an absorbing selection of landscapes, these features make this one of the most popular desert itineraries in Morocco.

Starting from the Draa Valley you head north around the Jebel Bou Debgane and then cross a large basin-like formation with Hassi Taffeta well in its centre. Descending the eastern rim you then cross the Oued Mird to the fort at Hassi Zguilma and begin the long north-north-east run up to Tafraoute. From here the track follows a valley to the tricky Oued Rheris crossing alongside and then continues over bumpy chotts to Taouz. After Taouz it's a sealed road run up to Merzouga by the amazing dunes of Erg Chebbi and so Rissani.

Because it's so smooth, this route could be done in a long day, but it would be a shame not to spend at least one night out in the desert. Any number of spots between Tafenna and Taouz would make great overnight stops. From KM121 onwards this route was updated in 2008. Auberges have mushroomed alongside the piste and are detailed in the text, while Erg Chebbi itself has a score of auberges facing the dunes in a 20km line north of Merzouga. See the website for recommendations, or the Moroccan guidebooks.

## Off road

Rough hairpin tracks lead steeply down into the basin of Tafenna, after which it's remarkably smooth (by Moroccan standards) until you get to the small dunes before Tafraoute. The toughest stage is winding in and out of the nasty hummock scrub, dunelettes and *feche-feche* of the **Oued Rheris** just before Hassi Remlia (KM156); **big bikes** may struggle here and even locals in **2WDs** avoid it. Beyond Remlia rough chotts lead to Taouz. The 2004 **mountain bike** updaters did this route in eight days but think it could be done in five. This is a popular route with both local tours and tourists alike.

## Route finding

Between Tagounite and KM18 you might find yourself blundering around the villages and adjacent irrigation canals, but from this point it's a clear run over Tafenna to Oued Mird where the lower loop that goes south of Jebel Bou Debgane joins this piste.

  The long smooth run from Hassi Zguilma fort (KM56) up to the eastward turn of the piste has a few turn-offs, so keep an eye on your bearing. 'Agoult' on the Michelin map does not appear to exist, but near here twin tyre markers lead you east over a featureless gravel plain, a few low dunes and a chott (the 'Lac') to Tafraoute. This is the only section that may require concentration.

  From Tafraoute (not marked on any map) to Hassi Remlia and the auberges around Ouzina is straightforward. From Ouzina get south of the Oued Ziz and then follow the tracks (sometimes splitting and rejoining) which all lead to Taouz, the road and the way to Rissani. The **map** is on pp176-7.

## Fuel and water

Tagounite plus Tafraoute and Remlia (from drums); Rissani (43km from Merzouga). Plenty, from villages and wells along the route. The longest water-less stretch is from the fort at KM56 to Tamassint, KM109.

## Suggested duration

Do-able in a long day but a night out in the desert or at the many auberges between KM122 and Merzouga is the way to go.

**0km**          **N29° 59.38'  W05° 35.08'**
**Tagounite** ZIZ fuel on the north side of town. Drive south into the town centre for 1.5km and turn left at N29° 58.6' W05° 35.0' opposite the military barracks. You may see a very faint sign for 'Blida' (a village marked on the Michelin map) on the east side of the main street. This **track** leads along canals to a palmerie.

**3.5 (279.5)**
Walled village on both sides of the track. Heading east-south-east. When you emerge from the village you'll soon pass a sign for 'central Tagounite' as you continue through the palmerie.

**7 (276)**
You reach a scrubby plain and 500m later the track turns almost north with the mass of **Jebel Bou Debgane** to the east. The track soon passes two concrete blocks and runs alongside a palmerie to the right.

**9 (274)**          **N29° 59.0'  W05° 30.8'**
**Blida**. Having crossed a canal with sluice gates where the track turns east-north-east and then a major ditch, you arrive at a junction with a small sign on a lamppost indicating 'Blida'. Turn left towards the red and white mast. Pass the mast on the left and a school on the right and continue through town towards the Jebel.

In a kilometre pass a health centre and come to a junction. Turn left and continue north with the Jebel to your right past white cairns.

### 12 (271)
Fork right. After 1500m you pass the village of Aissfou on the left with its long palmerie. Continue north-north-east.

### 16 (267)
Ruins on the left and another village 1500m later. Continue straight through it.

### 19 (264)      N30° 03.4'   W05° 29.0'
Junction. Turn right and continue north-east. The track gets sandy and bumpy, veering east-north-east.

### 23 (260)      N30° 04.5'   W05° 26.7'
A track joins from the west-north-west coming from Zagora – our track now turns east-south-east. The track is bumpy but up ahead you see it rising up the west rim of Tafenna.

### 28 (255)
The wide, smooth track starts to rise up the hamada and onto the ridge.

### 31 (252)
Crest of the ridge at 856m. The descent is very rough and stony. Soon you see the track cutting across the smooth flat centre of the 'basin' to the opposite ridge. At KM34 pass Hassi Tafenna **well** (N30° 04.5' W05° 20.2').

### 38 (245)
Begin to climb the track up the less rough eastern rim.

### 41 (242)
Hut on the right near the crest of the ridge (951m) which appears after 300m. From here a view stretches east over distant plateaux. Begin a very gradual descent over the next 3km.

### 45 (238)      N30° 06.6'   W05° 15.1'
Junction with a cairn on the hamada between the ridge and Oued Mird. Right leads south of Jebel Bou Debgane back to the Draa valley.

Take the left fork north-east across the hamada with a line of acacias running parallel to your left.

### 48 (235)
Cross a small oued with a line of acacias.

### 50 (233)      N30° 07.7'   W05° 12.4'
Cross a thicker band of trees as a track joins from the right. In less than a kilometre you get to some buildings and a small palmerie on the left of the track, with a pole marker on the right. The track becomes sandy for a few hundred metres.

### 53 (230)
Veer north-east towards a reddish escarpment.

### 56 (227)      N30° 09.4'   W05° 09.9'
Hassi Zguilma; a pink fort on a hill and military checkpoint. The track leaves to the north-north-east.

### 60 (223)
A track joins from the left. Smooth going.

### 66 (217)      N30° 13.9'   W05° 06.8'
Tracks diverge. Take the left fork going north-east with cone-shaped hill to your right.

### 70 (213)      N30° 15.7'   W05° 05.4'
Track splits to the right. Keep left, heading towards big red Ayers Rock-like monolith. After a kilometre more monoliths become visible ahead and to the right, north-north-east. Some corrugations.

### 75 (208)
A track joins from the right; having passed the red plateaux to the east, another track joins from the right 4km later (N30° 18.6' W05° 03.3').

### 81 (202)
Distinctive slab cairn with a hole, on the right of the piste. The track is still smooth: red sandy gravel. In a kilometre the track cuts across the piste with two white-painted cairns on the left.

### 84 (199)      N30° 21.8'   W05° 00.9'
Possibly a well on the right. The track becomes stonier with scrub and trees to the right.

MS – SAHARA

**90 (193)**          **N30° 25.5'  W04° 59.5'**
After you've started climbing a bit, a track joins from the right.

**95 (188)**          **N30° 27.4'  W04° 59.2'**
Having passed some soft sand, a cairn on the left and tussocks you reach a pair of tyres on either side of the now corrugated track. You see more tyre markers as the track heads north-north-east across a featureless gravel plain.

**98 (185)**          **N30° 29.1'  W04° 58.4'**
Two more tyre markers, another single tyre at KM100 and another pair on a slight rise to the left at KM102. Continue north-east across the gravel plain.

**109 (174)**          **N30° 33.3'  W04° 54.3'**
After you've passed another tyre at KM108, the village of **Tamassint** becomes visible a few hundred metres to the north-west (left). The terrain softens a bit and tracks become faint. Keep heading just east of north-east aiming for two more tyre markers ahead.

**112 (171)**          **N30° 34.7'  W04° 53.0'**
Two tyre markers on the right. Still on a fast, flat gravel piste. There is a single tyre at KM113, another pair at KM116 (N30° 36.2' W04° 51.6'), a single tyre a kilometre later and another pair with a cairn at KM118. After this there are a few cairns.

**121 (162)**          **N30° 38.15'  W04° 49.37'**
The track joins Route MS3. Keep right, heading east towards dunes. The going now gets slow and soft as you cross a low dune (plenty of tracks) and continue over the soft undulating sand.

**122 (161)**          **N30° 38.23'  W04° 48.71'**
Cross this dune easily on an improved surface. *Auberge Dinosaur Kem Kem* lies just to the south.

**127 (156)**          **N30° 38.58'  W04° 45.45'**
A marabout (shrine) is just to the north of the piste and *Auberge Marabout* to the south, beside the sand dune.

**129 (154)**          **N30° 38.48'  W04° 43.91'**
Pass another auberge (get used to it, it's not the last) and blue-grey rubble hills to

the south-east: Jebel Zireg with a radio mast on top. On the far side is Algeria. Soon you start across the seasonal chott known as Lake Maider.

**134 (149)**          **N30° 39.98'  W04° 41.48'**
Signs point to **Tafraoute** auberges nearby.

**136 (147)**          **N30° 40.16'  W04° 40.18'**
You're over the pass and entering a valley with a crenellated ridge to the north and dunes to the south.

**147 (136)**          **N30° 40.58'  W04° 33.43'**
A sandy section starts around here.

**151 (132)**          **N30° 40.18'  W04° 30.89'**
A track and a sign point promisingly north, possibly for the Col Mharech. Continue east on a bumpy piste.

**156 (127)**          **N30° 40.51'  W04° 28.36'**
Sign: 'Auberge Oasis Ramlia 7km'. Low dunes appear ahead. Brace yourself for many winding tracks around small dunes and bushes and nastier *feche-feche* powder.
    On big, heavy bikes it could be hard work. In a car I wandered too far south where the oued gets wider and only just scraped through. Consider lowering your tyre pressures and stay well north towards the gap in the range where the oued is narrower.

**162 (121)**          **N30° 41.14'  W04° 25.00**
*Auberge Ramlia*. A piste goes north. Head north-east on a stony track.

**164 (119)**          **N30° 41.97'  W04° 23.81'**
Junction of pistes.

**166 (117)**          **N30° 42.39'  W04° 22.98'**
*Aghbalou Ramlai Auberge* to the left with its name in stones on the hill behind. Soon there's a sandy descent towards a chott. Cross it following occasional cairns on either side.

**179 (104)**          **N30° 43.05'  W04° 19.10'**
Cross various chotts in between stretches of hamada.

**183 (100)**          **N30° 44.68'  W04° 12.74'**
Having just passed an auberge you now pass *Auberge Ouzima Rimal*, a nicer than

average place with dunes behind. In 2km you pass *Kasbah Ouzima Desert Hotel* and a kilometre later the *Erg Ouizima Auberge*.

**188 (95)       N30° 45.87' W04° 10.39'**
It's another auberge: the *Porte de Sahara*. Here you can cross over to the south side of the Oued Ziz to rejoin the track at KM193 via a village, but having tried that once it's simpler to continue straight ahead about 2km, crossing the oued around N30° 46.7' W04° 09.6'.

**193 (90)       N30° 46.70' W04° 08.65'**
A sign indicates 'Auberge Hassi Ouzima 2km'. The 'white-cairn/village' route joins from the right. Head north.

**197 (86)       N30° 48.66' W04° 08.23'**
Two tracks lead over a oued. The left one may be washed out. Occasional twin cairns feature alongside the track hereabouts.

**200 (83)       N30° 50.15' W04° 08.44'**
A track seems to join from left and soon the track forks but either fork will do. A kilometre later there are signs for various auberges. Another track joins from the left. Head along the edge of the oued.

**202 (81)       N30° 50.69' W04° 07.35'**
Junction. Turn left down into the oued among gravel hillocks.

**211 (72)       N30° 52.42' W04° 02.58'**
Pass along a sunken section of track. Black hamada follows.

**215 (68)       N30° 54.22' W03° 59.69'**
Cross over a rise with radio tower installation on the left. The tarmac is visible ahead.

**217 (66)       N30° 54.53' W03° 59.58'**
**Join the tarmac** at a sign: 'Centre Taouz' (to the left). Turn right for Merzouga, Erg Chebbi and Rissani.

**240 (43)       N31° 06.02' W04° 01.08'**
Junction at the north end of **Merzouga** with at least two dozen auberges running up alongside the dunes to suit all tastes and budgets. There's more on Erg Chebbi at the end of Route MS3.

**283       N31° 16.9' W04° 16.3'**
**Rissani** fuel station at the west end of town near the arches. ATMs, hotels, restos, shops, mechanics; it's all here.

# MS7   FOUM ZGUID – TAGOUNITE                    163KM
April 2008 ~ Mazda pickup

## Description
Many people are attracted to this route as a handy desert link between the sealed roads at Mhamid and Foum Zguid; the road via Agdz is twice as far but actually a great drive. For the first half this route follows the Jebel Bani to the north passing the usually dry chott of Lac Iriki. This is predominantly a rough, rocky trail that, depending on your suspension and how you slept last night, can make you wonder why they don't just seal it.

The nearby **dunes of Chegaga** are the main attraction. The transit will be much more fun if you get off the track to the south, bomb across Iriki and head into the small dunes as far as you like for a bit of exploration and experimentation.

With package tourists overnighting in the bivouacs of Erg Chegaga, this route is very popular and as a result nomad kids may desperately wave you down with empty water jugs from around KM75 onwards, but rest assured there are wells out here.

## Off road

Take it easy on your car's springs or your motorbike's wheels. In a car you sometimes just have to crawl along at walking pace. Coming through the dunes lining the Oued Mhamid at the end of the piste section you'll probably need **four-wheel drive**, while **bikers** will need to stand up and get pro-active. Lac Iriki might be considered an inland delta of the Oued Draa and although it never fills up any more, it frequently gets soggy. In a 4WD it's something to consider. On an **MTB** this route would be hard work along the rocky stages so make the most of the lake bed sections, or better still, try something else.

## Route finding

Side tracks come and go but route-finding is all too clear with the Jebel always to the north and either stone cairns or a rubbly track that you can't miss. At KM104 maps show a piste following the curve of the Jebel Bani all the way to Tagounite but few ever try this. The **map** for this route is on the opposite page.

## Fuel and water

Foum Zguid and Tagounite for fuel; water at each end plus the wells and encampments along the route.

## Suggested duration

This route is easily done in a day with several plush kasbah-style hotels out of Mhamid. Overnight camps en route may attract a nomad or two.

**0km              N30° 05.40'  W06° 52.66'**
**Foum Zguid** fuel at the north end of town For more see the end of Route MA9. Head south out of town.

**3 (160)              N30° 04.0'  W06° 52.0'**
Southern gate. Drive out of town along the tarmac and after a kilometre turn left, south-south-east **onto the piste** heading directly for a pink fort.
  Leaving Foum Zguid you really do feel like you are driving out of the Atlas ranges and into the Sahara.

**2 (161)**
Fort with possibly a passport check. Continue south-south-east on corrugations across a rocky plain. Saw-tooth ranges are visible on the southern horizon.

**13 (150)              N29° 57.9'  W06° 49.8'**
The track forks. Go left, south-east to a wide oued. In 700m exit the oued with a piste joining from the right.

**19 (145)**
As you drop into a dip a track joins from the left.

**21 (142)**
Fork. The main corrugated track curves right heading towards a large mesa (Jebel Hamsailikh).

**29 (134)**
Pass to the north of the mesa on your right and in half a kilometre cross a sandy oued with grassy tussocks.

**30 (133)**
Now you're back on a stony hamada and heading south-south-east towards Oued Mdaouer.

**33 (130)**
The piste curves around the north-east edge of Mdaouer Srhir.

**35 (128)              N29° 50.7'  W06° 40.3'**
The piste forks as you're heading east with the mesa behind you. Take the left fork heading east-north-east. Sand dunes are visible ahead.

**37 (126)**
Fast smooth going for a couple of kilometres. Make the most of it! Then you cross a

MS – SAHARA

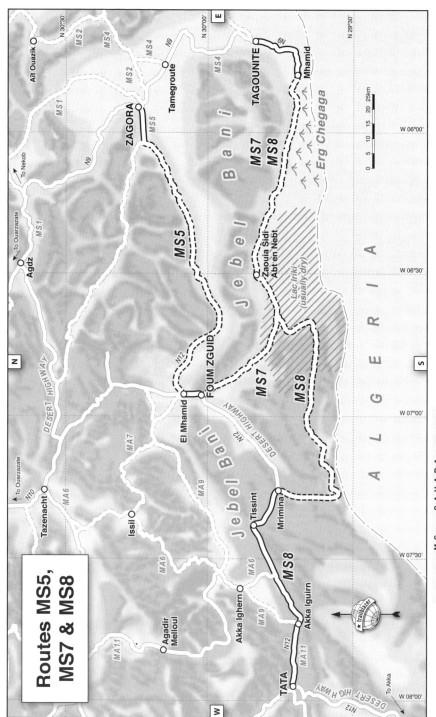

Routes MS5, MS7 & MS8

bumpy claypan and drive through a hummocky oued (KM39.6). Cairns may mark the piste at 100m intervals. This is the far western edge of the Iriki chott.

**41 (122)**
Another sandy oued crossing. Continue north-east past cairn markers.

**47 (116)      N29° 52.75'  W06° 34.60'**
Pink fort checkpoint and probably a bit of inane chatter with the soldiers. From here a smooth track skims across the lake bed all the way to Zaouia Sidi Abt; enjoy it because soon after it gets grim.

**65 (98)      N29° 58.2'  W06° 26.0'**
**Zaouia Sidi Abt en Nebt**. A few buildings and the mausoleum of Sidi Abt. In a kilometre leave the village to the east-south-east continuing over a stony track with occasional buildings on the left.

Brace yourself as here begins a bone-shaking 30km stage that can take up to two hours depending on if your car's a rental or not. Bikes will probably wonder what the fuss is about.

**72 (91)      N29° 58.57'  W06° 21.98'**
Pass a village and in a kilometre take the diversion to the left.

**75 (88)**
Pass a sign for a nomad school.

**77 (86)      N29° 57.89'  W06° 19.17'**
Checkpoint on a hill, a **well** 30m to the south and soon a very basic-looking camp site near another '*Ecole Nomade*'.

**80 (83)      N29° 56.91'  W06° 17.84'**
Junction; go straight, not right.

**97 (66)      N29° 54.29'  W06° 08.48'**
Forking right here might be better.

**99 (64)      N29° 53.07'  W06° 07.23'**
Junction with a piste going south into the dunes with a fort to the south. Soon you pass *Iriki Excursions* auberge. The stony section is over.

**104 (59)**
Junction for the track to Tagounite. Right is for Mhamid.

**106 (57)      N29° 52.55'  W06° 03.54'**
Cross the deep channel of Oued el Rharg.

**111 (52)      N29° 52.19'  W06° 00.54'**
Junction; head south-south-east over various wide and occasionally corrugated tracks. It may help to stick the KM138 waypoint in the GPS and just 'Go to', following whatever track's best for you.

**124 (39)      N29° 50.22'  W05° 53.02'**
Metre-high dunes begin as you near Mhamid.

**127 (36)      N29° 49.80'  W05° 51.39'**
Bumpy dried mud and sand banks with tamarisk tree mounds ahead. Work your way along whatever track is easiest while generally heading east and aiming to come down from the north onto KM138.

**138 (25)      N29° 50.25'  W05° 45.24'**
After a very sandy 100m or so you come to the corner of a grubby-looking camp-site. Carry on south-east towards the water and radio towers.

**139 (24)      N29° 49.91'  W05° 44.75'**
The main piste heading west out of Mhamid joins from the right. Rubbish all around and buildings ahead. The northern arc you've taken to come in may have missed the worst of the sand.

**142 (21)      N29° 49.68'  W05° 43.72'**
**Join the tarmac** leading into Mhamid, passing a few cafés and shops.

**143 (20)      N29° 49.49'  W05° 43.21'**
**Mhamid** roundabout. The village has become the jumping off point for starry night bivouacs out in Erg Chegaga so there are wall-to-wall nomad crafts and if you slow down the touts will be on you.

Sadly it seems the old *Hotel Sahara* by the roundabout may have had its day so if you don't fancy staying in town, there are several flashier kasbah-style hotels along the road a few kilometres north of town.

**163      N29° 59.38'  W05° 35.08'**
**Tagounite** ZIZMO northside. No café but there are a few in town, and with no 'things to see and do' as in Tamegroute up the road, you can walk around and do some shopping without a disguise.

# MS8   TATA – TISSINT – TAGOUNITE                    315KM
April 2008 ~ Mazda pickup

## Description
South of the Desert Highway, from around 40km east of Tata at Sidi Rezzoug to as far west as Zag on the closed road to Smara, the borderlands are a closed area. (Routes MW1 and especially MW6 skirt round this region.) If you try and venture south here you'll be spotted by the many patrols and observation posts and escorted back to the road. In fact it's surprising how far south you're allowed to roam in Morocco without being menaced by jumpy border guards, although those that don't stop you for a check will take a good look at you as you pass by.

This route takes the first opportunity in the east to get down into the borderlands and once it leaves the highway it picks up a former **Dakar Rally** track which, like Route MW2, is as well marked as any piste in Morocco. It works its way north of the fringes of the **Oued Draa** which marks the border hereabouts and then moves north towards the famed mud flats of **Lac Iriki** with a chance to set some personal land speed records or, it seems, just hoon about. At a pink fort you then join Route MS7 for the run into Mhamid and the tarmac up to Tagounite.

The day I did this route was pretty nasty, with scorching sand winds blowing in from the south and visibility of just a few kilometres at times. It was too hot to even get out of the car for very long so my impression of the route was a little tempered.

With only 207km of actual piste this is do-able in a day but why are you here if not to camp out in the desert once in a while?

## Off road
Things may get messy with a bit of ground water rising up through Iriki or the Oued Draa further south. The thought of getting a heavy **4WD** mired in the salty mud does not bear thinking about. Sticking to the track, **big bikes** will manage fine most of the time but it's clearly too long a run on a **bicycle**.

Though not on this route, the **dunes of Chegaga** are not far away and a worthwhile deviation if you're up for some dune driving. You always know that the flat lake bed or the stony track are to the north, and the Erg itself is dotted with tourist encampments. This route, or versions of it across Lac Iriki are popular and although I saw no other tourist cars until well past Zaouia Sidi, chances are you will.

## Route finding
It's a seemingly complex meander along the piste but is initially very well marked with Dakar cairns up to the pink fort at KM199 and largely Olaffed. After a zip across the lake bed at Zaouia Sidi Abt you then get locked into the tramlines of a stony track for a couple of hours followed by the challenge of surfing through the low dunes into Mhamid. The **map** is on p189.

## Fuel and water
Fuel only at each end or possibly Mhamid if you ask around. Once on the piste the only well spotted was around KM228.

**0km**          **N29° 44.31'  W07° 58.42'**
**Tata** fuel on the south side of town. Head into town and turn right to follow the wide boulevard heading east for Foum Zguid. For accommodation options in Tata see the end of Route MA6.

**49 (266)**        **N29° 50.33'  W07° 29.99'**
Pass the turn off north for Route MA6 and MA11 coming down from Akka Ighern and Tazenacht.

**70 (145)**        **N29° 54.42'  W07° 19.12'**
Frequent checkpoint in **Tissint** as the road bends sharply right after coming through a gap in Jebel Bani. There's a café right on the bend and several stores down the road. Head south out of town.

**87 (228)**        **N29° 49.53'  W07° 12.24'**
Just before Oued Mellah and a warning roadsign, **turn south onto a track** which soon becomes corrugated. There are Dakar Rally balises every 10m or so. Olaf runs parallel to the west and soon joins up.

**104 (211)**        **N29° 40.69'  W07° 13.80'**
An observation post is visible on the hill to the south-east and soon you see an army base ahead on the other side of a oued. This is not a place to be poking cameras around too conspicuously. What you're about to do now is loop south around the base, turn east and north again to KM113 then set off eastwards.

**108 (207)**        **N29° 38.93'  W07° 13.62'**
Having crossed a side oued near the barracks, you pass beneath the scrutiny of another observation hut on a hill to the east.

**109 (206)**        **N29° 38.58'  W07° 13.52'**
At this point you can cut a corner on Olaf by heading south-east to a prominent cairn on a hill about a kilometre away.

**110 (205)**        **N29° 37.85'  W07° 12.84'**
Rejoin Olaf and head north-east with a balise (cairns) every 5m or so.

**111 (204)**        **N29° 38.46'**
**W07° 12.31'**
Fork right following the cairns on mounds.

**111.5 (203.5)   N29° 38.79'  W07° 12.28'**
You reach Oued Mellah (or 'Oued Zguid' depending on your map) just before it spills into the Oued Draa right on the border. There may be salty pooled water as well as voracious flies. Work your way over the oued to the east.

**112.5 (202.5)   N29° 39.03'  W07° 11.96'**
Leave the oued here and err to the north-east passing over a patch of soft grey sand.

**113 (202)**        **N29° 39.43'  W07° 11.80'**
You're now at the top of a low pass, pointing east. Follow the sometimes corrugated track east past Dakar mounds. Low rubble hills all around.

**118 (197)**        **N29° 39.33'  W07° 09.49'**
Cross a kilometre-wide chott marked with cairns. According to Google Earth you're less than two miles from the Algerian border here, although Google Earth also depicts Mhamid roundabout (KM295) as less than a mile from the border. Few maps ever give the same position or even mark the border at all.

**121 (194)**        **N29° 39.94'  W07° 07.50'**
An observation post with a radio mast is visible on the hill 500m to the south-east. You're on a wide, corrugated track.

**125 (190)**        **N29° 41.42'  W07° 06.16'**
Two rocks on either side of track with 'CS' painted on them. A nice passage along a oued follows; it could be an OK camp spot.

**128 (187)**        **N29° 41.15'  W07° 04.07'**
Short bumpy section over a chalky-white surface.

**131 (184)**        **N29° 40.97'  W07° 02.87'**
The track rises out of a oued onto a stony hamada. You head north-east.

**132 (183)**        **N29° 41.64'  W07° 02.35'**
The track drops into a side oued, does a squiggle and then continues north-east again over another oued.

**137.5 (177.5)   N29° 43.49'  W07° 00.00'**
Cross 7°W on hamada (a chance to position yourself on a map with gridlines).

Nothing visible to south, jebel to the north and the Iriki chott ahead.

**144 (171)      N29° 44.01'  W06° 56.58'**
Sandy patch.

**146 (169)      N29° 43.90'  W06° 55.67'**
While heading east you cross the second north-south track in the last few minutes with another one about a kilometre ahead. Soon small dunes appear.

**153 (162)      N29° 43.41'  W06° 50.92'**
A piste marked on some maps and Olaffed crosses to the south-east. You continue directly east.

**158 (157)      N29° 43.50'  W06° 48.12'**
The track rises over a small pass with nice dunes to the south. This is possibly another nice camping spot, but not in a 40°C gale!

**168 (147)      N29° 43.21'  W06° 41.72'**
Jebel Zguilma visible not far to the south.

**174 (141)      N29° 43.23'  W06° 38.37'**
The track now turns to the north-east and soon even north-north-west for a bit as it crosses western Lac Iriki.

**180 (135)      N29° 45.05'  W06° 35.52'**
Key point. Having just crossed a oued you get to a fork, take the route with cairns to north-north-west. East leads onto Lac Iriki and **Chegaga** to probably rejoin this route with a northward arc at around KM251, a distance of about 60km to the east-north-east. It's something to consider when you think what lies beyond Zaouia Sidi Abt en Nebt at KM217...

**184 (131)      N29° 47.59'  W06° 36.87'**
Bumping along the western edge of the lakebed heading north-north-east with some sandy patches. After a while you'll pass the flat-topped Jebel Nouhsour to the west.

**190 (125)      N29° 49.64'  W06° 38.12'**
A sandy passage through a oued. If you keep up momentum there's no need to do the tyres.

**192 (123)      N29° 50.47'  W06° 37.76'**
Having picked up a track joining from the left you now curve north-east and then east following Dakar mounds across the lake bed.

**195 (120)      N29° 51.51'  W06° 35.85'**
Leave the lake bed and head through a pass with a shack on the left and a tyre marker soon after.

**197 (118)      N29° 52.49'  W06° 34.73'**
Tracks join from the right as you head north towards the pink fort.

**199 (116)      N29° 52.75'  W06° 34.60'**
Pink fort and checkpoint. From here a smooth track skims across the lake bed north-east all the way to Zaouia Sidi Abt.

**217 (98)      N29° 58.2'  W06° 26.0'**
Zaouia Sidi Abt en Nebt. A few buildings, a mosque and the mausoleum. In a kilometre you leave the village to the east-south-east continuing over a stony track with occasional buildings on the left. Brace yourself for a bone-shaking 30km stage that can take up to two hours.

**224 (91)      N29° 58.57'  W06° 21.98'**
Pass a village and in a kilometre take the diversion to the left. Sign for an *'Ecole Nomade'*.

**229 (86)      N29° 57.89'  W06° 19.17'**
There's an unmanned checkpoint on a hill with a **well** to the south and soon a rough-looking 'camping' near another Ecole Nomade.

**232 (83)      N29° 56.91'  W06° 17.84'**
Junction, go straight, not right.

**249 (66)      N29° 54.29'  W06° 08.48'**
Forking right here might be better.

**251 (64)      N29° 53.06'  W06° 07.23'**
Key point. Junction with a piste going south-west into the dunes to tourist encampments. There is a fort to the south. Soon you pass *Iriki Excursions* auberge. The worst of the stony section is over.

**256 (59)      N29° 52.67'  W06° 04.51'**
Early junction for the piste winding around north-east to Tagounite. Right (south-east) is for Mhamid.

**258 (57)         N29° 52.55'  W06° 03.54'**
Cross the Oued el Rharg. Directly south of here at N29° 50.95' W06° 02.65' there's a **waterhole** in the oued, according to a web report.

**263 (52)         N29° 52.19'  W06° 00.54'**
Junction with another track up to Tagounite. You head east-south-east over many wide and occasionally corrugated tracks. It may help to simply stick KM290 waypoint as a 'Go to' and reel yourself in whichever way is best. It seems erring to the north is less sandy.

**276 (39)         N29° 50.22'  W05° 53.02'**
Metre-high dunes begin here as you near Mhamid.

**279 (36)         N29° 49.80'  W05° 51.39'**
Bumpy dried mud and sand banks with tamarisk tree mounds ahead. Work your way along whatever track is easiest while generally heading east and aiming to come down from the north onto KM290.

**290 (25)         N29° 50.25'  W05° 45.24'**
After a very sandy stage you get to the corner of a grubby-looking campsite. Carry on south-east towards the water and radio towers.

**291 (24)         N29° 49.91'  W05° 44.75'**
The main piste heading west out of town joins from the right.

**294 (21)         N29° 49.68'  W05° 43.72'**
**Join the tarmac** leading into Mhamid, passing a few cafés and touristy shops.

**295 (20)         N29° 49.49'  W05° 43.21'**
**Mhamid** roundabout by the *Hotel Sahara*. For more on Mhamid see the end of Route MS7.

**315                N29° 59.38'  W05° 35.08'**
**Tagounite** ZIZ fuel station on the north side of town.

# MS9   OUARZAZATE – TAZENACHT                 77KM
November 2008 ~ Yamaha Ténéré

## Description
This is not really a true desert route but was probably as green as it gets when I did it. A handy short cut from Ouarzazate through low rounded hills and valleys towards either the Foum Zguid-, Sirwa- or Anti Atlas routes, it sets off following a wide new track to the turn-off at KM25. Soon after this point, from the 1612m high point and onwards you get great views of the Sirwa massif, under thick snow when I passed through in early November.

## Off road
The inter-village section between Imidar and Tisslite gets a bit rough but nothing a **4WD** or even a loaded Triumph Tiger can't manage as it won't last long. All a rider has to do is keep an even keel across the oueds and the descents. On a **mountain bike** it would be a pretty full day's ride as the final road section from near Anezal down to Tazenacht is hilly and twisty and so not a great place to be riding in the dark. If you need it, there's small *gîte d'étape* in Anezal.

## Route finding
Out of Ouarzazate minor tracks and the new wide track may confuse you until you get to the Imidar turn-off where the new track seems to plough on south, possibly to Tagangoute and so Tazenacht as shown on Google Maps. A possibly old Olaffed track traces or parallels this route, but compared to other Olaf

tracks, in places it seems oddly imprecise as if the track log recording interval of whoever logged it was set too low. The only traffic you're likely to see on this section are the Ouarzazate–based bike tour operators. The route **map** is miles back on p164.

## Fuel and water
Fuel at each end and maybe Anezal; water in the wells, the creeks and the two main villages on the piste.

## Suggested duration
Allow about two hours on a bike or up to three in a car to Tazenacht.

**0km          N30° 53.97'   W06° 54.66'**
*Mobil* fuel at the South **Ouarzazate** junction; one of a few around here. Take the south Ouarzazate bypass heading west towards Marrakech.

**2.2 (74.8)     N30° 54.41'   W06° 55.97'**
Pass the Olaf left turn (it joins up later) and at a sign indicating 'Fint 10km' turn left to follow the new track.

**16.5 (60.5)     N30° 50.42'   W07° 01.81'**
Rejoin Olaf coming from south-east above the palmy village of Taguenzalt.

**25 (52)          N30° 47.30'   W07° 04.01'**
Turn right off new road at sign for Imidar village. There was confusing road building going on here when I passed through.

**26.5 (50.5)     N30° 47.65'   W07° 04.76'**
Near **Imidar** continue straight along the oued, not into the village. Recross the oued a couple of times and pass through a defile into a valley. The track gets thin and little used until you reach Tisslite.

**29 (48)          N30° 46.99'   W07° 05.76'**
Exit the oued out to the right and ascend to the south-west.

**30 (47)          N30° 46.68'   W07° 06.60'**
**High point** on the piste section of this route at 1612m following a loose, washed-out climb. The possibly snow-capped peak of Jebel Sirwa is visible ahead, the actual 3305m summit is the small turret to the south. The views of Sirwa get better as you go on. From the pass drop back down onto the next valley.

**33 (44)          N30° 46.49'   W07° 07.98'**
Pass a stone goat enclosure and refuge and then drop into a oued and follow it for a while. It can get sandy.

**36.5 (40.5)     N30° 45.68'   W07° 09.32'**
Another goat fold and adjacent shelter.

**44.5 (32.5)     N30° 45.55'   W07° 12.71'**
Fenced off pink huts by a oued and nearby cultivation with a mine-head like ruin over the creek. The track detours around a small wash-out.

**45.5 (31.5)     N30° 45.43'   W07° 14.26'**
Pass a well north of the track just after crossing the oued again and as you curve south and uphill.

**46.5 (30.5)     N30° 44.82'   W07° 14.12'**
Enter **Tisslite** village (Tamassine on old maps) from the north.

**47 (30)          N30° 44.71'   W07° 14.17'**
In the middle of the village turn right and head out west. You'll soon pass a football field and follow power lines as the track improves.

**52.5 (24.5)     N30° 44.90'   W07° 17.13'**
**Join the N10** just over a kilometre south of **Anezal** and turn south for Tazenacht. This is quite a scenic drive in its own right, with large flat lay-bys popular with free camping campervans and a great **viewpoint** south into the desert at around KM65 (N30° 38.84'  W07° 16.28') following the 1715m **Tizi-n Bachkoum** pass.

**77               N30° 34.69'   W07° 12.34'**
*Shell* fuel on **Tazenacht's** north edge. There are a few hotels and restos in town. For more on Tazenacht see Route MA6.

MS – SAHARA

## MS10    FIGUIG TO THE ATLANTIC: THE DESERT HIGHWAY    1500KM
2008 – Mazda pickup and Yamaha Ténéré

The 1500-km network of sealed roads connecting Figuig to the Atlantic makes a classic and easy overland journey for those in a **rental car**, **motorhome**, riding a **touring motorcycle**, or for **cyclists** looking to get stuck into a long, mostly level road tour. The tarmac is in good shape and **fuel stops** are never more than 200km apart, even if you won't necessarily find European-style roadside services.

At times running within sight of the Algerian border, the entire route runs through the Moroccan Sahara and sees so little traffic that you may jump when a car overtakes you. In either direction and on a daily basis it'll offer as much stark desert scenery as your windscreen or visor can accommodate and, bikes excepted, it's possible to spend every night in some sort of hotel, or at worst a municipal campsite. In places it's even possible to get off the highway without damaging all but the lowest vehicle (and so breaking local 2WD car rental regulations). Places listed below in bold which are on, or close to, the Desert Highway have **fuel**, but other fuel sources may exist in small towns. Most of these towns will have **hotels** too. Besides your *LP* or *Rough Guide*, check the latest recommendations on the website's link or refer to the off-road routes in this book which end in a town you're interested in.

### Route description
From **Figuig** (where petrol may be limited, see p115) overlooking the Algerian border it's a striking run though the jebels along the N17 to **Bouarfa** which has lately transformed itself into a busy town in the middle of nowhere. From here you scoot back south towards the frontier following the N10 and passing **Bouanane** (basic hotel). A road branches from here up up to **Beni Tajite** and on to Missour; Route ME1. Back on the N10, soon after Boudenib you may choose to leave the relatively dull stretch of the Desert Highway which follows at the Oued Guir bridge. A diversion leads north and west up via **Gourama** from where you can work your way back down through the Ziz Gorge and down again to **Er Rachidia**, a sprawling modern university town.

Staying on the N10, you reach the junction just south of Rachidia where the N13 leads down the oasis-filled Ziz valley via **Aoufous** to **Erfoud** and **Rissani**. At Rissani most people will make the 90km round trip to admire the dunes of Erg Chebbi near Merzouga – fairly small by Saharan standards but unique to Morocco. Rissani can be a hassle, but on the bright side many of the auberges alongside the dunes north of Merzouga and listed in the guidebooks will be accessible along tracks not needing huge clearance if taken slowly.

Back in Rissani the N12 'Route of Fossils' runs south and west and in good weather is one of the best stretches of the Desert Highway, even if many of the trilobites you'll be offered are made by hand. You pass nameless ranges to the south, villages with long-ruined hilltop ksars and after **Alnif**, the volcanic spikes of Jebel Sarhro. Tazzarine and **Nekob** have cafés and hotels too, as does **Adgz** soon after the bridge over the Draa River. Here the 'Valley of the Casbahs' runs down to **Zagora** (a parallel to Rissani…), home of the famous '*Timbuktu, 52 jours*' sign. Taking this diversion the asphalt ends close to the Algerian border where overnight camel excursions head off into the low dunes of Chegaga. Note that

MS – SAHARA

some paper maps and guidebooks indicate a sealed road linking Zagora to just north of Foum Zguid. Although such a connection would make sense, in 2009 it was still Route MS5 but with a prospect of sealing.

The Desert Highway; not just for cars and bikes.

Not to worry, you're about to take a much more enjoyable drive from Agdz west along the R108, one of the most scenic and quietest stages of this whole trans-Moroccan tour, passing striking ranges, picturesque villages with tiny mosques, rustling palmeries and crumbling kasbahs as well as the occasional café and very little traffic.

At the junction with the R111, **Tazenacht**, just up the road, is worth the detour both for the spectacular viewpoint on the drive back, and if you're after buying a carpet in a relaxed, non-city souk setting. On the way back south you pass though the narrow walls of the **Tizi Taguergoust** pass which unravels dramatically to reveal the desert beyond. Of all the Moroccan so-called 'gateways to the desert' this one takes the prize. Otherwise, turn south from Agdz down the R111 and pass through the gap or 'foum' in the ranges into friendly **Foum Zguid** (more on p229). Its relaxed ambience and town square cafés are a far cry from places embedded further east on the tourist axis.

Leaving town on the N12 you really feel you're heading out into the Sahara; a thousand miles to the south, Timbuktu is the next town of any consequence. At Tissint you pass back through the ranges of the Jebel Bani and west of town can take a right turn and reverse Route MA11 up to **Taliouine**, a great drive over the Anti Atlas. Back on the Desert Highway, **Tata** has good hotels, restaurants, ATMs and camping right in town. If you've a day to spare you can take a great mountain drive north up to **Igherm** (the end of Route MA11) and loop back down the R109 to Tata.

Beyond Tata, there are a few shops and fuel at **Akka** if you know where to look (see Route MA3) and room to camp out in the desert if you so wish. Foum el Hassan has seen more prosperous days when it was a staging point for the now abandoned road to Tindouf in Algeria. The N12 carries on west here via **Aït Herbil** to **Bou Izakarn** on the coast road. Much nicer is the road down to enigmatic **Assa**. From here the border road south down to Zag and on to Smara is **closed** to tourists, though it's easy to get to Zag before anyone tells you this. Apart from Route MW6, there's a permitted highway out of Tan-Tan. And note the sealed road from the 'teapot' roundabout in Assa soon ends at Aoueinat Torkoz.

Out of Assa, if the sun is low a great stage beckons as the R103 climbs up over the **Targoumite Pass** with great views back to the desert before dropping down towards **Fask** with a basic café in the ZIZ as you enter town.

With a vehicle to park, if you don't fancy the bustle of Guelmim on the N1 coastal highway there's a reasonable hotel in Tighmert (called versions of 'Ait Bekkou' on maps and in some guidebooks, see Route MW5). Once you get to **Guelmim** you may find the faded charms of oceanside **Sidi Ifni** to be a touch more ambient a destination to end your tour than inland **Tan-Tan** which is merely faded, albeit with the lure of the untamed Western Sahara beyond.

MS – SAHARA

# MA ANTI ATLAS

## Outline of the Anti Atlas region

This region incorporates the more arid and so less populated southern and eastern ranges of the Anti Atlas chain, south of the N10 highway at Taliouine and west of the R103 at Foum Zguid. Running as they do right down along the Algerian border as far as Assa, many 'MA' routes are satisfyingly long while also combining a human and natural element, and all are readily accessible in a rental vehicle from Agadir, Marrakech or Ouarzazate.

In essence this area is the western extension of the MS Sahara zone, but with the addition of canyon and mountain routes and with far fewer tour groups.

The exact point where the Anti Atlas ends and High Atlas begins is hard to define on the ground, but geologically the Anti Atlas is part of a much older formation and today experiences a **drier climate**. This makes it a good proposition when the High Atlas may be snow bound or you're trying to shake off the rain.

## MA Routes

# MA1    TAFRAOUTE – TIZERKINE GORGE – AÏT HERBIL  106KM

April and November 2008 ~ Mazda pickup, Yamaha Ténéré

## Description

This is a satisfying way of getting back to Aït Herbil if you came up MA2, as well as a great way of getting down south in its own right. You climb steeply up out of Tafraoute on a road and at Tleta Tasserirt (not all maps show it, or in the right place) you break off to the east along a wide track. Soon this track turns into an old, narrow asphalt road near Taraout, but once it enters the upper Tizerkine Gorge this abandoned road becomes potholed and has in places been washed away. Not that you mind much as descending through the Tizerkine Gorge is most agreeable; another environmental transition as argan trees give way to palms.

By the time you've dropped 400m and get to what is probably Tizerkine village, the palms are thick enough to see your headlight beam on the ground and presently you join Route MA3 and follow it down to Afella (among its many other names). Here, right in the town's forded oued you turn south to follow the wide stony canyon of the Assif n Int (as far as its name can be deduced from old maps) passing some prehistoric engravings and a couple of nomad goat camps along the way. While it's fun to drive along a riverbed, the Assif lacks the villages, palmeries and dramatic ascents which led you here, although with no other southbound sealed roads for miles, it's a relatively quick way of getting down from Tafraoute to the N12 road and the desert around Akka and Assa. The Tizerkine stage was done on the bike; the Assif n Int canyon was done earlier in the car.

## Off road

Some stages in the Tizerkine Gorge (which should be considered a piste despite being mostly sealed) were washed away but nothing that can't be got around. There are no tough off-road ascents as on MA2 or drastic clearance issues, so **any vehicle** showing a bit of daylight around its ankles could manage this route. The Tizerkine Gorge stage would be fun on a **mountain bike** but I'd guess the unremitting shingle causeway along the Assif n Int canyon would be less so; you may as well reverse MA2 which is prettier.

## Route finding

Once off the normal sealed roads, which aren't especially busy apart from the short mine truck stages (see KM49), you won't see any traffic in the gorge or canyon and it's hard to get lost. Note that Souk el Had d'Afella-Ihrir is what appears on most paper maps but it's also known as Souk el Had Issi, Talate n Yissi on old maps and Google Maps, or just plain old 'Yissik'. 'Afella' is the locally distinctive word and so is what I use. This route is **mapped** on p213.

## Fuel and water

There is fuel at each end (not always at Aït Herbil) and probably in Afella too if you ask around. Once on the piste there are several wells along the oueds.

## Suggested duration

Half a day. From Afella to Aït Herbil (54km) takes about two hours in a car.

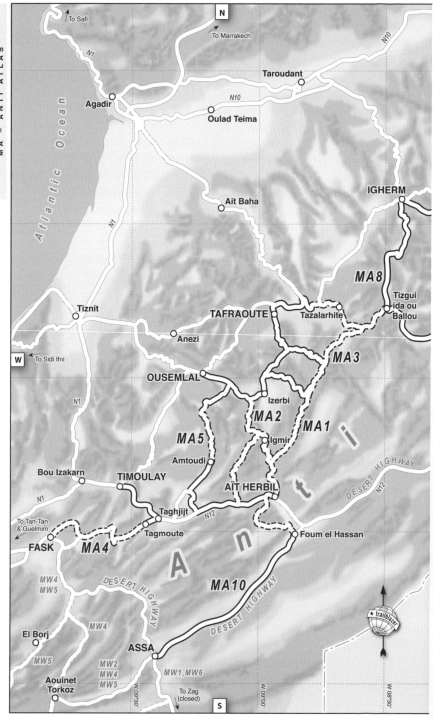

**N**

O Aoulouz

*MH8*

*MH9*

To Ouarzazate

To Agdz

DESERT HIGHWAY

TALIOUINE

TAZENACHT O

*N10*

*N10*

N 30°30'

M A – A N T I   A T L A S

*N10*

*MA6*

*N10*

*MA7*

*S*

*t*

*l*

Issil

*MA7*

*MA11*

*a*

Agadir
Melloul

*MA6*

To Zagora

El Mhamid O

*N12*

FOUM ZGUID O

*MS5*

Akka Ighern

*MA9*

N 30°00'

*t*

*A*

Tissint O

*N12*

DESERT HIGHWAY

*MA9*

*MS7*

TATA O

*N12*

*MA6*

*MA11*

Akka
Iguirn

*MS8*

O Imitek

To Tagounite

*N12*

*MS8*

DESERT HIGHWAY

**E**

N 29°30'

*MA3*

0    10    20    30km

O AKKA

N 29°00'

A L G E R I A

## Anti Atlas (MA)
## Routes Overview

**MA1** Tafraoute – Gorge – Aït Herbil
**MA2** Aït Herbil – Tafraoute
**MA3** Akka – Tafraoute
**MA4** Fask – Timoulay
**MA5** Ousemlal – Amtoudi – Aït Herbil
**MA6** Tazenacht – Issil – Tata
**MA7** Foum Zguid – Issil – Taliouine
**MA8** Tafraoute – Tazal' – Igherm
**MA9** Tata – Akka Ighern – Foum Zguid
**MA10** Ousemlal – Foum el Hassan – Assa
**MA11** Taliouine – Tata – Igherm

N 28°30'

**0km**          **N29° 43.20'  W08° 58.30'**
*AFRIQUIA* fuel station in **Tafraoute** town centre. (For hotel details see the end of Route MA3). Head south out of town.

**3 (103)**          **N29° 41.77'  W08° 57.74'**
At this junction keep left.

**7 (99)**          **N29° 39.80'  W08° 57.63'**
A road forks right for the famous **Painted Rocks** (the work of Belgian artist, Jean Verame from 1984) and Izerbi. You keep left and commence a 500m climb.

**19 (87)**          **N29° 36.80'  W08° 55.14'**
Junction and a milepost in Arabic and a wide track leading left to the nearby village of **Tleta Tasserirt**. **Take the dirt road** through the village.

**22 (84)**
Fork right here for the Gorges de Tizerkine. Left (Olaffed) leads north, probably to Tazalarhite on Route MA8.
     On the way to Tizerkine you soon get to the village of **Taraout** after which the wide track becomes an old broken road. In places it's washed away and you drive over stones, but never for long.

**32 (74)**
Deep but dry well on the left.

**36 (70)**          **N29° 35.12'  W08° 48.02'**
**Tizerkine** village where the broken road turns into a rubbly track. Carry on winding through the dark, shady palmerie.

**40 (66)**          **N29° 34.37'  W08° 46.32'**
You arrive and join Route MA3 which has come down from Timkyet a little to the north. Turn right and join MA3 the short distance to Afella.

**48 (58)**          **N29° 31.48'  W08° 48.03'**
An Olaffed track joins from the left, but probably just runs to the mine.

**49 (57)**          **N29° 30.10'  W08° 49.07'**
The **tarmac junction** at an elaborate milepost. The tarmac goes north-east (left) 16km to the Akka gold mine and on to KM50 on Route MA3.
     You carry straight on and soon get to **Afella**. On the right, is a basic café with a few not-so-cheap groceries.

**52 (54)**          **N29° 29.89'  W08° 49.28'**
Drop down to the oued and **leave the road**, south, into the Assif n Int oued. Initially this track is a diversion around the town for the heavy mine trucks.

**56.5 (49.5)**      **N29° 27.85'  W08° 50.41'**
At a sign: '*Graveurs 7km*' turn left off the truck piste. You're now entering a wide, shallow canyon along which winds a stony oued which you'll follow just about all the way to Aït Herbil.

**61 (45)**          **N29° 26.05'  W08° 50.96'**
A track goes off to the left for the engravings. The *Rough Guide* has some details with promises of elephants and rhinos.
     There are some intriguing abstract engraving sites in Morocco, particularly up in the northern High Atlas, but if these are anything like the crude depictions of fauna at the other end near Aït Herbil (see Route MA2) you may not be so impressed.

**68.5 (37.5)**      **N29° 22.62'  W08° 52.59'**
Pass two **wells** on the right and in about 5km pass a dry well.

**77 (29)**          **N29° 18.82'  W08° 54.15'**
A valley joins from the right near some goat nomad camps.

**84 (22)**          **N29° 16.36'  W08° 57.06'**
Pass a **cistern** on the left.

**89 (17)**          **N29° 14.79'  W08° 58.79'**
Don't turn left here to take a short cut, it gets too rough. Keep straight ahead to join the main route in 250m at N29° 14.78' W08° 58.92'. Here you meet Route MA2 heading north and is where you turn left, south, for Aït Herbil.

**96 (10)**          **N29° 12.04'  W08° 59.32"**
The **tarmac starts** near **Imouzlag** village and soon rises above the oued with great views of the settlement below. Just before you reach the N12 highway there are a couple of shops.

**106 (00)**         **N29° 07.99'  W08° 57.92'**
The basic *ZIZ* fuel station of **Aït Herbil** on the N12 highway. The nearest place to stay is the *Igmir Guest House*, 32km back up MA2.

# MA2    AÏT HERBIL – TAFRAOUTE                    97KM
March 2008 ~ Mazda pickup

## Description
For the distance you cover, this is the best short route in the Anti Atlas, and whichever direction you do it in you're in for a wonderful, winding traverse along the gorge of the Oued Smouguene through the eastern ranges of the Anti Atlas. On the way you pass cliff-side Berber villages followed by palm-shrouded Berber villages as far as Igmir, where the route suddenly climbs fit to burst your radiator's cork out onto the highlands and Berber hill villages (you'll have the full set now) along the tarmac to Tafraoute. At the very start of the route there's a chance to inspect rock engravings at Aït Herbil, though if you've seen examples in Algeria and Libya you may be disappointed.

If you're wondering whether to do this or MA1 then do them both. MA1 is a good way of getting back down to Aït Herbil and could even be packed with this route into one eventful day. Otherwise, allow half a day, though camping around KM29 or spending the night at the agreeable guest house at Igmir (KM35) is more fun and gives you a chance to meet the locals and appreciate the evening/dawn light on the burned orange gorge walls.

## Off road
This route was originally done in 2004 in a clapped-out Mercedes 190 (see the website for more details) so anything with more clearance will manage fine. The stony ruts and oued crossings through the gorge will make riding a bike while enjoying the scenery a bit tricky; coming down into Igmir on my Ténéré required some finesse and a head for heights. MTBs may find this route a better proposition in the opposite- and no less impressive direction, as from Igmir you may be walking – or pedalling at walking pace – much of the time.

## Route finding
On the lower sections the route is clear, though flooding may wash away sections and lead to stony detours. For some reason this well established and popular route is not depicted on any of the paper maps of Morocco, although the much less used MA1 sometimes is.

Local traffic serves the villages at either end of the gorge section but not all vehicles can manage the climb out of Igmir. Trucks coming from the north stop at around KM38 to get their loads ferried down in pickups. It's the same point to which villagers must come up, to get a signal on their mobiles.

Note that in the narrow, palmerie trails you may have to back up so others can get by. The **map** for this route is on p213.

## Fuel and water
Fuel at Aït Herbil (supplies can be intermittent) and Tafraoute with water from the many villages along the route. No wells were noted along the way but there is water here for sure.

## Suggested duration
Do-able in half a day unless you choose to overnight in the oued or at Igmir, or combine it with other MA routes.

**0km          N29° 07.97'  W08° 57.93'**
**Aït Herbil** fuel station on the N12 with a basic café but not much else.

To visit the **rock carvings** as described in the *Rough Guide*, drive on the track to the east of this route (rejoined at KM3.2, see below) which leads into the village of Aït Herbil. Continue north along the narrow main street and when you get to a road turning off to the right with a bougainvillaea-draped wall on the corner at the top end of town (N29° 08.7' W08° 57.1'), turn right and follow the track down to the oued.

Park by the oued at the base of the hill on which stands the old fort. Now walk east across the oued – it may take some scrambling up and over flood-carved banks. To the south-east, on the far side of the oued is a small palmerie and just north of that is a pile of grey tailings where well shafts have been excavated. Behind the grey tailings is a gully, and halfway up the hillside to the right (south) of this gully you will find engravings on the slabs (N29° 08.9' W08° 56.4').

Back at the vehicle, retrace your route to the bougainvillaea corner and here turn right (north) out of the village to rejoin the bypass road at KM3.2 (N29° 08.8' W08° 57.4'). This information dates from 2004.

**4.5 (92.5)**
Pass by **Aguerd** where the road rises above the village with impressive views across the oued. Soon the road drops down to the oued and crosses it via a concrete ford, passing cliffs of dramatically folded strata.

**10 (87)**
The **tarmac ends**.

**17 (80)          N29° 14.79'  W08° 58.79'**
Junction with Route MA1 which comes in from the right, along the wide oued from Souk el Had d'Afella-Ihrir.

**19 (78)**
Cross a oued and re-enter it soon. As you pass walled gardens by the piste at around N29° 16.02' W08° 59.23', the very scenic 10km section of this route begins, initially along the narrow oued and passing the village of **Tamesoult** (N29° 16.2' W08° 59.5').

**23.5 (73.5)          N29° 17.13'  W08° 59.58'**
Leave the narrowing oued up the bank to the right. Out the other side turn left uphill into the village where you'll see a couple of hand-painted signs at a junction (N29° 17.2' W08° 59.6') showing distances to Igmir, Tafraoute, etc. Follow the signs left out of the village below the cliffs. Soon you're back in the stony oued bottom or alongside it.

**26 (71)          N29° 17.54'  W09° 00.31'**
Anywhere around here is a great place to camp or have a break among the shady argan trees. The pressing of argan nuts (once they've been digested, softened up and passed on by goats) makes a highly-prized and nutty-flavoured oil, available at Igmir and widely sold in and around Tafraoute.

**31.5 (65.5)**
Leave the oued as you encounter walled enclosures and pylons on the outskirts of **Igmir**. Drive through an avenue of palms and trees. Soon you get to the *Igmir Guest House* (N29° 20.03' W09° 00.14') on the other side of the oued at the foot of a deep, narrow canyon. It's a great place to eat, spend the night or meet the locals if there's not a big tour group passing through. Half-board is around 200dh per person with three or more 3-bed rooms and shared toilets. There's a spacious salon decorated with local nic-nacs, plus a roof terrace.

You now leave the **Smougeune** valley, taking a very steep 5km ascent into the hills with great views of the track snaking back down into the valley to Igmir. Should you stop halfway up the ascent you may find the orange scree full of delicate seaweed fossils.

**40 (57)          N29° 20.71'  W09° 02.43'**
The piste forks at a detailed sign. Go right (north) for Tafraoute ('53km'). Left and south gets pretty rough; it's part of Route MA10.

**47.5 (49.5)          N29° 23.84'  W09° 04.29'**
Fork right off the old route to Tafraoute along the newer track.

**50 (47)          N29° 25.04'  W09° 03.61'**
Pass a track leading right, east down to

Agojgal (where you turn left for tracks leading to Izerbi) and **Aoukerda** (10km) which is marked on some paper maps and which can also be reached by 90 minutes' walk up the canyon from Igmir; ask at the guest house.

**52.5 (44.5)    N29° 26.40' W09° 03.44'**
Turn left at this junction towards **Tahwawat** village.

**53.5 (43.5)    N29° 27.08' W09° 03.74'**
Join the **sealed road** just east of Tahwawat at a yellow sign for *Igmir Guest House*. Turn right for Izerbi and Tafraoute.

**60 (37)**
You'll notice some striking private homes in **Izerbi**; the *Rough Guide* suggests they belong to an ex-housing minister from the town (and presumably his family), although a '*Disney-style chateau*' was not evident – nor was the fuel station indicated on the RKH map. There is barely a shop here.

**66 (31)    N29° 29.97' W09° 00.68'**
Junction right to Souk Had Afella Ighir (or something similar) on Routes MA1 and MA3. Carry on north and in a couple of kilometres you get to another junction, signed left for 'Tiznit 90'. Carry straight on and over the 1200m Tizi ou Manouz and down into the Ameln valley of Tafraoute.

**94 (3)    N29° 41.77' W08° 57.74'**
At this junction turn left for Tafraoute.

**97 (0)    N29° 43.20' W08° 58.30"**
Fuel station in **Tafraoute** town centre next to the *Hotel Tafraoute* (more details at the end of Route MA3). For **campsites** fork right at the fuel station and head north-west out of town for about 6km, turning up the **Ameln valley** on the road to Igherm. There are a couple there as well as slick-looking campsite-auberges such as the *Arganier*, but at double the price of the Tafraoute.

# MA3   AKKA – TIMKYET – TAFRAOUTE    201KM
March 2008 ~ Mazda pickup

## Description

Two hundred kilometres of action and spectacle that will leave you wishing you had eyes in the back of your head to take it all in. You start from the very desert floor out of Akka and head north up into an orogenic wonderland of Berber mountain villages as if from another era, where brightly-dressed womenfolk attend to the chores in a string of villages shrouded in their own glittering palmeries. The kids here are not averse to some stylo- and car-swinging action, but living where they do who can blame them the distraction. At the northern end at least, they may command you to stand and deliver with such sweet innocence that it's all part of the fun. While the chances are that in a car you'll complete this route with mild whiplash from the relentless jolting, you'll be able to use the recovery time to process the many wonders you saw and the encounters you had.

The scenery ranges from never dull to mind-boggling. From the 'Desert Highway' (see p196) you pass through Akka's extensive palmerie and scoot up a piste to meet the R109. Once you leave this road at Tizgui ida ou Ballou village (KM69.5) the drama comes in fast and doesn't let up until you emerge on the high plains (still at the same bone-shaking speed), only to have it return with a dazzling drop into Aouklid. From here you spin down through another string of palm-clad villages jammed alongside a gorge before you reach the tarmac for a well-earned and soothing hour's drive over to Tafraoute.

You can do it all in one exhausting day but a night out midway on the plateau or even in one of the gorge villages could not fail to be an adventure. The latter may not afford you a shred of privacy and it may be polite enquiring if it's even acceptable, but chances are you'll be dining out on the story for a while after.

## Off road

Up the piste from Akka is a piece of cake but once you leave the R109 at Tizgui ida ou Ballou this is not the place to be towing a caravan full of badly packed Ming vases. Even something like a Range Rover or a VX will need to have their tyre sidewalls if not their very sides watched carefully in the gorge. Many times in the riverbeds you'll see stone **width-markers** giving guidance to the clearance ahead. Unless you're leading a donkey piled up with hay, continue in anything wider than an average 4WD at your peril.

**Motorbikers** may struggle on this part of the route. The satisfaction of sitting in a car for hours in first or second while lapping it all in is not so easy on two wheels. To keep your balance, directional stability and on the look out for rocks in the shingle-filled riverbeds you need to ride too fast to enjoy the spectacle and interactions around you. As with bigger cars, wide alloy panniers and, dare I say it, BMW boxer engines will require careful positioning as on a bike you're stuck in either one of two loose stony ruts and at times rather close to the side rocks. And without ABS, the descent into Aouklid at KM112 will require careful use of the front brake on the loose stones.

This particular descent too may govern the direction in a regular car. Attempting MA3 in reverse it's possible a regular car won't manage this loose ascent; the climb up onto the plateau from the other end (the direction of this route description) is concreted on its steepest stages.

Any sort of storm down here does not bear thinking about. The run-off would rush down the bare rock walls into the gorges and surge through them in minutes. My impression was this route is too stony for all but the hardiest **mountain biker**. You'd be much better off walking.

## Route finding

This route, with many branches besides, is 98% Olaffed. As for paper maps, once off the R109 nothing in print at the time was worth much more than a windscreen shade. The widely-depicted route from near Aït Ballou down to 'Bou Zarif' and back up to Timkyet does not exist with the prominence shown (but see KM50.5 and KM69.5 opposite).

Once you leave the Tazegzaoute gorge (where this route continues clearly, despite what maps show), Timkyet will be the first village that relates to any modern map, although they haven't kept up with the many new roads between here and Tafraoute.

Note that Souk el Had d'Afella-Ihrir is what appears on most paper maps but it's also known as Souk el Had Issi, Talate n Yissi on old maps and Google Maps or just plain 'Yissik'. I settle on 'Afella'. Once off the highway at either end you may see a couple of local vans close to the tarmac. No local traffic seems to go over the top if it can help it. Where's the **map**? Page 222.

# Fuel and water

In Akka look for the green *AFRIQUIA* sign at the west end and north side of the main street. The guys here dispense diesel from an ancient hand pump at 7.75dh (national rate at the time was 7.4) and 'essence' (two-star petrol) out of five-litre jugs for 60dh. In Tafraoute you drive straight into a modern *AFRIQUIA* forecourt soon after you enter town from the south.

There are plenty of villages and some handy wells, complete with bucket and pulleys on this route. The high well at KM100 looks like a good place to fill right up.

# Suggested duration

A day will do you all the way to Tafraoute. Or start late and camp out.

**0km**        **N29° 23.39'  W08° 15.58'**
**Akka** fuel (see above). Leave town to the west, passing under the arch. In just over a kilometre (N29° 23.05' W08° 16.08') turn right, north, **onto the piste** at a sign: 'Imitek 33'. You're heading up the west side of the settlement towards a gap in the Jebel Bani range filled with Akka's palmerie and satellite villages.

**4 (197)        N29° 24.57'  W08° 16.00'**
Pass south of the first village of **Aït Antar** and then north of **Tagadirt** with the big palmerie below you.

**7.5 (193.5)        N29° 26.26'  W08° 16.13'**
Cross the main oued running through the gap by a deep **pool**. Here you can take a diversion a couple of kilometres to the north-west to try and locate some **rock engravings** by some old barracks. The *Rough Guide* has a map, though in 2004 we couldn't find them (possibly because our Mercedes ran out of clearance). Otherwise continue straight on northwards for Imitek on a wide, rubbly piste.

**25.5 (75.5)**
Top of a 720m pass.

**34 (167)        N29° 38.59'  W08° 16.33'**
A good double-bucket **well** with water at 30m. The white hut you can see up ahead is a checkpoint on the road and they're probably watching you.

**35 (166)        N29° 38.97'  W08° 16.25'**
Join the R109 **tarmac** by the observation hut just west of **Imitek**. Turn left or west.

**50.5 (150.5)        N29° 38.73'  W08° 25.24'**
Pass a sign to the south-west for 'BRPM' mine and 'Izgoui ida Oubaloul 62'. This could be the way 'Bou Zarif' (a name unused locally) and the mine is probably Iourirne signed at KM140.5. Whatever, contributor Eric De Nadai came through from KM140.5 with ease in 2008.

Along the R109 you'll observe many spectacular examples of crumpled anticlines (folded rock strata) to the east. It's about to get a whole lot more impressive.

**69.5 (131.5)        N29° 44.65'  W08° 31.01'**
**Tizgui ida ou** (or just 'Aït') **Ballou** village with a sign left for Tazegzaoute. Looking for another route from this village south to Bou Zarif as shown on the paper maps, I drove south about 5km to a village signed '**Ifri Oujou**', by which time it became clear that **Tazegzaoute** was the main route option through this area.

Old maps do show a piste beyond Ifri Oujou (Awjour Tamcoult or 'Tamsoult ou Ouijou' on Google Maps) to Bou Zarif via Intla, but they also show scores of other pistes in the area that may no longer be used.

These days 'Bou Zarif' (or whatever it is called now) may well be accessed from near Timkyet (KM122), from whose vicinity there are a number of mysterious east-bound tracks. The clear trail copied by all the paper maps and possibly Google Maps may well be another phantom piste.

**70 (131)        N29° 44.53'  W08° 31.39'**
Junction by a oued with a **well** not far to the left. Turn right, south-west.

**73 (128)  N29° 43.57'  W08° 32.47'**
Fork right here to take the high track above the oued rather than the stony track through it, to the village of **Sidi Al Haj Ou Ali**. Up ahead you'll see the striking zig-zag erosion pattern of twisted and near-vertical strata (this book's cover) which even the pylons can't spoil.

**76 (125)  N29° 42.95'  W08° 33.97'**
Cross the oued at the end of the village. As you wind along the track look back; you'll soon see the ruins of an old agadir (fortified storehouse) perched on the ridge. Carry on below the ranges into the narrowing gorge. On a big or loaded bike you'll need to concentrate intently for the next 20km along the river bed.

**80 (121)**
The palmerie hiding the villages along this narrow gorge begins. In 3km you'll pass tri-lingual graffiti on the gorge wall (the subject matter is pan-global).

**87 (114)  N29° 40.38'  W08° 34.92'**
The gorge opens out with a **well** on the right. Right on cue there are some trees for a shady break.

**93 (108)  N29° 40.54'  W08° 37.03'**
Finally after what feels like hours in wonderland, leave the oued near the village of **Ifassras** and less than 200m later at N29° 40.55' W08° 37.10' fork left for what will turn out to be the way to Timkyet. Right here also leads up onto the plateau; KM49 on Route MA8, which is 2km north of KM108, below. The climb begins.

In the Tazegzaoute gorge.

**97.5 (103.5)  N29° 39.27'  W08° 37.96'**
After a slabby oued crossing, on a bike or in a car you may get into third gear for a few hundred metres. It's something definitely worth noting. Then, within a kilometre of this point, you get to a cleared area by the side of the track.

**99 (102)  N29° 38.28'  W08° 38.41'**
The spread out village of **Aït Alha**. Turn right out of the oued where an out-of-place *Coke* sign reminds you what century it is. Keep right up the valley. The track gets very steep from here onwards. In about a kilometre (N29° 38.36' W08° 38.77') you get to a **well** (10m) on the left with a bucket. The well winch can also help haul a car uphill. There are a couple more **wells** soon after.

**101 (100)**
You've climbed 200m out of the gorge in just over 2km, at times on concrete ramps. The sage bush plateau now around you is comparatively bleak and dreary after what's gone before, but you may spot gazelles up here. It's something to take your mind off things as, for cars at least, the going still remains slow. On a bike you can at last relax a bit and look around; trouble is there is now not so much to look at anymore. In less than a kilometre (N29° 37.88' W08° 39.64') you pass a lone farmhouse on the right.

**108 (93)  N29° 40.54'  W08° 41.47'**
Key junction. Straight on (north-west) leads to Tafraoute reversing Route MA8, you turn left, signed for Aouklid (and so Timkyet and Souk Had Afella Ighir). In 400m at N29° 40.45' W08° 41.71' another sign promises 'Aouklid 7km' and to the right 'Tafraoute 43' (MA8). Within a kilometre of this sign you pass the abandoned village of **Idouwayghd** and soon after a track 'triangles' in from the right (ie: also from Tafraoute along MA8).

**111.5 (89.5)  N29° 39.01'  W08° 42.45'**
You pass the 1862m **high point** of this route and the steep, loose descent into Aouklid begins, something that might be quite tricky in the opposite direction for a regular car.

**114.5 (86.5)    N29° 38.06' W08° 42.72'**
Although it's not marked on any maps the village of **Akoulid** marks your return from the plateau to the gorges and the domain of ground squirrels. From here there's a near-continuous line of mostly unmapped villages with adjacent gardens all the way to the tarmac.

**116.5 (84.5)    N29° 37.54' W08° 43.30'**
Don't go right, below the mosque here, but keep left in the oued.

**122 (79)    N29° 37.14' W08° 44.60'**
Enter a palmerie and the gardens of **Timkyet**, you're back on the paper maps.

**124.5 (76.5)    N29° 36.44' W08° 44.91'**
Turn right and head to the next village.

**127.5 (73.5)    N29° 35.55' W08° 45.84'**
Unmarked **Tamegroute** village with a handy shop opposite a squat mosque or zaouia.

**131.5 (69.5)    N29° 34.37' W08° 46.32'**
Keep left for Afella. Coming in from the right is Route MA1 from Tafraoute (40km) also on its way to Afella where it heads off down the oued to Aït Herbil. If you've not had enough of the rough stuff then reversing MA1 at this point is an initially scenic if not necessarily quicker way back to Tafraoute along the lovely Tizerkine Gorge.

Back on the track to Afella, there's an Arabic sign to the left shortly, you go straight and soon cross a ford.

**137 (64)    N29° 32.18' W08° 47.53'**
Pass a left turn by some gardens and buildings. Go straight on.

**140.5 (60.5)    N29° 30.71' W08° 48.79'**
At an elaborate milepost join the tarmac leading north-east to the Akka gold mine at **Iourirne** (16km) and eventually KM50.5 – a handy way back towards Tata.

From here on you may pass a regular stream of mine lorries on the road ahead; where possible they take to a parallel haul track criss-crossing the tarmac to stop the road surface getting mangled. At the speed they drive it seems they're getting paid by the ton, not by the day.

Within a kilometre you reach '**Afella**' with a basic café/shop on the right before you cross the oued. As you head down to the oued Route MA1 leaves to the left down to Aït Herbil and on the far side of the oued a piste slips off to the north-west.

For Tafraoute head west on good tarmac, passing roadside villages with striking villas along a valley and over a pass on a road that only features (well, most of it) on Google Maps until you reach …

**170 (31)    N29° 29.97' W09° 00.68'**
… the junction with the Izerbi-Tafraoute road which does feature on most paper maps. A sign proclaims: 'Tafraoute 32' to the right or north. Once you've obliged, in a couple of kilometres you get to a junction, signed west for 'Tiznit 90'. Carry straight on and over the 1200m pass of Tizi ou Manouz and down into the Ameln valley of Tafraoute.

**194 (7)    N29° 39.80' W08° 57.64'**
A road joins from the right: part of Route MA1.

**198 (3)    N29° 41.77' W08° 57.74'**
At the junction turn left for Tafraoute.

**201    N29° 43.20' W08° 58.30'**
Fuel station in **Tafraoute** town centre. I stayed at the *Hotel Tafraoute*, a cheapie rightly recommended in the *Rough Guide* with the entrance right in the petrol station forecourt where you can park. It's not the quietest location but what town centre is? A room with a bathroom over the hall was 80dh, breakfast another 20dh and when it finally arrived, dinner was 68dh. The staff here were very friendly and some spoke English.

If you've come from the deep south or have forgotten what Zagora and Rissani were like, Tafraoute is back in tout country and chances are you won't even have the keys out of the ignition before they're on to you. But compared to what you'll get out east, they're pretty lame.

**Campsites** seem to be mostly about 6km out of town up the **Ameln valley**.

This road, the R106, continues via Igherm to Taliouine (170km) and is a great ride on a motorbike or bicycle along remarkably quiet country roads.

# MA4    FASK – TAGHJIJT – TIMOULAY                84KM
March 2008 ~ Mazda pickup

## Description
This route links the Guelmim-Assa road with the N12 along some windy valleys past the occasional nomad, folds of rock and a village or two. The valleys
and jebels in this region are not laid out in the usual linear arrangement but
curl and loop around each other and the creek courses, and so the piste follows
the same detours to cover the relatively short distance between the highways.
At the far end the villages and palmeries of Tagmoute and Taghjijt (pronounced 'Tarjijt' with the two 'j's like the 's' in 'treasure') are both nice places
for a wander, and if you're coming up from the 'MW' region, you're lined up
nicely for the 'MA' Anti Atlas routes. Big jebels rise up close to the track pushing it this way and that, but on a clear day the highlights are the quiet villages
nestling in the valleys.

## Off road
Initially the track is not in good condition (for the more used direct start see
KM22, p211) and although the jebels hem you in, route finding may need some
thought in places as far as KM22. There's not much traffic up to Igherm
Iguezzoulene, but after that tarmac roads are never far away.

## Route finding
For once paper maps show this short route as accurately as their scales allow,
though both the Michelin and the RKH and maybe others too, label it the 'N12'
national highway, and as usual the RKH lavishes it with asphalt and makes up
a few more tracks in the vicinity. Far from it, it's a rough piste but **big motorbikes** will manage it fine, and although it's not that smooth, **bicycles** can make
use of the short distance and regular water stages. The **map** for this route is on
p212.

## Fuel and water
There's fuel in Fask and Timoulay, as well as Aït Herbil to the east and Bou
Izakarn to the west. It's also available at Taghjijt if you ask around. There's
water in a couple of wells along the route as well as the villages.

## Suggested duration
Allow three hours or so in a 4WD, less on bikes and more in a 2WD.

**0km              N28° 59.11'  W09° 49.60'**
ZIZ fuel and café at the east end of **Fask**.
Head east out of town.

**1.3 (82.7)**
At a bend leave the highway to the left
and **take to the piste**, eastwards.

**4 (80)          N28° 58.91'  W09° 47.36'**
Pass a **well** on the left and possibly a tent
on the right. The track here is washed-out
and stony.

**5.5 (78.5)        N28° 59.03'  W09° 46.47'**
Enter a oued and drive along in it north
on tracks. In 500m at N28° 59.22'  W09°
46.27' leave the oued to the east. Soon a
track joins from the right and in 700m you
re-cross the oued to the west side.

**8.5 (75.5)**
As you cross N28° the basin of the oued,
or Assif Tawimaght as it's known, opens
out ahead.

**11 (73)**          **N29° 01.39'  W09° 45.23'**
A track joins from the left as you go north into the basin to begin a big curve back round to the south. In 600m at N29° 01.69' W09° 45.16' there's a small walled garden by a 10m-deep **well**. Soon you cross the Assif Tawimaght to the east side.

**13.5 (70.5)**     **N29° 02.25'  W09° 44.30'**
Junction, you turn right or east.

**16 (68)**          **N29° 02.42'  W09° 42.82'**
Pass south of some buildings by a **well**. The piste now starts to go south to get round a spur of the Adrar Tawimaght.

**21 (63)**          **N29° 00.01'  W09° 42.44'**
Turn sharp to the left as a track joins from the right.

**22 (62)**          **N28° 59.74'  W09° 42.26'**
Junction a bit after this waypoint. Turn left, north-east, and pick up Olaf if you have it.
      The Olaffed route probably starts at a clear piste that leaves the Assa highway about 9km south-east of Fask at N28° 55.93' W09° 46.97'. It heads east and then north-east up the side of the Adrar Zegmouz to this point, about 13km from the highway, or all in all about the same distance as this route up to now, but following a more commonly-used track.

**25 (59)**          **N29° 00.30'  W09° 40.58'**
Pass north of **Igherm Iguezzoulene** village's gardens and white-domed zaouia. Three or 4km north-east of the village you make a detour where the banks of a oued have been washed away.

**31.5 (52.5)**     **N29° 01.46'  W09° 37.72'**
Junction with a **tar road** that goes directly north to **Timoulay**. You could call it a day here, however it's well worth stringing this route out by carrying on east through a pass in the ranges heading for the mass of Adrar Touzannaga.

**35 (49)**          **N29° 01.18'  W09° 35.61'**
Sharp turn right, south, by a garden at the base of Adrar Touzannaga.

**39.5 (44.5)**     **N28° 59.15'  W09° 35.46'**
Curling round the Adrar you carry on east-north-east along the oued north of the village of **Ksaba Aït Moussa ou Daoud**.

**45 (39)**          **N28° 59.99'  W09° 30.57'**
There are many tracks, some sandy, as you cross back up over N29°. This area up to Taghjijt is especially well rendered on Google Earth from 2004. All the landmarks described below are clearly visible.

**52 (32)**          **N29° 01.55'  W09° 28.89'**
Cross an irrigation ditch and then turn right, east, towards the village of Tagmoute visible ahead. In a kilometre you turn right to cross a oued just east of a small dam and then turn left back towards Tagmoute.

**54 (30)**          **N29° 01.82'  W09° 27.66'**
On the south-west outskirts of Tagmoute you pass to the south of a walled compound with an old mosque inside. After the end of the wall carry on south-east for 150m then turn left, north-east, for 300m to reach the next waypoint.

**54.5 (29.5)**     **N29° 01.86'  W09° 27.60'**
**Join the tarmac** (postdating Google Earth) in **Tagmoute**, an old village with many brightly-coloured doors, a regional feature it seems, although you'll see similar doors all over Morocco.

**59 (25)**          **N29° 03.09'  W09° 25.78'**
Having left Tagmoute you're passing **Taghjijt** and its dense palmerie to the left. Soon you bend north through the palmerie, curve back to the right and reach the N12 at the next waypoint.

**61 (23)**          **N29° 03.64'  W09° 25.22'**
Turn left on the N12 opposite the town arch. Or pop into the *Oasis Café* here for an *omelette sauvage*. After that, head west for the *Shell* in Timoulay or pick a spot to camp in Taghjijt's palmerie. The *Hotel Tarhjijt* on the east end of town appears to be semi-abandoned – you don't really want to stay or even eat there.

**84**                **N29° 10.06'  W09° 34.21'**
Basic *Shell* station in the strung-out village of **Timoulay**. There are cashpoints and another *Shell* in **Bou Izkarn** down the road on the N1 coastal highway, but after a quick look around, that's just about all it's got going for it.

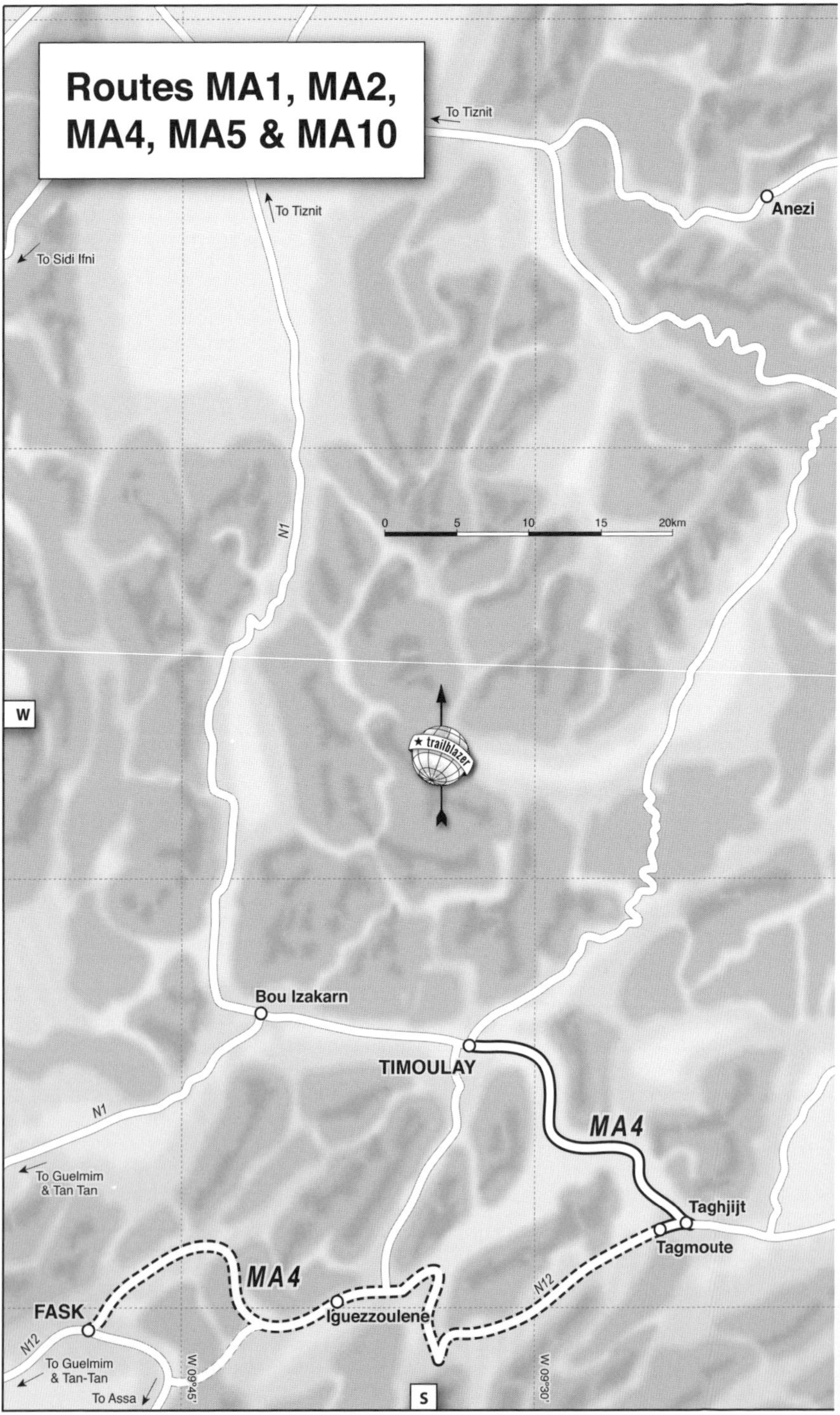

MA – ANTI ATLAS

# Routes MA1, MA2, MA4, MA5 & MA10

To Tiznit

Anezi

To Tiznit

To Sidi Ifni

N1

0   5   10   15   20km

W

trailblazer

Bou Izakarn

TIMOULAY

MA 4

To Guelmim & Tan Tan

N1

Taghjijt

Tagmoute

N12

MA 4

FASK

Iguezzoulene

N12

To Guelmim & Tan-Tan

To Assa

W 09°45'

W 09°30'

S

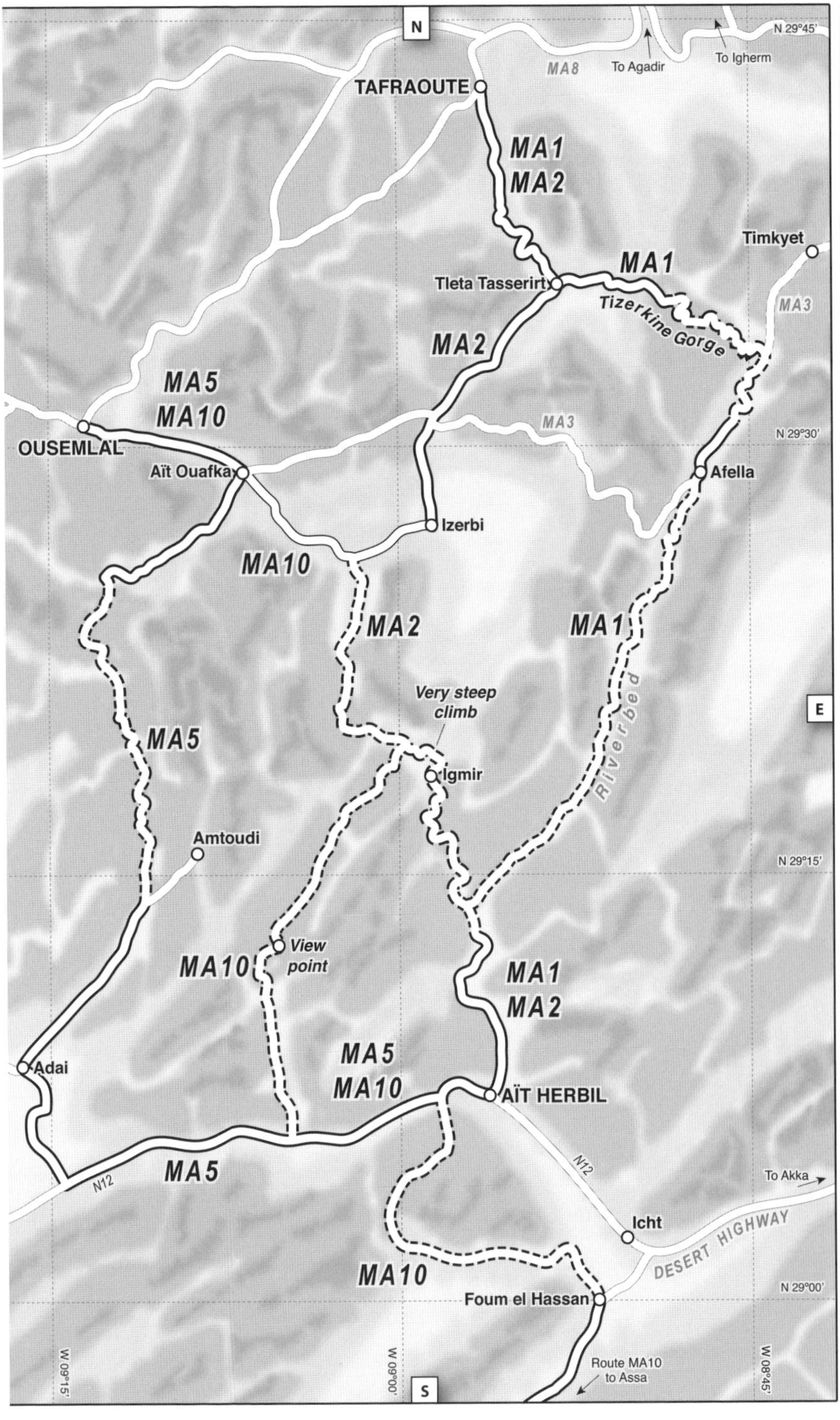
N
N 29°45'
To Agadir
To Igherm
MA8
TAFRAOUTE
MA1
MA2
Timkyet
MA1
Tleta Tasserirt
Tizerkine Gorge
MA3
MA2
MA5
MA10
OUSEMLAL
MA3
N 29°30'
Aït Ouafka
Afella
Izerbi
MA10
MA2
MA1
Very steep climb
Riverbed
E
MA5
Igmir
Amtoudi
N 29°15'
View point
MA10
MA1
MA2
MA5
MA10
Adai
AÏT HERBIL
MA5
N12
N12
To Akka
Icht
DESERT HIGHWAY
MA10
N 29°00'
Foum el Hassan
W 09°15'
W 09°00'
W 08°45'
Route MA10 to Assa
S

# MA5   OUSEMLAL – AMTOUDI – AÏT HERBIL          119KM

April and November 2008 ~ Mazda pickup and Yamaha Ténéré

## Description

MA5 is another way of dropping down onto the desert floor from the north, but fuel and a couple of shops are all you'll find at either end of this route, so realistically you'd want to start from Tafraoute or thereabouts and consider wild camping at the far end (a few miles after KM88 down Route MA10 would do, or on the sand sheet east along the N12 past Icht). Being a short route between fuel stations, MA5 may well work better combined in a loop with Routes MA1, -2 and -10 based out of the guest house at Igmir halfway up Route MA2, certainly on an unladen bike.

The route itself may be nothing special but the highlight is the visit to **Amtoudi** where a finely restored fortified stone storehouse or 'agadir' looms over the edge of the escarpment above the canyon-bound settlement . You can easily walk or be muled up to the top and enjoy a fascinating guided tour of the interior by the guardian. You'll find storage rooms, beehives, a small museum and of course great views down the valley from where you came. Outside the walls ancient petroglyphs suggest, as is so often the case with these places, that the locale has been occupied for millennia.

From Amtoudi you head south across the plain to the N12 and turn east for Aït Herbil.

## Off road

For your suspension the wake up call comes around 19km south of Ouafka as you rise up onto the plateau. Here you join the southbound track linking a village or two and drop down a short gorge towards the Amtoudi junction where you rejoin the road. This section of the route can be easily done in anything you've got, though a mountain bike may find the hammering/scenery ratio a bit skewed compared to other routes around here.

## Route finding

No great dramas await you as long as you can follow these instructions and operate your vehicle. There are villages all along the route, so as far as passing traffic goes you shouldn't be stranded for long. The **map** is on p213.

## Fuel and water

Fuel at each end only (though Aït Herbil can occasionally run out) and a couple of wells in the villages on the way through.

## Suggested duration

A couple of hours driving or riding time, but you'd want to spend as least as long exploring the environs of Amtoudi.

The fortified storehouse at Amtoudi.
© Peter Hartleb.

**0km          N29° 31.57'  W09° 14.73'**
*Petromin* fuel on the west side of **Jemaa Ida Ousemlal** to give it its full title; a few shops though nowhere to stay. The guy here said there was a hotel 'Khandouz' a couple of kilometres out west but I couldn't find it. Fill up and head in the other direction, east through town towards Ouafka.

**11 (108)        N29° 30.10'  W09° 08.49'**
Junction in **Souk Khemis de Aït Ouafka** or just 'Ouafka'. The road to the north-east comes down from Tafraoute – an alternative start for this route. Turn right or south at the crossroads and follow the tar road up into the hills. This road and the track you'll follow are missing or incorrectly positioned on many paper maps.

**30 (89)         N29° 24.36'  W09° 15.27'**
After passing through a few villages, at the apex of a right-hand hairpin just after a village ('**Aghoudid**' on old maps) you turn left and south-east **onto the piste**. After three kilometres and a bend to the south you pass through **Aït Ali ou Hamad** village with its distinctive crenellated mosque. Continue south-south-east along a broad track.

**37 (82)         N29° 21.17'  W09° 13.46'**
You pass a hut on the left and soon the short descent into the valley begins, passing a small, stepped waterfall and deserty cacti on the way.

**43 (76)         N29° 18.97'  W09° 12.87'**
Six kilometres later you've dropped 300m and enter the village of **Targa Oukhadir** alongside its oued. In a kilometre and a half you pass what are presumably the ruins of old Oukhadir on the right.

**56 (63)         N29° 13.27'  W09° 13.50'**
You **join the road** by a sign to the villages you've just come from (the distance to Ouafka is out by 10km) and a building on a hill. Turn sharp left or north for 4km to **Amtoudi** which is shown on some maps as '**Id Aissa**'.

As you reach Amtoudi the **sealed road ends** by a basic **auberge** and coach park. In the car I drove onwards for another kilometre or so, over and along the oued

and parked on the north-west side by some houses below the agadir (N29° 14.65' W09° 11.11'). From here I walked straight up the gully (shady in the morning) until I picked up the mule path at a hairpin; all in all about 25 minutes effort to get to the top where the old guardian was waiting for me, key in hand. Allow up to an hour for a good look around inside. The site gets a few tour groups from January to March; at other times it'll be all yours. You pay the guardian what you like.

According to the guidebooks, there's another auberge in the village as well as another even more dramatic agadir perched a little further up the valley as well as a palm-filed canyon. If you like these sorts of places – the essence of southern Morocco in my opinion – but are not planning to stay overnight then allow at least half a day to explore Amtoudi's agadirs and canyon.

When you've had your fill, turn back south past the point where you joined the road and carry on 11km to the village of ...

**77 (42)**
... **Souk Tnine Adai** (to give one spelling; and note that the cumulative distances from here on assume you took the 10km round trip to Amtoudi). Here bear left at the road bollard and head south-east around the hill and across the plain for the N12.

**86 (33)         N29° 04.89'  W09° 15.64'**
At the N12 turn left or east for Aït Herbil. In about 15km at N29° 06.53' W09° 07.53' just before some trees, you pass the point where Route MA10 comes down from the north.

**119            N29° 07.97'  W08° 57.93'**
**Aït Herbil** fuel station with a basic café but not much else.

For somewhere to stay the *Igmir Guest House* is 32km up Route MA2; allow an hour to get there. In Foum el Hassan about 25km further on, the hotel mentioned in one of the guides was too rough to be recognisable late one night and you don't want to stay at the semi-abandoned 'hotel' on the east edge of Taghjijt last time I looked. Hopefully you're reading all this before you got here.

# MA6   TAZENACHT – ISSIL – TATA          186KM
March 2008 ~ Mazda pickup

## Description

Depending on where you are and where you want to end up, both this or Route MA7 (which it overlaps for a couple of kilometres) take a diagonal route up and over the main southern range of the Anti Atlas, in this case the **Jebel Timkouka** which separates the desert from the more temperate plateaux of the north. In doing so these routes inch their way up canyons and past villages that barely feature on any map.

Once you leave Tazenacht and the N10, you tick off the villages of the Issil plain with the 2000m ridge of the Jebel Timkouka looming ahead. Presently, a U-shaped groove becomes evident on the horizon, and once past Issil you'll be heading up the flanks of the Jebel and through that gap. Here, a sometimes tortuous and dramatic descent begins down to the valley floor. You return to villages spread around ageing kasbahs towards Akka Ighern (as spelled locally most of the time; paper maps give various versions) down on the plain from where the tarmac from Taliouine (Route MA11) sweeps you to the N12, 60km from Tata to the west, a great town to recover in.

This route is do-able in a day but better to do some carpet browsing or lunch in Tazenacht, camp out on the Jebel or in the desert and carry on next morning, so enjoying the evening and morning light in the desert.

If you get a taste for this area, I met someone who took a third route over the Jebel starting 13km south of the N10 junction at N30° 21.98′ W07° 45.64′ on the Taliouine road north of Agadir Melloul (MA11). It goes via Asarrakh (found on some paper maps but not along the route the RKH map shows).

## Off road

Getting up to the Timkouka Pass is not so hard; getting back down the south side is a slow and rocky run that, even downhill, will take it out of your vehicle. But once at the oued at KM60 the roughest stage is over. A **robust 2WD** ought to manage it as very little low range crawling is required and with the absence of sand, **bikes** large and small can just stand up on the footrests and let the suspension do its job.

Nevertheless, it can be tiring done all in one day so at Akka Ighern this route takes the easy way out by following the tarmac to the N12 and so west for Tata. If you fancy spinning out the piste for as long as possible, then reverse Route MA9 a few kilometres south of Akka Ighern; see KM109. Both this and MA7 would be a great but rough ride on a full suspension **MTB**.

## Route finding

Although nothing appears on today's paper maps, route finding is easy with little chance of getting lost in the mountains. I saw no traffic until Akka Ighern and beyond Issil you'd not expect any. **Issil** is a useful pivot on which to mix and match this route with MA7, making all four corners: Tata, Foum Zguid, Tazenacht and Taliouine linkable with each other, and bits of MA9 could be thrown in there too. If you really want to test your vehicle then do as I did (unknowingly) and follow MA7 up to Issil to pick up this route going back south so combining to make one of the most satisfying routes in the Anti Atlas.

The subsequent broken leaf springs and dizzy spells were a small price to pay. The **map** for this route is on p223.

## Fuel and water
Tazenacht and Tata for fuel. There aren't so many wells between the villages but they at least are close together in distance if not in time.

## Suggested duration
Easily do-able in a day but if you've got the gear in the back and the weather overhead, it's much more fun to camp out in the wilds.

**0km          N30° 34.39'  W07° 12.56'**
*AFRIQUIA* fuel at the west end of **Tazenacht**. Head out of town for Taliouine.

Then again, stop! This town is worth spending some time in. It's well known for its **carpets**; you'll see them displayed all over the main road, but there doesn't seem to be any of the accompanying hassle you may get in the cities. It makes a great place to browse and even buy without pressure, and potentially at better prices too. The carpets are the work of local Berber co-ops and the sheep you may pass out on the Issil plain provide the raw material you'll see dyed and drying in some village backyards.

If you're serious, the time to get here is very early for the Friday or Saturday morning souks. Northern dealers come down to fill their vans for the tourist souks of Marrakech, Meknes and Fes where a gullible or indifferent customer can easily pay ten times what they would down here. The 2007 *Rough Guide* seems to play this positive carpet-buying aspect down, but otherwise has a useful account of Tazenacht which has a few hotels, cafés and no less than four fuel stations.

**13.5 (172.5)    N30° 29.90'  W07° 18.84'**
Turn south **off the highway** alongside a wall and drive through **Zaouia Sidi Abdallah ou-Mhand**. You'll see his shrine round the back as well as an old mosque. In 500m pass a water tower on the southeast corner of the village.

**20 (166)        N30° 26.81'  W07° 20.51'**
Route MA7 joins from the right. You retrace it south as far as Issil.

**22.5 (163.5)**
Pass by a water tower on the left with the village of **Zawyat Taliza** down on the right.

**25 (161)        N30° 24.79'  W07° 18.76'**
Pass the village of **Tiwiyine** set on the east side of a cone hill while you go round on the west side.

**31.5 (154.5)    N30° 21.81'  W07° 16.94'**
Cross a oued and continue south.

**38.5 (147.5)**
Pass an orchard and gardens in the oued.

**40 (146)        N30° 17.95'  W07° 17.50'**
Junction near **Issil** visible just to the south-east (along with the rest of Route MA7 in reverse). Fork right here to the west of Issil and in a kilometre or so pass N30° 17.37' W07° 17.98'. You're now heading directly for the Jebel Timkouka up whose side you'll soon be crawling.

**43 (143)        N30° 16.62'  W07° 19.19'**
Pass a **well** with a bucket.

**45 (141)        N30° 16.28'  W07° 20.04'**
The village of **Wantkou** is at the base of the ridge. Before it you turn right and ascend the ridge on a rough track towards the pass.

**47 (139)**
You're passing along a kind of corniche high above the Issil plain with great views to the north, especially late in the day.

**48 (138)        N30° 16.31'  W07° 21.28'**
A windy, 1830m pass marked with a tomb in a walled enclosure and still great views to the north. To the south a canyon unwinds back down to the desert floor; a slow, rough stage in a car but a

spectacular one. With photo stops (or repairs…) it may take an hour to drive in a car to the next waypoint.

**60 (126)          N30° 13.39'  W07° 22.73'**
The 700m descent is over as you cross the oued.

**62 (124)**
Drive along the oued passing some trees and rise out of it in a kilometre.

**64 (122)          N30° 12.07'  W07° 23.23'**
Leave another oued and head west into the hills, passing a deep, but dry well as you exit a branch oued 1500m later.

**68 (118)          N30° 11.09'  W07° 25.42'**
You come over a rise and a valley opens up ahead with straight tracks leading to the south-west. In less than a kilometre you cross a oued with caves dug into the low banks.

**76 (110)          N30° 09.46'  W07° 29.05'**
Junction with an oil-drum-lid sign in Arabic indicating '80km' to somewhere. Turn left. Right appears to be another one of those Olaf dead ends after 10km.

**77 (109)          N30° 08.75'  W07° 29.47'**
Another junction, turn left here towards the distant palms, even though pylons crossing the hill on the horizon directly ahead suggest that direction.

**79 (107)          N30° 08.11'  W07° 29.00'**
Cross the wide, palm-lined oued. Soon after, some palms by the track can make a good place for a shady break.

**80 (106)          N30° 07.75'  W07° 28.28'**
Enter the village of 'Ighern Warfaln' (according to old maps) and cause the usual commotion.

About 150m on, curve right and head about another 150m south-west, then turn left for 150m east-south-east and get to this key point: N30° 07.58' W07° 28.19' in a oued passing through the middle of the village. Turn left down this oued over bare rock slabs; it doesn't feel right but it's the right way. As you pass through the defile, to either side are finely-built stone buildings and a ruined ksar.

**84 (102)**
Pass a junction with a track coming up left from the valley below.

**87 (99)          N30° 06.29'  W07° 27.18'**
Cross a big oued by some pylons, meeting a track on the other side, probably coming from nearby **Agmour** with its cream-coloured mosque and orange buildings. A stone signpost nearby features various village names unknown to most cartographers.

**88 (98)**
Cross a sandy oued by a low cliff.

**94 (92)          N30° 03.47'  W07° 27.06'**
From the east joins a piste leading to Route MA9 which features on many paper maps. Pylons start here too. Continue south-west over hamada.

**102 (84)**
**Akka Ighern** (though even local road signs aren't consistent) appears ahead in a sandy basin. Once you get to town drive down a wide, dusty boulevard.

**104.5 (81.5)    N29° 59.50'  W07° 31.83'**
You soon reach the **tarmac road** coming down from Taliouine (Route MA11) near a red and white radio tower and some mature trees. Turn left here, south-east.

**109 (77)          N29° 57.58'  W07° 32.91'**
Fork; keep left on the main tarmac road. Right may well join up with Route MA9, but the easier way to pick up that route is 2.5km down the road at N29° 58.64' W07° 32.59'. If you've not had enough of a beating coming down the Jebel, this little-used track is for you.

**122 (64)          N29° 52.11'  W07° 29.74'**
Pass the village of **Kasba el Joua** on the left as the road bends right.

**126 (60)          N29° 50.33'  W07° 29.99'**
Junction with the N12 opposite the Jebel Bani range. Turn right for Tata.

**186                N29° 44.31'  W07° 58.42'**
Fuel stations on the south-west edge of **Tata**. For more see the box opposite.

## TATA

Tata is the provincial capital, as big as a place gets down here and dubbed the 'Siena of the Sahara' on account of its hundreds of sienna-daubed colonnade arches shading the side-walks.

It has two **fuel stations** facing each other on the far side of town on the road to Akka. Coming from the east down the wide boulevard, when you get to a T-junction in town just past the barracks, most of the town and the municipal campsite are to the right or north; the road to Igherm. For the two main **hotels** and fuel turn left. The Rough Guide has a handy map, *al hamdullilai*!

The **campsite** (N29° 44.84' W07° 58.39') used by long-term RV-ers is pretty much in the middle of town by a yellow 'Pigier' sign on the town's main road which carries on to Igherm. There are also a couple of hotels along this street: the *Essalam* and the *Sahara* a few doors down. Neither may be too flash upstairs but both are great places to eat: half a roast chicken with salad, chips, plus a drink or two at the *Essalam* was 65dh.

Just after dusk is the time for *le prome-nade* when, market day excepted, the town briefly becomes energised. In an hour it's all over and they're back home watching dubbed Brazilian soaps.

As on previous visits, I stayed in the tiled interior of the near-empty *Hotel Renaissance*, five minutes walk from the town centre and which you'll pass on the way to the fuel stations. A storage room over the road for the bike was offered without asking and the hotel has indeed had a bit of a revival since we got squeezed into a tiny room here in 2004. Half board was 220dh (room only 120dh, breakfast 20dh) with an en-suite room and access to the roof to cool off if need be.

For a moment I thought I'd made a mis-take going for an evening meal here (espe-cially as there is a great choice in town) and would get the dreaded warmed-up leftovers which can lay travellers low. But unlike in 2004, they made the effort to prepare fresh food. I got what I was given: soup, meatball tajine, potatoes and rice, plus fruit.

Just down the road next to one of the fuel stations is the flashier *Hotel Tata, Relais des Sables*. With a name like that you know they're ready for cheched-up tour groups. We ate there one time which for some reason took them by surprise.

*MA – ANTI ATLAS*

# MA7   FOUM ZGUID – ISSIL – TALIOUINE                    178KM
April 2008 ~ Mazda pickup

## Description

A spectacular and isolated transit up from the desert floor, up along a serpen-tine canyon track passing through villages hidden in a tectonic crumple zone and lost to any map maker. Up and over the **Jebel Timkouka** you crawl at lit-tle more than a hobbled donkey's pace to emerge above the Issil plain won-dering what day it is and looking over a viewpoint from One Million Years BC, but without the fur bikinis.

No maps really can do this route justice and you'll end the day in Taliouine grinning at a steaming tajine which will probably smile right back. It's do-able in a day, a great route on lighter bikes linking two chilled towns and adds up to southern Morocco in a nutshell.

## Off road

Get set for some gnarly off-road action: hours of inching round steep hairpin turns (which may put paid to a **2WDs** transmission), several villages and some palmeries. As long as you nurture your tyres and rims, a **trail bike** will be great fun on this route, a loaded **mountain biker** will have a tough time but won't forget it in a hurry.

## Route finding

Not on any map but pretty well Olaffed and with little opportunity to go wrong as where it's not Olaffed, it doesn't matter too much. Just sit back and enjoy the ride. The route **map** is on p223.

## Fuel and water

For fuel you have Foum Zguid plus two or three places before Taliouine itself, and for water there are a couple of wells, the villages and pools in the oueds.

## Suggested duration

Easily do-able in a day as long as nothing breaks.

**0km          N30° 05.40' W06° 52.66'**
*AFRIQUIA* fuel on the north side of **Foum Zguid** with unleaded. There is more on this town at the end of Route MA9. Leave to the north.

**18 (160)          N30° 14.90' W06° 51.05'**
Turn west onto a wide track.

**31 (147)          N30° 13.62' W06° 58.67'**
A track comes up from the south from El Mhamid with another one just before a red and white radio tower by the village of **Nsoula**.

**36.5 (141.5)          N30° 13.37' W07° 01.80'**
Turn north for Tlite. Here it comes...

**39.5 (138.5)**
Cross the oued into **Tlite** and then turn back down into the oued by a ruined ksar, passing an old graveyard by a palmerie.

**44 (134)          N30° 16.21' W07° 03.74'**
Pass the old village of **Tawrirt n Tilas** on purple stone dust. You now rise out of the valley with the pylons and a water tower towards a radio mast on the ridge.

**46 (132)**
Pass a ruined ksar on the right by a palmy oued and in a kilometre pass above **Aghgoumi** village, heading for the gap in the ranges. Once you're through the gap you pass lush palm gardens on the right.

**48 (130)          N30° 17.60' W07° 05.44'**
Fork right out of the oued as the blue arrow on the rock suggests and proceed steeply up into the pass.

**50.5 (127.5)          N30° 18.24' W07° 05.98'**
Come through the pass at 1150m and descend again.

**53.5 (124.5)          N30° 19.11' W07° 06.64'**
An inter-range basin opens up with the small village of **Amtezguine** tucked in alongside its gardens.

**55.5 (122.5)          N30° 19.71' W07° 06.99'**
Keep left and head into the oued through a wall-lined palmerie on both sides, not into Amtezguine. At one point you're on a concrete embankment.

**56.5 (121.5)          N30° 19.82' W07° 07.30'**
At another blue arrow turn right and then steeply hairpin left out of the village (rejoining Olaf which went through it). Leave the village heading south-west and rise up over a gorge. In a kilometre cross a shingly oued and continue uphill, passing a perfectly cleared square on the left soon after (as at KM98.5 on Route MA3). Some tight hairpins follow as you crawl west in first gear above the valley far below.

**63 (115)          N30° 19.69' W07° 09.47'**
You're at 1495m after a long, slow but dramatic ascent.

**65 (113)**
The track improves a bit as you see buildings and the parched terrace plots of **Zawyat Ainas** ahead.

**70 (108)          N30° 17.68' W07° 12.17'**
**High point** at 1724m, and '15km' from Issil, according to a sign. At the top Olaf goes left, you go right and join up in a couple of kilometres.

**72 (106)**

A track crosses the piste and in a kilometre another track joins from the right at N30° 16.85'  W07° 12.56'.

**76 (102)        N30° 16.15'  W07° 12.87'**

Pass a lonely village with a pink mosque.

**78 (100)        N30° 15.81'  W07° 14.74'**

Come over a 1635m pass as a canyon opens out to your left. Within 500m you round a bend and suddenly the **Issil plain** opens up before you, dotted with isolated outcrops: a dramatic Saharan vista which the late afternoon light won't spoil at all. You're finally out of the mountains which have absorbed your concentration for hours.

**81 (97)        N30° 16.62'  W07° 15.57'**

Pass a **well** on the left and head for Issil.

**85 (93)        N30° 17.57'  W07° 17.18'**

You find yourself by a **well** and the round red water tower of **Issil**. There may be a shop here but not much else. Leave Issil to the north-west.

**86 (92)        N30° 17.95'  W07° 17.50'**

Pick up the northbound track for the Taliouine highway.

**88 (90)**

Cross a oued with gardens alongside.

**94 (84)        N30° 21.81'  W07° 16.94'**

Cross a oued and continue north.

**101 (77)        N30° 24.79'  W07° 18.76'**

Pass to the west of the village alongside a cone hill.

**106 (72)        N30° 26.81'  W07° 20.51'**

Split right here for the direct route northeast to Tazenacht (see MA6) or continue straight for the N10 to Taliouine.

**111 (67)        N30° 28.87'  W07° 21.58'**

**Join the N10 road** and turn west towards Taliouine. Soon you'll pass a lone ZIZ, possibly Kourkouda, just before heading up a pass, as well as a basic SHELL about 22km before Taliouine at N30° 28.14' W07° 46.54' after the village of **Tinfat** where Route MH9 comes in from the north.

**174 (4)        N30° 31.49'  W07° 53.22'**

ZIZ on the west end of Taliouine, a few kilometres from the town centre.

**178        N30° 31.91'  W07° 55.33'**

Having passed the two auberges, this is the fuel station in **Taliouine** town centre.

According to the guidebooks the *Souktane* is the place to stay in town but I tried the *Askaoun* one time and the *Safran* over the road on another occasion. Here both dinner and breakfast were great but my room (all en-suite, it must be said) was just twice the size of the bed and as plain as the *Anzal* in Igherm. All in all the *Safran* did not add up to the 270dh half-board bill. For less than that, opposite Erg Chebbi I got a room out of *Designer Kasbahs Review*.

Over the road and six months earlier the *Askaoun* was trying hard to please and my recollection was a more agreeable salon as you walked in, as good food and a much bigger en-suite bedroom for about 120dh.

# MA8   TAFRAOUTE – TAZALARHITE – IGHERM        135KM

November 2008 ~ Yamaha Ténéré

## Description

This is a version of Route MA3 in reverse, a great transit up through the Ameln valley and Tazalarhite on top of the Tizkhit plateau, uninhabited apart from a couple of plucky farmsteads. On the far side you drop off down legally borderline grades into the deep canyon on the Oued or 'Assif' Oumdar. Here ensues a slow but satisfying passage along the riverbed past a string of palm-clad villages and lush gardens labelled as **Tazegzaoute** on the maps. Then, as the canyon opens out an hour or so downstream, the dramatic angular erosion

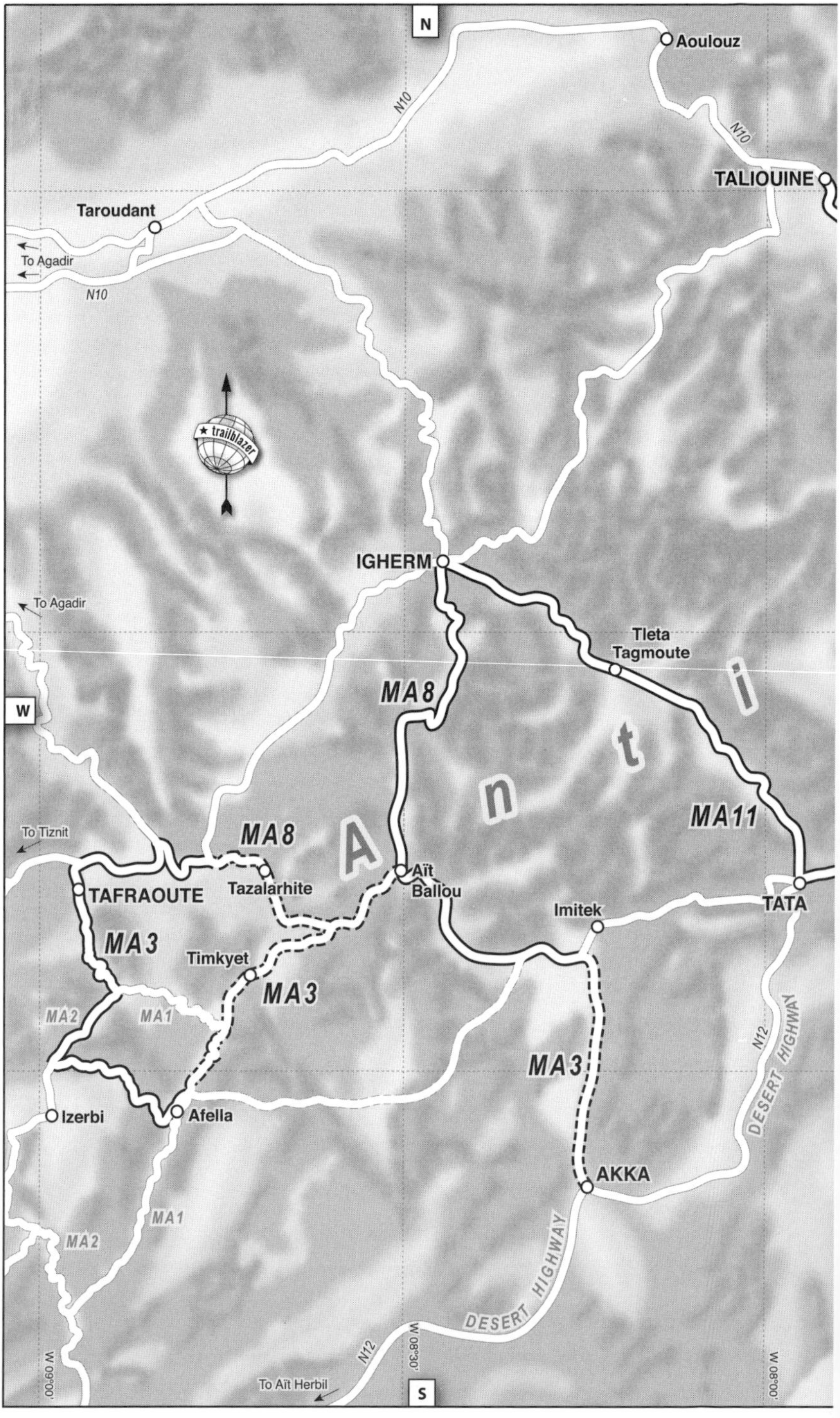
N
Aoulouz
N10
N10
TALIOUINE
Taroudant
To Agadir
N10
trailblazer
IGHERM
To Agadir
Tleta
Tagmoute
MA8
W
Anti
MA11
To Tiznit
MA8
Aït
Ballou
TAFRAOUTE
Tazalarhite
Imitek
TATA
MA3
Timkyet
MA3
MA2
MA1
N12
DESERT HIGHWAY
MA3
Izerbi
Afella
AKKA
MA1
MA2
DESERT HIGHWAY
N12
W 09°00'
W 08°30'
W 08°00'
To Aït Herbil
S

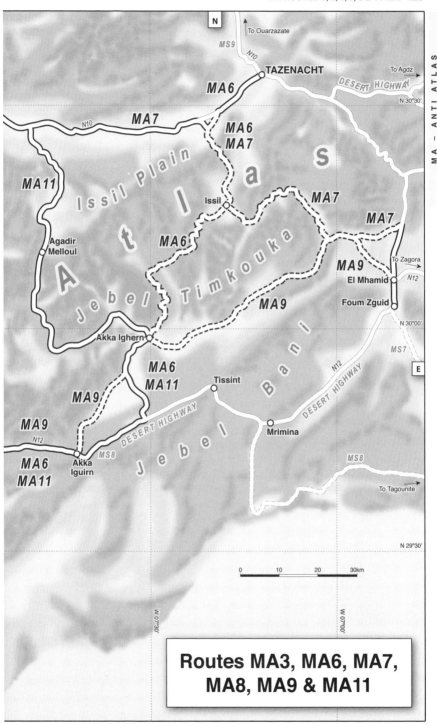

Routes MA3, MA6, MA7, MA8, MA9 & MA11

MA – ANTI ATLAS

of the cliffs is unlike anything else you've seen in Morocco. Soon you're back on the highway, heading north. As a place to celebrate a great day on the piste, **Igherm** is a bit of an anticlimax, but give yourself another hour and you could be in Tata, Taroudant or Taliouine.

## Off road

In good weather the only restriction on this route is the 23km passage along the Assif Oumdar (KM60-83) and possibly muddy stages up on the flat plateau top. Apart from the need for good brakes to get down to the riverbed, something like a big Land Cruiser will have to watch the width on some of the narrow passages in the gorge. Many times in the riverbed you'll see stone **width-markers** giving guidance to what can pass ahead; ignore them at your peril.

**Motorbikers** may find the riverbed section hard work. Depending on how your bike is set up and its load, to keep your balance and directional stability in the shingle-filled riverbeds you'll need to ride too fast to enjoy the spectacle and interactions around you. Lowering tyre pressures would help but risks punctures on the sharper rocks; with harder tyres you can take the hits at the speed you need to maintain. As with bigger cars, wide alloy panniers may at times be a liability as you're stuck in either one of two loose shingle ruts, close to the side rocks at times. On a big, loaded bike, riding this tricky 23km stage without a break will take forearms like Popeye. Finally, whatever you're on or in, if black clouds are gathering and grumbling overhead, the bed of the Assif is no place to linger.

## Route finding

On road or track there are several junctions to get right, so plan ahead and read carefully (just like any other *Morocco Overland* route, then). Both times I took this route I was the only vehicle on the piste apart from a local pickup or two at the easy ends. Turn to p222 for the **map** for this route.

## Fuel and water

Fuel at each end only and water from a couple of wells on the plateau and on the steep descent into Ifassas.

## Suggested duration

Easy to do in a day, though ending it in Igherm may not be too thrilling. Once at the road at KM89 you can head down to more tourist-agreeable Tata (see box on p219) or take the mountain route down to Tata once in Igherm (the end of Route MA11 in reverse). Camping out on the plateau would be windy and bleak, and in the gorge most probably the opposite.

**0km** N29° 43.20' W08° 58.32'
*AFRIQUIA* fuel in **Tafraoute** town centre by the *Hotel Tafraoute* (for more on accommodation here see p209). Head north out of town along the main road.

**4 (131)** N29° 45.14' W08° 57.89'
At this junction turn right for the **Ameln**

valley and the road to Igherm. Head east up a valley past campsites and other auberges below the 2300m Jebel El Kest; it's a long ascent. At the head of the valley, as you go round a sharp left-hand hairpin, the road shown from here on many maps to Agard, just south of Tafraoute (and seemingly a more direct route), does not exist, at least with the prominence it's given.

**22 (113)**          **N29° 44.53' W08° 49.90'**
Soon after the hairpin mentioned above, at this junction leave the Aït Baha road and turn right for Igherm, passing through the village of **Titeki**.

**33 (102)**          **N29° 46.50' W08° 46.79'**
Pass through a village of ox-blood red painted houses (as often round here, village names where given are only in Arabic (**Azgour** is the name on old maps). As you go uphill, just after a like-coloured mosque on the right, turn right or south-east **onto a track**. There is a white block inscribed with Arabic. Soon down this track you get to a minor fork to the right by a block with 'Tata' written on it; keep left or straight for Tazalarhite.

**37 (98)**          **N29° 46.41' W08° 44.81'**
Pass through a village (Afassfas Imdafane?) as you climb east and then south up the hill side.

**41 (94)**          **N29° 45.06' W08° 43.74'**
You top out at nearly 1900m at the mining village of **Tazalarhite**; its old town perched on a rock with newer houses spread around below. To the north you may also see a layer of snow capping the western end of the High Atlas as it drops towards Agadir.

Pass round the west side of the village, heading south-east. In a kilometre you get to a track forking left; keep right. And the same again in less than another kilometre; keep right at KM42 (N29° 44.61' W08° 43.33'). These tracks off to the left look as if they're associated with the mine.

You're now setting off to traverse the treeless 1800m plateau which old maps call **Tizkhit**. The shallow vales and hillsides are dotted with a sagey scrub and rocks. There's the occasional pastoral enclosure and maybe the odd gazelle bounding away from you at high speed.

**47 (88)**          **N29° 42.57' W08° 42.36'**
A lone farm with a **well**, surrounding cultivation and a few trees.

**49 (86)**          **N29° 41.53' W08° 41.39'**
Arrive at a plastered block. Turning left or

south-east here leads down to Ifassas at KM66 below, possibly via the village of Mazdal, taking one side of a triangle. This route carries on straight south.

**51 (84)**          **N29° 40.53' W08° 41.47'**
Meet Route MA3 at another stone block. MA3 turns to your right or south-west here for Timkyet and Afella. You carry straight on, or south-south-east.

**58 (77)**          **N29° 38.22' W08° 39.32'**
Having turned north-east and passing the other lone plateau farmhouse on the left, at this point you drop off the Tizkhit and commence a very steep descent. You'll appreciate the places where they've concreted ramps over the track.

**60 (75)**          **N29° 38.28' W08° 38.41'**
Brake hard for the village of **Aït Alha** or you'll end up in someone's living room. Once through the village turn left into the oued.

**66 (69)**          **N29° 40.54' W08° 37.03'**
Arrive at the village of **Ifassras** and pass the junction at N29° 40.55' W08° 37.10' where the track from KM49 comes down. You now set off to crawl along the shingly riverbed of the Assif Oumdar towards Tazegzaoute and Aït Ballou; great fun to crawl along in a car listening to the birds and the bees and the stylo pleas, a bit more demanding on a motorbike.

You pass through thick palmeries and gardens jammed in below a string of villages perched above the banks; it's hard to know which one is actually **Tazegzaoute** or where it starts or ends. Whatever, it's worth taking a break now and then from the rattling vehicle just to take it all in.

This track was notably not significantly worse following The Rains of late 2008 than it was six months earlier. Like many of these deep, narrow Anti Atlas gorges, a flash flood would be intense but is spent in a few hours.

**79 (56)**          **N29° 41.66' W08° 34.63'**
The palmerie ends and the gorge opens out below distinctively eroded zig-zag formations on the left. From now on towards the highway, look back to see them at their best.

**83 (52)        N29° 42.95'  W08° 33.97'**
Cross the oued at the west end of the village of **Sidi Al Haj Ou Ali** (so called on old maps – or it could be any one of the eight names indicated on the block at KM89, below) and pass some striking villas, presumably built by prodigal sons who've done well up north. Many towns and villages in this part of Morocco have such lavish-looking dwellings set among the more traditional mud-brickery.

**86 (49)        N29° 43.57'  W08° 32.47'**
After switch-backing down from a high point with a great view behind you, meet a track coming up from the oued on your right and carry on north-east.

**88.5 (46.5)     N29° 44.53'  W08° 31.39'**
Cross the Oumdar oued one last time and on the north bank turn towards the village of **Aït Ballou** visible just ahead.

**89 (46)        N29° 44.72'  W08° 31.04'**
Having passed around the north side of **Aït Ballou**, you **join the R109 highway** at a white stone block with many village names and head north for Igherm. Presently you'll pass through a village with a ksar or fortress on the right. The presence of a couple of restos here means it's a tour bus stop.

**135        N30° 05.26'  W08° 27.67'**
**Igherm** SHELL just before the crossroads and by the little souk. If you're wondering where to go next, a winding tarred road leads right at the crossroads by the *Anzal*, down to Tagmoute and Tata.

Coming from Tafraoute, after what you've seen by the road and on the trail, comparatively neglected and grubby Igherm is not a particularly sumptuous place to end a great day out; its touristic appeal adding up to less than the five roads which meet here. But it does have two hotels: at the cross roads the *Hotel Anzal* has wide screen Al-Jazeera in the big tiled bar and perfunctory service until you've earned your stripes. A 50dh room here is as plain as a bag of flour: two beds, a door plus a bulb and a window, with basins in the hall and a shower if you ask. With a soup and bread for dinner and bread and jam for breakfast my bill came to 85dh, an all-time low and they'll let you stash your bike in their lock-up over the street.

If you don't fancy the *Anzal*, the *Hotel Rendezvous*, north over the crossroads from the SHELL and left, on the road to Taroudant (and the crossroads for Tafraoute and Taliouine) looked empty but has twice as many floors and may well be a bit flashier.

# MA9   TATA – AKKA IGHERN – FOUM ZGUID        150KM
November 2008 ~ Yamaha Ténéré

## Description
This alternative to the perfectly usable N12 'Desert Highway' linking the towns at each end is a former Dakar Rally piste; probably what was just part of a much longer day for them. For you it's a fine day out too, following a valley between the long Jebel Bani ridge to the south and the mass of the Anti Atlas to the north. There is a relatively rough and little-used start once you leave the highway at Akka Iguirn (as written on local road signs, maps all differ) until you reach the gardens south of Akka Ighern, a major crossroads hereabouts. You briefly join the sealed road to Taliouine but leave it at the town centre to follow what turns out to be a pleasingly smooth and open desert track offering some broad acacias for a shady break. You'll spot goat nomads to the south and then the track suddenly widens as if you've reached the boundary of a municipality with a bigger road-building budget.

In a way the fun is over once you're belting along this track, slowing only to get round the mangled concrete fords and bridges wrecked by The Rains of October 2008. Towards the end you have a choice to follow a flood-damaged piste all the way to El Mhamid and the road to Foum Zguid, or just carry on east and take the road south. Either way, Foum Zguid is as good a place to end the day as Tata was to start.

## Off road
A flat route with no great dramas and Olaf at your side most of the time. Only the oued crossings or rougher sections at each end might give a big bike with road tyres something to think about. A **2WD** could manage this route too, certainly by taking the road up to Akka Ighern from near Kasba el Joua (about 23km east of Akka Iguirn) and then taking the quick way out at the end. On a **mountain bike** the well at KM37.5 is handy, but taking the recommended 2WD route may be less arduous too, allowing you to save your energy for the agreeable eastern stages.

## Route finding
Nothing too taxing with this book in your hand; the road and the piste ought to unroll dutifully ahead. Off the N12 highway there was no traffic as far as Akka Ighern, a couple of cars around town, then a couple more on the wide track to the El Mhamid turn off. The route **map** is on p223.

## Fuel and water
There's fuel at each end only, water in the few wells and the more numerous villages.

## Suggested duration
Easily do-able in a short day and with the best camping spots east of Akka Ighern, or of course, anywhere that takes your fancy.

**0km**          N29° 44.31'  W07° 58.42'
**Tata** fuel on the south side of town. Head into town and turn right to follow the wide boulevard heading east for Foum Zguid. For accommodation options in Tata see the box on p219.

**28 (122)**          N29° 45.84'  W07° 42.03'
Turn left off the road at **Akka Iguirn** and follow the track north through the village and out the other end.

**31.5 (118.5)**     N29° 47.64'  W07° 42.31'
A bigger track joins from the right; you've seemingly followed a deviation to get over a oued.

**33 (117)**          N29° 48.41'  W07° 42.24'
Leave the oued to the east and uphill. Bikes will prefer the steep, stony ramp on the left as the route to the right looks like

deep sand for a couple of hundred metres. They join up in less than a kilometre.

**34.5 (115.5)**
A thin track leads off to the left (probably to Wismine village); keep right. In a kilometre you head up a low pass above the oued on loose gravel, not really a place you want to accelerate hard on a bike. On top unfolds a stony hamada. Head east-north-east.

**37.5 (112.5)**     N29° 49.64'  W07° 40.34'
A **well** (15m with a rope and a bottle) and trough by a stone hut just after crossing the Oued Targant. Soon after you fork right (left goes north-west to Wismine) and soon after that, at around KM40 (N29° 49.67'  W07° 40.14') a track joins from the right.

**39 (111)          N29° 50.15'  W07° 39.66'**
Cross a track, possibly a way from Wismine directly south-east to the highway via the Targant village track (see below).

**45 (105)          N29° 52.96'  W07° 38.06'**
Cross another track leading left or northwest to Targant; right here leads 13km back to the N12 highway at N29° 47.96' W07°34.23'. Carry on ahead and pass another couple of village access tracks over the next kilometre or so. The route then winds uphill either side of the eroded main track. At the top you can see the palmerie and mosques of Tiskamoudine far ahead. In 3.5km another village access track joins from the left near some pylons.

**53 (97)          N29° 56.04'  W07° 34.88'**
Junction by a hill to the east near **Issarghine** village. The track to the right goes to the Akka Ighern road (Route MA11) back to the N12. You keep ahead or left on a rubbly track.

**56.5 (93.5)          N29° 57.66'  W07° 34.17'**
A track joins from the right with a water tower on the right. In 500m you pass some irrigated gardens, crossing the built-up water channels over the track; **Tiskamoudine**. Akka Ighern is now visible ahead.

**57.5 (92.5)          N29° 58.29'  W07° 33.65'**
By a wall you join a more prominent track coming up from Tiskamoudine and turn left to follow it north-east and then east to the Akka Ighern road.

**59.5 (90.5)          N29° 58.64'  W07° 32.59'**
**Join the tarmac** road (Route MA11) by a pylon branch line and turn left or northeast for Akka Ighern.

**62.5 (87.5)          N29° 59.67'  W07° 31.76'**
**Akka Ighern** town centre by the radio towers and mature trees. Straight on are a shop and a café or two, as well as tarmac all the way to the N10 and eventually Taliouine – Route MA11 and well worth following another time.
  You turn right off the tarmac down a wide, dusty boulevard for 500m and at N29° 59.82'  W07° 31.52', by a square

water tower, turn right again (east) and head out of town. From here on the track is much smoother.

**69 (81)          N29° 59.01'  W07° 27.83'**
You cross a oued by some big, shady acacias. Anywhere off the track here would make a nice lunch spot or even a camp. The surface is smooth gravel and sand so for a while at least you're not pinned down to the track's course through the rubble; rare in Morocco!

**74.5 (75.5)          N30° 00.052'  W07° 25.04'**
Fork left here towards a white sign. Right leads to a village and would probably join up later. In 1500m there's another turn off south to the same village.

**80.5 (69.5)          N30° 01.51'  W07° 22.16'**
A track joins from the right at a small cairn. Soon another joins from the left.

**81.5 (68.5)          N30° 01.80'  W07° 21.60'**
Come out of a oued crossing with a military observation post on the ridge ahead and turn right around the south side of the ridge. Left leads north up to Agmour and so Route MA6. In 500m Olaf branches off south to a dead end, probably a nomad camp access track.

**84 (66)          N30° 01.94'  W07° 20.26'**
The smooth and windy twin-rut piste suddenly becomes a wide, smooth track.

**101 (49)**
A garden before the village of **Isngarn**. They may get repaired in time, but there are now a few deviations around broken bridges and fords over the next few kilometres as you pass the distant village of Timgissint with its access tracks leading north.

**124 (26)          N30° 13.37'  W07° 01.79'**
Sign north: 'Tlite 8km' (Route MA7) at the modest 860m **high point** of this route. Carry on ahead.

**128 (22)          N30° 13.93'  W06° 59.48'**
Olaf leads south towards Foum Zguid via the village of **Nsoula** or 'Aoufelgach' on some modern maps. You carry on straight for the newer route south.

**130 (20)**         **N30° 13.61'  W06° 58.62'**
Turn south off the main track to follow what proved to be a rough finale to El Mhamid village and the tarmac leading down to Foum Zguid.

This section was logged after a deadly flood a week or two earlier and although it's bound to have become better used by the time you read this, these last 20km took me nearly an hour. If you've had enough (or are heading north for Tazenacht or Agdz) stay on the main track for another 13km or so until you reach the tarmac 18km north of Foum Zguid's fuel station. Otherwise, purists turn south now.

**131 (19)**         **N30° 13.23'  W06° 57.85'**
Arrive at a few houses and pass round to the north side and then turn right or south again where a track comes in from the north-east. In a kilometre Olaf comes in from the right or north-west at N30° 12.61' W06° 57.81'. Join Olaf and follow it for a while to the south-east.

**135 (15)**         **N30° 11.55'  W06° 57.01'**
Cross a stony and sanded-up oued. A kilometre later Olaf slips off the left of the GPS screen while you follow a dead straight track to the south-east.

**141 (9)**         **N30° 09.53'  W06° 54.23'**
By a building, a wall and some pylons the track was a dry riverbed when I came through.

**142 (8)**         **N30° 09.28'  W06° 53.94'**
Tricky crossing down and up the banks of the Oued Mhamid (although it's bound to have got easier). Carry on along the rough stony track towards El Mhamid which is visible ahead.

**144 (6)**         **N30° 07.86'  W06° 53.07'**
Outskirts of El Mhamid, a useful point to head for if doing this route in reverse. Drop down through the village to the road.

**145 (5)**         **N30° 07.68'  W06° 52.86'**
**Join the tarmac** in the village opposite a white sign indicating 'Ecole' and a huge graveyard which makes you think either **El Mhamid** has been around for a very long time or they all smoke too much. (Actually one of the guidebooks suggests that multiple fake headstones were a com-

---

## NORMAL PLACES, ORDINARY PEOPLE

**Foum Zguid**, 'the gateway to the Sahara'. Anywhere else such an epithet would signal alarms bells for roving bands of 'blue men' in oversized turbans, but here it's no exaggeration and for once, no reason to keep moving. Sure, there are stores in the square selling colourful wares. Tourists head there after staggering out of big 4WDs following a night being minstrelled in an Erg Chebbi bivouac and a dawn ride on a camel.

But as in much bigger Tata, the people of Foum Zguid have so far managed to get it right as far as welcoming visitors is concerned, neither hyperactive or sullen, just chilled or 'normal'. 'How is that?' I asked the guys at the café, compared to places at the other end of Routes MS5 or -7? '*Nous ne sommes pas les "hommes bleux"*' the guy explained with some pride, pointing out his normal clothes '*nous sommes les gens simple*' as in 'ordinary' rather than dim-witted.

They knew well that tourists in places like Zagora who try so much as a walk up town risked getting pecked to death by touts and, if it happens too often too virulently elsewhere, will join the defeated who vow never to return to Morocco.

In the ten years since I first visited both Zagora and Foum Zguid the ambience of both places has not changed significantly. I look forward to stopping off at Foum Zguid, but the last time I was in Zagora we arrived late (already trailing a wake of moped touts) and left early.

Zagora is a big tourist town of course with not enough catering and hospitality work to go around, but **Mhamid**, that other *porte du Sahara* is about as big as Foum Zguid. You'd need thick skin to walk around there too, judging by the last time I hesitated, thought about it and then pressed on.

mon ploy to try and confuse jackals digging up the graves.)

**150**　　　**N30° 05.40'　W06° 52.66'**
Pass through the 'foum' or gap in the
range and arrive at the *Afriquia* fuel station (unleaded) on the north edge of
**Foum Zguid** (pronounced 'Zgyd' not
Zgoo-id). The town centre's cafés and
*checheries* are half a kilometre down the
road.

I had a great feed at the *Restaurant
Chegaga* on the corner. Salad, brochettes
and chips with a *Hawaii*, a plate of fruit for
afters and the obligatory **freshly-
squeezed orange** juice required of any
pilgrim stopping in Foum Zguid came to
a hefty 85dh. I felt I'd earned it hammering the last few kilometres into town.

For **somewhere to stay** the *Hotel Bani*
signed on the way into town is visible on
the south side of the square. Assuming I
walked into the right place, it didn't look
any better closer up or inside, but it's
bound to be cheap.

Carry on down the road to Tata and
you'll soon get to the small **campsite** on
the right which was OK a couple of years
earlier, if a bit pricey. This time I tried the
**Auberge Iriki** a bit further on, signed
down a side road to the right. The guy
was keen, there was room for cars in the
locked yard and a twin en-suite with half
board was 190dh. Just the room with
breakfast would have been 120dh.

There's a nice salon in the typical style
and a roof terrace on top for hot nights or
watching your clothes dry. The food was
not too exciting: a small Moroccan salad, a
pile of chicken cous-cous and a plate of
fruit. On my visit the place was a bit noisy
with crying babies round the back, kids
yapping out front and then the drumming
started after dark – but there's always ear
plugs or the open desert just down the
road.

# MA10　OUSEMLAL – FOUM EL HASSAN – ASSA　　195km

November 2008 ~ Yamaha Ténéré

## Description

Here's yet another way of getting down off the Anti Atlas to the desert, but as
with Route MA5, nothing can quite match the wonders of MA2 up the Oued
Smouguene. This route follows MA2 along its less impressive off-road stage
before splitting off to cross the plateau to the west. I had fond hopes of more
palmeries and hidden villages, but all I got was a rough track, enlivened not
inconsiderably by the impressive viewpoint at KM66.

From here you drop down, cross the plain below and head east a short dis-
tance along the N12 to pick up a track which winds in and out of the jebels like
Route MA4. You reach Foum el Hassan, passing nomad camps along the way.
You then follow the 'Desert Highway' south-west to Assa.

## Off road

After the block at KM46 where the tracks splits for Igmir (Route MA2), the
piste you follow is little-used and so soon becomes rough up to the KM66
viewpoint before the big descent. The second section is in better shape and
won't give **any off-road vehicle** any trouble; even regular cars could manage
it and it's short enough to be a fun taster or indeed a quiet place to camp out.
**Mountain bikes** will enjoy this stage more too, but from Foum el Hassan – no
oasis despite the palms – it's a long road ride to anywhere else.

## Route finding

The first piste stage is a straightforward if rough descent with little to confuse
you. The winding route of the second section requires a tiny bit more concen-

tration. On these piste sections you're unlikely to come across any traffic other than the mule caravans of the nomads. The **map** for this route is on p213.

## Fuel and water
Ousemlal and Assa only. You could try asking around at Foum el Hassan but it didn't work for me. No wells were noted on the piste apart from at KM113, but there must be some out there for the nomads. Otherwise try the villages.

## Suggested duration
End-to-end in a day is not difficult, but breaking it up with a camp out north of Foum el Hassan would be more fun.

**0km          N29° 31.57'   W09° 14.73'**
PETROMIN fuel on the west side of **Jemaa Ida Ousemlal** to give it its full title. The town has quite a few shops and I was told there was a hotel 'Khandouz' a couple of kilometres out west but I couldn't find it. Fill up and head in the other direction, east through town towards Ouafka.

**11 (184)**
Junction on the east side of Souk Khemis de Aït **Ouafka**. The road to the north-east comes down from Tafraoute – an alternative start for this route. Carry on eastwards.

**32 (163)        N29° 27.08'   W09° 03.74'**
**Take the piste** which leaves the sealed road to the south, just east of **Tahwawat** village at a yellow sign for the *Igmir Guest House*. In about 1.5km at N29° 26.40' W09° 03.44' turn right and follow this track south towards Igmir.

On the way you may notice a track joining from the right and another leading off left, but the main way is clear. (Full details of the turn offs are in Route MA2).

**46 (149)        N29° 20.71'   W09° 02.43'**
The piste forks at a detailed sign block. Turn right (south-west) and wind slowly into a shallow valley. Left leads down to Igmir on Route MA2.

**60 (135)        N29° 15.27'   W09° 05.56'**
At this fork keep left. The route up ahead is little used and as a result is in bad shape.

Although it's an unlikely prospect, according to some maps, right at this fork leads south-west to **Amtoudi** just 10km away (on Route MA5). I gave it a go for

about half an hour but soon got confused in a maze of mineral exploration tracks heading off in all directions and evidence of recent prospecting. There was no clear sign of a single through-route leading towards Amtoudi, or indeed anywhere useful, though in a cross-country sense it may well be possible.

Certainly it's occasionally done with tourists on mules. Looking at the geological formation across this region on Google Earth (not evident at ground level) makes the exploration activities more understandable. Navigating back to the fork I was sure glad of the GPS track and couple of waypoints I'd logged on the way out; without this it would have been easy to get disorientated out here.

Back on Route MA10, in 4 or 5km you pass the **high point** at around 1112m.

**66 (129)        N29° 12.69'   W09° 06.82'**
You arrive at a pauseworthy **viewpoint** where the escarpment drops away dramatically towards the N12 and the jebels beyond.

The track winds down to the plain without too much difficulty (or at least the view takes your mind off things). Once you've dropped 350m and are back on the flats, head directly south, passing tracks leading east to the villages of Talilit and later **Tagigalt**, close to the road.

**78 (117)        N29° 06.55'   W09° 07.55'**
**Join the N12 highway** close to two cairns just west of some trees. Turn left, or east.

**88 (107)        N29° 07.37'   W09° 01.87'**
**Leave the road** and turn right down a track leading southwards. (The Olaf start is about 3.5km further on, just after some

Armco on a bend and gets to the way-point below having covered an additional 7km along some enjoyable shaley riverbeds and nomad camps).

**92.5 (102.5)     N29° 05.22'   W09° 01.36'**
Olaf joins from the east.

**100 (95)     N29° 02.47'   W09° 01.14'**
You curve south then south-east then east round the Jebel Tastaft and at this point fork left. A kilometre later you pass a stone building as you cross a oued.

**104 (91)     N29° 02.12'   W08° 58.84'**
A bigger track joins from the right or south-west by some ruins. It's Olaffed and appears to join the road halfway to Assa at around N28° 42.9'  W09° 14.7'.

**110 (85)     N29° 01.97'   W08° 55.40'**
Here you head into a big oued then cross back to the north bank and carry on along a smooth track, leaving Olaf. Soon you spy the mosque and radio towers of Foum el Hassan through the gap in the range.

**112 (83)     N29° 02.48'   W08° 54.36'**
Arrive at a junction with a big track coming down from the Aït Herbil road to the north. Turn right into the oued again. The shingle and sand ruts can be tricky on a big bike.

**113 (82)     N29° 01.95'   W08° 54.37'**
Pass a **well** (6m) high on the east bank of the oued by some big trees.

**115 (80)     N29° 01.04'   W08° 53.59'**
**Join the tarmac** at a concrete ford on the west side of **Foum el Hassan**. Turn south-west for Assa.

Despite its long outdated prominence on maps and road signs, Foum el Hassan is a poor border village with some stores and a basic hotel somewhere. In colonial times it was a garrison (as it is today) on the long-abandoned road to Algeria, via the mysterious 'Tour de Merkala' – probably a natural formation.

**195     N28° 37.05'   W09° 27.05'**
ZIZMO at the west end of Assa. For a hotel in town see the end of Route MW2.

# MA11  TALIOUINE – TATA – IGHERM     276KM
November 2008 ~ Yamaha Ténéré

There's a direct road route from Taliouine to Igherm, about 100km to the south-west along the R106, and a great drive up through the hills it is. Although nearly three times as long, MA11 takes a big arc to the south-east, over the crest of the Anti Atlas, down to the desert floor and back up again; the sort of scenic drive you want to discover in Morocco. Only sealed in the last few years, most maps miss out classifying this route correctly as tarmac, or even depicting it at all, but barring heavy rains it'll be open to all vehicles large and small, and bicycles will find it a great ride, certainly as far as Tata (fuel and hotels) before the big climb back up to Igherm. See pp222-3 for the map.

## Route description
Kilometre zero is at the auberges at the east end of **Taliouine**. Head east, away from town past the turn off for the mountain road to Askaoun (another great 50km drive this, past some lovely mountain villages but a dead end unless you have the clearance). Back down below, you pass the old kasbah to the south,

cross the oued and pass a ZIZ a couple of kilometres out of town. Here starts a steep climb up to 1500m where, at KM15, you leave the N10 to the south and head into the ranges. The road climbs slowly up across the plateau to the small town of **Agadir Melloul** at KM49 (a few shops and a café). A couple of kilometres on, the road peaks around 1860m at the Tizi n Ounzour and then rolls off the Anti Atlas crags through a short narrow canyon where flash floods sometimes scour the road. You emerge in a narrow valley as the metres tumble from your altimeter and your ears unpop. Suddenly the air is warmer and the scenery more arid.

The stone-clad village of **Tisfriouine** crops up on a bend at KM71, a desert settlement with an old shrine by the mosque. Four kilometres later, your arrival on the desert fringe is underlined by a dense roadside palmerie then, after crossing 30°N, the road takes a sudden turn to the east and even northeast to circumvent the spur of a ridge. This is the start of the transit of the Admal valley, as agreeable and quiet a place to lunch as anywhere along this route. Even with a low-slung road vehicle it's not hard to find a spot to get off the road and enjoy a break, or even out of site beneath the jebels to enjoy a night out in the desert at around 1000m.

Back on the road, at KM106 you turn south where a confluence of oueds have carved a gap in the ridge. Within 10km you're in **Akka Ighern**, a small town with a couple of cafés and a shop as well as surrounding palmeries and market gardens. Set at the edge of a flat basin surrounded by mountains, at the roundabout by the trees, Routes MA6, -7 and -8 head for the hills while you track south across the floodplain to the N12 'Desert Highway' and at KM138, just after **Ksaba el Joua**, turn west for Tata.

Behind the Jebel Bani ridge the Sahara rolls away unbroken for a thousand miles to Timbuktu, and as you drive down the boulevard into laid-back **Tata**, the biggest town for miles around, you'll find the two better hotels and **fuel** (KM197) to the left. Turn right for main street with several **cafés** and **hotel restaurants**, as well as **ATMs** and a spacious, central **campsite**.

Continue up this street, through the town's palmerie, over the Oued Tata and north out of town for the final stage back up into the ranges and Igherm. Initially you follow the valley upstream, passing striking, twisted rock strata and distant nomads' tents until you emerge at another rim-rocked basin. On the far side at KM235 is **Souk Tleta Tagmoute** and at the town centre (a couple of shops), bear right and wind on through the settlement. Soon you'll pass the *Gite Tagmout* and presently pass the remains of the old town. The valley narrows and the road may be washed-out as it crosses and re-crosses the oued and you pass more palmeries jammed alongside the banks.

The climb begins as the road folds back on itself like a strand of tagliatelle, away from the desert and back up into the scrubby heights of the Anti Atlas. Winding north and then west, presently it flattens out and suddenly at KM276 you're at the crossroads that is Igherm town centre right by the basic *Hotel Anzal* (for more on the town see the end of Route MA8). For the SHELL and the shops turn left. Should you have a few miles left in you this road, the R109 continues with no less drama for just over 100km back down to Tata.

## Outline of the West region

This small region north of the Mauritanian border adds up to a half dozen routes either side of the **Oued Draa** valley and is probably the least visited region featured in this book. The routes and terrain are again Saharan in character but without the full elevation of the Anti Atlas or the tourists and the associated infrastructure found further east. Chances are you'll see no one on these pistes apart from the ancient Landrover 'mules' transporting the **Saharawi** who you'll meet out in the desert and the villages; former nomads now relegated to tending flocks of goats and sheep for the army garrisons and coastal resorts.

North of the Draa, MW3 is a satisfying run, although south of the Jebel Ouarkaziz (Routes MW1 and 6) you could meet military patrolling for Polisario activity. It's best not to stray any nearer the border than these routes do, but within this region you could make your own links between the key points and roads to the west.

In winter the **weather** here ought to be reliably cool and rain-free; a good time to be in the desert. As noted on Route MW6, even disregarding the 40°C-plus temperatures, storms in summer or at any time can be sudden and violent, and temporarily cut off routes.

## MW Routes

# MW1 TAN-TAN – JEBEL OUARKAZIZ – ASSA        268KM
April 2008 ~ Mazda pickup

## Description
This is a desolate traverse inland to Assa, following the south side of the **Jebel Ouarkaziz**. Running north-east with barely a break for nearly 300km, the ridge made a natural barrier during the 1980s Polisario war and, at the handful of passes in the range, defensive walls and trenches with gun emplacements were built to plug the gaps.

You pass through the first of these 'mini berms' at KM76, head out into the former Polisario badlands and then turn in again towards the end of the route at KM225. These installations can make you understandably anxious about the presence of mines which are said to exist elsewhere along the Moroccan borders, but these walls are wartime relics compared to the main militarised **Berm**, further south which today marks the de facto border, dividing the Western Sahara between Morocco, and the so-called Polisario Free Zone inland (see the map on p253; it's best not to show this map to army types).

With the jebels distant and low and no palm-ringed settlements to speak of, the scenery here lacks the variety of the best of Morocco, but it's a satisfyingly long desert run rarely visited by tourists or it seems, anyone else.

## Off road
The narrow valley stage after KM78 is a bit of a crawl and may filter out the average **road car**, but is not characteristic of what lies ahead. If you make it to KM94 you're back out in the open and on your way. On a **motorbike** there's no problem other than the long hammering and possibly the fuel range. For **bicycles** MW1, lean as it is on known wells, will be a bit much. There are more enjoyable routes to pedal around here.

## Route finding
Most of the time the Ouarkaziz ridge or parallel formations lie close to the north. Things can get muddied around KM150 for a bit, but keep plugging away just north of east and you'll eventually get somewhere useful. With no villages after Mseid and even nomadic tents unknown mid-route, this is a desolate track as you wind along and through small passes and across dusty chotts. After Mseid I saw no vehicles until Assa, although I did follow recent Land Rover tyre tracks most of the way. When I did it, Olaf mysteriously petered out at KM90.

If you think it all might be over too quickly, you could string this route out by heading for Labouirat on Route MW6 at KM135 and then following MW6 one way or the other. The route **map** is on pp248-9.

## Fuel and water
Fuel at each end with nothing in between. Water is from just a couple of tanks and wells as marked.

## Suggested duration
You could bang this out in a day but it's best enjoyed with an overnight stop in the middle of nowhere. Have I said that already?

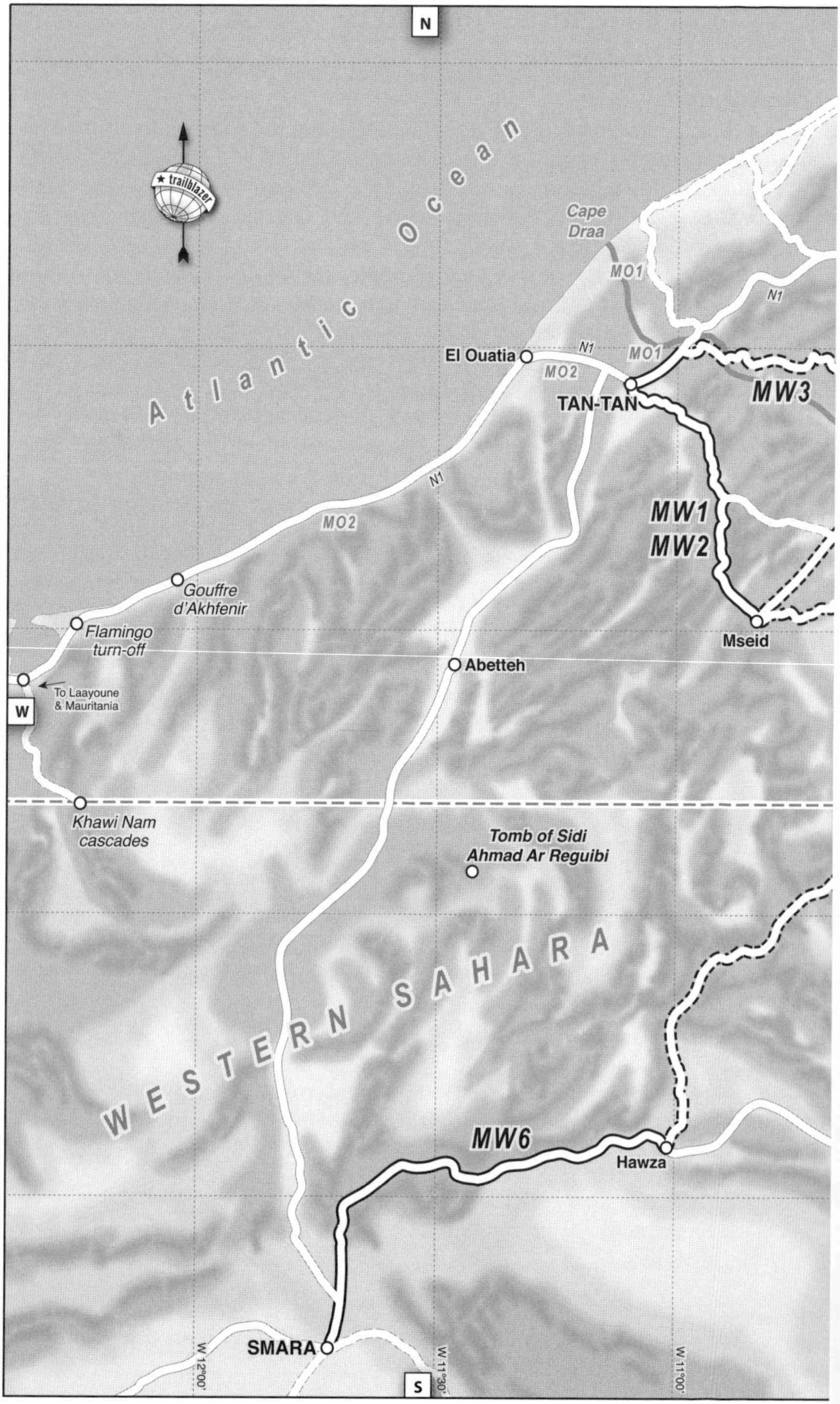
N
trailblazer
Atlantic Ocean
Cape Draa
MO1
N1
El Ouatia
MO2
TAN-TAN
MW3
MW1
MW2
Mseid
Gouffre d'Akhfenir
Flamingo turn-off
Abetteh
To Laayoune & Mauritania
W
Khawi Nam cascades
Tomb of Sidi Ahmad Ar Reguibi
WESTERN SAHARA
MW6
Hawza
SMARA
W 12°00'
W 11°30'
W 11°00'
S

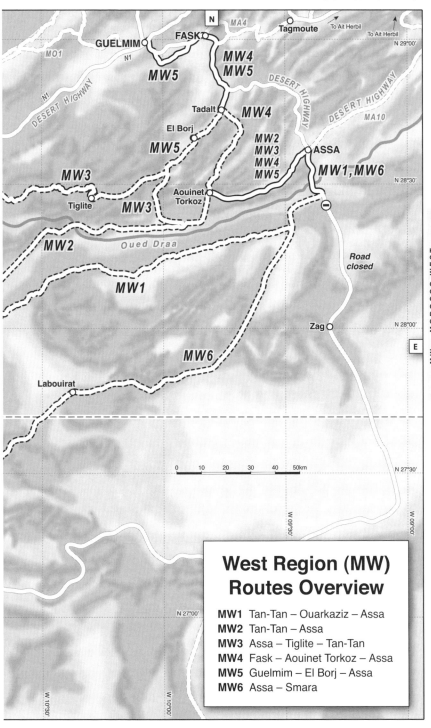

## West Region (MW)
## Routes Overview

**MW1** Tan-Tan – Ouarkaziz – Assa
**MW2** Tan-Tan – Assa
**MW3** Assa – Tiglite – Tan-Tan
**MW4** Fask – Aouinet Torkoz – Assa
**MW5** Guelmim – El Borj – Assa
**MW6** Assa – Smara

**0km          N28° 26.03'  W11° 04.75'**
**Tan-Tan** east fuel station. Head into town but after 400m turn left at the sign 'Lemseid 68km'. Follow the road inland.

**27 (241)        N28° 17.08'  W10° 54.22'**
**Tilemsen** village. In a few kilometres the road rises up and over a ridge with good viewpoints back and ahead at KM37.

**58.5 (209.5)    N28° 04.30'  W10° 52.79'**
Possible turn off to the east to pick up Route MW2.

**68 (200)        N28° 00.90'  W10° 48.88'**
The **tar ends** in **Mseid** ('Lemseid'), a basic nomad village at the base of the Jebel Tassout by a big gap in the range. Drive into the village, turn right (south-west) and head south through the wide pass.

**69 (199)        N28° 00.48'  W10° 48.88'**
Just as you come through the pass, by some solar panels and a **well** pump, turn east along the back side of the Jebel Tassout, passing some tents and buildings. There are many tracks here going to various nomad encampments. Make your way any which way to KM74.

**74 (194)        N28° 01.06'  W10° 46.26'**
Key point: a small cairn in the oued with a **well** 500m to the north. At the cairn turn right, south, out of the oued towards a low berm you'll have seen running across the valley, looking like a buried pipeline.

**76 (192)        N28° 01.26'  W10° 45.27'**
Cross over the berm, and again a kilometre later as you head up to a pass.

**78 (190)        N28° 01.01'  W10° 44.40'**
Head into the pass through the Jebel Ouarkaziz and on the other side, turn left or east and head into a narrow, stony valley. It's slow going but do-able without resorting to low range. There may be various deviations to get round washed-out sections in the next few kilometres until the valley ends.

**80 (188)        N28° 00.61'  W10° 43.32'**
**Well** (20m).

**87 (181)        N28° 01.68'  W10° 39.89'**
Palms. Always nice to see some palms!

**90 (178)        N28° 02.26'  W10° 38.43'**
Olaf ended here in 2008, but carry on north-east as you emerge from the valley – a clear track continues.

**94 (174)        N28° 03.75'  W10° 36.27'**
Fork right to the east. The terrain finally opens up and the track speeds up.

**104 (164)       N28° 05.92'  W10° 31.45'**
Having done a dog-leg down to some standing stones, a track joins from the right (marked on the old French map).

**110 (158)       N28° 07.42'  W10° 28.58'**
Some tall cairns. Continue north-east.

**113 (155)       N28° 08.75'  W10° 27.80'**
Hassi Tagueleimet, now a **cistern** with water inside. This is the last known well on this route until the pass at KM227.

**115.5 (152.5)   N28° 09.47'  W10° 26.56'**
Possible early split to the south for the **Labouirat** route. You continue east around the north of a hill to enter a oued and go along it.

**125 (143)       N28° 11.22'  W10° 21.93'**
Semi-abandoned nomad camp with domed mud charcoal ovens.

**128 (140)       N28° 11.36'  W10° 20.46'**
Remains of a very old truck.

**135 (133)       N28° 12.09'  W10° 16.38'**
Junction. There's a white building just to the south by a pass, probably the track as marked on the Michelin map as the 'P1600' to **Labouirat**, about 75km to the south-east. (KM118 on Route MW6). You continue east.

**137 (131)       N28° 12.15'  W10° 15.04'**
Fork right to the south-east towards a big chott. In a kilometre at N28° 11.64'  W10° 14.64' you head east into a pass and cross a oued with palms and bluish rocks. Could be a nice spot to camp.

**145 (123)       N28° 10.62'  W10° 10.38'**
Fork left here; up ahead is a shallow pass out onto the Aster chott to the east. Although the resolution on Google Earth is pretty poor in this sector, from this point it looks like a wide open run south-

east for about 40km to Labouirat on MW6 via a couple of shallow passes.

**146.5 (121.5)  N28° 10.60'  W10° 08.97'**
Former camp with more charcoal ovens and a kilometre to the east, a crumbling block marked with Berber writing and bullet holes. A track seems to lead north from here although there's no break in the Jebel Ouarkaziz. It could be to 'Amon' or 'Amot' as marked on some maps, possibly a well.

**150 (118)  N28° 10.26'  W10° 07.09'**
Pass a large, stone-cobbled circle with an arrow on the ground, pointing east – a desert air strip? Around here you start heading north-east. The tracks multiply and become ill-defined as you pass along the Oued Tigzert.

**159 (109)  N28° 12.00'  W10° 02.86'**
After possibly blundering around for a bit, pick up a track heading north-east at this point. The track winds around over the bumpy, dried mud of the Oued Tigzert. After a while you notice an unusually long and straight line of trees to the south, marking a oued line.

**171 (97)  N28° 14.51'  W09° 57.34'**
Fork right.

**188 (80)  N28° 16.41'  W09° 47.68'**
Turn north-east through a small pass. Continue north-east, then north-north-east.

**202 (66)  N28° 18.34'  W09° 39.40**
Cross a oued, possibly a good camping place. Up ahead, nomad tents may appear as the terrain opens out. Behind the hills visible 50km to the south-east is **Zag** on the closed border road to Smara. You don't want to go there.

**212 (56)  N28° 19.12'  W09° 33.31'**
The track drops down into a camp-worthy oued with some trees.

**221 (47)  N28° 20.24'  W09° 28.94'**
Pass a **white tank** just to the south of the track.

**222 (46)  N28° 20.46'  W09° 28.89'**
You join a prominent northbound track. This is KM48 on Route MW6 via Labouirat, 71km away – and Smara, about 344km to the south.

**225 (43)  N28° 22.04'  W09° 29.14'**
Pass through a defensive wall across the first gap in the Jebel Ouarkaziz since Mseid and head into the pass.

**227 (41)  N28° 22.87'  W09° 29.40'**
In the pass there's a **well** to the right, used by nomads, as well as crumbling walls and gun emplacements all around.

**228 (40)  N28° 23.44'  W09° 29.49'**
Emerging from the pass, fork right and follow this inter-jebel valley eastwards. This point is KM42 on Route MW6.

**235 (33)  N28° 25.90'  W09° 24.75'**
A deep **well** (35m) by the piste, just after a pylon.

**236 (32)  N28° 26.07'  W09° 24.46'**
Join the **Assa-Zag highway** at a broken rusty sign saying 'El Arbouyet 68'. From here it's 32km to Assa fuel, crossing the Oued Draa on the way.

**268 (0)  N28° 37.05'  W09° 27.03'**
Assa fuel and café on the west end of town. For directions to the **hotel** see the box on p242.

MW – MOROCCO WEST

## MW2  TAN-TAN – ASSA  238KM

February 1999, part updated April 2008 ~ Mazda pickup

### Description

Part of an old Dakar route from the late 1990s, this version of Tan-Tan to Assa is not as interesting as it looks and, depending on your suspension and tyre pressures, the bumpy terrain can become tiring, but get used to it – this is 'Mo-rocky-o'. The piste passes through typical south Moroccan scenery, crossing stony hamada and for a while passing along the terminal stages of the **Oued Draa** as it flows west between parallel mountain ranges.

## Off road

Doing it in a cart-sprung **Land Cruiser** won't have left the best impression but this is a rough, stony trail, churned-up by run off feeding the Draa. **Motorcycles** will be less affected, but **MTBs** will find it a long, tough slog.

## Route finding

Jammed between the ranges and at times boulder fields, route finding does not present many variables, though you'll have to wing it along the undriven stage from KM58.5 to KM67. Once you pick the trail of 'Dakar' cairns built up on mounds of bulldozed earth (up to KM189), a single track leads you clearly north-east to Aouinet Torkoz and the road to Assa.

This route does not appear on any map until you near Aouinet Torkoz, yet it's one of the best-marked pistes in the Sahara. There are so many cairns on this route that you could almost stumble from one to the next blindfolded. You won't see much traffic on this route other than the odd nomad's Landrover. For the route **map** see pp248-9.

## Fuel and water

Fuel at Tan-Tan and Assa and several wells along the way.

## Suggested duration

With an early start you can easily get to Assa in a day.

**0km          N28° 26.03'  W11° 04.75'**
**Tan-Tan** east ('north') fuel station. Head into town but after 400m turn left at sign 'Lemseid 68km' and follow the road inland.

**37 (201)**
Having passed **Tilemsen** village 10 kilometres ago, the road tops out on this ridge with good viewpoints back and forth.

**58.5 (179.5)    N28° 04.30'  W10° 52.79'**
**Turn off the road** to the east, noted in 2008. The next waypoint and the route description up to KM170 date back to 1999, with the distances corrected.

**67 (171)          N28° 05.5'  W10° 48.3'**
A piste crosses at right angles, the 'left' track possibly being the one you've just arrived on from KM58.5. Continue north-north-east up the valley.

**80 (158)          N28° 10.7'  W10° 43.3'**
Having just come through a bumpy sec-

tion, you head out across smooth clay pans. The frequent cairns continue on either side of the track. After a few kilometres you draw close to the ridge on your left.

**90 (148)          N28° 14.2'  W10° 38.8'**
In a kilometre you enter some churned up chotts with lots of scrubby vegetation.

**93 (145)          N28° 15.2'  W10° 37.6'**
The piste becomes very stony and starts to rise over low hills. In a few kilometres you come north through a pass and soon see white buildings to the left and right. Stay on the right-hand track, following the cairns. The track runs east-north-east.

**97 (141)**
Pass a concrete building to the right at the foot of the escarpment.

**99 (139)**
The track crosses a broad, vegetated oued. On the other side the track forks: go right,

following the cairns into the hills, east-south-east, seemingly crossing back into the valley you've just come over from.

**100 (138)          N28° 17.3'  W10° 34.8'**
Emerge into a parallel valley.

**105 (133)          N28° 18.2'  W10° 32.2'**
Pass a double-lidded **well** on the right of the track just before a oued (in 1999 one well was dry, the other locked). Over the next few kilometres there are several very stony oued crossings.

**110 (128)          N28° 18.6'  W10° 29.6'**
Head east across a wide gravel valley with several nomad tents along the foot of the escarpment to the south. In 3km head into another valley and soon pass a concrete building with a green door on the left of the piste. It's very stony going for a few hundred metres.

**120 (118)          N28° 19.7'  W10° 24.2'**
Waypoint. In a kilometre you see a distinctive strip of red rock on an outcrop to the left. You're now entering the course of the **Oued Draa** as it takes a northern turn through the Jebel Amermerdene range. The track becomes even stonier, making progress very slow for a couple of kilometres.

**125 (113)**
Climb up onto a stony plateau as the track smoothes out.

**130 (108)          N28° 22.1'  W10° 20.4'**
In two kilometres you cross a oued with a small palmerie enclosed by a circular stone wall.

**133 (105)          N28° 21.5'  W10° 19.5'**
Fork right following cairns heading east with occasional stony patches and minor diverging tracks.

**140 (98)          N28° 20.4'  W10° 16.1'**
Still on a stony plain with occasional rough oued crossings. Continue east.

**144 (94)**
To the left is a concrete building with two red doors. The terrain is becoming sandy with a few trees as the pace speeds up.

Anywhere in the next few kilometres would make a good spot to camp.

**150 (88)          N28° 21.1'  W10° 10.2'**
Waypoint. Still a fast smooth surface with some... the only word is 'stony' – patches.

**164 (74)          N28° 22.7'  W10° 02.4'**
Pass a concrete building to the right as the terrain gets rougher.

**170 (68)          N28° 22.9'  W09° 59.3'**
Fast going over a very smooth clay pan. Around this point, recorded in 2008, you meet tracks coming down from the north: Routes MW3 and MW5.

**177 (61)          N28° 23.92'  W09° 55.41'**
The smooth clay pan ends but the good surface continues.

**180 (58)          N28° 24.06'  W09° 53.81'**
Fork left here away from the oued on your right.

**181 (57)          N28° 24.48'  W09° 53.46'**
Leave the oued and head for this junction waypoint then continue north-north-east for **Aouinet Torkoz**.

**190 (48)          N28° 29.00'  W09° 51.20'**
Enter the old western part of **Aouinet Torkoz** village with possibly a couple of stores but not much else.

Drive east over the oued to newer side of town where the **tarmac starts** and meet the crossroads where Route MW4 comes in from the north. Follow the tarmac east to Assa. You'll pass a couple of roadside **wells** and tanks on the way.

**236 (2)**
On arriving at the 'teapot' roundabout on the outskirts of **Assa**, the town centre is straight ahead and there's a hotel to the right (see p242).

For fuel, turn left at the roundabout, follow the road round to the north and at the main road turn left, passing Assa Park (see box on p242 for more on Assa).

**238          N28° 37.05'  W09° 27.05'**
Z_IZ_ fuel station and café at the west end of Assa.

---

### ASSA

A focal point for nearly all the routes in this region, **Assa** is a curiosity; a clean and in parts, prosperous-looking town with more money spent on municipal street furnishings than many other places down south, not least somewhere like Foum el Hassan up the road. Maybe the mayor was owed a favour.

Relying on outdated paper maps, both guidebooks miss out Assa or even mapping the sealed roads which run through, between Foum el Hassan and Guelmim, an impressive stretch of the 1500km long 'Desert Highway'.

Check out the well-tended **town park** on the main road near the fuel station. Above the beds of seasonal flowers, it includes a witty life-sized diorama of gazelles browsing innocently on an outcrop while beneath them a cunning jackal stalks, ready to pounce. There's nothing else like it in southern Morocco.

Just down the road on the way to Aouinet Torkoz is the as yet unrecognised '**teapot roundabout**' where a jaunty trio of oversized jugs dispense a brew. According to Wikipedia, the next known teapot roundabouts are both in Algeria, both over 1500km to the south-east. One is in the old oil town of In Amenas close to the Libyan border, the other opposite the *Air Algerie* office in Tamanrasset.

Although I've not checked it out, I hear there is a small **hotel** in Assa, the only one for at least 100km in any direction. At the teapot roundabout a kilometre or so from the Ziz, take the road branching south-east towards an Arabic inscription on the hillside. Hopefully the *Hotel Nidaros* is a couple of hundred metres on; if not, ask around in town. There's a Google Earth map (pre-dating much of Assa's current infrastructure) on the website.

---

## MW3   ASSA – TIGLITE – TAN-TAN                     231KM
April 2008 ~ Mazda pickup

### Description

A great run through the western end of Jebel Bani through to the coastal ranges, finishing off right in the reeds of the **Oued Draa** as it nears the sea. It's all here: deserted desert blacktop, palmy gorges with inviting waterholes, fast tracks over bleak uplands passing more hidden gorges, cosy valleys and brightly-painted villages against the dun background of the Sahara.

### Off road

Just about do-able in a **2WD** with bent up bumpers and some bridging planks. After rain things could get muddy in the Oued Draa towards the end (there's an alternative escape route), or in the deep gorges converging around Tiglite.

Providing the rider has been on a prolonged spinach diet and isn't overloaded, this route could be done on an **Africa Twin**, Triumph Tiger and the like. Just make the most of the restful section up to Tiglite, because after that you'll need some stamina to get to Tan-Tan in one piece.

On a **mountain bike** this would be a tough three or four-day haul. But with enough water on the way and places to rest, if you're on top form, give it a go. Just remember the end stage may wear you out and there's not much traffic to depend on.

### Route finding

Easy enough, Olaf is by your side to all but the bitter end at KM198. At worst just hammer your way westwards until you hit the coastal highway or expire from the effort. Options include starting from Fask via El Borj (see Route

MW5). You may come across a local car or two as far as Tiglite but I saw no moving cars on the route. The **map** is on pp248-9.

## Fuel and water
Assa and Tan-Tan and possibly available in remote villages like Tiglite and Aouinet Ighoman. There are many wells and waterholes as listed, plus villages and doubtless more sources unseen.

## Suggested duration
Allow a day and a half in a 4WD, two full days in a regular car or a day on a fast, light moto. As mentioned below left, an MTB rider would need three or four days and a solid sense of commitment.

**0km          N28° 37.05'  W09° 27.05'**
Assa ZIZMO on the west side of town. Head into town but turn right, south, after 500m. Follow the road round to the 'teapot roundabout' and take a right, south-west, for Aouinet Torkoz.

For more on Assa, including a hotel, see the box opposite.

**39 (192)      N28° 27.94'  W09° 46.11'**
**Well** by the road.

**47 (184)**
As you arrive in Aouinet, drive straight over a crossroads where Route MW4 comes in from the north and over the oued to the old side of town. **The tar ends**.

**48 (183)      N28° 28.99'  W09° 51.20'**
Leave town here and head south-south-west.

**58 (173)      N28° 24.48'  W09° 53.46'**
Fork left down to the oued.

**59 (172)      N28° 24.06'  W09° 53.81'**
Once near the oued head out onto a smooth clay pan and at KM62 follow old Dakar Rally cairns across the pan.

In the desert a natural surface doesn't get any smoother than this so enjoy it while you can.

**66 (165)      N28° 23.89'  W09° 58.25'**
The northern split you left at KM58 runs in from the right as you near the western edge of the pan.

**67 (164)      N28° 23.84'  W09° 59.01'**
Another track joins from the right. Soon

you reach a **well** (4m) and may see some nomad tents to the north. Various tracks start running in from the left but your destination is clear: the gap in the range directly ahead.

**73 (158)      N28° 24.55'  W10° 02.60'**
The main junction, among many others. Head north here.

**76 (155)**
**Taskala** village in the pass. A few nomad *raïma* or tents were bundled up by the oued below the village.

**76.5 (154.5)  N28° 26.19'  W10° 03.21'**
Leave the village at a **cistern** by a pink hut.

**78 (153)**
A track goes off to the right.

**82 (149)**
The winding ascent into the gorge begins. After a few kilometres and some hairpins you may pass some deep **waterholes** in the riverbed on the right.

**87 (144)**
Cross a small oued with pink oleanders (in April at least). In a couple of kilometres you're out of the gorge and on a 500m, upland plateau.

**91.5 (139.5)  N28° 30.87'  W10° 01.18'**
If you're in a mad rush take the fork left here, it rejoins the track at KM96.5, cutting off the elbow and saving a couple of kilometres.

**94 (137)          N28° 32.32'  W10° 00.29'**
A track joins the 'elbow' from the east, possibly a direct route from Aouinet.

**95 (136)**
'Blue bag' Junction with the track from El Borj and Tadalt (Routes MW4 and 5). In 700m or so you cross a dense, palmy oued with more pink flowers and frogs in the pools. There could be seasonal overnight mozzies, but it's a shady spot for lunch.

**96 (135)          N28° 32.33'  W10° 01.28'**
Main junction where you join the El Borj-Tiglite track. Tabayoudet mountain is ahead and in a few hundred metres at N28° 32.51'  W10° 01.45' the short cut from KM91.5 probably joins from the left.

The track now becomes smooth and fast, and in 2008 was marked by stone cairns stuffed with blue plastic bags (hence 'Blue bag' junction). It could be due for sealing, although elsewhere in the Anti Atlas they've signified the residue of mineral prospecting.

**121 (110)          N28° 28.31'  W10° 13.47'**
The Oued El Merked below right becomes a deep gorge.

**124 (107)          N28° 28.51'  W10° 15.08'**
The southern outskirts of **Tiglite** in the wide canyon of the Oued Tiglite. The fast section is over, but the surface continues to be good for a bit. Turn north through a gap in the range.

**131 (100)          N28° 28.23'  W10° 18.89'**
Near one of Tiglite's palmeries keep right. Follow the track north and east through the settlement until the next waypoint.

**133 (98)          N28° 29.20'  W10° 17.91'**
Don't cross the oued, but keep left and take the steep, well-graded track out of the canyon.

Within a kilometre, and halfway up the 200m climb, all of a sudden the perfect hard-packed surface becomes terrible. A 2WD's problems may begin here.

**138 (93)**
You're now out of the canyon on a plateau where the surface becomes better. There's a good flat spot for a camp hereabouts.

**142 (89)          N28° 30.18'  W10° 19.37'**
Buildings ahead and pylons. Go right or keep straight; the tracks join up soon.

**145 (86)          N28° 29.83'  W10° 21.38'**
Follow the track and usually the pylons. Side tracks lead off to nomad camps.

**161 (70)          N28° 30.04'  W10° 31.28'**
Aouinet Ain Oussa (or **Aouinet Ighoman** on the Michelin map). Go left at the junction as you come into town and head for a palmerie and old mosque on the west side, towards the pass.

**163 (68)          N28° 30.10'  W10° 32.22'**
You're on the way out of Aouinet, passing through the gap in the range with a wide basin ahead bordered by the Jebel Rich to the south.

**164 (67)          N28° 29.90'  W10° 32.80'**
Three pistes diverge, the right Olaf track may be best, but whichever way you go, aim towards the next waypoint.

**174 (57)          N28° 28.72'  W10° 38.81'**
Join Olaf at this point if you're not on it already. The village of **Kheneg el Adam** is visible to the north-west.

**176.5 (54.5)    N28° 29.30'  W10° 40.22'**
Junction with white stones. Go straight (west) here to pick up the waypoint at KM185.

Then again, if you've got time on your hands, turn north a kilometre or so to explore the abandoned village of **El Ayoun du Draa** (as it's known on some maps: N28° 30.14'  W10° 40.71'; water) then make your way to KM185 via another occupied village.

**185 (46)          N28° 29.20'  W10° 44.21'**
On the main track heading west.

**186 (45)**
Another track joins from the left and from here on gets washed out and bendy: you'll need clearance.

**188 (43)          N28° 29.52'  W10° 46.16'**
**Cistern** with water at arm's reach, and another one soon after.

**189 (42)**
The track gets gnarly and slows you down, but in a good way.

**192 (39)**
Coastal scenery and vegetation begins to emerge.

**195 (36)    N28° 29.51'  W10° 49.74'**
A **well** to the south. Olaf is running parallel along an old hillside track to the north.

**196 (35)    N28° 29.69'  W10° 50.33'**
Join Olaf at a pass where the track swings right to get round the stony wash-out ahead. Cacti and coastal vegetation appear as well as a village visible below.

**198 (33)    N28° 30.28'  W10° 50.84'**
Cross the oued in the small village of **Ain Kerma** with gardens and maybe some people around. After the descent, out of the village take the left split if you're heading for Tan-Tan.

If you want to head north on the N1 then Olaf sets off that way, probably to reach the coastal highway in about 11km at around N28° 33.7' W10° 54.5'. Once on the highway, from this waypoint you're about 104km south of the next fuel at Guelmim.

**199 (32)**
Back on the Tan-Tan route, head into rolling hills which lead along a narrow, shaley gully for a couple of kilometres.

**202 (29)    N28° 30.19'  W10° 52.78'**
The gully opens out with hills all around.

**203 (28)    N28° 29.85'  W10° 53.14'**
Pass the deep **Guelta ez Zerga** in the Oued Draa; a good place for a swim or a wash. Out of the oued turn right, with pylons visible ahead.

**207 (24)    N28° 30.90'  W10° 54.69'**
Pass through a flood-worn defile alongside the Draa's grassy banks. Within half a kilometre or so, N28° 30.92' W10° 55.21' could be a short cut on the way to KM212. In a bit you pass under the big pylon cables straddling the wide riverbed.

Entrance to Tan-Tan.
A different kind of speed hump.

**209 (22)    N28° 31.27'  W10° 56.17'**
If you didn't try to follow the short cut above you must turn left here, even though you can see cars being stopped on the Draa Bridge checkpoint less than a kilometre away.

Fun though it would be to drive out of the Draa and onto the N1 like the Creature from the Black Lagoon, when I tried it, the way along either bank was blocked by trees or muddy pools, and even if you could make it, it's possible the police at the checkpoint will spot you scurrying about in the reeds before you can adequately explain yourself.

**212 (19)    N28° 30.51'  W10° 56.16'**
Having followed the winding track, come round a bend to a dam. Here turn right, steeply up a rubbly hill to overlook your route. Or staying down at the dam level and crossing it to the left may work too, as the highway is very near.

**215 (16)    N28° 30.43'  W10° 57.58'**
**Join the N1** 16km north of Tan-Tan and south of the Draa Bridge by some painted bollards and just north of some Armco.

**231    N28° 26.04'  W11° 04.72'**
Tan-Tan fuel on the east side of town with two more in town. For a bit more on the town, see the end of Route MO1.

MW – MOROCCO WEST

# MW4  FASK – ASSA                    121KM
April 2008 ~ Mazda pickup

## Description
An easy desert run with just 39km of piste over the hills to the Draa valley and east to Assa. The highlight is rising up above the gorge as you pass over the watershed and begin your descent to Aouinet Torkoz. You can extend this route into a loop by picking up MW5 out of Aouinet and reversing it back to the junction below at KM33; a great day out in either direction.

## Off road
Barring the usual calamities there are no difficulties to speak of on this route for anything with wheels bigger than a BMX bike.

## Route finding
Easy, but you won't see much traffic between El Borj and Aouinet.

## Fuel and water
Fask and Assa for fuel, plus there are a few wells along the route as detailed.

## Suggested duration
You can do this one in just a couple of hours or spin it out with other local routes to make a day of it.

**0km**          **N28° 59.12'  W09° 49.57'**
ZIZ and café in **Fask**. Head south-east for Assa.

**22 (99)**          **N28° 50.35'  W09° 43.33'**
Turn south for Tadalt.

**32 (89)**          **N28° 45.78'  W09° 45.90'**
Cross **Tadalt** oued. Soon the **tarmac ends**.

**33 (98)**          **N28° 45.26'  W09° 45.79'**
Fork left here and follow a stony track towards the ridge. Right is Route MW5.

**49 (72)**          **N28° 38.61'  W09° 43.34'**
Very deep **well** (50m +).

**53 (68)**          **N28° 37.28'  W09° 45.10'**
A **tank** with a bucket and water at just 3m. After KM59 the track and scenery improve as you rise over the gorge.

**60 (61)**          **N28° 34.79'  W09° 47.86'**
Drop down to the riverbed and cross the stony oued a couple of times.

**65 (56)**          **N28° 32.98'  W09° 48.94'**
Deep **well** (50m).

**69 (52)**          **N28° 31.53'  W09° 50.86'**
Rough sign pointing right for 'Bord Six swimming pool' less than 3km away. On closer inspection it was unoccupied.

**71 (50)**          **N28° 30.78'  W09° 51.43'**
**Rejoin the tarmac** north of **Aouinet Torkoz** (called something else as you near town where there may be a checkpoint). There's not much at all in Aouinet.

**74 (47)**          **N28° 28.97'  W09° 50.87'**
Turn left in the village centre and head for **Assa**.

**119.5 (1.5)**          **N28° 36.40'  W09° 26.81'**
Teapot roundabout. Turn left for the fuel station, straight ahead for the town centre, right for the only hotel in town.

**120.5 (500m)  N28° 36.97'  W09° 26.79'**
Turn left here at the main road, pass Assa's park and in 500m you get to the ZIZMO.

**121**          **N28° 37.05'  W09° 27.03'**
Fuel station and café. For more details on **Assa**, see the box on p242.

# MW5   Guelmim – El Borj – Assa                    196KM
April 2008 ~ Mazda pickup

## Description
This is an interesting way of getting from Guelmim on the coastal highway inland to Assa. You pass through Asrir and at Tighmert (called versions of 'Ait Bekkou' on paper maps) you can wander through the palmerie or surreptitiously enjoy the *Facomtour Hotel*'s range of semi-erotic artworks.

The road drive is no eyesore, but things get interesting as you leave the Assa highway and even more so when the tar ends. The highlight is the passage over the Jebel Bani down the palm-lined gorge to the saltpans alongside the **Oued Draa**, south of the village of Taskala. Soon after you're back on the tarmac at Aouinet Torkoz.

A word about **Guelmim**. Neither guidebook is too positive about stopping here, most probably because the town may have once oversold its claim to be another one of Morocco's 'Gateways to the Sahara' with all that that entails. It is indeed the last big 'northern' town before marginally cultivable fields give way to the desert sands of the Western Sahara, and if you need things doing or bought, this is the place to do it. But be warned, the weekly 'camel' market is now said to be a sham put on for day trippers out of Agadir. It's also the most likely time and place you'll bump into 'Blue Men' who, despite the widely-parroted belief, are no more 'Tuareg' than George Clooney in a denim kaftan. There's more about that on the website.

## Off road
This route is manageable with care in a **regular car** or two-up on a **big bike**. With the long leads in and out on tar and a good spread of wells it's also a fair proposition over a couple of days on a **mountain bike**. For pushbikes and non off-road vehicles, the only rough section might be the descent from Jebel Bani through to Taskala on the desert floor.

## Route finding
Straightforward, you won't need GPS. There are a few piste junctions south of Taskala village but if you get in a pickle it's only 20-odd kilometres east-north-east to Aouinet Torkoz where most of these tracks are destined anyway. From here a tar road runs east to Assa.

You'll see a few cars an hour on the tarmac up to the Tadalt turn-off. Beyond El Borj you might see a local Landrover and maybe a car will pass you out of Aouinet to Assa. The route **map** is on pp248-9.

## Fuel and water
Guelmim, Fask and Assa have fuel stations and there are a few wells here and there; see pp250-1.

## Suggested duration
With engine power it's easily done in a slow day; with pedals or time to spare enjoy a camp out somewhere in the hills south of El Borj on the road to Taskala.

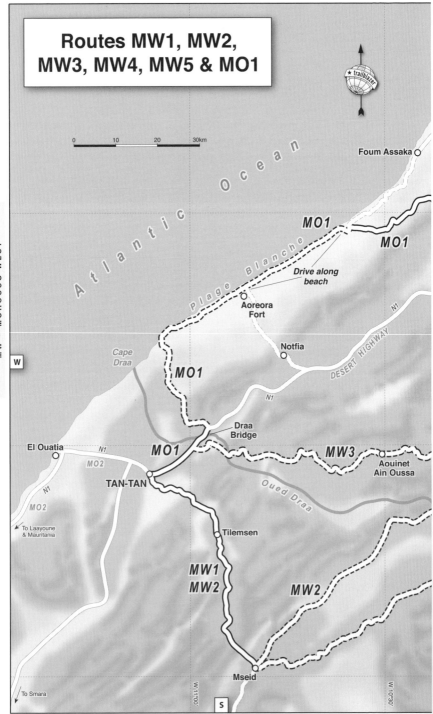

Routes MW1, MW2,
MW3, MW4, MW5 & MO1

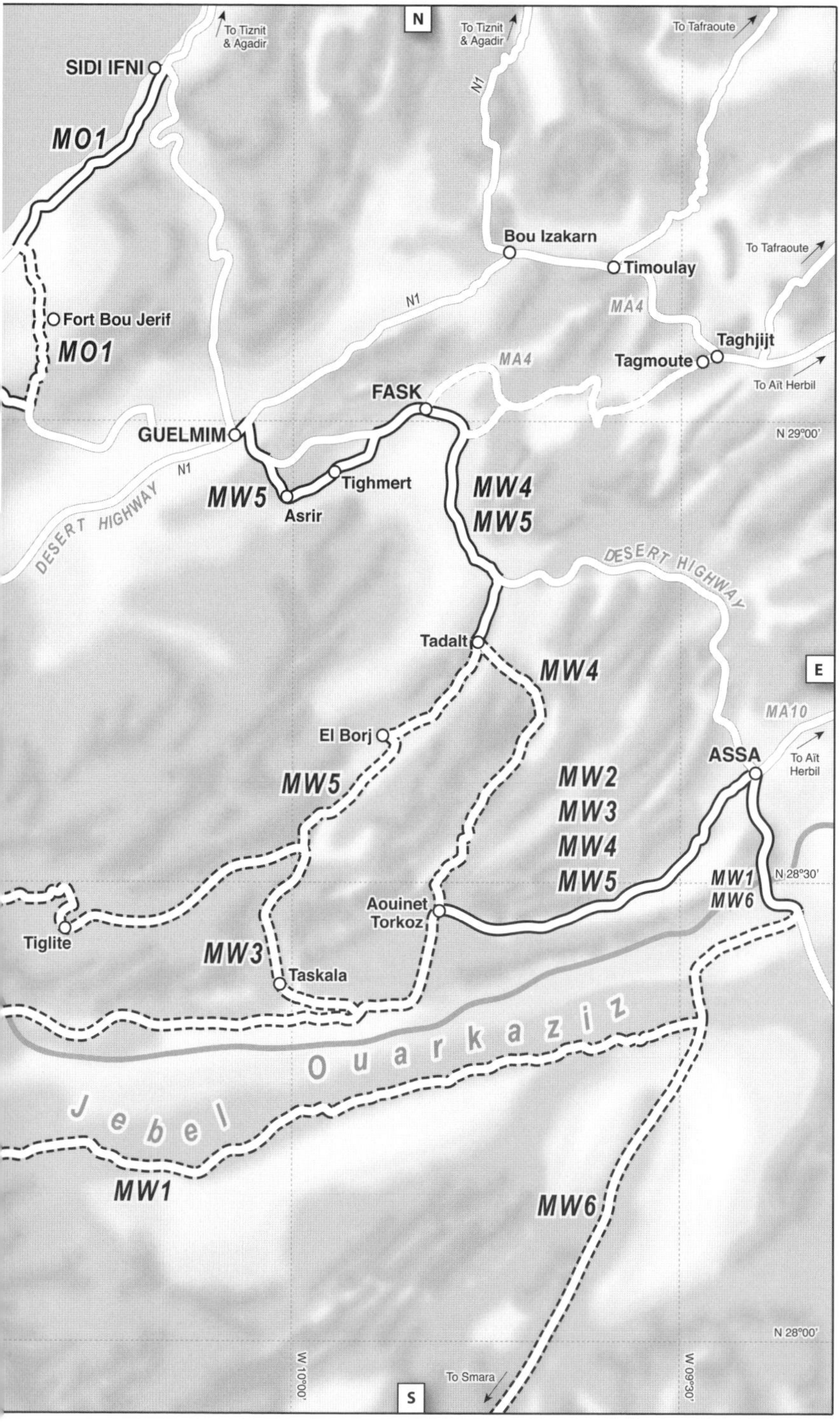
N
To Tiznit & Agadir
To Tiznit & Agadir
To Tafraoute
SIDI IFNI
MO1
N1
Bou Izakarn
To Tafraoute
Timoulay
N1
Fort Bou Jerif
MA4
MO1
Taghjijt
MA4
Tagmoute
To Aït Herbil
FASK
GUELMIM
N 29°00'
N1
Tighmert
MW5
Asrir
MW4
MW5
DESERT HIGHWAY
DESERT HIGHWAY
Tadalt
MW4
E
MA10
El Borj
ASSA
To Aït Herbil
MW5
MW2
MW3
MW4
MW5
MW1
MW6
N 28°30'
Aouinet Torkoz
Tiglite
MW3
Taskala
Jebel Ouarkaziz
MW1
MW6
N 28°00'
W 10°00'
To Smara
W 09°30'
S

**0km**          **N28° 58.70'  W10° 04.61'**
**Guelmim** fuel; a SHELL on south side of town. Follow the road north-east into town. At 1.5km cross the bridge over the oued and turn right. Fork immediately left and follow this road south-east to a roundabout. Go over the roundabout and curve right and then left getting to another roundabout and a kind of square by the town's main market. Carry on ahead and leave Guelmim to the south-east.

**6 (190)          N28° 57.97'  W10° 01.84'**
Turn right here for **Asrir** on a single-width tar road.

**11.5 (184.5)    N28° 55.39'  W10° 00.83'**
A piste leaves right heading south-west, parallel to the coastal highway (as shown on some maps).

**13 (183)**
Turn right and bypass most of Asrir.

**19 (177)          N28° 56.75'  W09° 57.35'**
Turn right here for **Tighmert** and right again into the *Facomtour Hotel* where you can camp in the front yard or take an en-suite room with breakfast for around 120dh; dinner was not an option as I was the only guest. It's a fair price as the hotel is another one of those ornate relics that feels like they moved the highway and things haven't been the same since.

Inside the central hall is a stage for re-enacting the legendarily seductive *guedra* – the regional name for a form of belly dance performed by the local Berber women (examples on 🖳 www.youtube.com) and which may explain the paintings.

In 2008 Yamaha used the dowdy *Facomtour* as a staging point on the press launch of their new XT660Z Ténéré. No wonder the subsequent reviews were a bit lukewarm...

**21 (175)          N28° 57.16'  W09° 55.52'**
Back on the road heading east, fork left here at an unsigned junction.

**23 (173)**
Turn right onto the main Guelmim–Fask R103 road.

**33 (163)          N28° 59.10'  W09° 49.61'**
ZIZ fuel, shop and café on the far side of Fask. In 1500m at a right-hand bend you pass the turn off for Route MA4.

**54 (142)          N28° 51.11'  W09° 43.79'**
Pass a **well** on the right side of the road, with nomad tents nearby and striking ranges all around.

**56 (140)**
Turn right for Tadalt and El Borj.

**66 (130)**
Pass **Tadalt** village on the right.

**67 (129)          N28° 45.26'  W09° 45.79'**
Soon after the village **the tarmac ends** and shortly the track forks; turn right into a wide flat valley heading south-west. (The left fork is Route MW4, a shorter and even easier alternative to this route.)

The track soon gets corrugated; make the most of side branches or use a much smoother wide track further south.

**83 (13)          N28° 39.51'  W09° 53.04'**
**El Borj** village with an arch and saplings lining the entry. Once in town fork left and left again up the hill.

**84 (112)          N28° 39.21'  W09° 53.16'**
Leave El Borj to the south and then south-west. The piste rises up to follow a line of pylons. In 10km you cross a 600m pass with another pass two kilometres later.

**101 (95)          N28° 32.92'  W10° 00.16'**
Junction at a oued with shady trees on the right: fork left here. Straight on leads to Tiglite and Tan-Tan (Route MW3).

**102 (94)          N28° 32.45'  W10° 00.77'**
'Blue bag' junction, turn left for Assa. Right here soon picks up Route MW3.

**103 (93)          N28° 32.32'  W10° 00.29'**
A track joins the route's 'elbow' from the left and may lead directly to Aouinet Torkoz. Soon there's a nice ouedside camp spot.

**104 (92)          N28° 31.57'  W10° 00.94'**
A track joins from the right (see Route MW3). Within a couple of kilometres you drop off the 500m-high plateau to descend though a winding, palmy gorge.

**109 (87)**          **N28° 29.88'  W10° 02.71'**
Possible **waterholes** in the creek bed on
the left.

**118 (78)**
A track joins from the left.

**120 (76)**          **N28° 26.19'  W10° 03.21'**
Pass a **cistern** and enter the small
nomadic settlement of **Taskala** situated in
a gap in the Jebel Bani range. Up ahead
the desert opens out with distant ranges
and Route MW2 comes in from the west.

**123 (73)**          **N28° 24.55'  W10° 02.59'**
Fork left.

**124 (72)**          **N28° 24.27'  W10° 01.92'**
Fork left again.

**126 (70)**
A track joins from the left.

**129 (67)**          **N28° 23.84'  W09° 59.01'**
Pass a **well** by the piste (4m) and possibly
some nomad tents to the north. Fork right.

**131.5 (64.5)**     **N28° 23.89'  W09° 58.24'**
Start of a smooth, fast clay pan.

**135 (59)**          **N28° 23.92'  W09° 55.41'**
Cairns run across the pan for a couple of
kilometres.

**138 (56)**          **N28° 24.06'  W09° 53.89'**
Fork left here.

**139 (57)**          **N28° 24.48'  W09° 53.46'**
Leave a oued and head north-north-east
up to Aouinet Torkoz.

**148 (48)**          **N28° 28.10'  W09° 51.20'**
Enter the old part of **Aouinet Torkoz** village. There's possibly a store or two but
nothing else here. Drive east over the
oued to the newer side of town where **the
tarmac starts** and pass over the crossroads
where Route MW4 comes down from the
north. Follow the tarmac east to Assa.
You'll pass a couple of roadside **wells** and
cisterns on the way.

**194.5 (1.5)**
On arriving at 'teapot roundabout', Assa
centre is straight ahead, the hotel is to the
right (see p242).
　For fuel and the café turn left at the
roundabout and follow the road round to
the north, turn left at the end and they're
500m down the road past the park.

**196**          **N28° 37.05'  W09° 27.05'**
Zɪz fuel station and café on the west side
of Assa. For more on Assa see the box on
p242.

# MW6  ASSA – SMARA                                391KM
July 2003, part updated April 2008 ~ Lada Niva (Franck Simonnet)

## Description
Running down to the **Saguia el Hamra** in the Western Sahara, MW6 has all the
ingredients of a classic Sahara route with a diversity of landscape and terrain:
mountains, reg, fast sections, numerous oued crossings, rocky piste and even
your old friend, corrugations – all in a remote setting you rarely find in 'mainland' Morocco.
　The region was the scene of Polisario battles in the 1980s, and today you'll
spot the *raïmas* (tents) of Reguibat nomads by the route.

## Off road
The terrain is rocky between KM194 and KM249 with some sand near the end.
On a bike the only problem is the range and on a **big motorbike** the only other
problem is the sandy sections. This route is probably too long and rough to
take on in a **2WD** or of course an unsupported **mountain bike**.

## Route finding

Most of this route was used in a Dakar Rally and is still well marked and easy to follow. After joining the Dakar piste at KM56, follow the cairns on earth mounds every 500m. Crossing the Ga'at Lewar, markers are cairns but from here to KM321 Rally cairns are always present. The track can be done with **three waypoints**: Labouirat (KM118), Hawza (KM281) and Smara.

Franck saw only light local traffic (but it was July). Don't stay on the highway beyond KM32 to Zag – this road is closed to tourists. The **map** is on pp236-7.

## Fuel and water

Assa and Smara have fuel. Water at the start and the end of the route, at a well and at the two main towns of Labouirat and Hawza. In between there are wells at KM32, -42, -191 and KM237.

## Suggested duration

It's hard to imagine doing this route without at least one night out in the desert.

**0km**      **N28° 37.05' W09° 27.05'**
ZIZ fuel station and café on the west end of **Assa**. Head east into town. For more on Assa see the box on p242.

**3 (388)**      **N28° 36.7' W09° 25.9'**
Pass through Assa and just before KM3 where the road heads east to Foum el Hassan, go right for Zag. On the way you'll cross a bridge over the Oued Draa.

**32 (359)**      **N28° 26.1' W09° 24.5'**
**Leave the road** before the gap in the Jebel Ouarkaziz at a broken sign 'El Arbouyet 68' on your right. You pass a deep **well** in 500m. Carry on west along the valley.

**42 (349)**      **N28° 23.4' W09° 29.5'**
At this junction turn south to pass through the Jebel Ouarkaziz. In the pass there's a **well** on the left. Soon you'll cross over three defensive walls.

**45 (346)**      **N28° 22.0' W09° 29.1'**
Leave the Jebel after the third wall. The track becomes corrugated before the junction with the Dakar route.

**48 (344)**      **N28°20.46' W09°28.89'**
Route MW1 leaves the piste to the right here to head west for Mseid and Tan-Tan.

**56 (335)**      **N28° 17.1' W09° 32.4'**
Junction with the former Dakar track. Head off west-south-west on a fast piste.

**67 (324)**
Cross a oued with vegetation.

**82 (309)**      **N28° 12.4' W09° 47.1'**
Cross the multiple courses of the Oued Oum Doul. Bearing south-west.

**103 (288 )**      **N28° 04.3' W09° 54.4'**
Vehicle wreck. Head south.

**118 (273)**      **N27° 57.2' W09° 57.4'**
**Labouirat**. Leave the village to the west. You are between hills on fast reg.

**149 (242)**      **N27° 53.0' W10° 14.6'**
Cross the sandy Oued Gnifida Tarf with An-Nous hill to the south. Bearing south-west.

**172 (219)**      **N27° 45.1' W10° 24.5'**
Two buildings on your left: Sidi Ahmed al Kenti. Sandy.

**191 (200)**      **N27° 37.0' W10° 31.3'**
Cross the Oued Afra with a **well** on the far side and head south-west. In 2003 I waited eight hours to cross the floodwaters!

**201 (190)**      **N27° 32.8' W10° 33.6'**
Climb onto a plateau along a rocky track. Around here you can see Reguibat *raïmas*.

**214 (177)**      **N27° 29.0' W10° 38.9'**
Crossing with other pistes. Head south.

**225 (166)          N27° 23.5'  W10° 39.8'**
A Dakar track leads back to Mseid, about 70km to the north.

**237 (154)          N27° 17.2'  W10° 39.0'**
Follow the oued west. In 4km there's a **well** (N27° 16.9'  W10° 43.8'). Climb onto a plateau before a drop with great views.

**251 (140)          N27° 15.8'  W10° 45.0'**
Leave the Jebel. Fast section follows.

**266 (125)          N27° 09.3'  W10° 50.2'**
End of the fast section. You can now see the old Spanish tarmac ahead. After the plateau, head west.

**281 (110)          N27° 06.7'  W10° 57.9'**
**Hawza** checkpoint. In April 2009 a new tarmac road from Smara reached this point, running a few kilometres north of the old route along the Spanish tarmac.

Stuck near KM237. Full story at west-africa2006.blogspot.com. © David French

**369 (22)          N26° 54.1'  W11° 46.2'**
Junction, turn south (wpt. unverified).

**391          N26° 44.6'  W11° 41.7'**
**Smara** fuel after a checkpoint. Lodgings here often booked out by the UN. See p266.

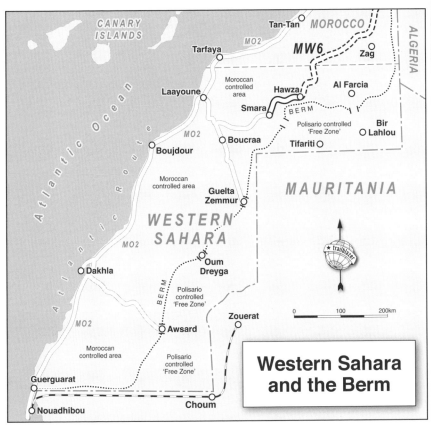

## Western Sahara and the Berm

# MO  OCEAN

## Outline of the Ocean region

The other continental shelf.

The two routes here add up to a short excursion along the desert's oceanic edge, partly right on a tidal beach – and a much longer transit along the N1 south to the Mauritanian border. One could be considered a beachside novelty, the other the start of a trans-continental adventure.

The maritime influence here means the **climate** along Morocco's Atlantic coast is manifested in less severe extremes than elsewhere in the country. In summer temperatures along the coastal strip remain moderate, so that undertaking the Atlantic Route at this time need not necessarily be the stifling effort that you'd encounter further inland.

Of course as soon as you move away from the coast at this time, (as you will do in Mauritania should you stick to the sealed road heading south to Nouakchott) temperatures will soar back up to the 45°C norm of mid-summer, with associated sandstorms. Winter of course is a much more agreeable time to be cruising along the Atlantic shore.

## MO Routes

# MO1   SIDI IFNI – PLAGE BLANCHE – TAN-TAN   194km

April 2008 ~ Mazda pickup

## Description

Quite possibly the first route you do in this book if you've come down via Essaouira and are taking a big sweep eastwards. Sidi Ifni, a former Spanish enclave (like still extant Ceuta and Melilla) is a mellow place to start the day. From here a dead-end coastal road leads past the turn-off for an inland track to the ruins of Fort Bou Jerif and the nearby tourist lodge ('FBJ'). A short piste from here leads back to a sealed road between Guelmim and Plage Blanche on the Atlantic. Guelmim (see p247) is an alternative starting point for this route if you want to get straight to the beach. Once by the Atlantic, you want to be sure to get the timing right for the 27km beach run.

Once safely off the beach and on the way to Cape Draa, you'll pass the clifftop shacks of fishermen who make a living here, as well as some impressive viewpoints over the crashing surf below. On leaving the coast multiple tracks make the inland run not always so clear, but eventually you'll pass by the spectacularly-located *Ksar Tafnidilt* hotel, the highway and so Tan-Tan.

The scrubby inland coastal scenery around here is not so enthralling, but cruising by the surf or looking down from the sea cliffs certainly is.

## Off road

Driving or riding on a tidal beach is always a lottery, but generally the firmer sand is nearer the surf where you can get away without reducing tyre pressures. Of course, bogged down and desperately deflating four tyres at once with the tide lapping around your ankles you may think otherwise. Ideally don't start this stage more than an hour after low tide. 'FBJ' at KM45 has tide times, or try somewhere like ⌨ www.easytide.ukho.gov.uk, search ('Predict') under 'Sidi Ifni' and then subtract about 10 minutes for **Plage Blanche**. Note that tide tables times may not match the actual **local time**.

If you do strike vehicle trouble on the beach (see box p258), as long as you can crawl up onto the low dunes piled up between the high tide mark and the cliffs you'll at least have some time to work it out.

The crux is getting off the beach through the soft sand ruts at KM112 and up the sandy ascent at KM113.5. A 4WD won't have much trouble, but because this track rises *and* curves it's hard to take a run up, especially on a big bike or in a road car or van. Reducing tyre pressures may do the trick. Beyond this point there's not much to stop you apart from some dunes around KM160.

## Route finding

It gets thin away from the cliffs and I saw no other traffic other than a car on the beach and some army cars on the cliff top. The route **map** is on pp248-9.

## Fuel and water

Sidi and Tan-Tan for fuel with a few wells as marked.

## Suggested duration

You can do this route in one long day assuming the tides match up, or overnight in comfort at FBJ or Ksar Tafnidilt.

**0km**        **N29° 22.71'   W10° 10.57'**
**Sidi Ifni** fuel. Head inland, up hill past the blue colonnades and turn right at the junction for the road to Tan-Tan.

**3 (191)**
Turn left here past the rubbish dump and the sign for 'Tan-Tan', not right for the new port.

**17 (177)**      **N29° 16.35'   W10° 15.28'**
Pass a sign – one of many sometimes confusing ones hereabouts, but just keep on the tarmac and head straight on past Sidi Oarzrik whose low dome mosque you'll soon see by the sea.

**25 (169)**      **N29° 13.88'   W10° 18.41'**
A piste to the left leads to an old mine and maybe Ait Tlata Sbouya.

**33 (161)**      **N29° 10.61'   W10° 20.99'**
Sign indicating 'FBJ 12km'. Turn left here **off the road**.

**35.5 (158.5)**    **N29° 09.31'   W10° 20.61'**
Tracks cross. Right leads to Sidi Massoud and possibly over the upper Oued Noun and around to *FBJ*. Carry on south, passing at least **three wells** close to the track with water at a few metres.

**40.5 (153.5)**    **N29° 06.99'   W10° 19.57'**
Sign. Turn right for FBJ. The track can get washed out around here.

**43 (151)**      **N29° 05.76'   W10° 20.12'**
Come over a rise and get a view of the huge Fort Bou Jerif ruins dating from the 1920s.

**44.5 (149.5)**    **N29° 05.10'   W10° 20.01'**
A track joins from the right, possibly coming up from the difficult route out of Foum Assaka. See box below.

**45 (149)**      **N29° 04.92'   W10° 19.88'**
*Fort Bou Jerif* upmarket tourist camp near the fort ruins. Ten years after my previous visit I still feel the location among the scrubby hills is not so inspiring, no matter how well the place has developed.

These days it seems *FBJ* is more about attracting tour groups in their quads and stripped-down jeeps to enjoy snake charming entertainment by night, rather than an overlanders' meeting point as some guidebooks outdatedly suggest. The owner seems nice enough but not all his staff match up. However the **food** here is as good as anything you'll eat in Morocco. Half board in a '*raïma*' tent costs 280dh per person.

Out of FBJ turn left (or just drive straight past it) and soon fork right and follow the white painted side cairns to the road.

**54 (140)**      **N29° 00.42'   W10° 20.70'**
Meet **the tar road** from Guelmim and turn right for Plage Blanche.

---

### OUED NOUN AND BEYOND

At KM33 the tarmac continues on to Foum Assaka, the mouth of the **Oued Noun**, where something may be under construction. But once you drive down into the gorge and over the bridge, tracks suddenly become much more difficult. If you head inland, upstream, on the south-west side of the oued, the track turns up a narrow, stony creek bed which, according to the old French maps, leads past Sidi Massoud to Fort Bou Jerif. I only got about a kilometre up this creek from where it looked like the hardest way out of Oued Noun.

Turning right at the bridge and heading down towards the sea involves crossing a couple of rock steps within 500m, easing down onto the banks of the oued and then who knows what once you reach the coast in another 500m.

It seems this is the old, and possibly washed-out way round, now replaced by an easier route which heads straight up from the bridge past a walled graveyard (visible on Google Earth) directly south-west up the valley side along tracks which eventually curve around onto the headland where there is some cultivation.

Old maps show this once lead 20km to an aerodrome at N29° W10° 30'. This track does not seem to connect with the first 'up the creek' option, but that remains for someone else to find out for sure.

**84 (110)  N28° 57.78'  W10° 36.23'**
Arrive at **Plage Blanche**, a few official-looking buildings with antennae, an abandoned restaurant and other junk. Continue past them down into the oued with dunes on the right and work your way to the beach.

**85 (109)  N28° 57.80'  W10° 36.92'**
**On the beach**. I've read warnings of nail-filled planks and getting strangled in fishermen's lines, but saw nothing other than pure off-white sand here and one other 4WD.

Don't overshoot the Aoreora fort exit in 27km. The ship wreck and suddenly softening sand at around N28° 50.23' W10° 52.10' are good warnings, although I hear at the lowest tide you can get up to 10km past Aoreora before turning back.

**112 (82)  N28° 50.76'  W10° 50.79'**
**Aoreora** fort visible on the hill; the end of the beach run. Turn inland crossing soft sand ruts and head into oued mouth.

**113.5 (80.5)  N28° 50.44'  W10° 50.14'**
A track continues up the oued to Notfia and the N1 Atlantic Highway, but at this point you turn back to take a steep and loose sandy ascent right (north-west) out of the oued. Low range or, on a bike, a good run up may be needed. It would take quite a skilled driver to get a regular car up here.

**114 (80)  N28° 50.26'  W10° 50.37'**
The top of the sandy ascent. Soon you turn right, back towards the fort.

**115 (79)  N28° 50.43'  W10° 50.67'**
A fork close to the fort, turn left (south-west). Tracks can get faint and diverge from here on, but generally it's hard to get too disorientated with the cliffs sometimes right by your side.

**124 (70)  N28° 48.49'  W10° 55.43'**
Some shacks, an army observation tower and maybe even a helicopter.

**127 (67)  N28° 48.09'  W10° 56.91'**
More fishermen's shacks, great views over the sea and white cairns. Possibly an army checkpoint and a **well** too.

**131 (63)  N28° 47.00'  W10° 59.11'**
Keep right at this fork passing a hilltop graveyard on the left. Within a kilometre the track comes right up to the cliff edge with great views to make you wonder – can surfing really be so hard to learn?

**137 (57)  N28° 45.76'  W11° 02.21'**
Several shacks and fishermen's tents – a good chance to buy a fresh fish.

**141 (53)  N28° 44.61'  W11° 04.07'**
Pass near a pink fort with radio masts.

**142.5 (51.5)  N28° 43.80'  W11° 04.40'**
I turned inland here heading south and even south-east later, but on reflection it would have been fun to carry on along the coast right to the **Draa estuary** and then follow it inland. Going this way you'd meet this route at KM155 and will have covered about the same distance.

**147 (47)  N28° 42.12'  W11° 03.02'**
An oblique cross junction, cross over it and continue south-south-east.

**148 (46)  N28° 41.59'  W11° 02.82'**
A junction with a track from the left. Continue straight although the track is not so clear.

**150.5 (43.5)  N28° 40.19'  W11° 03.13'**
You're on a clear track with corrugations (always a good sign). Dreary scrub all around.

**153.5 (40.5)  N28° 38.69'  W11° 02.95'**
The track rises up onto a small plateau.

**155 (39)  N28° 37.85'  W11° 03.05'**
A junction marked with stones where the alternative route from **Cape Draa** mentioned at KM142.5 joins from the right.

**155.5 (38.5)  N28° 37.63'  W11° 02.87'**
Arrive at a viewpoint over a basin and the Oued Draa ahead. An old track used to curve round this basin's eastern rim; this direct route drops into it and crosses it in a south-easterly direction to the south-eastern rim.

**156 (38)  N28° 37.48'  W11° 02.76'**
Fork left to the south-east.

MO – OCEAN

**160 (34)        N28° 36.20'  W11° 01.26'**
You've reached the other side of the basin, with mesas (flat-topped hills or table mountains) all around. Soon the old rim track joins from the left and together you descend into a valley. The terrain gets a bit more demanding from here on.

**160.5 (33.5)    N28° 36.10'  W11° 01.05'**
Ease down a notably rocky descent. Dunes appear and this could be a nice place to camp. In a kilometre the track diverges but soon joins up again.

**162.5 (31.5)    N28° 35.08'  W11° 00.78'**
A short ascent up a small dune. Two kilometres later there are corrugations and distant pylons to the south-west.

**165.5 (28.5)    N28° 33.54'  W11° 00.53'**
The Oued Draa is visible to the west just before a stony drop in and out of a oued.

**167 (27)        N28° 33.01'  W11° 00.31'**
A stony rise with pylons a few kilometres ahead, a palm tree and so possibly water.

**168.5 (25.5)    N28° 32.51'  W10° 59.78'**
Reach a T-junction. Turn left (north-east) towards the old fort of Tafnidilt. South-west seems to go into the Oued Draa with many tracks and presumably directly to Tan-Tan.

## THE SHIPWRECK FROM HELL

I didn't know what exactly the deal was with **Plage Blanche**, where it started and where it ended and the staff at FBJ weren't too helpful. Their literature suggested the Plage was some 40km long, but not to go beyond the shipwreck. So I figured once I got on the beach I'd watch out for the wreck or 40km on the beach. I was already pushing my luck with the timing, getting on the beach 45 minutes after low tide, but how long does it take to do forty clicks on flat beach sand?

Around KM27 and maybe half an hour on the beach I noticed some soldier-looking guys cavorting in the surf and a fort on a hill, but carried on regardless into suddenly softening sand.

I'm no stranger to nice, dry, predictable desert sand, but sinking on a tidal beach has a much more menacing quality. I steered towards the surf and then up to the beach searching for a firmer surface. This didn't feel right. Then up ahead the Shipwreck from Hell lay rusting on the beach like a skull on a stick. Was this the wreck from the *FBJ* notebook but only at KM30? I figured it must be and turned round with difficulty to head back and ask the guys on the beach.

Still with plenty of air in the tyres to be let out if necessary, I powered back along my soggy tracks, pushing hard in low range when suddenly a BANG exploded from somewhere. Puncture? Burst radiator hose? A con-rod looking to escape and make a dash for the Canaries?

Already stressed and wanting to get back to the proper desert, suddenly my mouth became very dry as I hopped out to inspect the tyres. All was well.

Looking under the lid I'd guessed close enough. Incredibly, or maybe not, while pushing at near full throttle in low range the huge induction pressure had blasted a hose off the Allisport intercooler. I looked right at the surf, now just 20 metres away, crammed the hose onto the scalding spout and grabbed a ten mil from the tool roll under the seat, tightened the clip and hoped it would stay there. It's remarkable how focussed you become at these high-pressure moments with quite a lot at stake. Your own mental 'intercooler' kicks in.

The car started fine and trying not to push too hard in low 2nd, I crawled back along the beach to the firmer sand, appalled to see my tracks from just 10 minutes ago had already been washed over by the incoming tide.

The bathing soldiers were from the fort I'd seen on the cliff top which of course was **Aoreora**. I turned up the oued mouth and breathed a sigh of relief once I got safely beyond the high tide mark.

Just as the first day's work on the original edition of *Sahara Overland* had nearly come to grief while crossing a flooded river in Tunisia (and already in a replacement car!) so it seemed the first route for *Morocco Overland* had required a fiery baptism.

**169 (25)      N28° 32.77'  W10° 59.57'**
*Ksar Tafnidilt* hotel on a hillside looking over the old ruined fort of the same name. A great location and although I only looked around, if it's that time of day then this place will be much better than anything you'll find in Tan-Tan. Half board in a raïma was 245dh or from 335dh in a room.

**174.5 (19.5)   N28° 32.22'  W10° 56.59'**
From *Ksar Tafnidilt* the track leads east and braids a bit to cross a oued with a washed-out bridge just before meeting **the old coast road**. Turn right at the old tar road and soon you reach…

**175 (19)       N28° 31.97'  W10° 56.56'**
… the N1 coastal highway marked with a 'Ksar Tafnidilt' sign. Turn right (south-west) and soon you'll get to the Draa Bridge checkpoint for a chat with a policeman.

**194          N28° 26.04'  W11° 04.72'**
**Tan-Tan** fuel on the east side of town with two more stations in town. You can get a good feed here when the restos in town seem a bit reluctant. Buy a chunk of meat from the butcher who'll mince it and give it to matey next door who'll come back with fresh meatballs, salad, chips and a water for about 50dh. To rinse off a salty vehicle in the car wash costs 20dh.

Tan-Tan, so good they named it twice? Not really. Once you pass the famous twin camels acting as a gateway into town (and indeed the Western Sahara) that's about it.

# MO2   THE ATLANTIC ROUTE TO MAURITANIA          1147KM
Based on material from José Brito and Tim Cullis.

The N1 highway through the **Western Sahara** to Mauritania is sealed all the way and can be covered in **three days**. Along with the inland scenery, the towns are nothing special and it can take quite an effort to find diversions from the unending blacktop; the most obvious being dramatic sea cliffs coming close to the road at regular intervals. **Laayoune** is the regional capital and military base surrounded by the *bidonvilles* (shanty towns) of the disposed Saharawi nomads. As you head south, traffic progressively thins out, especially once past Dakhla.

The so-called 'Atlantic Route' to Mauritania opened up to tourists in the 1990s by which time the two classic trans-Sahara routes through Algeria were no longer safe. Although security threats in the Western Sahara from the Polisario Front had diminished by this stage, until 2002 a military convoy of dubious value escorted vehicles twice a week from Dakhla along the final 340km to the border post with Mauritania.

These days all traffic flows **unescorted** along the coastal N1 highway and as far as tourists are concerned the southbound transit of the Western Sahara is limited to this road. South of Smara, extended **excursions inland** will eventually bring you up against the heavily-militarised series of trenches, walls, minefields and natural barriers known as 'the **Berm**' (see map p253). At around 2000km long, the de facto border effectively runs unbroken from Guerguarat close to Mauritania's Atlantic border right up to the Jebel Ouarkaziz facing Algeria, east of Assa.

Because of this, the seemingly plausible alternative road to Mauritania shown on maps running from Laayoune to Bir Mogrein via Galtat Zemmour is these days no longer viable. You need to pass through the off-limits Berm and into the Polisario Free Zone before getting to Mauritania; something the Moroccans won't allow. Sure, in its last decade in Africa, the Dakar Rally annually entered northern Mauritania via Galtat (or latterly Smara), but this probably involved well-established arrangements and incentives with local officials. In recent years smuggling operations, as well as possibly related deadly attacks on army bases and patrols in northern Mauritania attributed to Al-Qaeda of the Islamic Maghreb (AQIM), mean that the coast road to Mauritania remains the only option and for years has been entirely safe.

## Western Sahara history

With the old horizontal border south of Tan-Tan still identified on most maps (much to Morocco's irritation) the Western Sahara comprises the former late-19th-century colony of Spanish Sahara made up of two territories: the **Saguia el Hamra** and **Rio de Oro** to the south. Following successful wars of independence right across Africa in the 1950s and 60s, this marginal colony was abandoned by Spain in favour of Morocco, rather than the mostly nomadic indigenous population. Calling themselves the **Saharawi** ('Saharans'), in 1973 they formed the **Polisario Front** (Popular Front for the Liberation of Sequia al Hamra and Rio de Oro) who in February 1976 announced the independent Saharawi Arab Democratic Republic (SADR).

Morocco's response was the 'Green March' in November of that year when about 350,000 unarmed Moroccans marched into the territory. Annexation by Morocco followed in 1979 and so came war with Polisario guerrillas – supported by Algeria and for a time, Mauritania. (Today's closed border with Morocco and Algeria has its origins in this unresolved dispute).

A UN ceasefire was finally agreed in 1991 on condition of a referendum to decide the legal status of the territory. This referendum repeatedly gets postponed while Morocco continues to encourage migration from the north to help outnumber the Saharawi in any referendum, entrench its occupation and develop the territory. While the Polisario cause is viewed by some in the West as a struggle for self-determination akin to Tibet, realistically it has about as much chance of succeeding.

## Geography

Away from the coast the Western Sahara is an **arid limestone plateau** covered with small bushes, local dunes, low outcrops and escarpments, and shallow water courses. Elevation is generally around 200m, meeting the sea in cliffs up to 60m high. The highest point is 701m near **Galtat Zemmour**, the lowest is the **Sebkha Tah** salt pan at -55m (KM211) and with only one major oued: the **Saguia el Hamra** ('Red Canal'). Like its northern counterpart the Oued Draa, the Sequia rarely flows, but unlike the rest of the Sahara, the influence of the Atlantic gives the Western Sahara a less extreme temperature range. Humid oceanic winds help create a relatively **mild micro-climate** with fog delivering moisture up to 30km inland. Because of this, the coastal band constitutes a 'corridor' between sub-Saharan and Mediterranean ecosystems, supporting northern species like the hare, African wildcat and Egyptian mongoose as well as porcupines, honey badgers and striped weasels from sub-Saharan regions.

Compared to the mixed and Berber population of Morocco, the indigenous people of this region are distinctively Arabic or **Moorish** in appearance and manner, and nomadic by tradition. The **Reguibat** and the Delim are today the dominant tribes of the Saharawi confederation, but as elsewhere in the Sahara, the desert's lean resources along with the collapse of the nomadic lifestyle (formerly based as much on raiding and hostage-taking as pastoralism) has moulded a less outgoing temperament than you'll find among the Berbers of the more fertile north.

Full-blooded Reguibat nomads like to trace their lineage back five centuries to a legendary Yemeni holy man, Sidi Ahmad al Reguibi. His still-venerated shrine is about 105km south of Tan-Tan alongside the Oued Chbika (N28° 00.4'  W11° 25.1') in a region also noted for its many pre-Islamic 'antennae' tombs. The French aviator and writer Antoine de Saint-Exupéry described many edgy encounters with the fearsome Reguibat in books like *Wind, Sand and Stars*. Earlier, European mariners shipwrecked or lured onto the western Saharan shore were much less lucky, as Dean King's book *Skeletons on the Zahara* vividly and gruesomely describes, dispelling any quaint notions of nomadic chivalry or hospitality.

## Lodging and camping

The towns of Tan-Tan, Laayoune, Boujdour and Dakhla have **hotels** for all budgets; elsewhere you get what you're given and that won't always add up to be much. *Motel Barbas* (KM1056) is about 86km before the border and is your last chance to buy cheap fuel before entering Mauritania.

At the time of writing **camping sites** are few and currently include a spot 90km south of Tan-Tan just after the Oued el Oua'ar bridge by the ocean (N28° 10.47'  W11° 52.92'); *Camping Le Roi Bedoin* (N27° 27.70'  W13° 03.09') west of the N1 and about 35km before Laayoune (see KM272); *Camping Lamsiyed* (N27° 02.49'  W13° 05.70') about 15km south-east of Laayoune on the road to Smara (with an excellent view over the valley of the Sequia al Hamra); *Camping Nil* west of Laayoune (see KM320) and *Camping Moussafir* in Dakhla after KM807.

**Bush camping** is also an option, but do it well away from the road as traffic runs all night long. If you decide to bush camp after dark it's better to turn inland, away from the windy cliff edge. It's also less hassle, safer and cleaner not to camp too close to any settlements. Finally, bush camping is not advisable south of Dakhla due to the small risk of landmines. If you plan to do so, stick to well-defined tracks but recognise that the absence of warning signs does not mean mines are not present.

## Driving and traffic

From Tan-Tan to Laayoune traffic is regular with the usual menace of West Africa-bound car dealers perfecting 'kamikaze' overtaking moves on

MO – OCEAN

Laayoune. Some people just can't resist a bargain.

ancient, overloaded Land Rover Santanas. New or old, vehicle lights can often add up to merely the reflected glow of a cigarette so, along with the danger of wandering dromedaries it's best not to **drive at night** and beware of the sunset glare if heading south. South of Laayoune traffic decreases, although there's enough to help in case of a breakdown. Beyond Dakhla junction traffic drops right off and the formerly wide road from Tan-Tan becomes narrow.

Sandstorms in spring are common, notably along the N1 north of Tan-Tan and the Gulf of Cintra (N23°). The crossing of the salt pans or 'sebkhas' of Khnifis (N27° 57.6′  W12° 16.6′), Tantawlet (N22° 43.1′  W16° 19.7′) and Fares (N22° 32.6′  W16° 23.2′) is especially windy and prone to brief **duststorms** too. In a duststorm slow down and turn on the headlights and hazard lights. If progress becomes too difficult, park well away from the road. Following a duststorm or even just a strong wind, small dunes might cover the road. Typical sections to watch out for on-road dunes include the southern exit of Laayoune, the Gulf of Cintra and all the salt depressions or sebkhas. Even if there are no full-on sandstorms, the north-easterly wind is always present. If you're driving a tall vehicle the difference in fuel consumption between heading south or north will be noticeable.

In winter, rainstorms are not so rare. In fact it's common north of Tarfaya for the road to be blocked after heavy rainfall. Many of the usually dry oueds briefly become fast running creeks that may be too risky to ford. In such a situation it's better to see if the locals are going for it, but anyway such flash floods usually run their course in a few hours.

## Police checkpoints

Due partly to the unresolved legal status of the Western Sahara there are several police checkpoints along the road as well as either side of larger towns like Laayoune, Cape Boujdour and Dakhla. Passing these checkpoints can be expedited by handing out pre-printed copies of your details or *fiches* which will be laboriously entered into a ledger once you're on your way. See 'Documents' on the website for a Word template to fill out and print off; at least a dozen will be especially useful on the Atlantic Route. As with much of the N1 right up to Tangiers, watch out for **speed traps** too; a typical spot is on the southern exit of Laayoune. The route **maps** are on pp264-5.

## TAN-TAN TO THE MAURITANIAN BORDER                                1147KM
January 2008 ~ BMW R1200GS Adventure (Tim Cullis)

**0km**          **N28° 26.03′  W11° 04.75′**
**Fuel** station at the eastern end of **Tan-Tan**. South of here you're unlikely to find unleaded (*sans plomb*) petrol, however from KM113 fuel prices (see p61 or the website) are subsidised by about 40% and you might well see smugglers transporting this low-duty fuel back north.

Head west towards El Ouatia, aka: Tan-Tan Plage. After 8km pass the entrance to Tan-Tan airport on the left.

**26 (1121)     N28° 29.12′  W11° 19.37′**
At the **El Ouatia** turn off you can see the sea in the near distance. Keep left at the junction and continue on the N1. The road straight ahead goes into El Ouatia town, the port of Tan-Tan and a pleasant little beach resort. *Villa Ocean* situated right on the beach at N28° 29.89′  W11° 20.04′ is owned by a French couple and can accommodate six people. Add approximately 5km for the diversion to *Villa Ocean* and

back to the junction. Over the next 80km, the road runs alongside the ocean along low cliffs broken by three river estuaries.

**113 (1034)      N28° 06.42' W12° 02.28'**
**Sidi Akhfenir** is the first point south of Tan-Tan with **cheap fuel**. Immediately after a naval building on the right and before the town, you can pull over to see the Gouffre d'Akhfenir, a large sea cave with a collapsed roof. The result is a circular cove with an underground entrance to the sea.

**122 (1025)      N28° 04.29' W12° 07.94'**
The piste heading south here leads to the seasonal cascades of Khawi Nam at N27° 40.95' W12° 13.18'. This would be a diversion of approximately 120km there and back. Alternatively it's possible to continue south and west from the cascades and meet the main road again at Laayoune.

**137 (1010)      N28° 00.25' W12° 14.57'**
A sandy track heading north leads to the **Naila** flamingo sanctuary at N28° 02.06' W12° 14.15' situated at a lagoon on the estuary of the Sebkha Tarzgha.

**146 (1001)      N27° 56.48' W12° 17.46'**
You're now driving at the same level as the Sebkha Tarzgha, a smooth, flat plain only 5m above sea level and which can get flooded after rain. It's tempting to drive out onto the salt flat but beware of breaking through the crust. The salt that is leached out of the soil by the rain is a valuable commodity and is extracted for sale.

**152 (995)      N27° 54.04' W12° 20.18'**
After climbing up from the depression, you come to a point where you can overlook the Salines Tarzgha saltworks. The last 30-odd kilometres before Tarfaya you'll find sandy beaches rather than cliffs along the shore.

**211 (936)      N27° 56.91' W12° 52.93'**
Tarfaya junction. Keep left to continue south on the N1. Straight on leads to the fishing town of **Tarfaya** (**fuel**), site of a former trading post called Port Victoria built by a Scottish adventurer Donald Mackenzie in 1879. His original fort lies just offshore at Cape Juby, overlooked at

N27° 56.70' W12° 55.53', alongside a memorial to Antoine de Saint-Exupéry (there's also a Saint-Exupéry museum in town).

Only 12m above sea level, Cape Juby is known as the graveyard of sailors and many wrecks litter the beach to the north. Diverting into Tarfaya and then taking the loop to rejoin the road to the south adds approximately 8km.

South of Tarfaya the road moves away from the coast running alongside the **Sebkha Tah**, at 55m below sea level, the lowest point in Morocco.

**244 (903)      N27° 40.28' W12° 57.36'**
The former border post of Tah or **Hassi Laoroud** (**fuel**) was at one stage the frontier between Spanish Morocco to the north and Spanish Sahara to the south.

The Tarfaya Strip and the rest of Spanish Protectorate of Morocco (including Sidi Ifni) was handed over to Morocco in 1958, but the Spanish held on to their two Saharan colonies: **Saguia el Hamra** and **Rio de Oro**. After the Spanish signalled they were abandoning these colonies too, the tiny settlement of Tah was the entry point in 1976 for Morocco's 'Green March' led by King Hassan II.

**252 (895)      N27° 35.63' W12° 57.09'**
To the west of the road is the northern rim of **Sebkha Um Ed Deboaa**, another massive salt depression some 30m below sea level. The piste that leaves the road here heading west then south along the southern rim of the depression eventually leads to the campsite mentioned below.

**272 (875)      N27° 26.43' W13° 01.38'**
Heading west from this point along the track for 4km brings you to *Camping Le Roi Bedouin* (N27° 27.70' W13° 03.09'), a popular stop for overlanders, situated next to a calcified waterfall on the southern edge of Sebkha Um Ed Deboaa. Luc and Martine provide tents and 'bungalows' to rent and Martine makes a mean camel and date tajine. Any leftovers are fed to the goats who return the favour by producing goat's cheese.

**305 (842)      N27° 11.77' W13° 10.39'**
Laayoune junction. Take the right fork to continue on the N1 into **Laayoune** (**fuel**).

**Route MO2**
NORTH

To Sidi Ifni
El Ouatia
TAN-TAN
MO1
MW3
N1
MW1
MW2
MO2
Mseid
N 28°00'
Abetteh
Gouffre
d'Akhfenir
Flamingo
turn-off
Salines
Tarzgha
Khawi Nam
cascades
Cape
Juby
Tarfaya
To Assa
Tah
MW6
E
Sebkha
Tah, -55m
N 27°00'
Camping
Le Roi Bedouin
Smara
Tbeila Rock
LAAYOUNE
Laayoune
Plage
El Marsa
N1
N 26°00'
Lemsid
★ trailblazer
W 15°00'
W E S T E R N   S A H A R A
Boujdour
N 25°00'
MO2
N1

0   25   50   75   100km

TO SOUTH MAP
Echtoucan
S

N
W 12°00'
W 13°00'
W 14°00'

N
W

MO – OCEAN

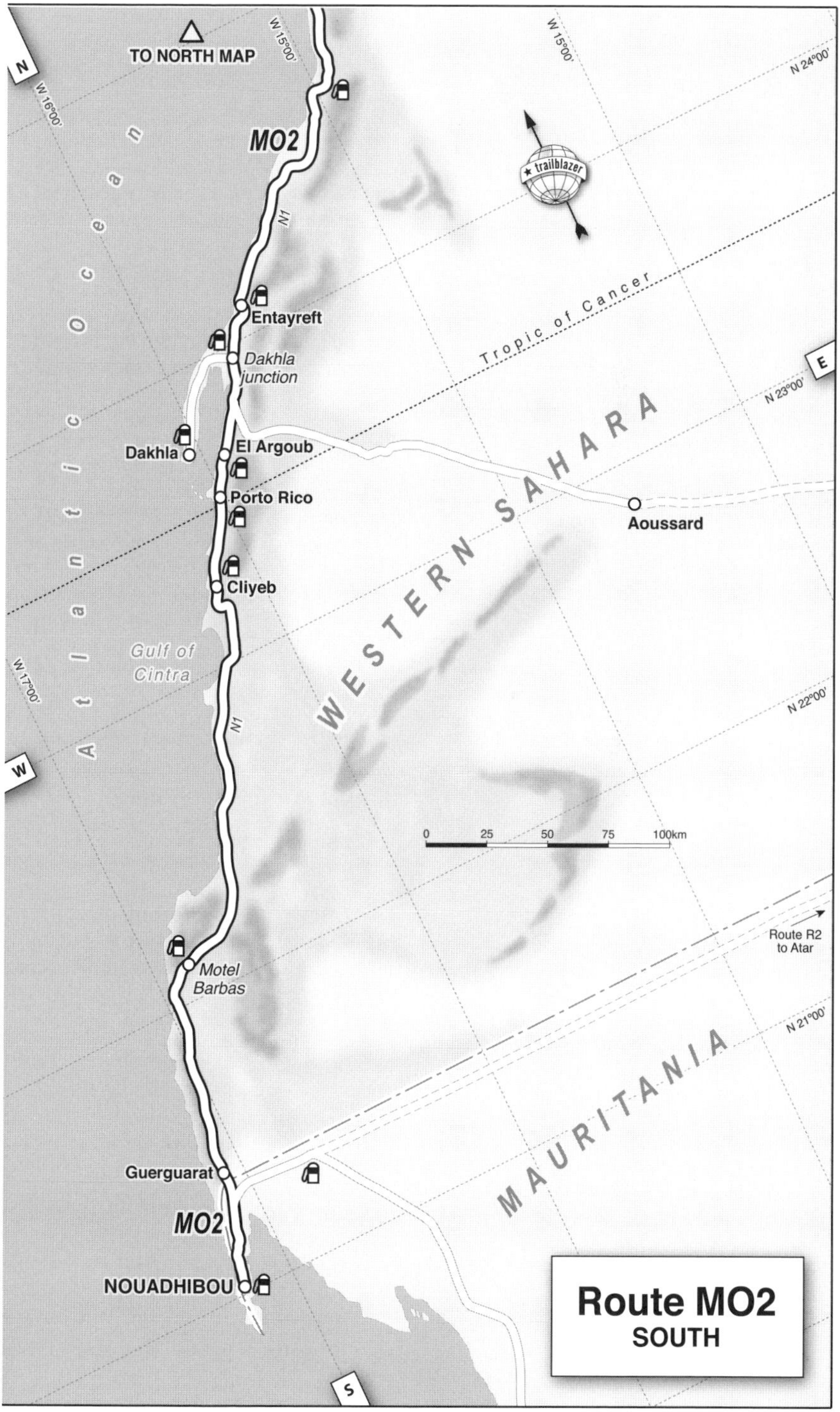
TO NORTH MAP
N
W 16°00'
W 15°00'
W 15°00'
N 24°00'
MO2
trailblazer
N1
Entayreft
Dakhla junction
Tropic of Cancer
E
N 23°00'
Dakhla
El Argoub
Porto Rico
WESTERN SAHARA
Aoussard
Cliyeb
Atlantic Ocean
Gulf of Cintra
W 17°00'
N1
N 22°00'
W
0 25 50 75 100km
Route R2 to Atar
Motel Barbas
N 21°00'
MAURITANIA
Guerguarat
MO2
NOUADHIBOU
S
Route MO2
SOUTH

KM500, Boujdour.

As you approach the town you come to the steep-sided **Saguia el Hamra** which has been dammed to create a shallow lagoon. The N1 turns west here, heading once more towards the ocean. Turning inland leads 240km to **Smara** (see p253; Route MW6).

Morocco has lavished millions on the provincial capital with upmarket hotels, a hospital, a 30,000-seat stadium and the impressive Place Mechouar central square. But as in Smara's less fancy examples, Laayoune's best **hotels** are permanently block-booked by UN observers brought in to monitor the ceasefire. They're often to be seen in white 4x4s and Russian-built helicopters.

You leave Laayoune on a four-lane highway running between the sand dunes of Erg Lakhbayta which sometimes overwhelm the road. Bulldozers are supposed to prevent this by shifting sand from the windward side, but keep a keen look out for sand drifts.

**320 (827)      N27° 09.57'  W13° 20.19'**
About 15km west of town, following a left bend to the south-west and just after a **fuel** station, turn right and then first left and follow the road for 5km to *Camping Nil* (N27°10.60'  W13° 23.55'), a shadeless 'parking lot' **campsite** by Laayoune Plage more suited to motorhomes. There are said to be more **hotels** down here too.

**336 (811)      N27° 06.13'  W13° 24.56'**
The road approaches the ocean at El Marsa. A beltway that crosses over the

road runs from the huge terminal by the jetty to the Bou Kra phosphate mine some 100km to the south-east.

**405 (742)      N26° 36.00'  W13° 43.62'**
The only place on the 164km between El Marsa and Boujdour is formerly sleepy **Lemsid** (**fuel**), now being expanded as part of Morocco's investment in Western Sahara. Twenty kilometres further on is a track leading to some interesting sandstone outcrops at N26° 25.92' W13° 54.31'.

**500 (647)      N26° 07.60'  W14° 29.05'**
The entrance to **Boujdour** (**fuel** and other services) is marked by an archway and massive sculptures of leaping swordfish and ostriches. The latter were said to be commonplace around Boujdour until a few decades ago; the former presumably represent the town's current prosperity.

The following stretch south of Boujdour is monotonous but there are a couple of exceptions: a huge sandy beach that starts about 15km south of Boujdour and 60m-high cliffs that begin about 65km from Boujdour (from N25° 35.1' to N25° 33.3').

**644 (503)      N24° 54.65'  W14° 49.19'**
A few shacks mark **Echtoucan** (aka: Nwifed), little more than a pair of fuel stations and a café. There's more **fuel** in the Gor Touf area (N24° 40.00' W14° 52.32'), and at around KM670 (477) the road becomes more interesting with bends running around some small hills. Diversions include the steep banks of the Oued Lakra (N24° 37.9' W14° 53.2'); a sand-covered sebkha in the Skaymat area (roughly from N24° 29.6' W15° 01.4' to N24° 25.0' W15° 06.2'); and finally more high cliffs near the Dakhla crossroads (N24° 22.9' to N24° 10.1).

**784 (363)      N24° 03.64'  W15° 34.21'**
**Entayreft fuel** station.

**807 (340)      N23° 53.56'  W15° 40.38'**
**Dakhla Junction**, checkpoint and **fuel**. Turn right for Dakhla; continue straight on for the N1 to Mauritania. It's 45km from the junction to **Dakhla** at the end of

MO - OCEAN

the peninsula and well worth the detour for an overnight stop in town. Dakhla, or 'Villa Cisneros' as it was formerly known, was the capital of Spain's Rio de Oro ('River of Gold') province.

**Wild camping** is possible at N23° 54.03' W15° 47.24' and N23° 49.86' W15° 51.92', whilst further down the peninsula *Camping Moussafir* is 5km from the town.

**846 (301)          N23° 36.29'  W15° 52.19'**
Back on the N1, **El Argoub** (**fuel**, and again 5km later) is now a quiet little town situated on the coast a couple of kilometres off the main road and immediately opposite Dakhla across the bay.

**861 (286)          N23° 28.97'  W15° 56.56'**
Porto Rico is a rubbish-strewn *bidonville* situated in a spectacular location.

**868 (279)          N23° 26.00'  W15° 58.20'**
Congratulations, you've just crossed the Tropic of Cancer. From here on you'll start to see many signs warning of **minefields** either side of the road.

Over the next 180km the road runs mainly along high cliffs overlooking the ocean, with salt depressions at intervals on either side of the road.

**898 (249)          N23° 12.48'  W16° 05.75'**
**Cliyeb fuel** station. The next attraction is the huge Gulf of Cintra with more than 40km of coastline (from N23° 10' to N22° 52') opening to the ocean in an almost perfect semi-circle.

Other interesting stopping points include the western limit of the Sebkha Tantawlet (N22° 43.1' W16° 19.7'), 30m high rocky cliffs (N22° 34.6' W16° 21.4'), and the western limit of the Sebkha Fares (N22° 32.0' W16° 23.9').

**1056 (91)          N22° 03.27'  W16° 44.84'**
*Motel Barbas* is a welcoming haven in the middle of nowhere, comprising two **fuel** stations and a hotel, café and shop as well as unofficial money changing services. It's about 86km to the Moroccan border post so many people choose to overnight here and get stuck into the border as soon as it opens next morning.

**1142 (5)          N21° 21.80'  W16° 57.64'**
Having passed the fort and former border post of Guerguarat, the current Moroccan **border post** is now right on the frontier.

**Exit procedures** can take between one and two hours: first go to the gendarmerie to register, then the police for a passport stamp, then the Douane (Customs) who'll formalise the exit of your vehicle and possibly make a brief vehicle search.

You can now move about 50m down the road to finally register with the military. Once that's done and your passport is checked again you're let out to navigate the 5km of piste to the Mauritanian counterpart.

Either side of the clearly defined tracks (which branch out and rejoin) are minefields so do not stray (see the website for a map link). The general consensus southbound is to follow tracks to the east for the easiest route. As recently as 2007 tourists were killed while straying (entirely unnecessarily it must be said) a couple of kilometres east of the track, but despite this, it's all much less perilous than it sounds and regular 2WD cars and road bikes can easily manage the track.

On the way through No Man's Land you may get waved down by **money changers** who are more keen to exchange euros than dirhams for Mauritanian ouguiya.

**1147          N21° 20.02'  W16° 56.83'**
The impressive border post of Mauritania may not be in use so carry on down the road another 300m to the ramshackle collection of huts and a caravan to pass through the police and Customs controls, as well as official money changing and motor insurance outlets.

For details on entering **Mauritania** see this route's online page. You'll also find an updated download for the 520-km 'R2' piste from *Sahara Overland* which heads inland along the railway to Atar (4WD needed).

After the border the next **fuel** is Nouadhibou, 70km to the south-west or at Bou Lanouar, 45km along the all-sealed road south to Nouakchott (450km).

MO – OCEAN

MANTEC SERVICES (UK) LTD
Unit 4, Smart Drive, Haunchwood Park Industrial Estate,
Galley Common, Nuneaton, Warwickshire. CV10 9SP.
Telephone: 024 7639 5368  International (+44) 24 7639 5368
Facsimile: 024 7639 5369  International (+44) 24 7639 5369
Company Registration No. 4342191 Directors: I.Gough, S.Gough

sales@mantec.co.uk

www.mantec.co.uk

# David Lambeth
## Rally & Overland

- **Overland & Rally bike preparation & parts.**
- **Ready built bikes bought & sold.**
- **Yamaha XT & Tenere specialist.**
- **UK agent for the Tuareg Moroccan rally.**

**Boston, Lincolnshire, UK**
**0044 (0) 1205 871 945**
# www.davidlambeth.co.uk

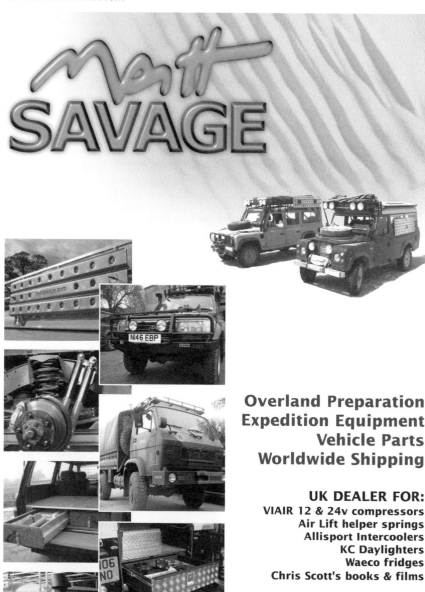

# *Matt* SAVAGE

**Overland Preparation**
**Expedition Equipment**
**Vehicle Parts**
**Worldwide Shipping**

**UK DEALER FOR:**
VIAIR 12 & 24v compressors
Air Lift helper springs
Allisport Intercoolers
KC Daylighters
Waeco fridges
Chris Scott's books & films

tel +44 (0) 1629 55855
sales@mattsavage.com

# www.mattsavage.com

new ideas for motorbikes

TOURATECH

EVERYTHING YOU need FOR YOUR next ADVENTURE

Touratech UK Ltd,
Unit 14 , Woodlands Business Park,
Ystradgynlais, South Wales,
UK, SA9 1JW.
info@touratech.co.uk
Tel: +44(0) 1639 841765
WWW.TOURATECH.COM

Catalogue for free!

# WAYPOINT ▪ TOURS
## CATERED 4X4 EXPEDITIONS

### WWW.WAYPOINT-TOURS.COM

*It's 45°C, you are miles off piste when the dust storm hits and your vehicle bogs down in the sand. Would you know what to do when it all goes wrong?*

**Learn from the experts in desert survival.**

We run a 10 day intensive Desert Survival Training Course in the Moroccan Sahara. Go to the website or e-mail info@desertadventures.co.uk for more information.

## www.desertadventures.co.uk

# INDEX

# TRAILBLAZER

| | |
|---|---|
| Adventure Cycle-Touring Handbook | 1st edn out now |
| Adventure Motorcycling Handbook | 5th edn out now |
| Australia by Rail | 5th edn out now |
| Azerbaijan | 4th edn mid 2009 |
| China Rail Handbook | 1st edn early 2010 |
| Coast to Coast (British Walking Guide) | 3rd edn out now |
| Cornwall Coast Path (British Walking Guide) | 3rd edn out now |
| Corsica Trekking – GR20 | 1st edn out now |
| Cotswold Way (British Walking Guide) | 1st edn out now |
| Dolomites Trekking – AV1 & AV2 | 2nd edn out now |
| Inca Trail, Cusco & Machu Picchu | 4th edn mid 2009 |
| Indian Rail Handbook | 1st edn late 2009 |
| Hadrian's Wall Path (British Walking Guide) | 2nd edn out now |
| Himalaya by Bike – a route and planning guide | 1st edn out now |
| Japan by Rail | 2nd edn out now |
| Kilimanjaro – the trekking guide (includes Mt Meru) | 2nd edn out now |
| Mediterranean Handbook | 1st edn out now |
| Morocco Overland (4WD/motorcycling/cycling) | 1st edn out now |
| Moroccan Atlas – The Trekking Guide | 1st edn mid 2009 |
| Nepal Mountaineering Guide | 1st edn late 2009 |
| New Zealand – The Great Walks | 2nd edn mid 2009 |
| North Downs Way (British Walking Guide) | 1st edn out now |
| Norway's Arctic Highway | 1st edn out now |
| Offa's Dyke Path (British Walking Guide) | 2nd edn out now |
| Overlanders' Handbook – worldwide driving guide | 1st edn Jan 2010 |
| Pembrokeshire Coast Path (British Walking Guide) | 2nd edn out now |
| Pennine Way (British Walking Guide) | 2nd edn out now |
| The Ridgeway (British Walking Guide) | 2nd edn out now |
| Siberian BAM Guide – rail, rivers & road | 2nd edn out now |
| The Silk Roads – a route and planning guide | 2nd edn out now |
| Sahara Overland – a route and planning guide | 2nd edn out now |
| Scottish Highlands – The Hillwalking Guide | 2nd edn mid 2009 |
| South Downs Way (British Walking Guide) | 3rd edn out now |
| Tibet Overland – mountain biking & jeep touring | 1st edn out now |
| Tour du Mont Blanc | 1st edn out now |
| Trans-Canada Rail Guide | 4th edn out now |
| Trans-Siberian Handbook | 7th edn out now |
| Trekking in the Annapurna Region | 4th edn out now |
| Trekking in the Everest Region | 5th edn out now |
| Trekking in Ladakh | 3rd edn out now |
| Trekking in the Pyrenees | 3rd edn out now |
| The Walker's Haute Route – Mont Blanc to Matterhorn | 1st edn out now |
| West Highland Way (British Walking Guide) | 3rd edn out now |

For more information about Trailblazer and our expanding range of guides, for guidebook updates or for credit card mail order sales visit our website:

## www.trailblazer-guides.com

### ROUTE GUIDES FOR THE ADVENTUROUS TRAVELLER